Honorifics Explained

Throughout the Del Rey Manga books, you will find Japanese honorifics left intact in the translations. For those not familiar with how the Japanese use honorifics and, more important, how they differ from American honorifics, we present this brief overview.

Politeness has always been a critical facet of Japanese culture. Ever since the feudal era, when Japan was a highly stratified society, use of honorifics—which can be defined as polite speech that indicates relationship or status—has played an essential role in the Japanese language. When addressing someone in Japanese, an honorific usually takes the form of a suffix attached to one's name (example: "Asuna-san"), is used as a title at the end of one's name, or appears in place of the name itself (example: "Negi-sensei," or simply "Sensei!").

Honorifics can be expressions of respect or endearment. In the context of manga and anime, honorifics give insight into the nature of the relationship between characters. Many English translations leave out these important honorifics and therefore distort the feel of the original Japanese. Because Japanese honorifics contain nuances that English honorifics lack, it is our policy at Del Rey not to translate them. Here, instead, is a guide to some of the honorifics you may encounter in Del Rey Manga.

-san: This is the most common honorific and is equivalent to Mr., Miss, Ms., or Mrs. It is the all-purpose honorific and can be used in any situation where politeness is required.

-sama: This is one level higher than "-san" and is used to confer great respect.

-dono: This comes from the word "tono," which means "lord." It is an even higher level than "-sama" and confers utmost respect.

-kun: This suffix is used at the end of boys' names to express familiarity or endearment. It is also sometimes used by men among friends, or when addressing someone younger or of a lower station.

-chan: This is used to express endearment, mostly toward girls. It is also used for little boys, pets, and even among lovers. It gives a sense of childish cuteness.

Bozu: This is an informal way to refer to a boy, similar to the English terms "kid" and "squirt."

Sempai/Senpai: This title suggests that the addressee is one's senior in a group or organization. It is most often used in a school setting, where underclassmen refer to their upperclassmen as "sempai." It can also be used in the workplace, such as when a newer employee addresses an employee who has seniority in the company.

Kohai: This is the opposite of "sempai" and is used toward underclassmen in school or newcomers in the workplace. It connotes that the addressee is of a lower station.

Sensei: Literally meaning "one who has come before," this title is used for teachers, doctors, or masters of any profession or art.

-[blank]: This is usually forgotten in these lists, but it is perhaps the most significant difference between Japanese and English. The lack of honorific means that the speaker has permission to address the person in a very intimate way. Usually, only family, spouses, or very close friends have this kind of permission. Known as *yobisute*, it can be gratifying when someone who has earned the intimacy starts to call one by one's name without an honorific. But when that intimacy hasn't been earned, it can be very insulting.

My Heavenly Hockey Club

6

AI MORINAGA

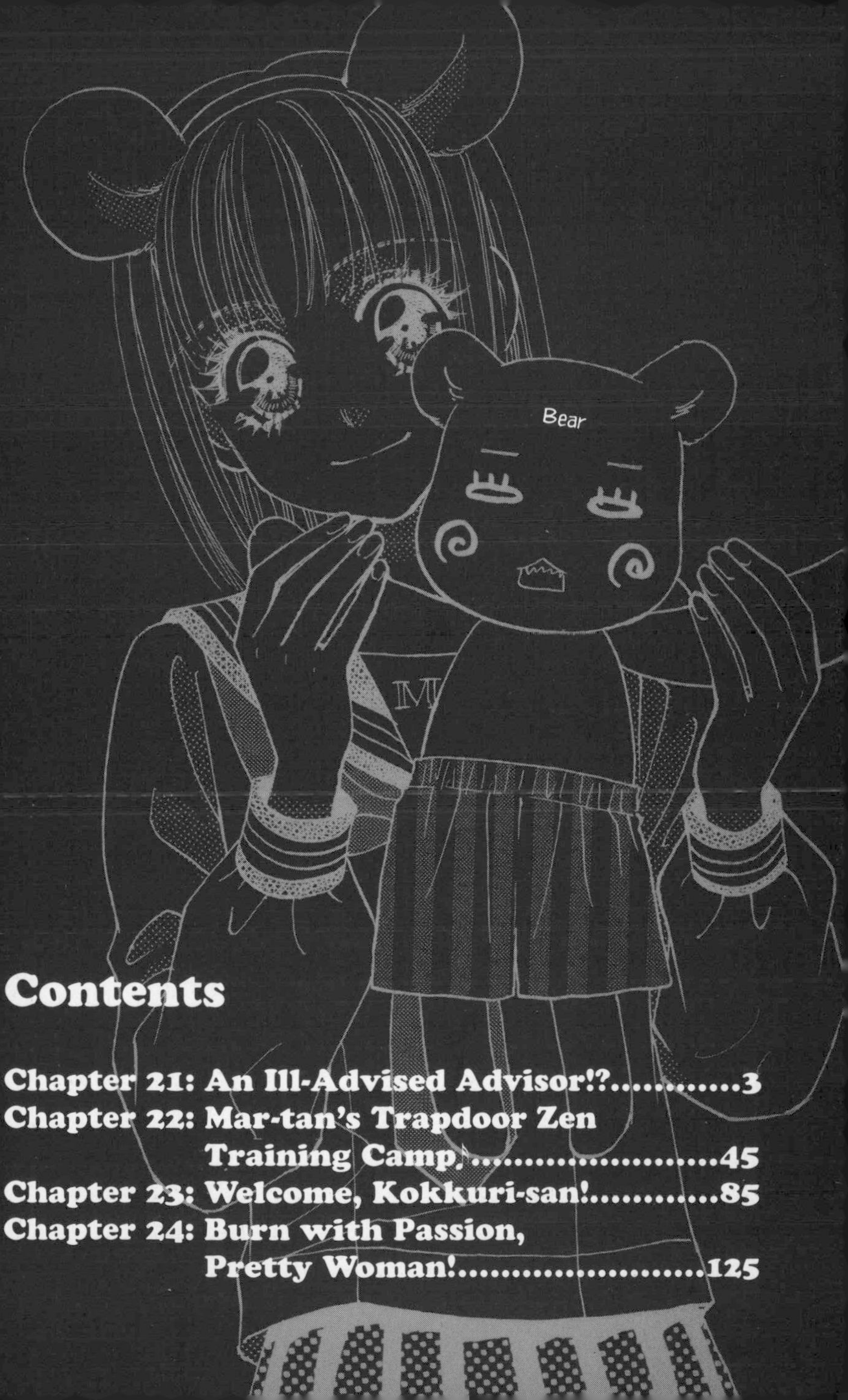
Bear

Contents

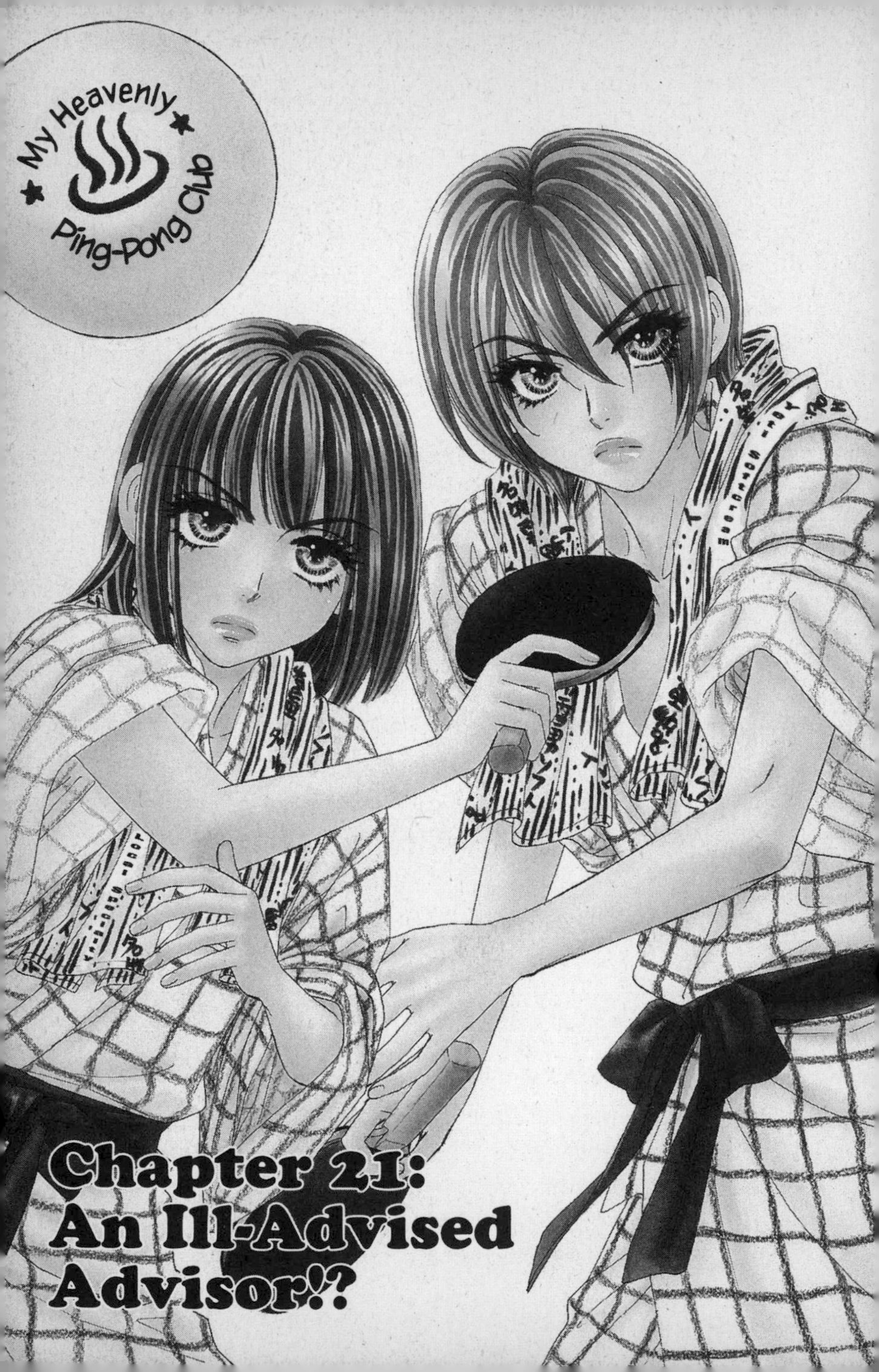
My Heavenly Ping-Pong Club
Chapter 21: An Ill-Advised Advisor!?

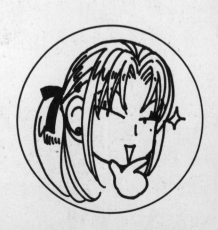

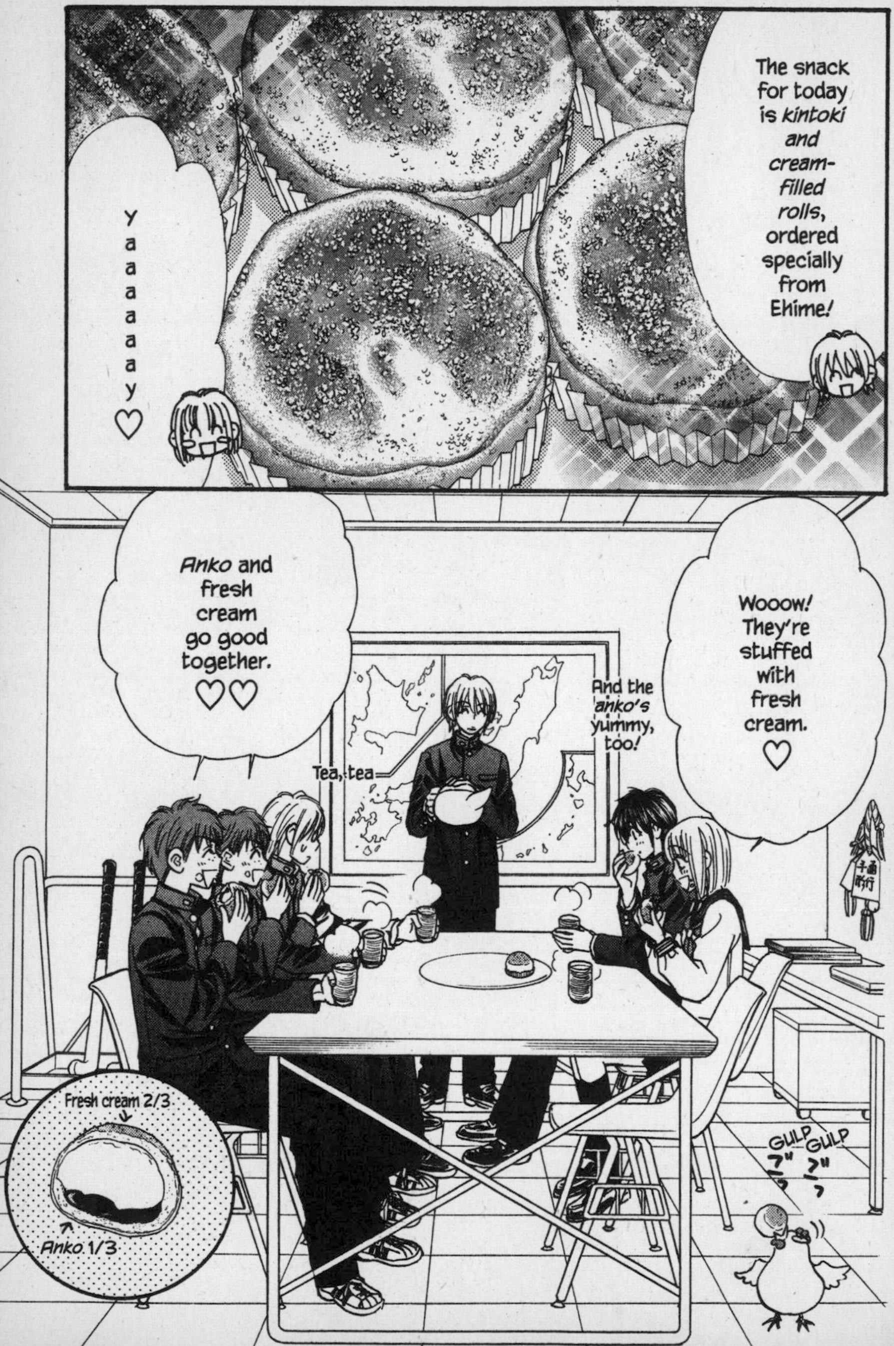
The snack for today is *kintoki* and cream-filled rolls, ordered specially from Ehime!
Yaaaaaaay ♡
Wooow! They're stuffed with fresh cream. ♡
And the *anko's* yummy, too!
Tea, tea
Anko and fresh cream go good together. ♡♡
Fresh cream 2/3
Anko 1/3
GULP GULP

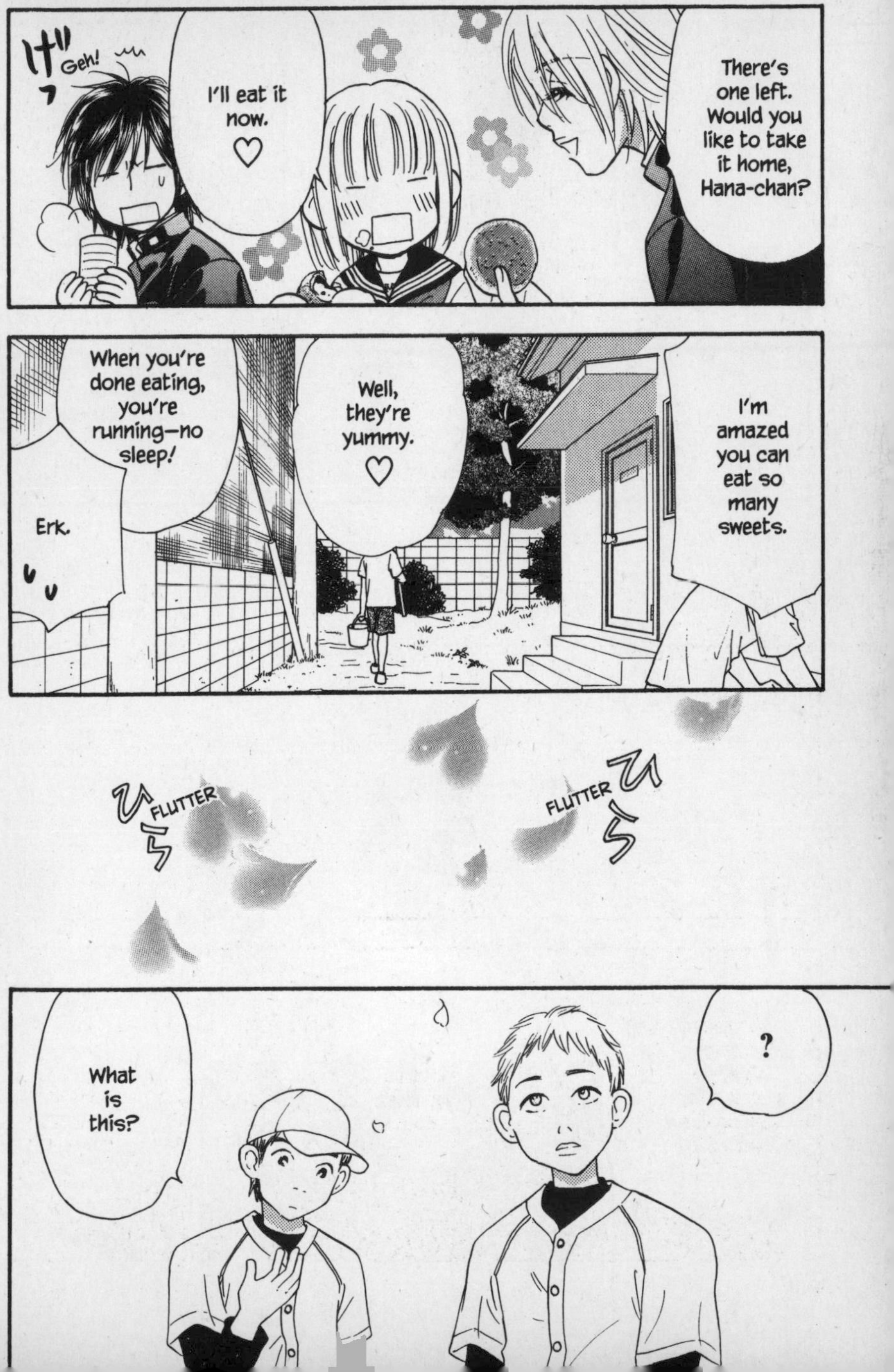
There's one left. Would you like to take it home, Hana-chan?
I'll eat it now. ♡
Geh!
I'm amazed you can eat so many sweets.
Well, they're yummy. ♡
When you're done eating, you're running—no sleep!
Erk.
FLUTTER
FLUTTER
?
What is this?

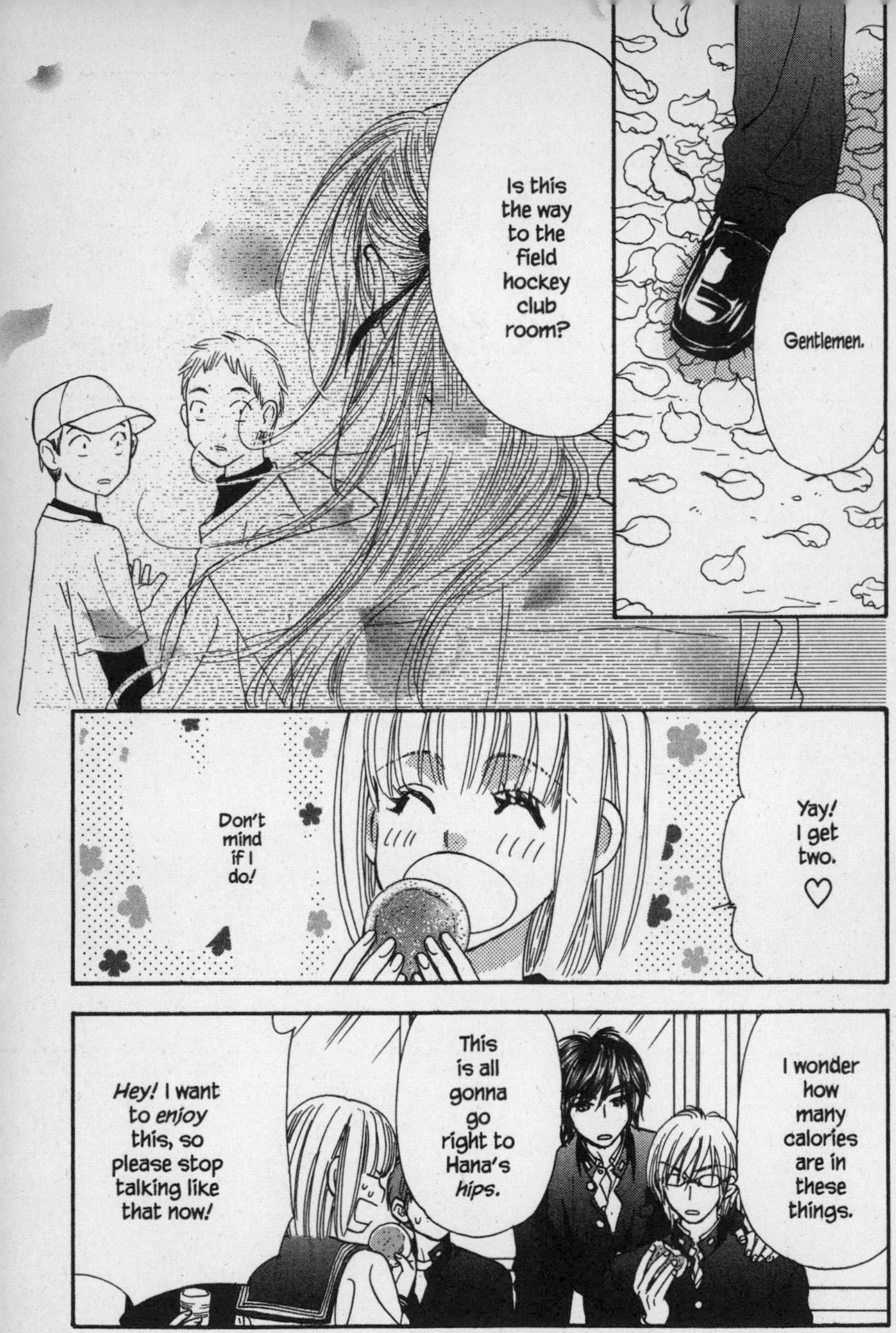
Gentlemen.
Is this the way to the field hockey club room?
Yay! I get two. ♡
Don't mind if I do!
I wonder how many calories are in these things.
This is all gonna go right to Hana's *hips.*
Hey! I want to *enjoy* this, so please stop talking like that now!

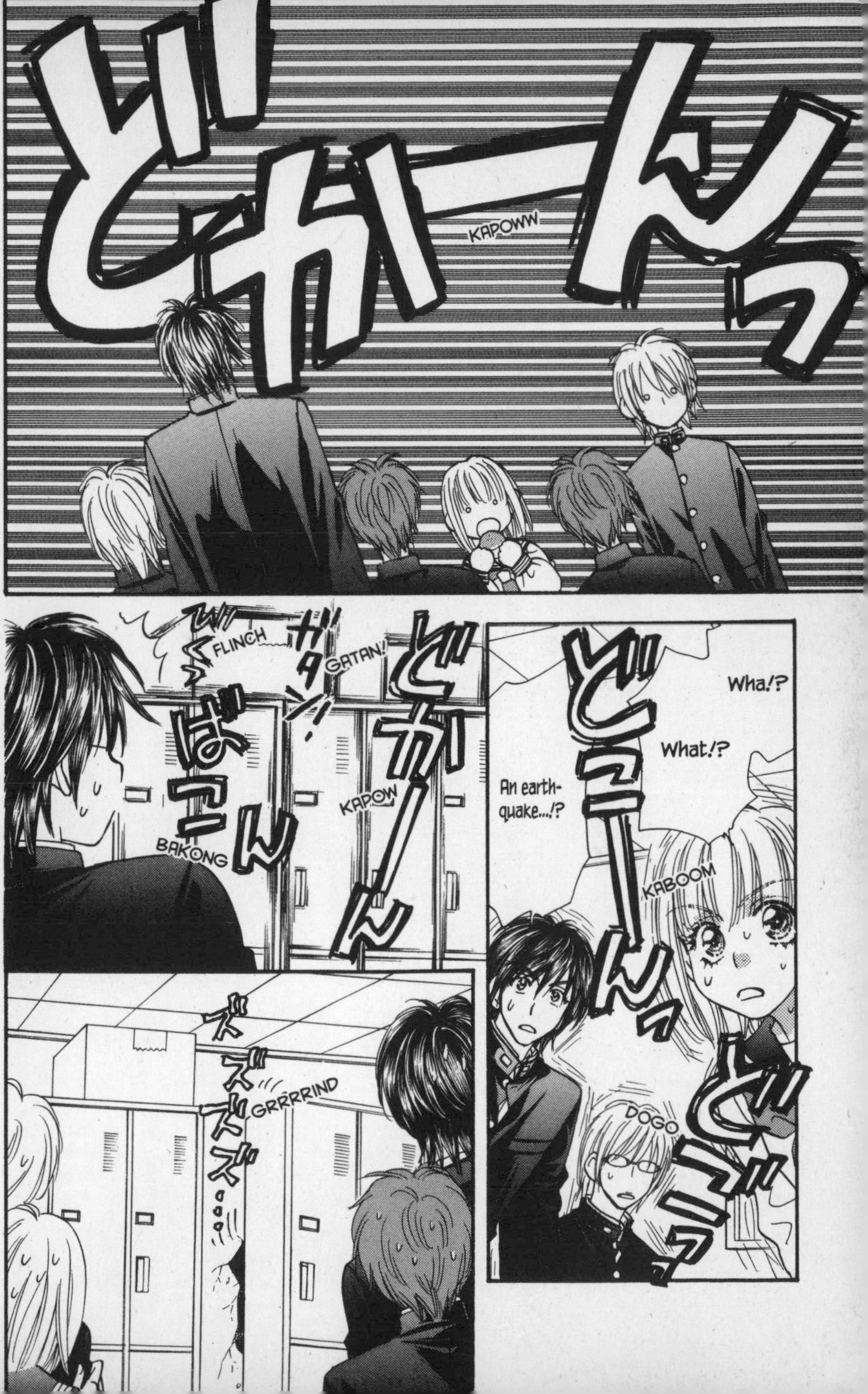

KAPOWW
Wha!?
What!?
An earth-quake...!?
KABOOM
DOGO
FLINCH
GATAN!
KAPOW
BAKONG
GRRRRIND

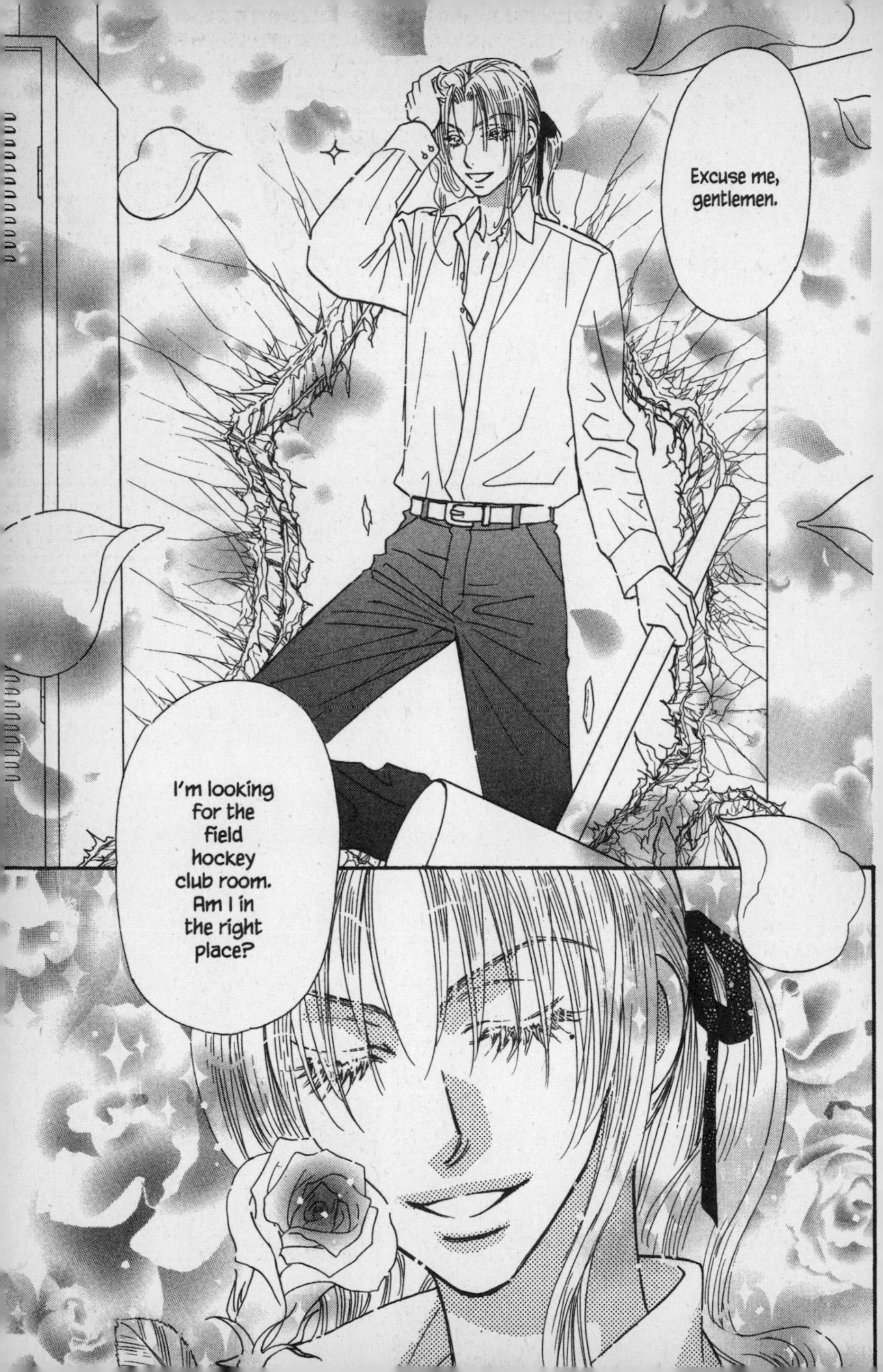
Excuse me, gentlemen.
I'm looking for the field hockey club room. Am I in the right place?

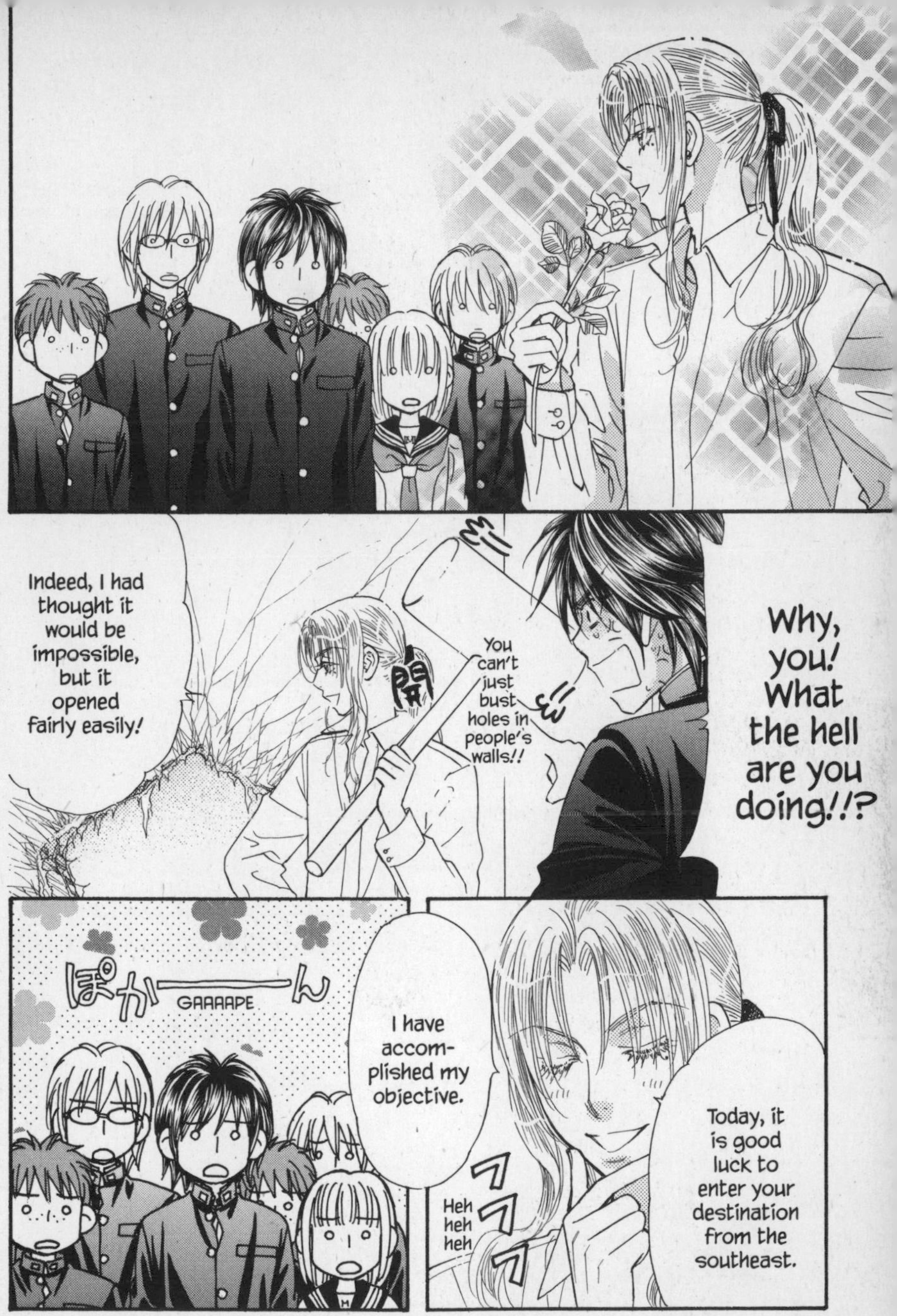
Why, you! What the hell are you doing!!?
You can't just bust holes in people's walls!!
開
Indeed, I had thought it would be impossible, but it opened fairly easily!
I have accomplished my objective.
Today, it is good luck to enter your destination from the southeast.
Heh heh heh
ぽかーーーん
GAAAAPE

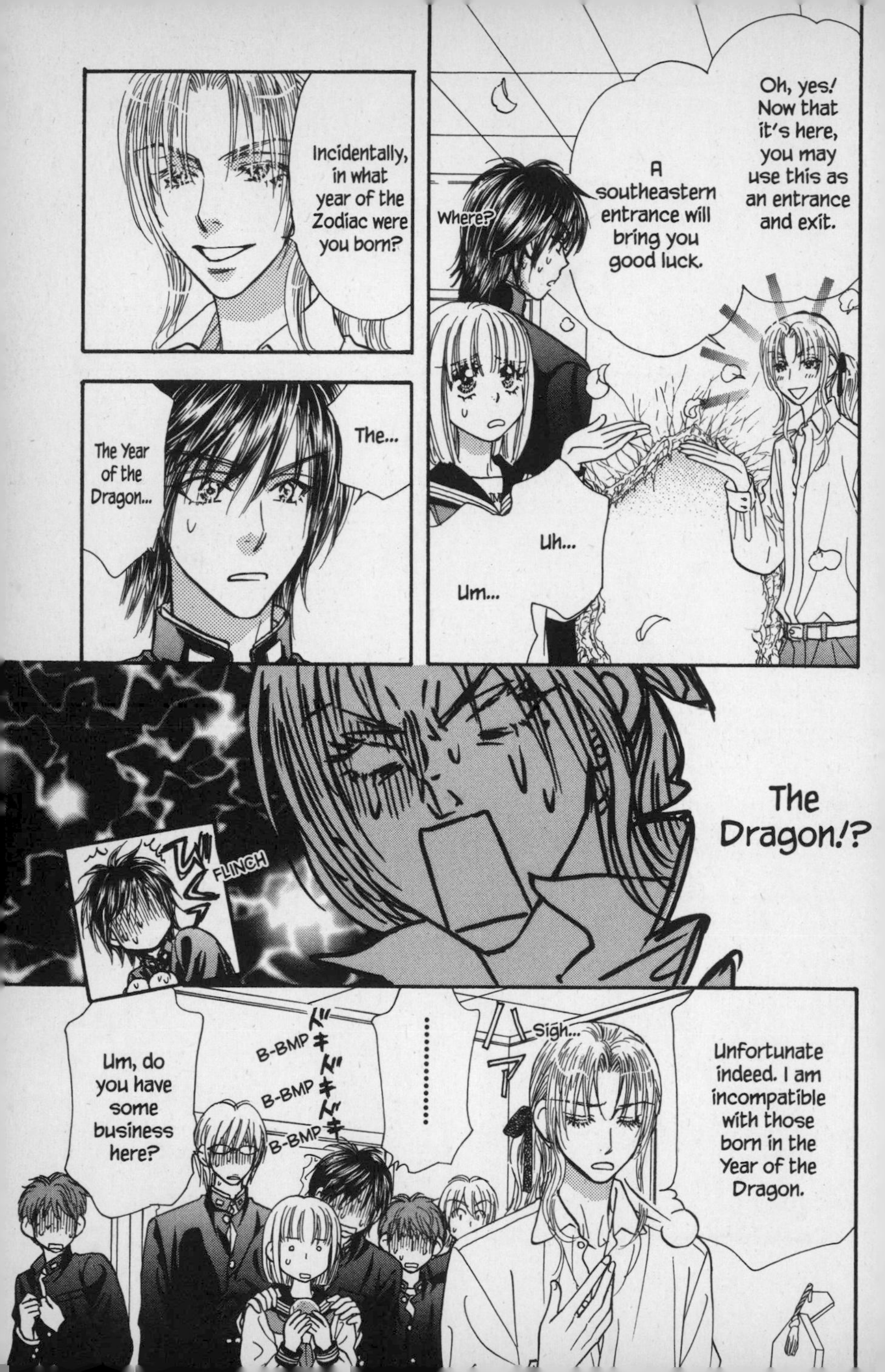
Oh, yes! Now that it's here, you may use this as an entrance and exit.
A southeastern entrance will bring you good luck.
Where?
Uh...
Um...
Incidentally, in what year of the Zodiac were you born?
The...
The Year of the Dragon...
The Dragon!?
FLINCH
Unfortunate indeed. I am incompatible with those born in the Year of the Dragon.
Sigh...
......
B-BMP
B-BMP
B-BMP
Um, do you have some business here?

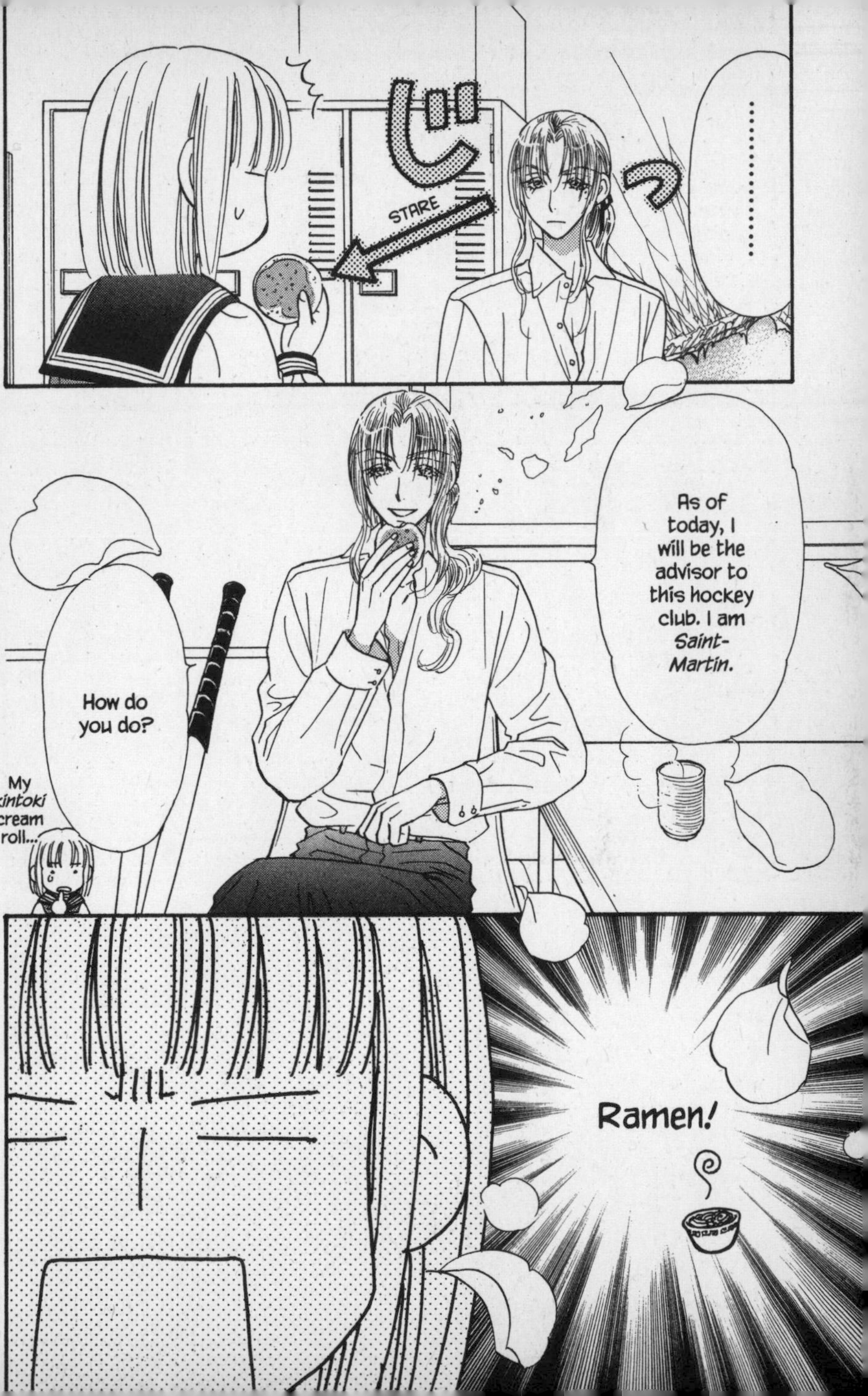

......
じっ
STARE
As of today, I will be the advisor to this hockey club. I am Saint-Martin.
How do you do?
My kintoki cream roll...
Ramen!

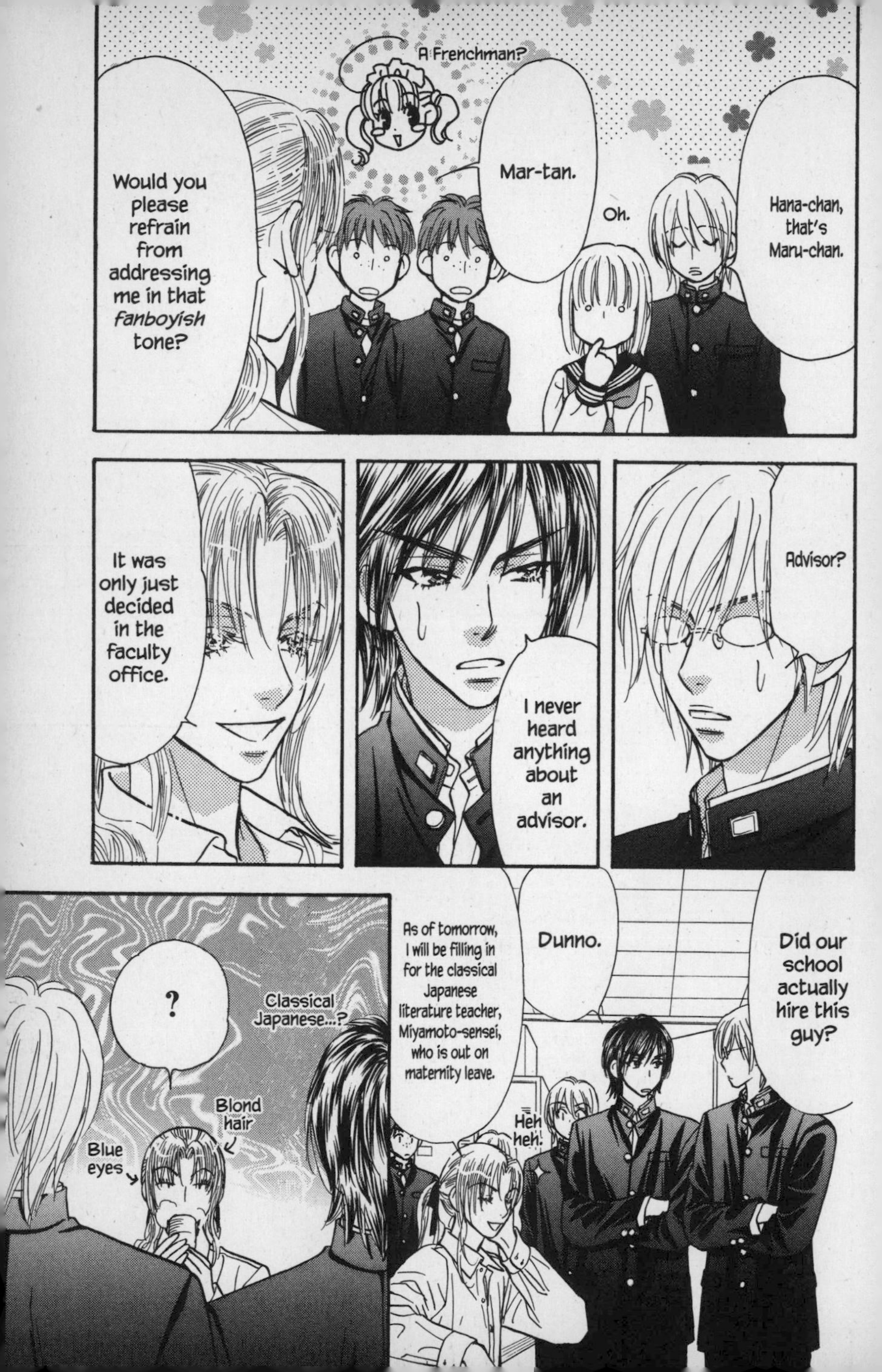
Hana-chan, that's Maru-chan.
Oh.
Mar-tan.
A Frenchman?
Would you please refrain from addressing me in that *fanboyish* tone?
Advisor?
I never heard anything about an advisor.
It was only just decided in the faculty office.
Did our school actually hire this guy?
Dunno.
Heh heh.
As of tomorrow, I will be filling in for the classical Japanese literature teacher, Miyamoto-sensei, who is out on maternity leave.
?
Classical Japanese...?
Blond hair
Blue eyes

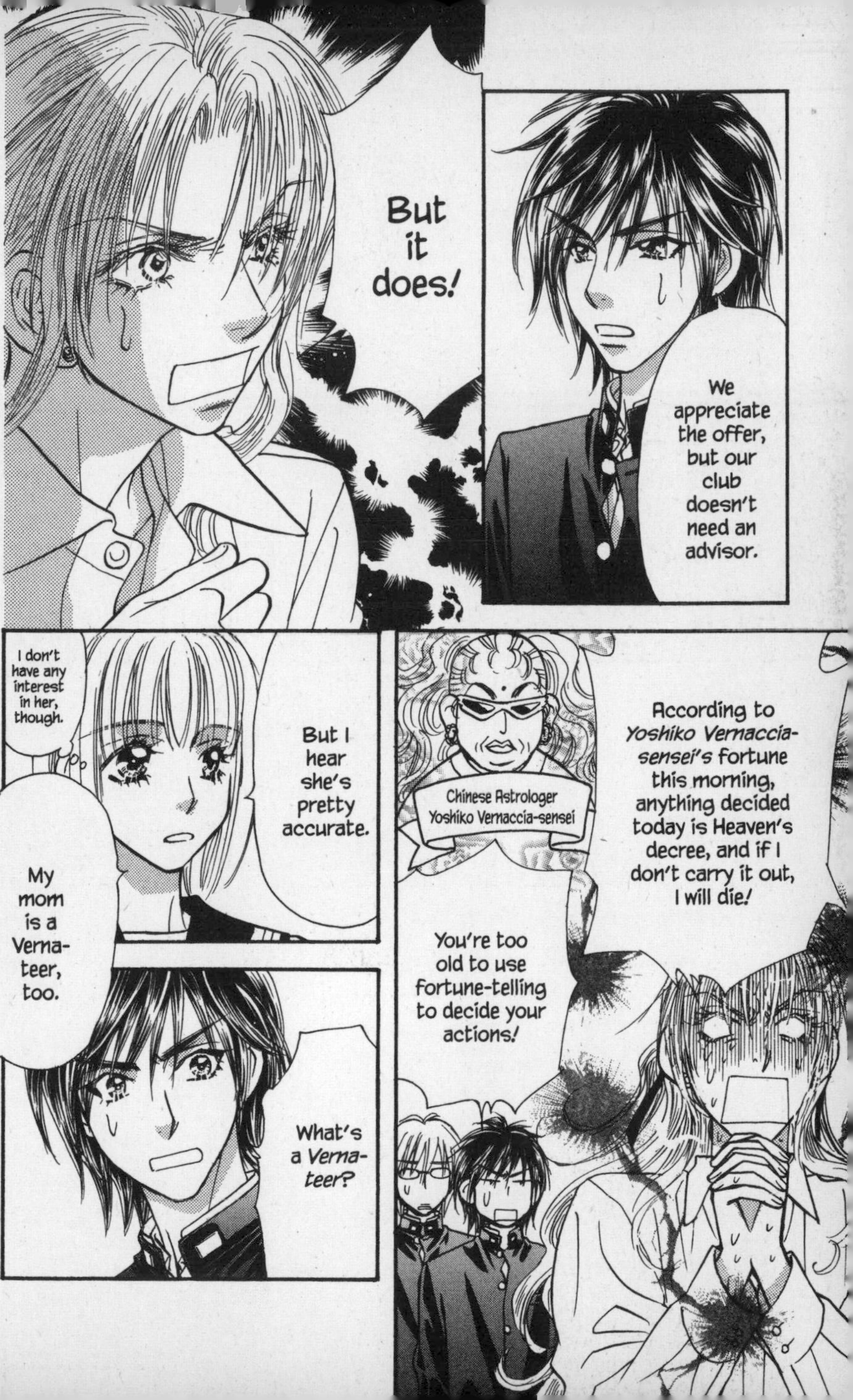
We appreciate the offer, but our club doesn't need an advisor.
But it does!
According to *Yoshiko Vernaccia-sensei's* fortune this morning, anything decided today is Heaven's decree, and if I don't carry it out, I will die!
Chinese Astrologer Yoshiko Vernaccia-sensei
You're too old to use fortune-telling to decide your actions!
But I hear she's pretty accurate.
I don't have any interest in her, though.
My mom is a Verna-teer, too.
What's a *Verna-teer*?

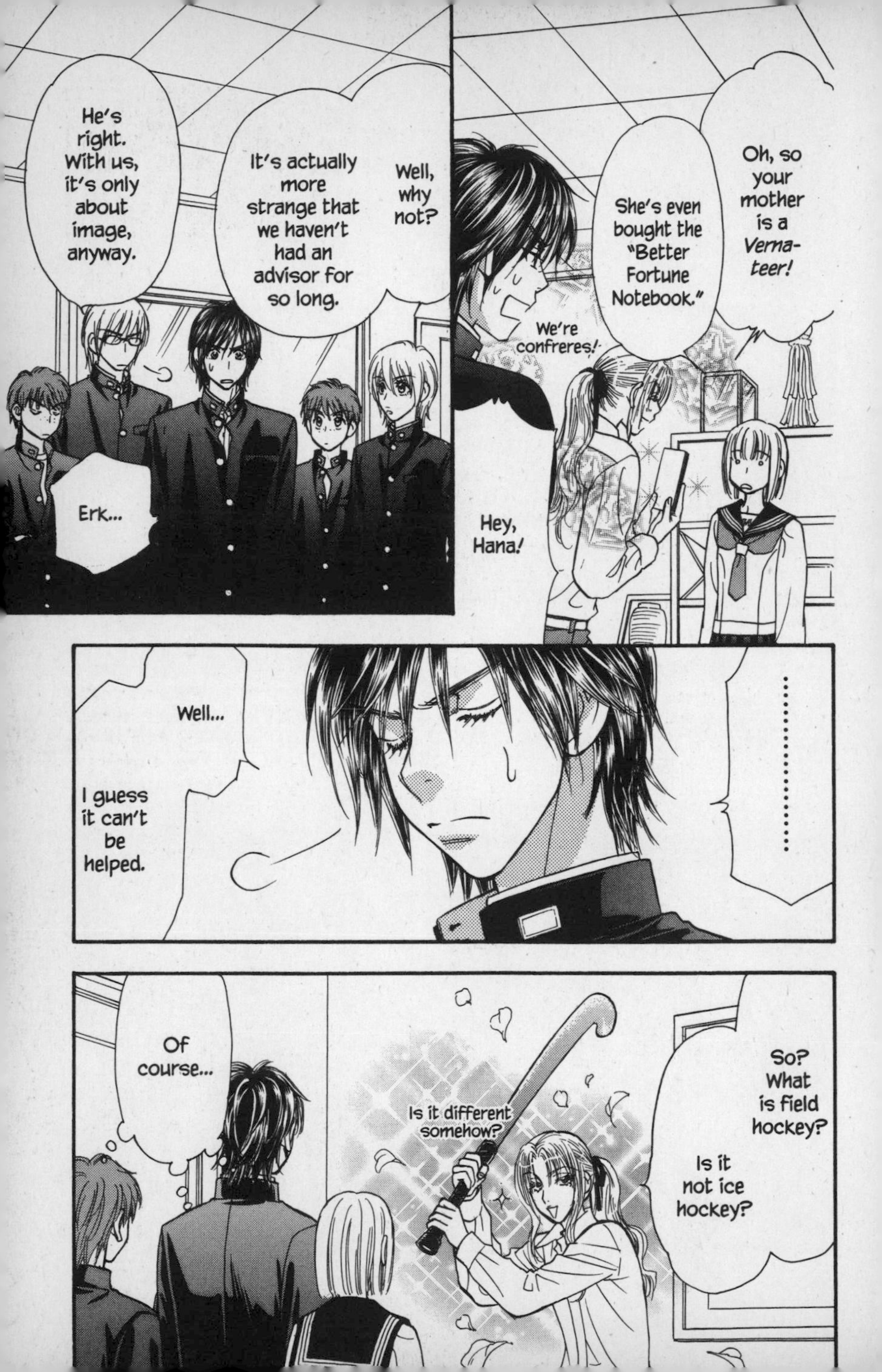
Oh, so your mother is a *Verna-teer!*
She's even bought the "Better Fortune Notebook."
We're confreres!
Hey, Hana!
Well, why not?
It's actually more strange that we haven't had an advisor for so long.
He's right. With us, it's only about image, anyway.
Erk...
....
Well...
I guess it can't be helped.
So? What is field hockey?
Is it not ice hockey?
Is it different somehow?
Of course...

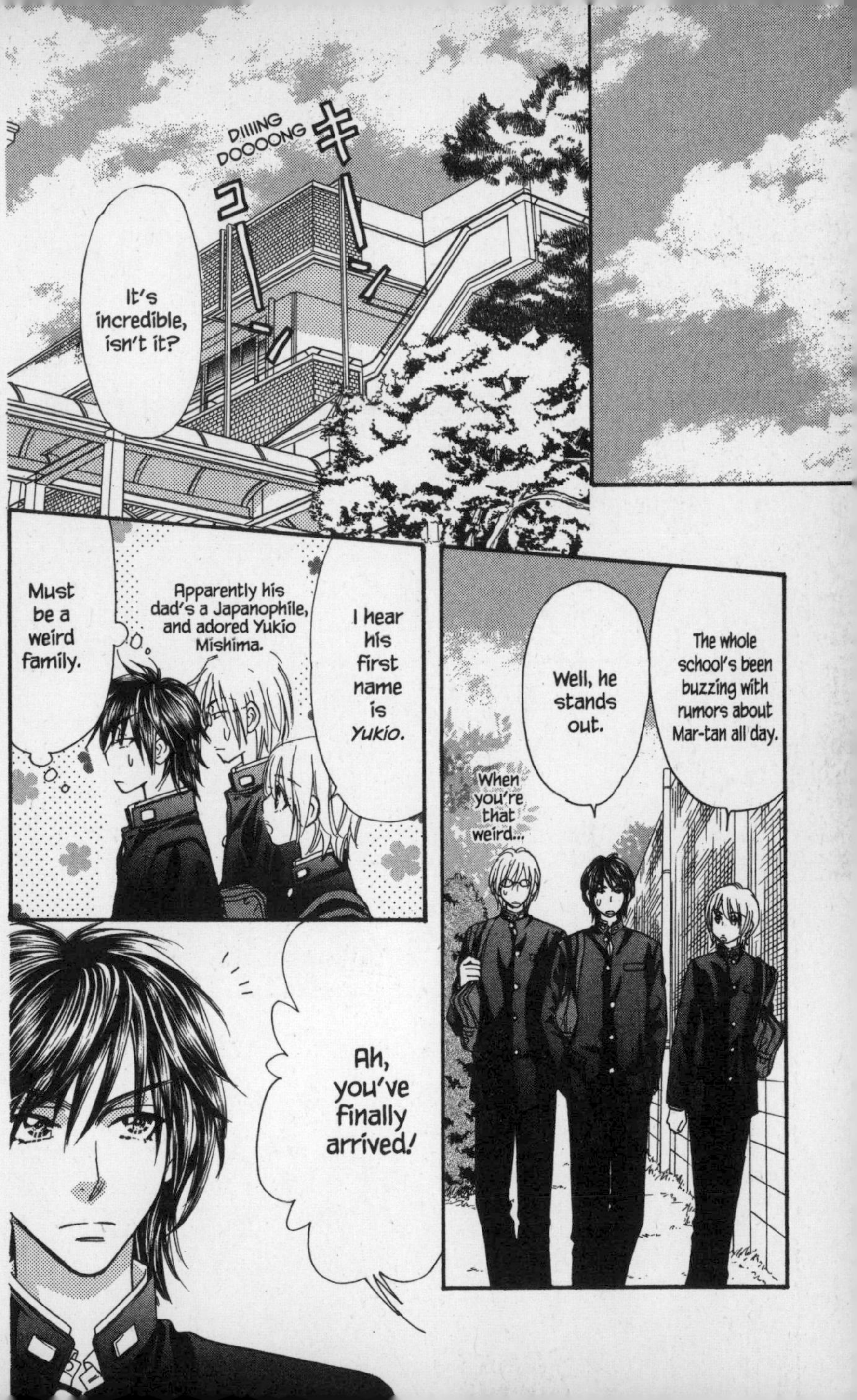
DIIIING DOOOONG
It's incredible, isn't it?
The whole school's been buzzing with rumors about Mar-tan all day.
Well, he stands out.
When you're that weird...
I hear his first name is *Yukio*.
Apparently his dad's a Japanophile, and adored Yukio Mishima.
Must be a weird family.
Ah, you've finally arrived!

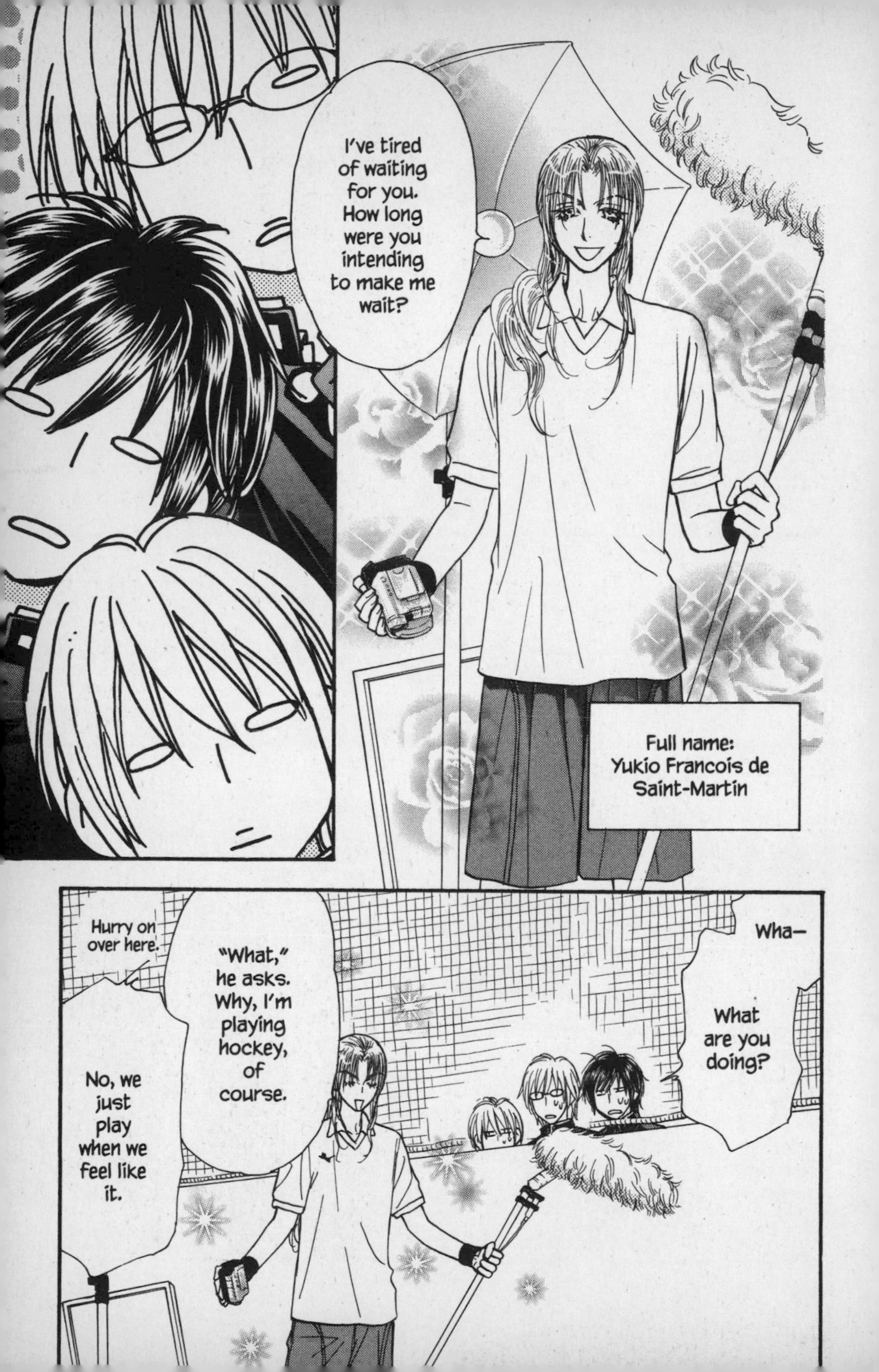
I've tired of waiting for you. How long were you intending to make me wait?
Full name: Yukio Francois de Saint-Martin
Wha—
What are you doing?
"What," he asks. Why, I'm playing hockey, of course.
Hurry on over here.
No, we just play when we feel like it.

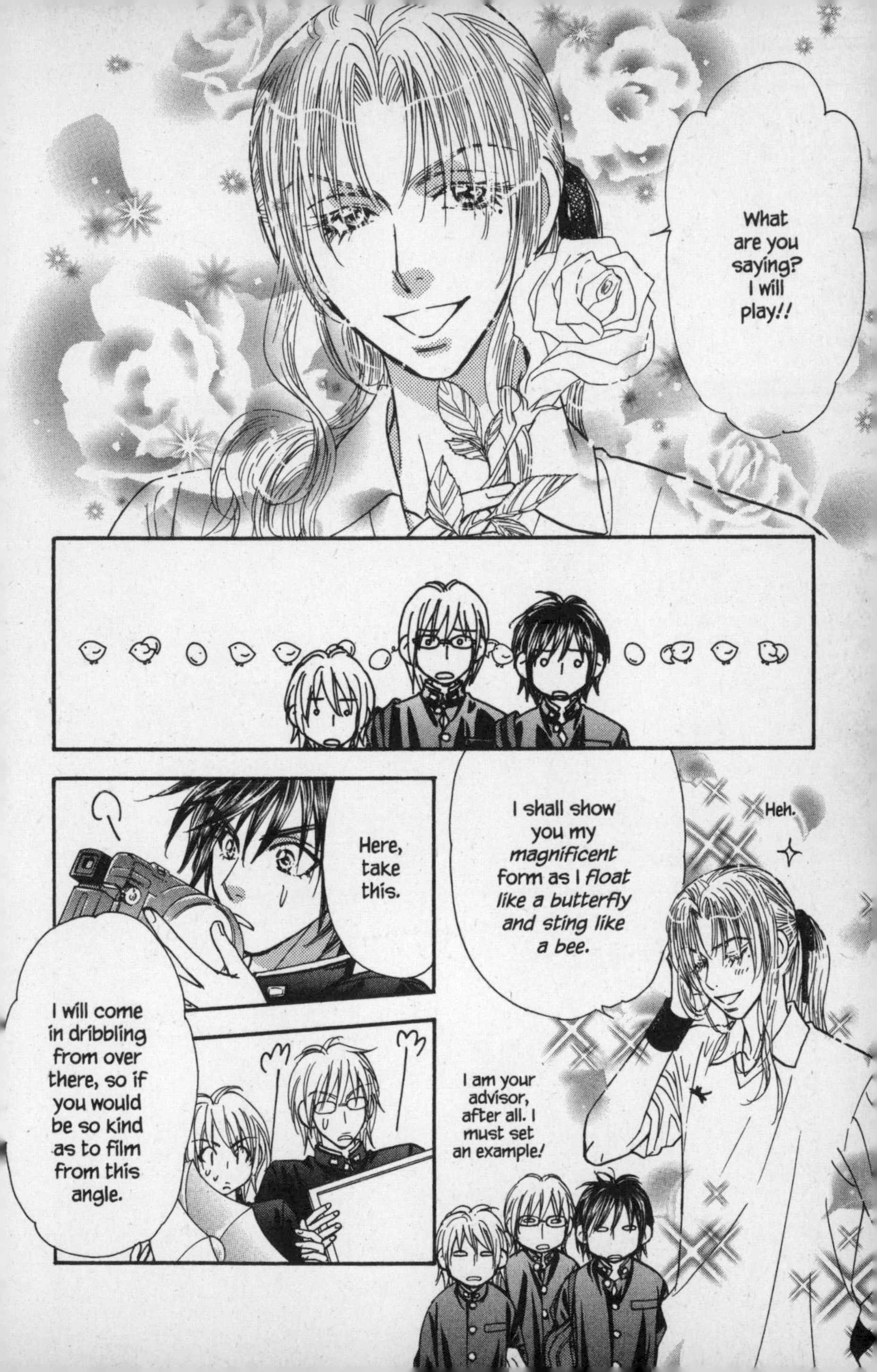
What are you saying? I will play!!
Heh.
I shall show you my *magnificent* form as I *float like a butterfly and sting like a bee.*
I am your advisor, after all. I must set an example!
Here, take this.
I will come in dribbling from over there, so if you would be so kind as to film from this angle.

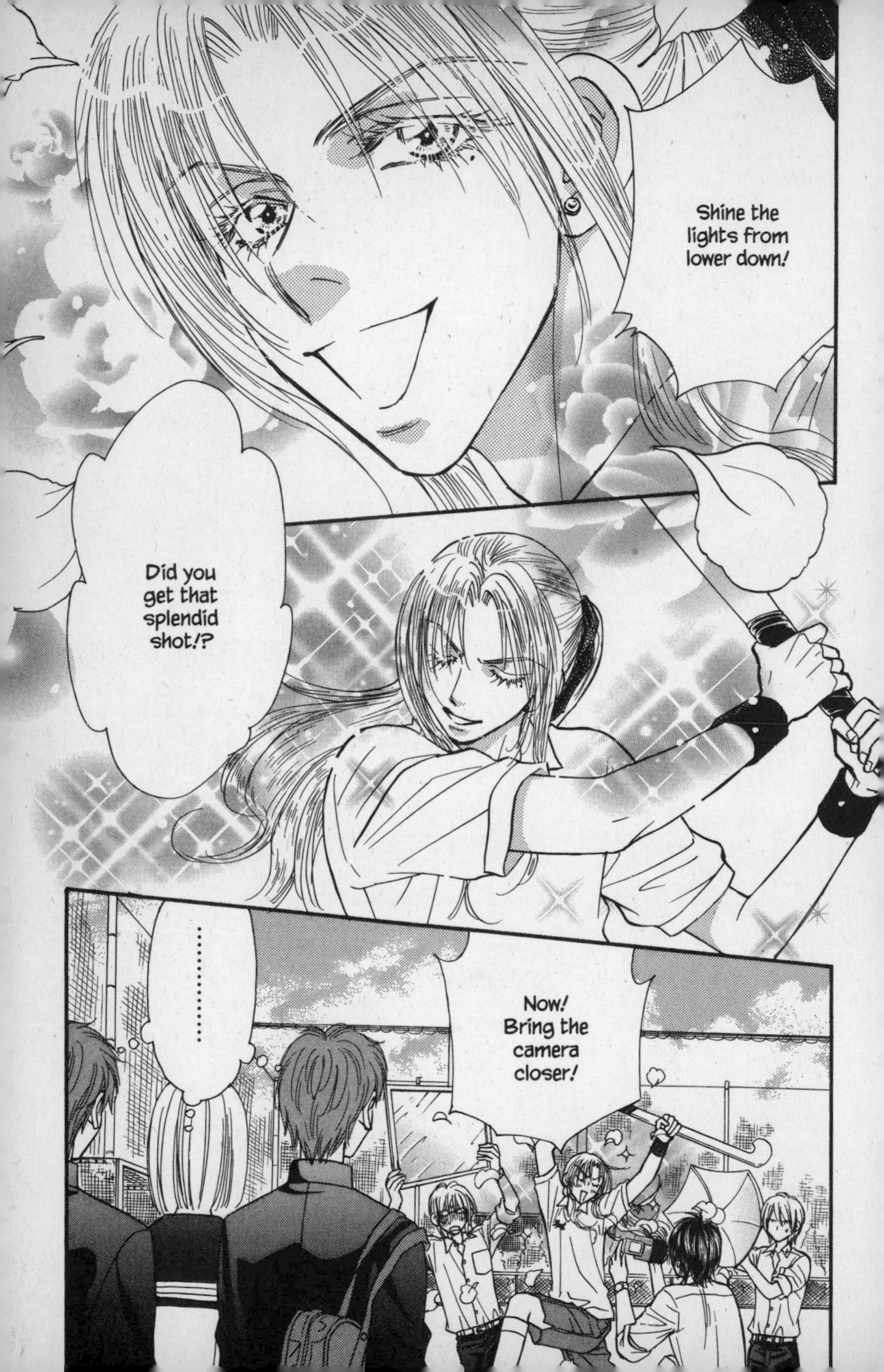
Shine the lights from lower down!
Did you get that splendid shot!?
Now! Bring the camera closer!
......

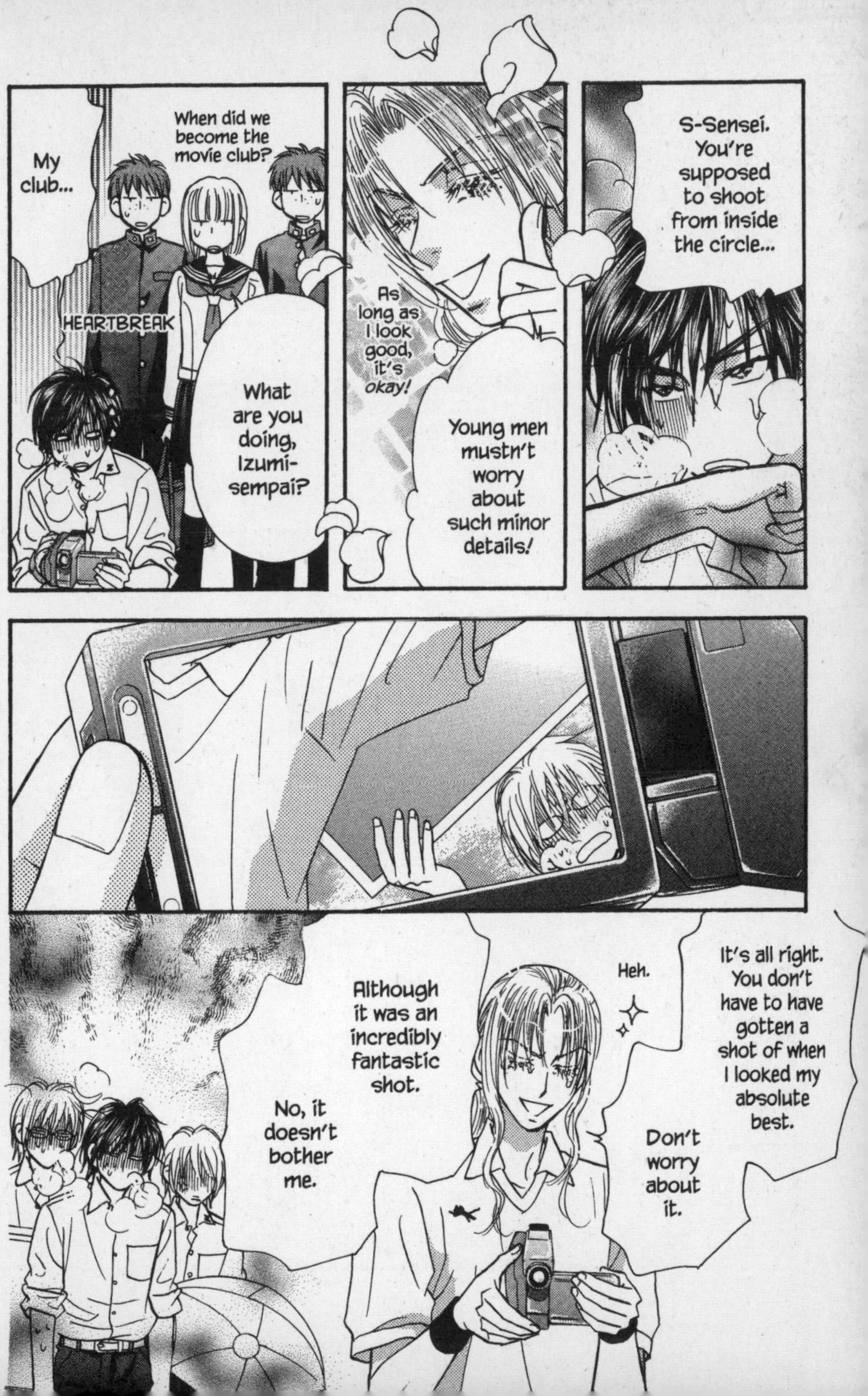

S-Sensei. You're supposed to shoot from inside the circle...
Young men mustn't worry about such minor details!
As long as I look good, it's *okay!*
When did we become the movie club?
My club...
HEARTBREAK
What are you doing, Izumi-sempai?
It's all right. You don't have to have gotten a shot of when I looked my absolute best.
Heh.
Don't worry about it.
Although it was an incredibly fantastic shot.
No, it doesn't bother me.

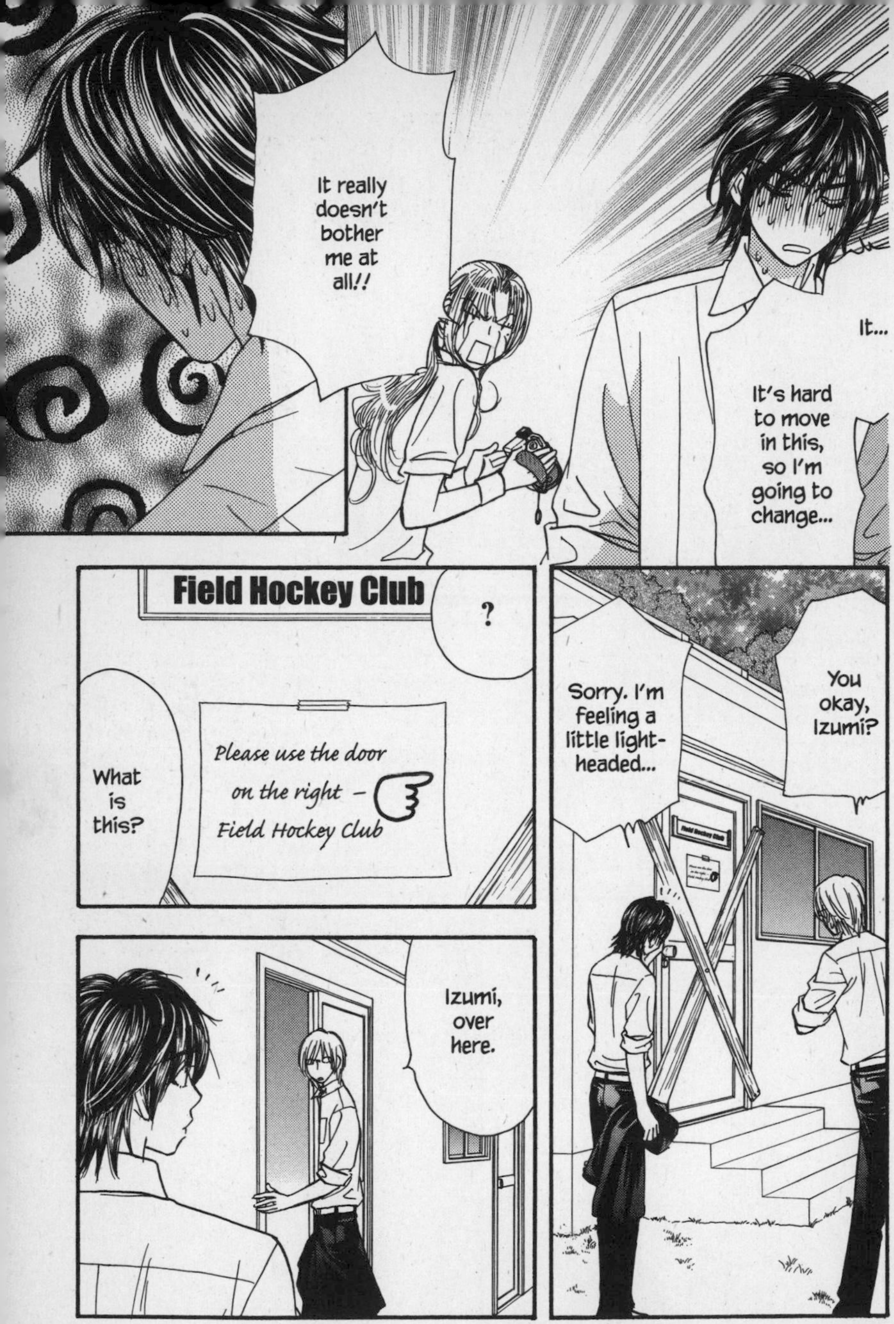
It...
It's hard to move in this, so I'm going to change...
It really doesn't bother me at all!!
You okay, Izumi?
Sorry. I'm feeling a little light-headed...
?
Field Hockey Club
Please use the door on the right – Field Hockey Club
What is this?
Izumi, over here.

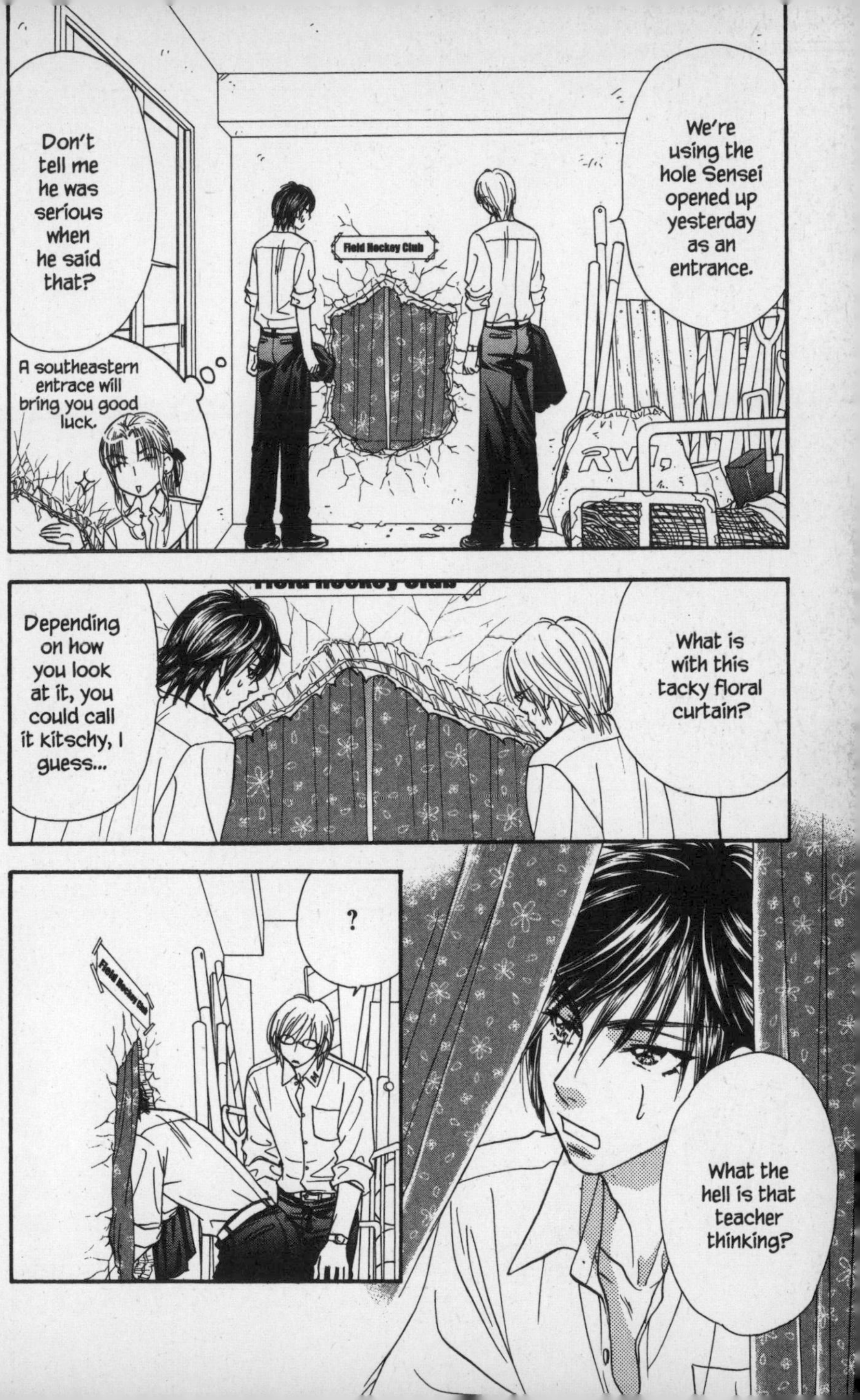
We're using the hole Sensei opened up yesterday as an entrance.
Field Hockey Club
Don't tell me he was serious when he said that?
A southeastern entrace will bring you good luck.
What is with this tacky floral curtain?
Depending on how you look at it, you could call it kitschy, I guess...
What the hell is that teacher thinking?
?
Field Hockey Club

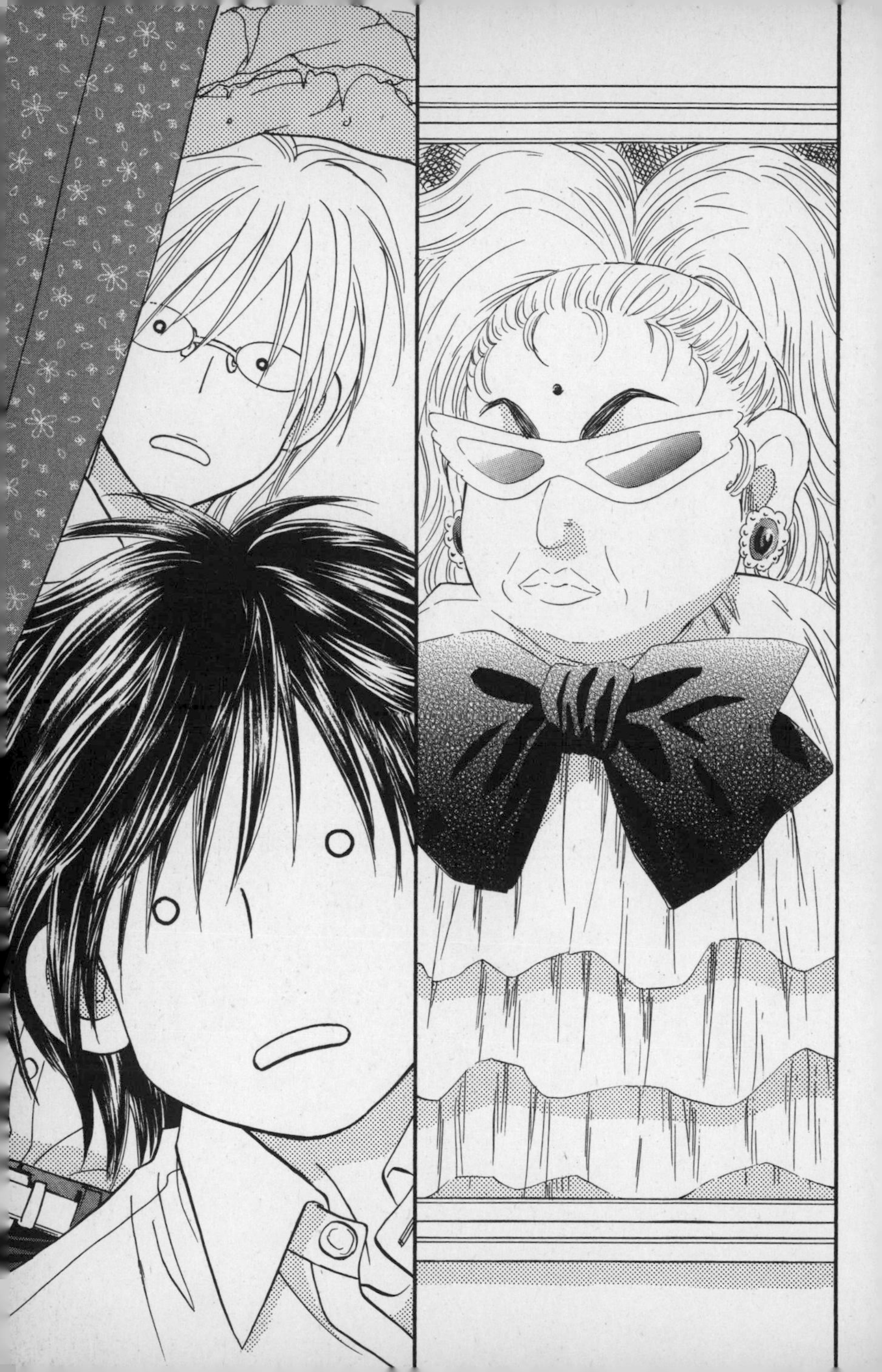

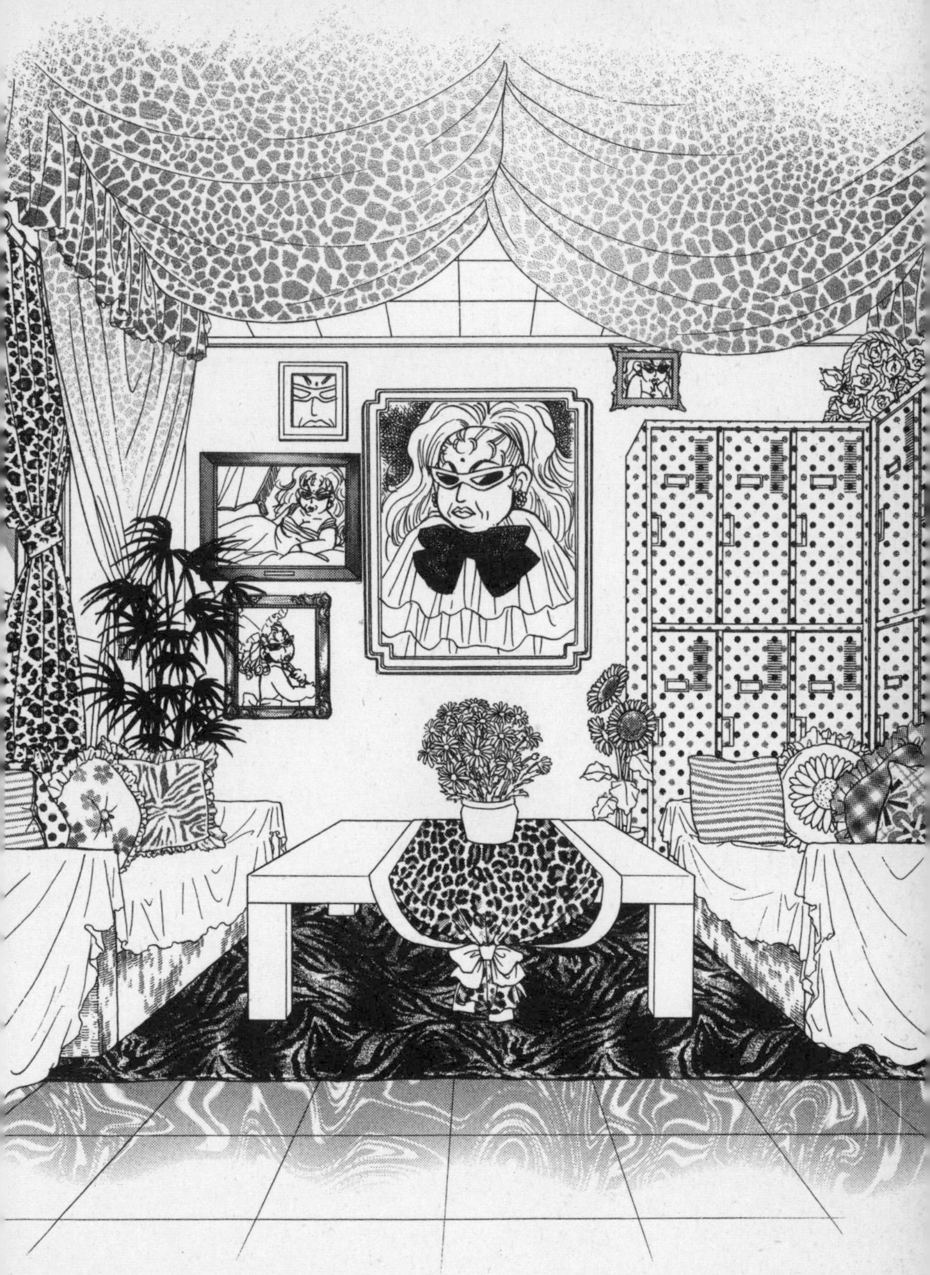

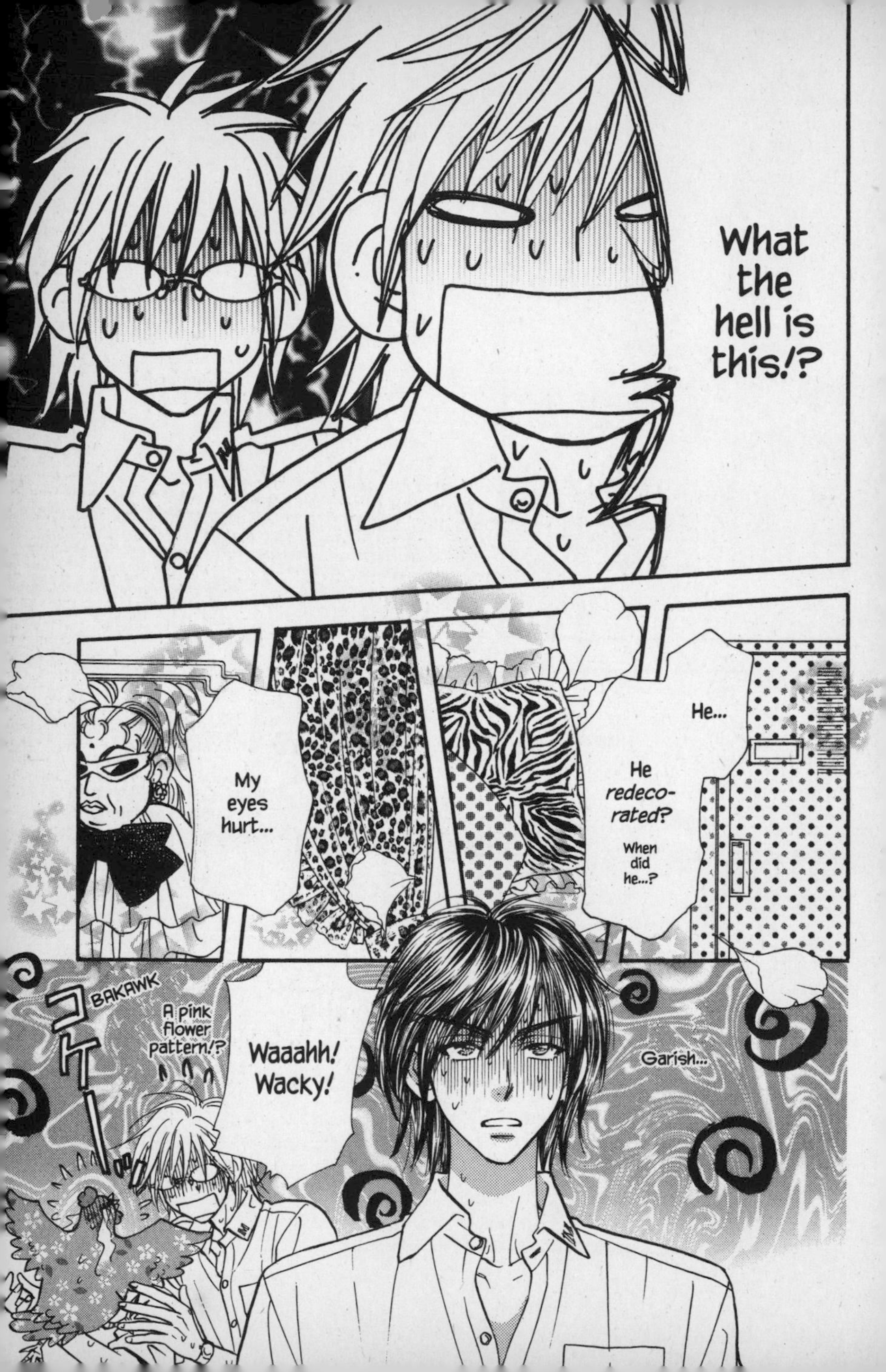
What the hell is this!?
He...
He redecorated?
When did he...?
My eyes hurt...
Garish...
Waaahh! Wacky!
A pink flower pattern!?
BAKAWK

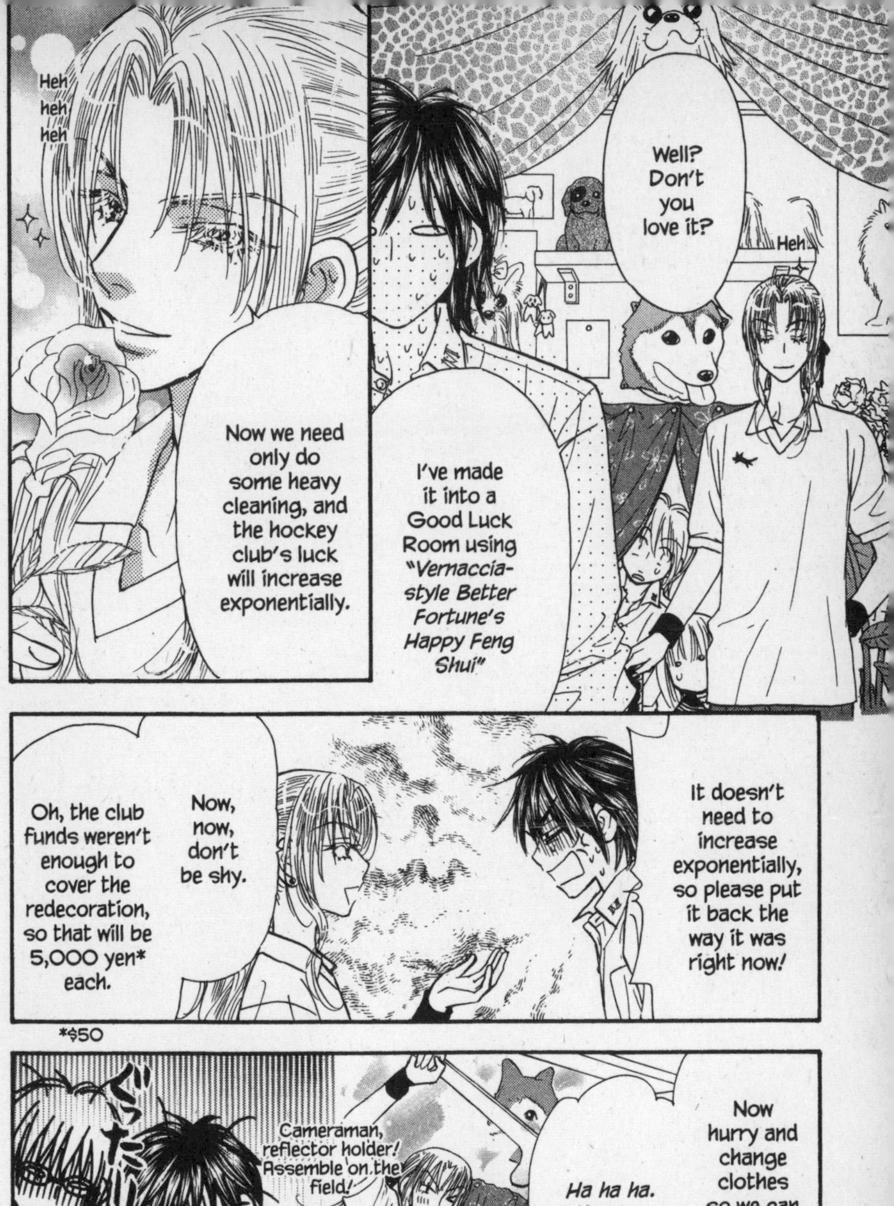
Heh
Well? Don't you love it?
I've made it into a Good Luck Room using "Vernaccia-style Better Fortune's Happy Feng Shui"
Heh heh heh
Now we need only do some heavy cleaning, and the hockey club's luck will increase exponentially.
It doesn't need to increase exponentially, so please put it back the way it was right now!
Now, now, don't be shy.
Oh, the club funds weren't enough to cover the redecoration, so that will be 5,000 yen* each.

*$50

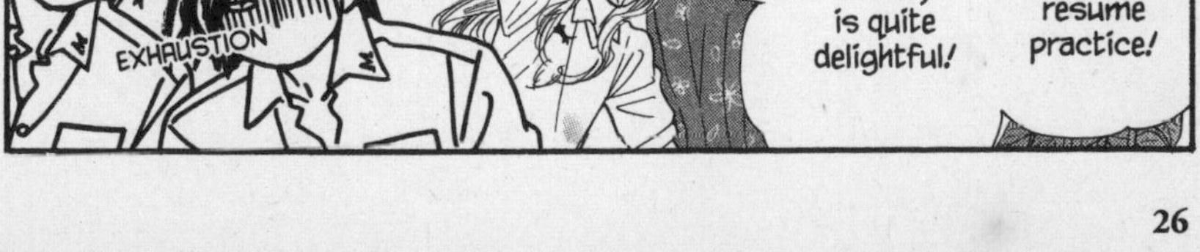
Now hurry and change clothes so we can resume practice!
Ha ha ha. Hockey is quite delightful!
Cameraman, reflector holder! Assemble on the field!
EXHAUSTION

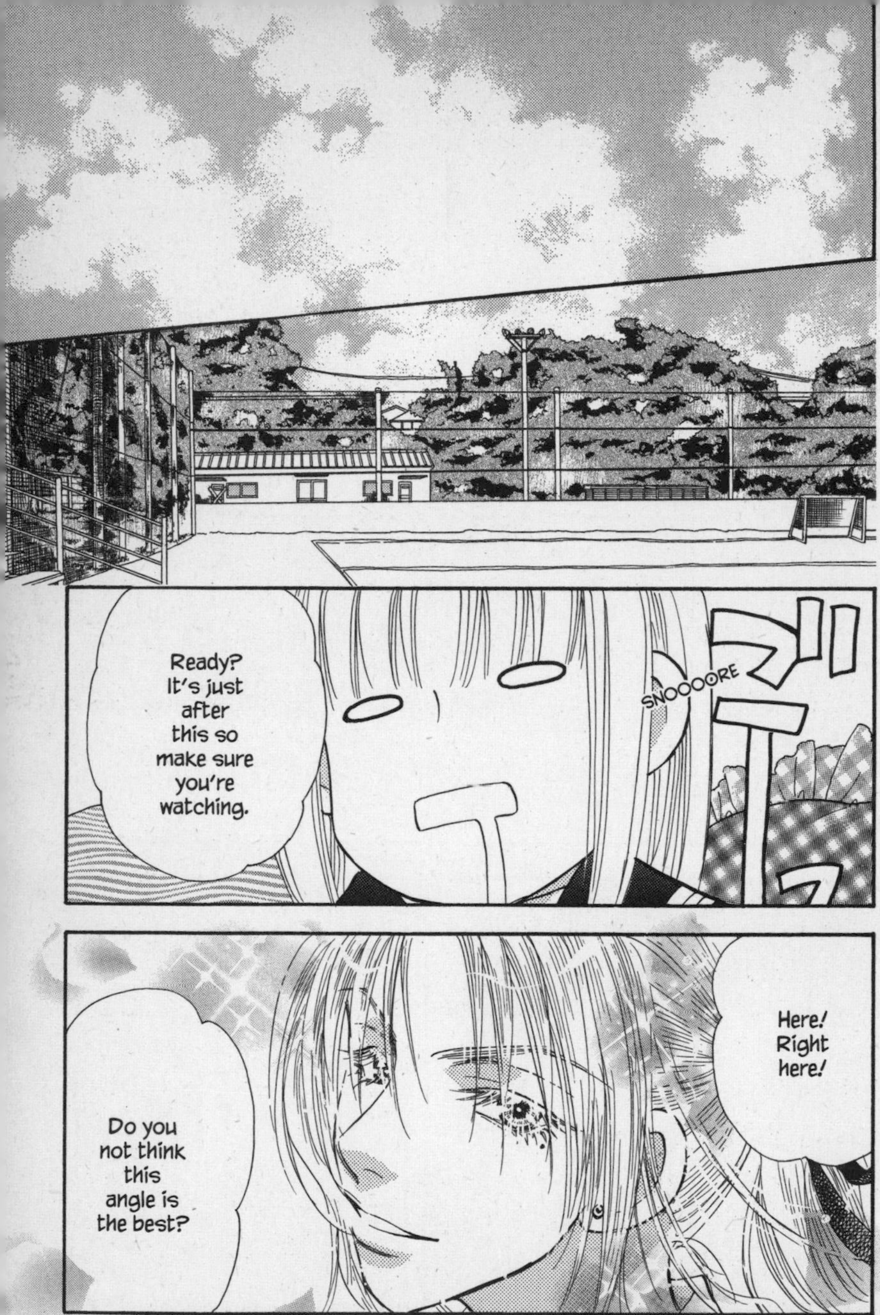
SNOOOORE
Ready? It's just after this so make sure you're watching.
Here! Right here!
Do you not think this angle is the best?

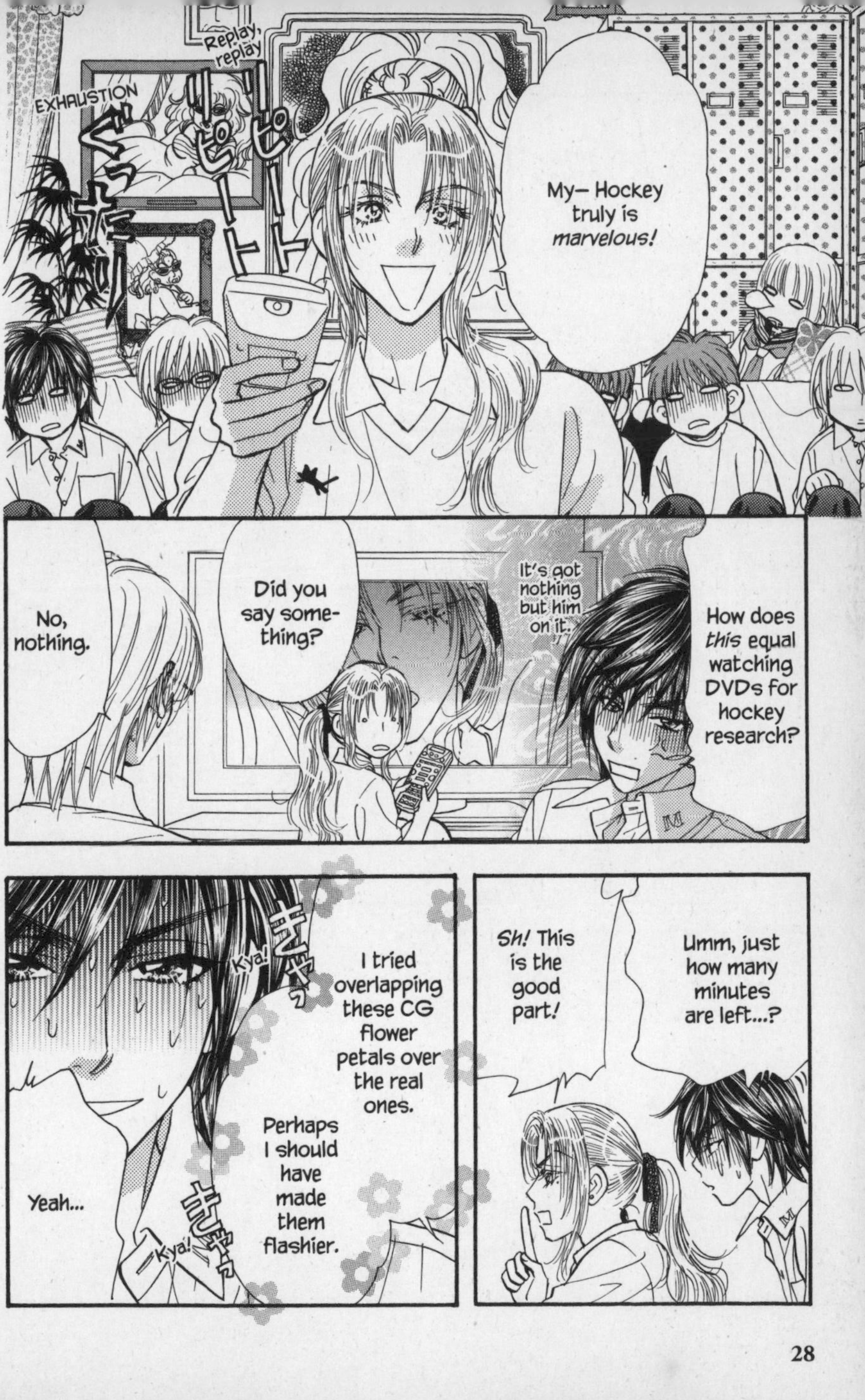
My— Hockey truly is *marvelous!*
リピート リピート
Replay, replay
ぐったり
EXHAUSTION
How does *this* equal watching DVDs for hockey research?
It's got nothing but him on it.
Did you say some-thing?
No, nothing.
Umm, just how many minutes are left...?
Sh! This is the good part!
I tried overlapping these CG flower petals over the real ones.
Perhaps I should have made them flashier.
きゃっ
Kya!
きゃっ
Kya!
Yeah...

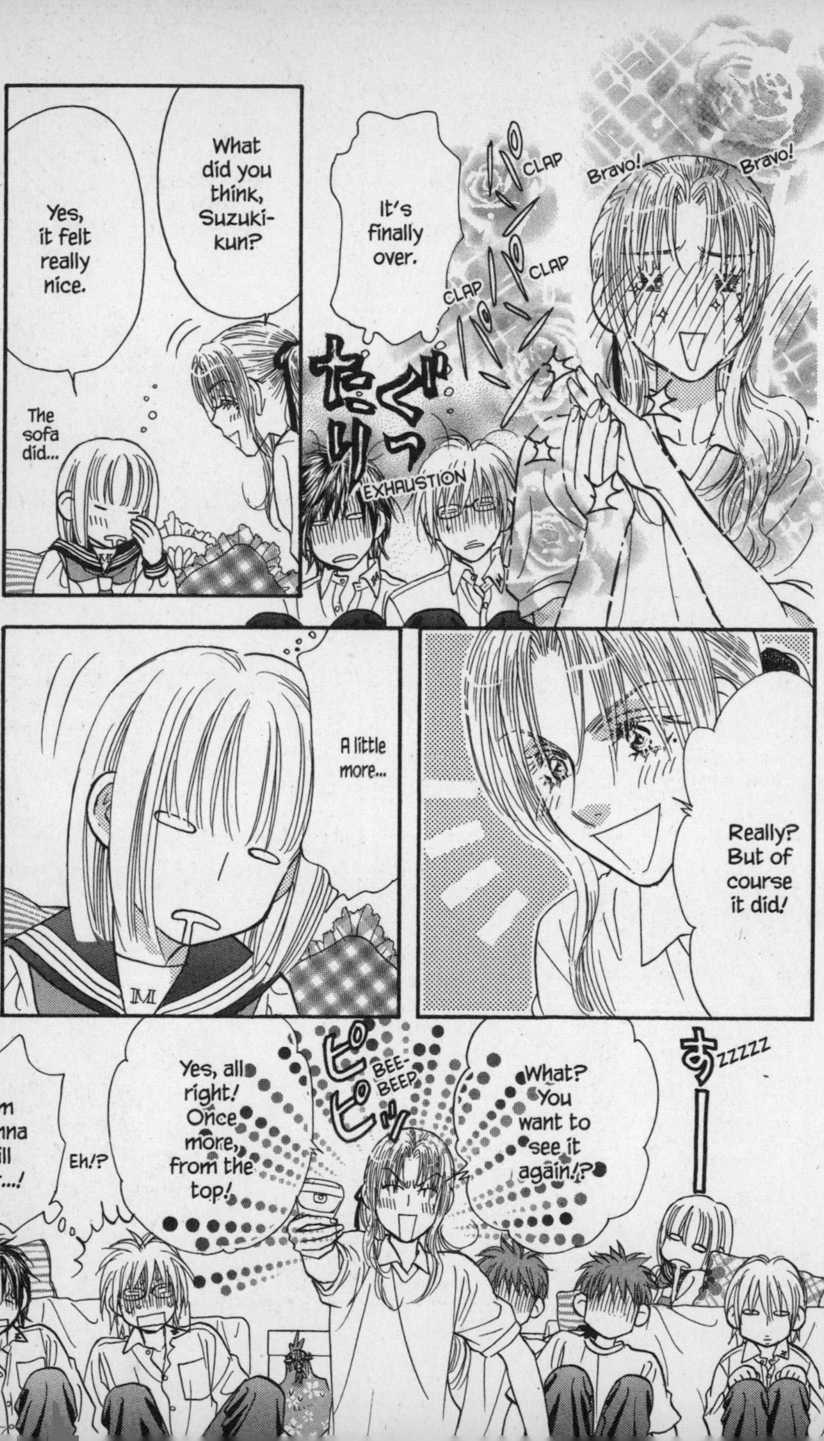
Bravo!
Bravo!
CLAP
CLAP
CLAP
It's finally over.
EXHAUSTION
What did you think, Suzuki-kun?
Yes, it felt really nice.
The sofa did...
Really? But of course it did!
A little more...
ZZZZZ
What? You want to see it again!?
BEE-BEEP
Yes, all right! Once more, from the top!
Eh!?
I'm gonna kill her...!

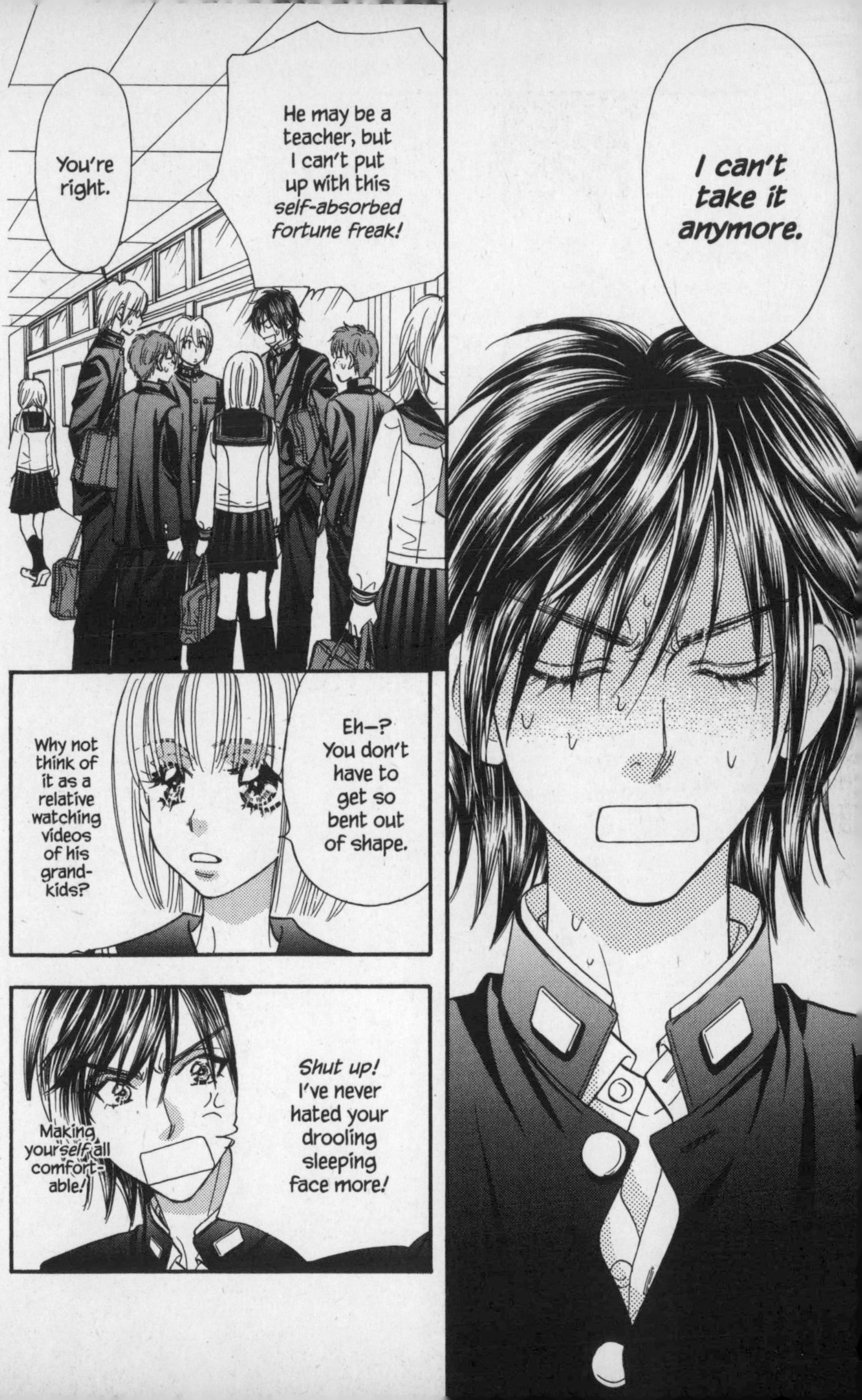
I can't take it anymore.
He may be a teacher, but I can't put up with this self-absorbed fortune freak!
You're right.
Eh—? You don't have to get so bent out of shape.
Why not think of it as a relative watching videos of his grand-kids?
Shut up! I've never hated your drooling sleeping face more!
Making yourself all comfort-able!

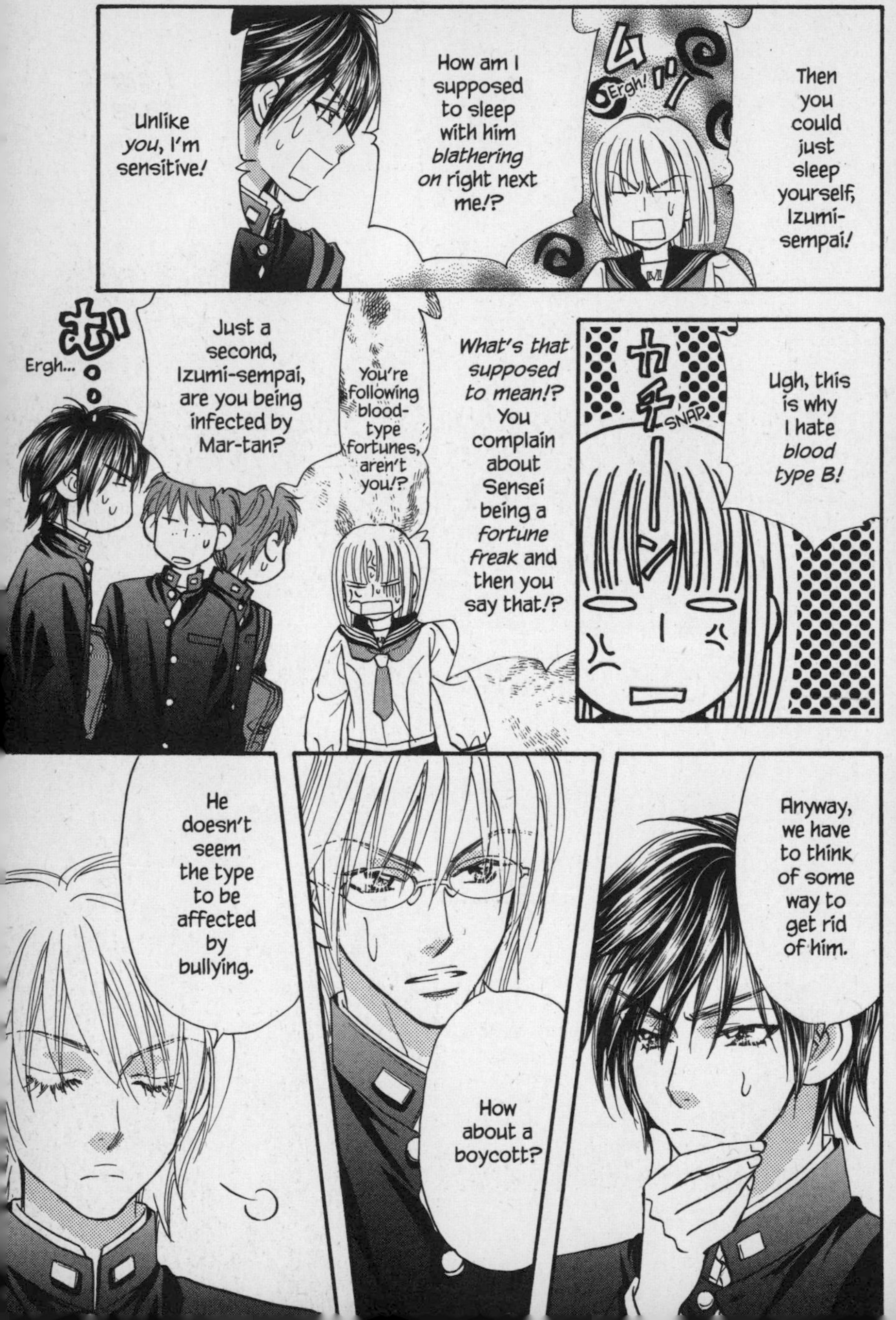
Then you could just sleep yourself, Izumi-sempai!
Ergh!
How am I supposed to sleep with him *blathering on* right next me!?
Unlike *you*, I'm sensitive!
Ugh, this is why I hate *blood type B!*
SNAP
What's that supposed to mean!? You complain about Sensei being a *fortune freak* and then you say that!?
You're following blood-type fortunes, aren't you!?
Just a second, Izumi-sempai, are you being infected by Mar-tan?
Ergh...
Anyway, we have to think of some way to get rid of him.
How about a boycott?
He doesn't seem the type to be affected by bullying.

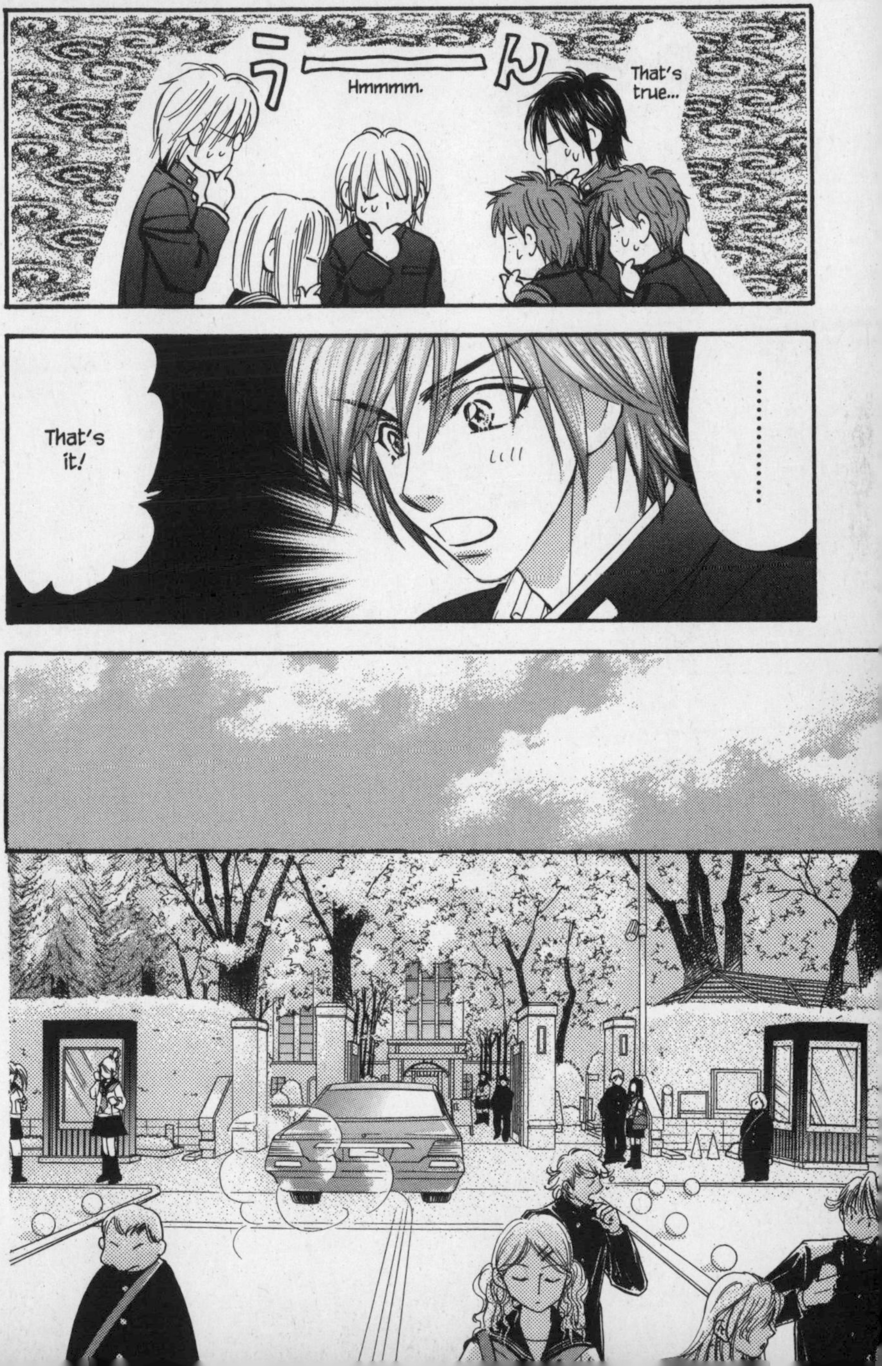
That's true...
うーん
Hmmmm.
....
That's it!

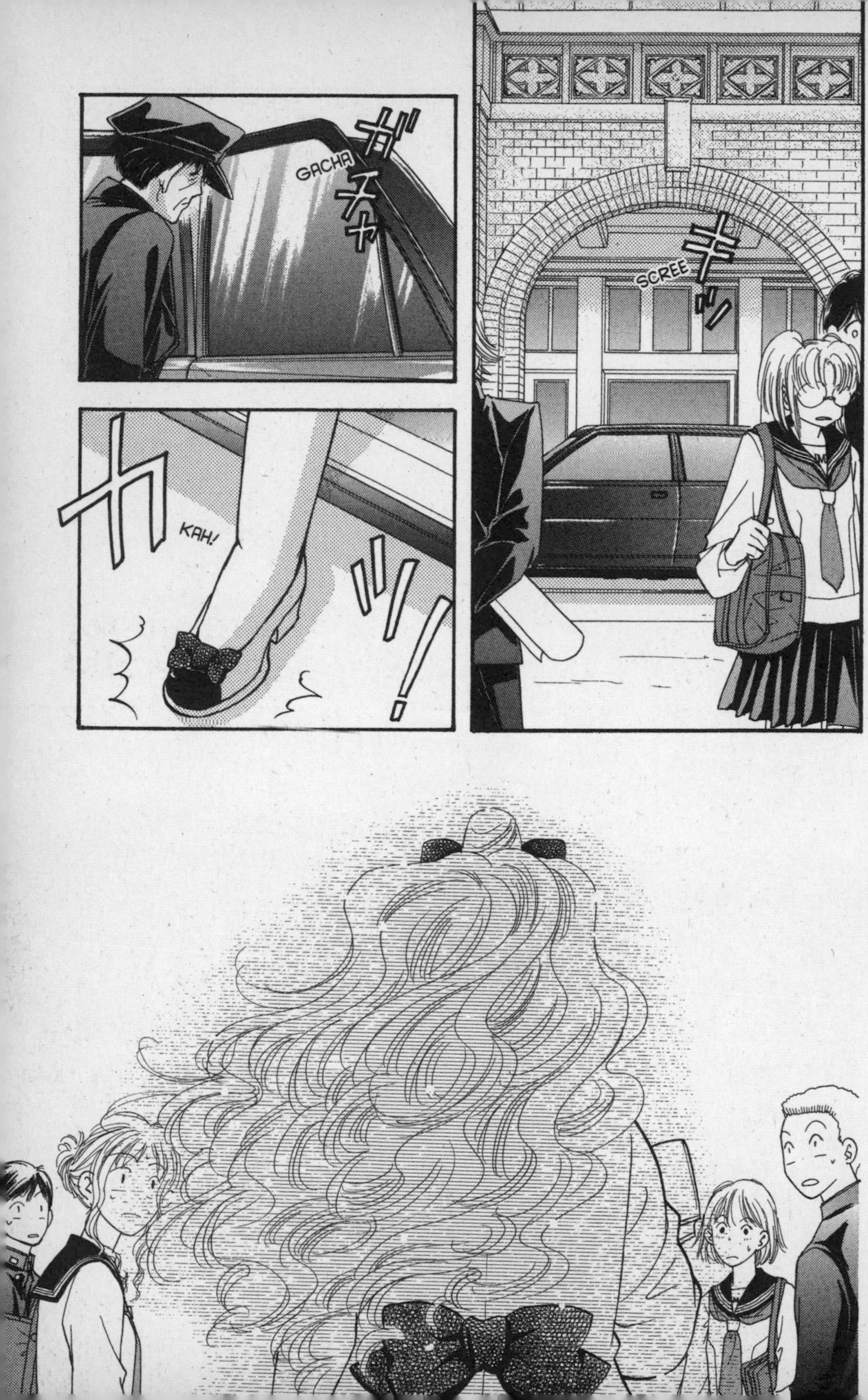
SCREE
GACHA
KAH!

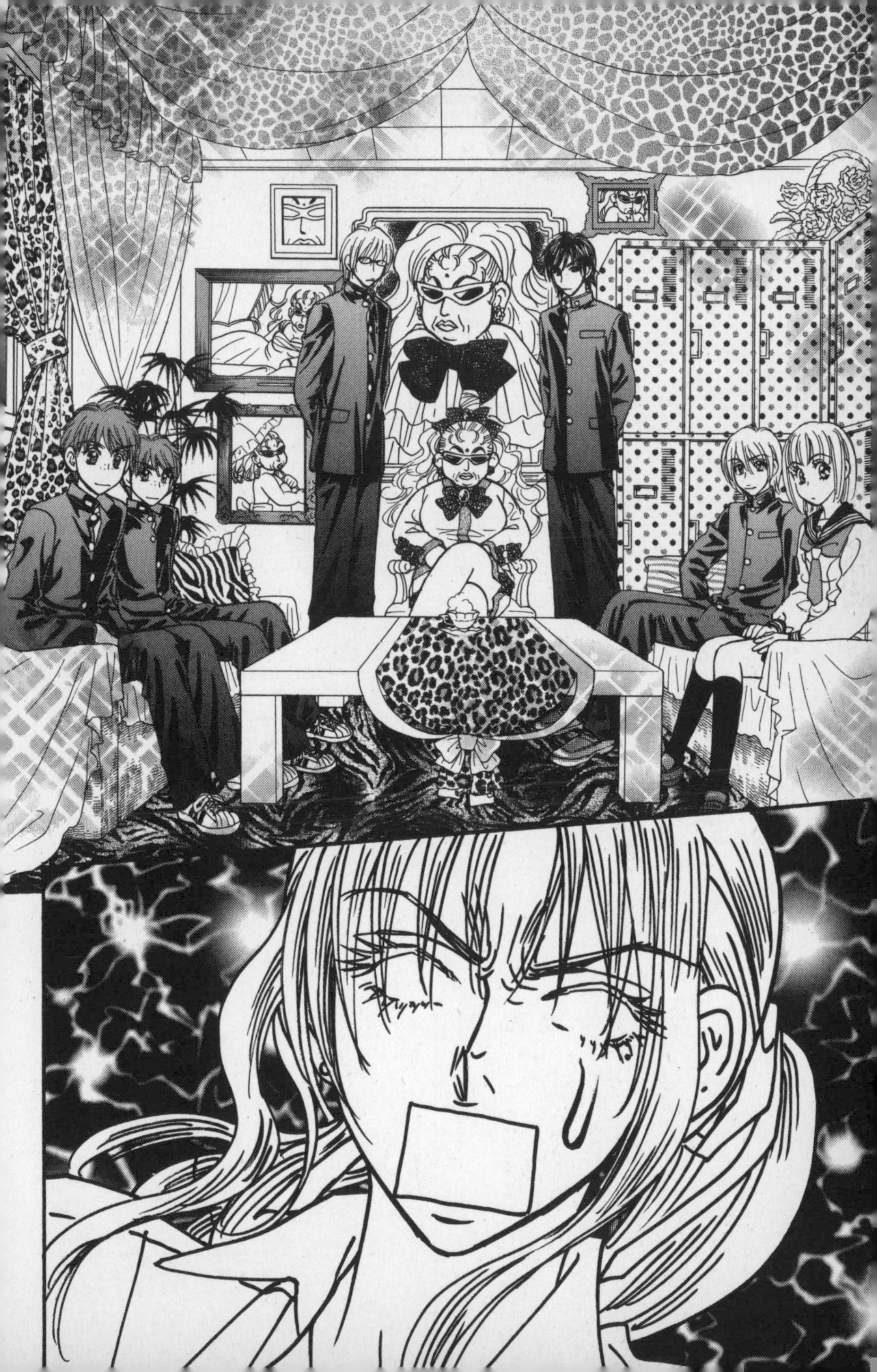

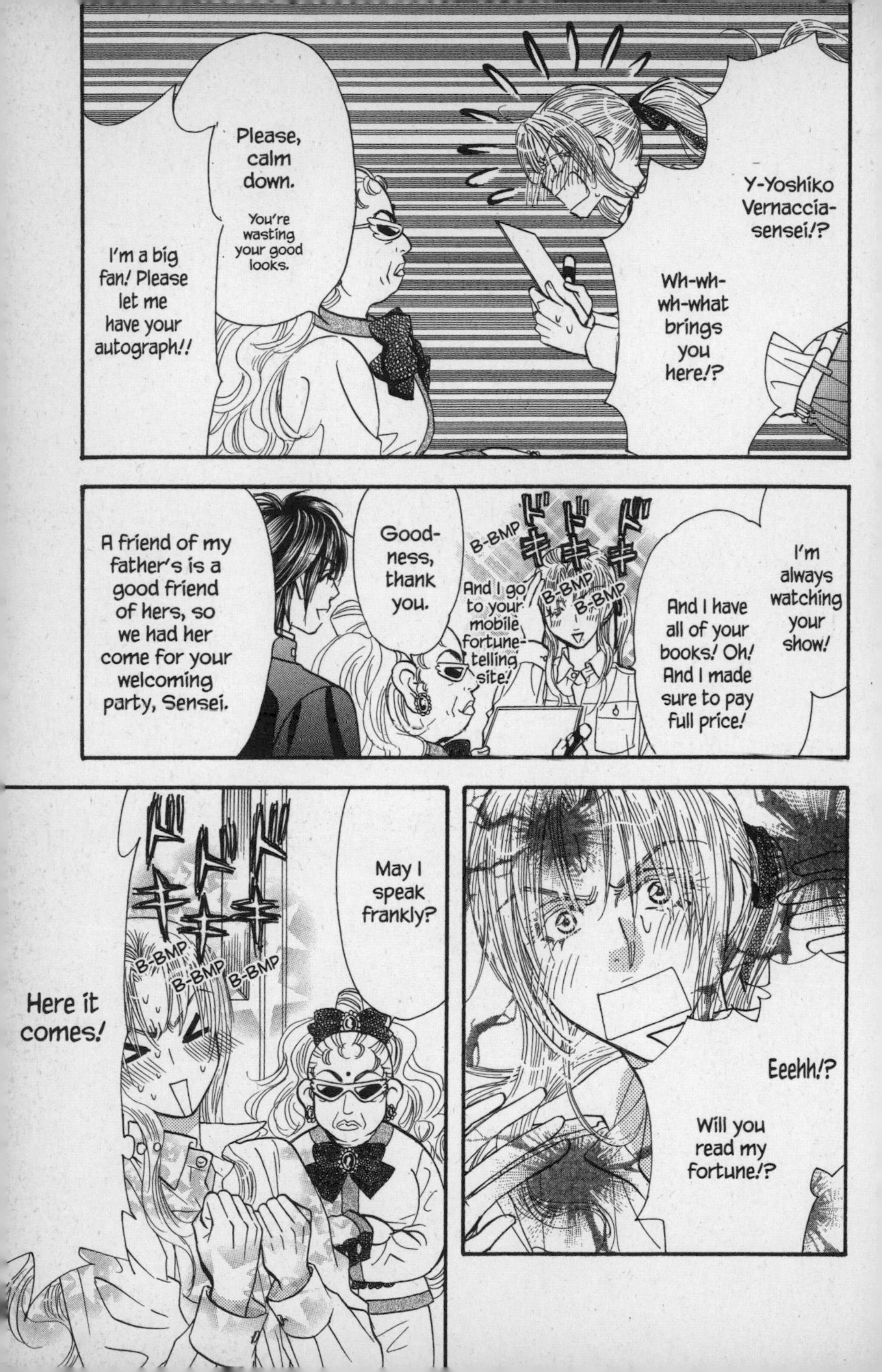
Y-Yoshiko Vernaccia-sensei!?
Wh-wh-wh-what brings you here!?
Please, calm down.
You're wasting your good looks.
I'm a big fan! Please let me have your autograph!!
I'm always watching your show!
And I have all of your books! Oh! And I made sure to pay full price!
B-BMP B-BMP B-BMP
And I go to your mobile fortune-telling site!
Good-ness, thank you.
A friend of my father's is a good friend of hers, so we had her come for your welcoming party, Sensei.
Eeehh!?
Will you read my fortune!?
May I speak frankly?
B-BMP B-BMP B-BMP
Here it comes!

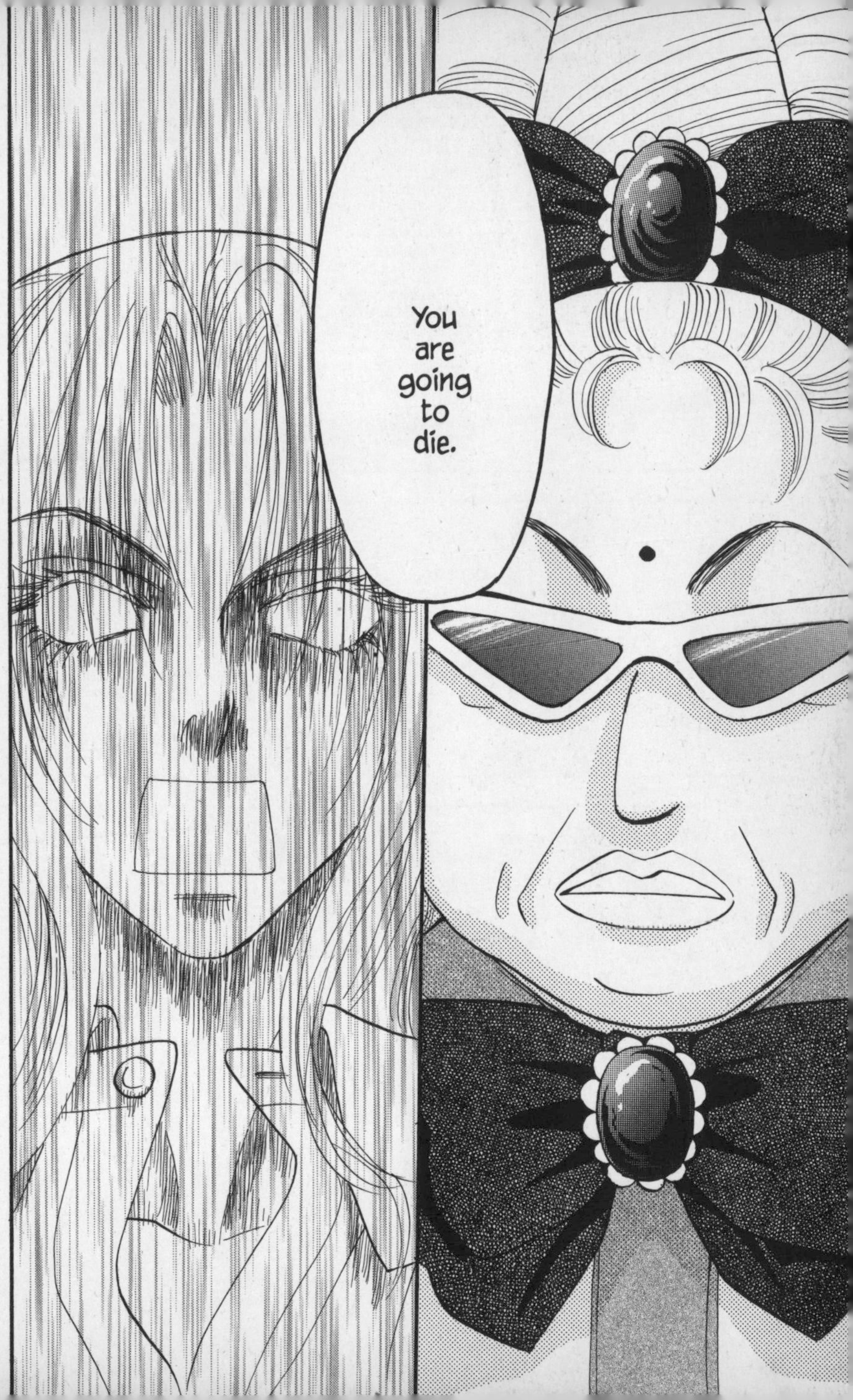
You are going to die.

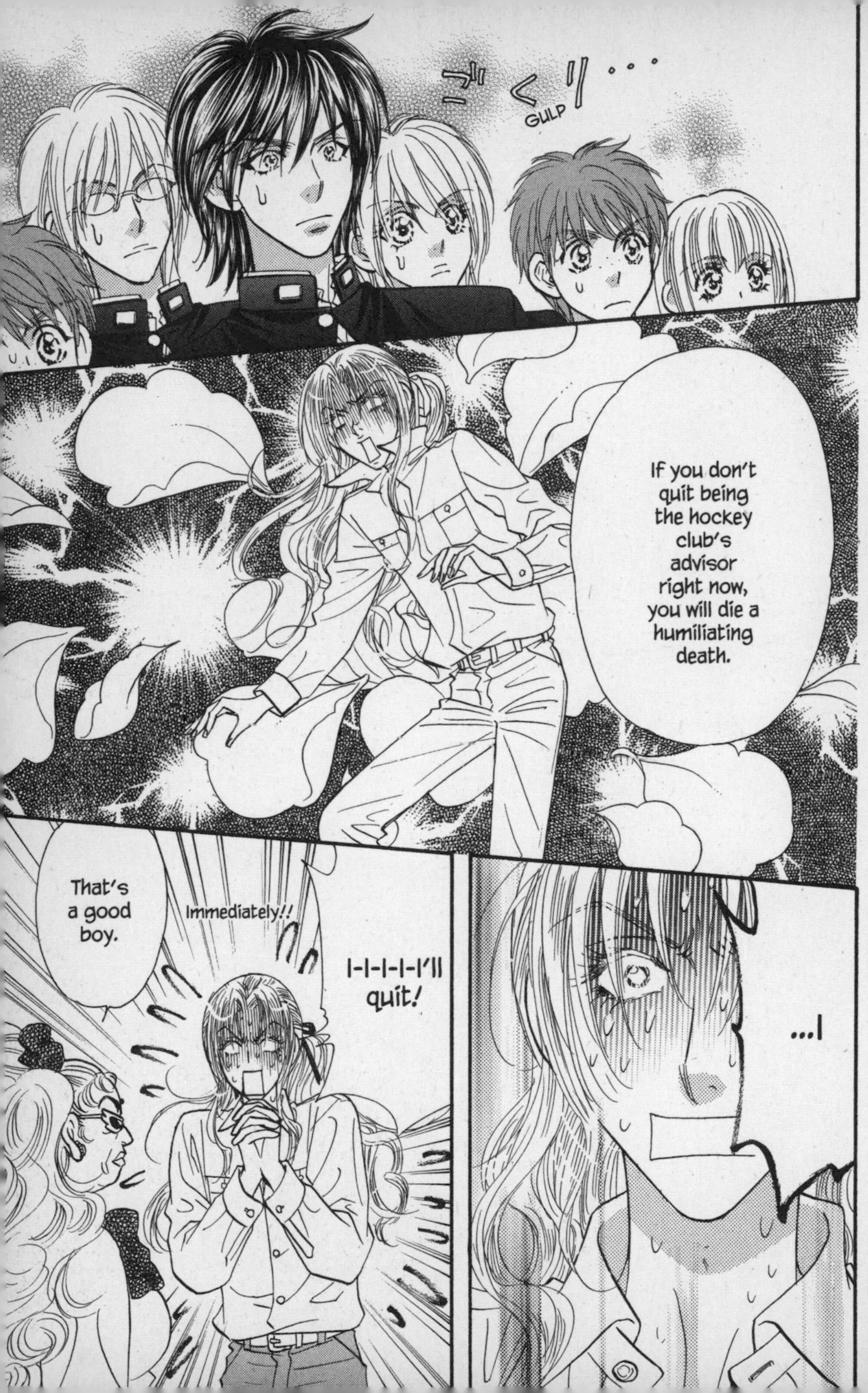
ごくり…
GULP
If you don't quit being the hockey club's advisor right now, you will die a humiliating death.
...I
I-I-I-I-I'll quit!
Immediately!!
That's a good boy.

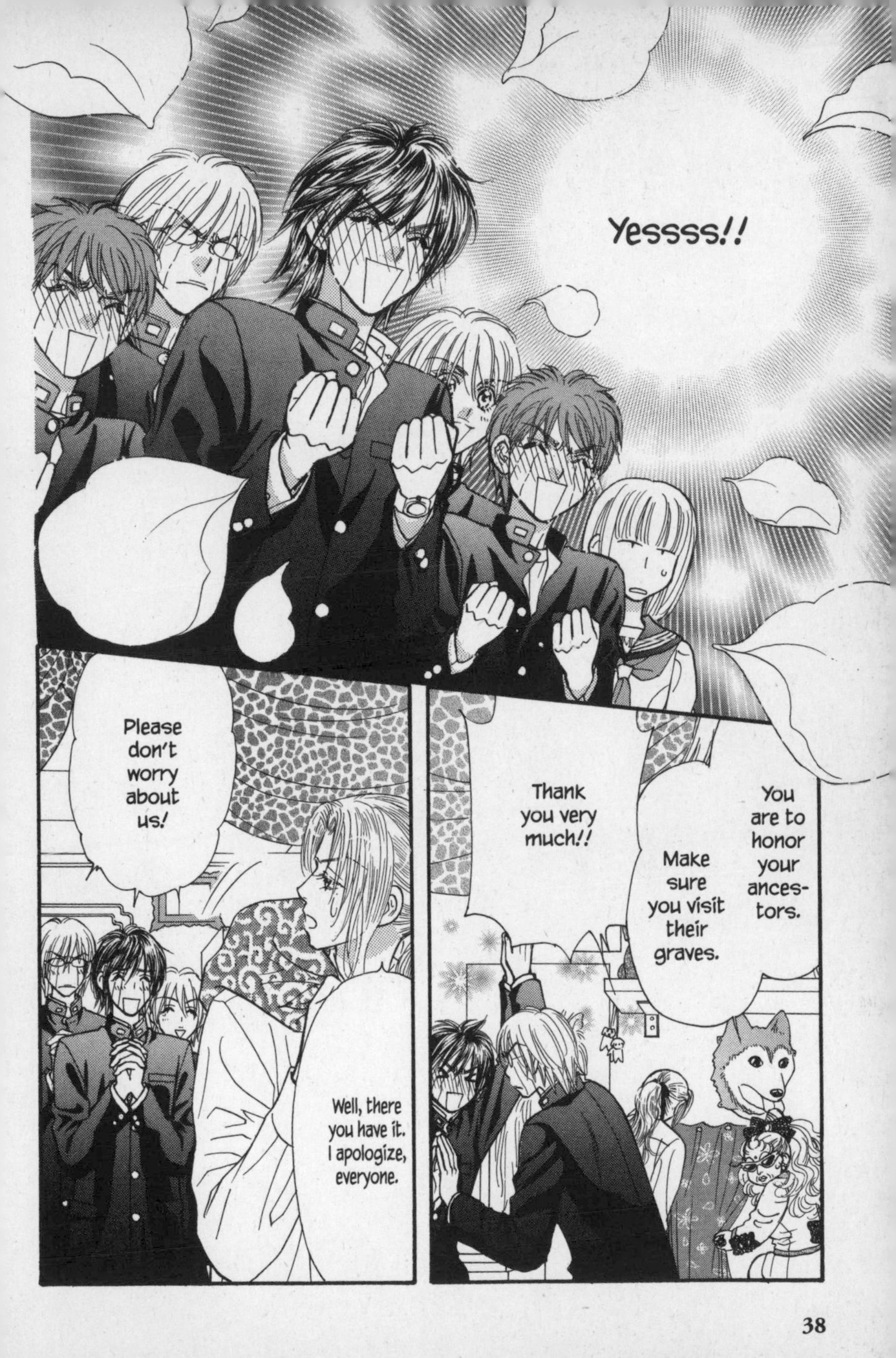
Yessss!!
You are to honor your ancestors.
Make sure you visit their graves.
Thank you very much!!
Well, there you have it. I apologize, everyone.
Please don't worry about us!

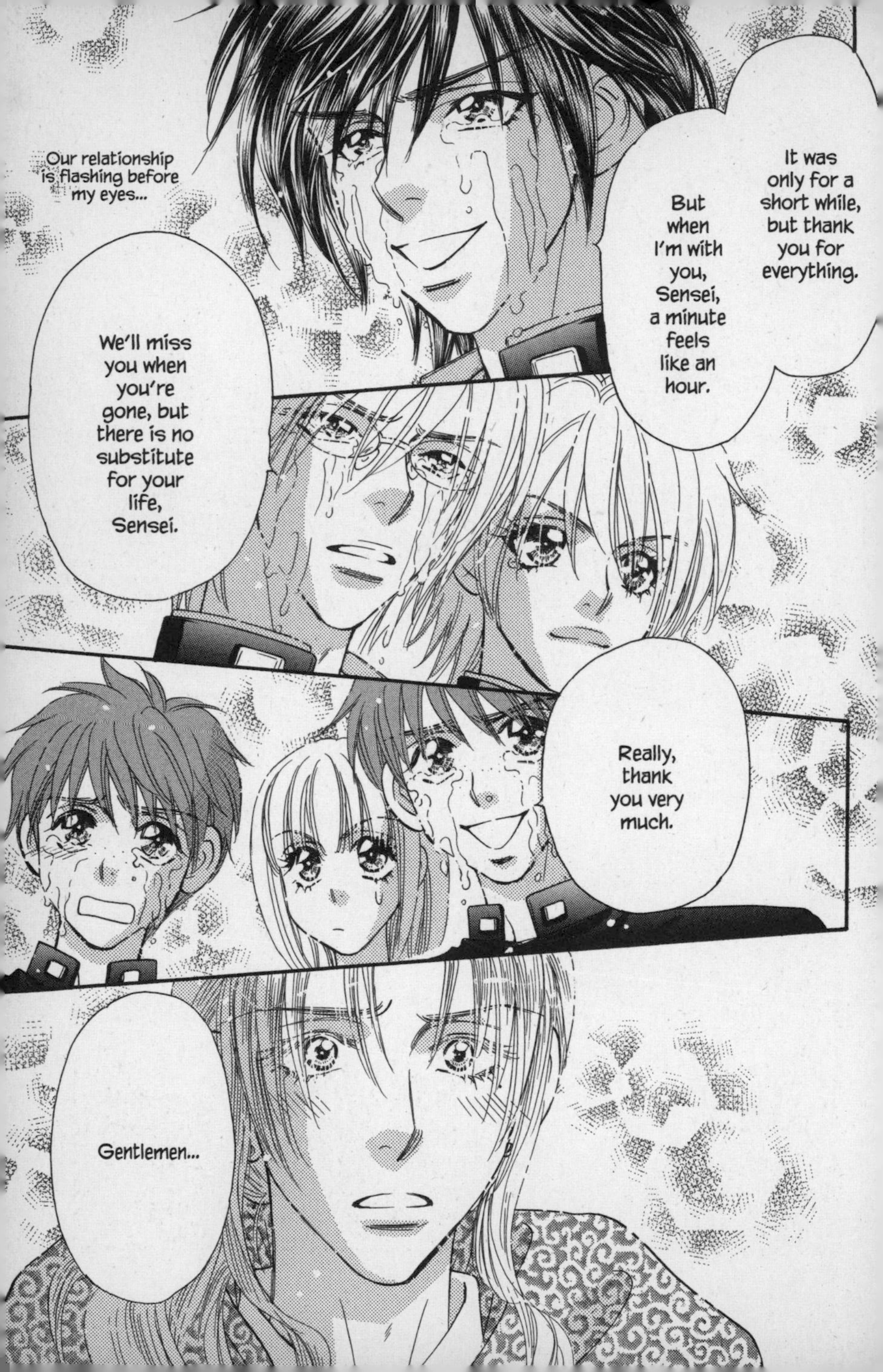
It was only for a short while, but thank you for everything.
But when I'm with you, Sensei, a minute feels like an hour.
Our relationship is flashing before my eyes...
We'll miss you when you're gone, but there is no substitute for your life, Sensei.
Really, thank you very much.
Gentlemen...

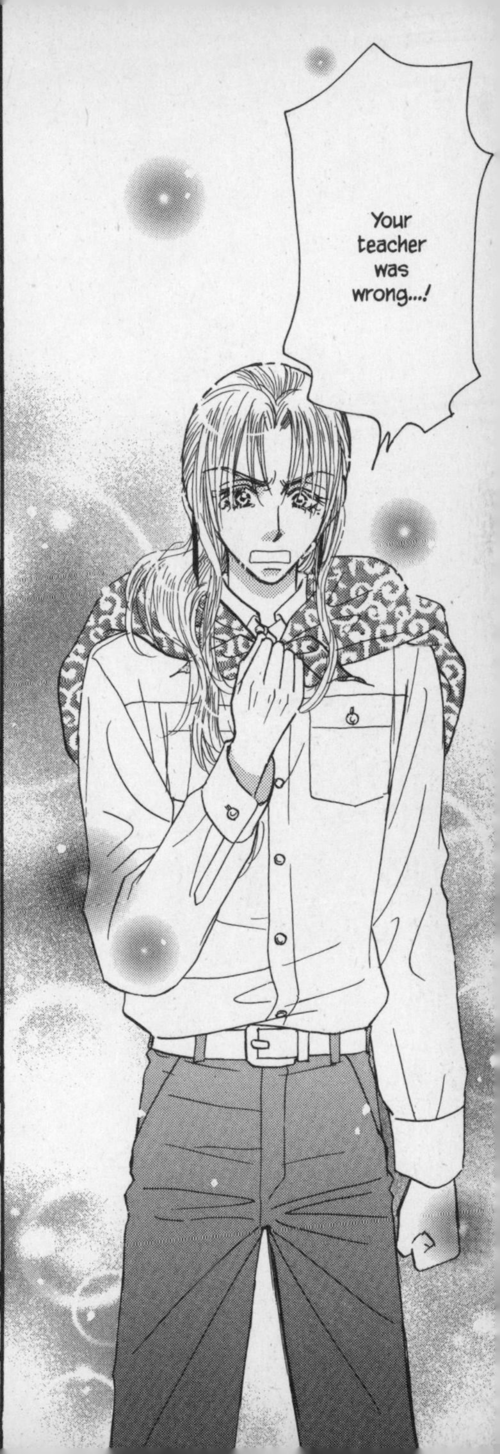
Your teacher was wrong...!
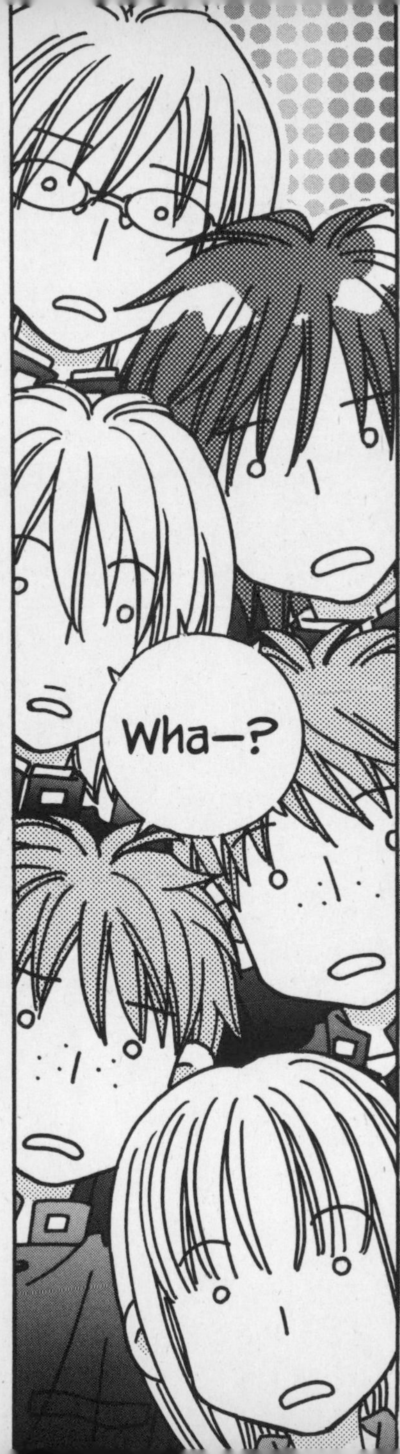
Wha-?

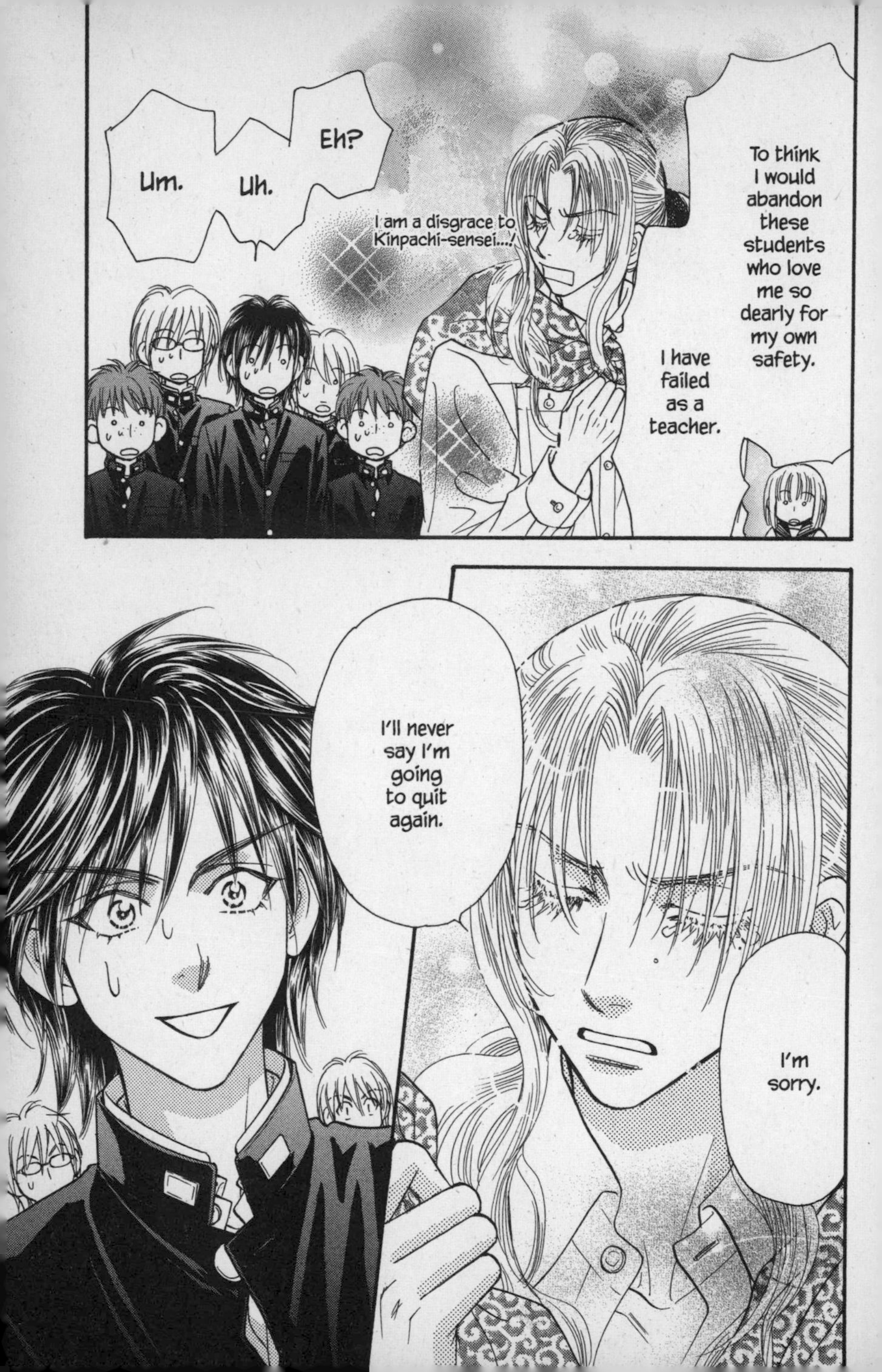
To think I would abandon these students who love me so dearly for my own safety.
I have failed as a teacher.
I am a disgrace to Kinpachi-sensei...!
Eh?
Uh.
Um.
I'm sorry.
I'll never say I'm going to quit again.

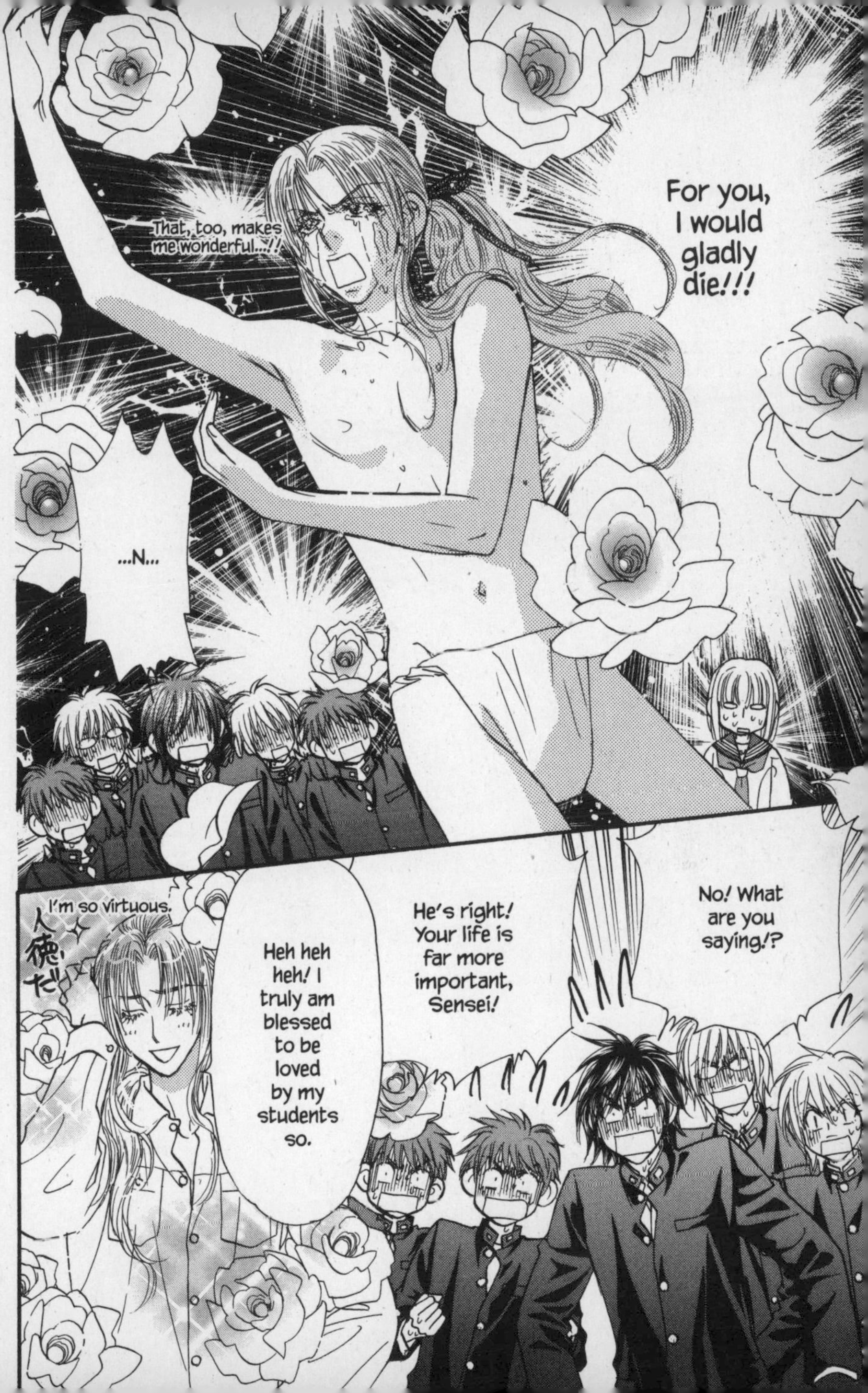
For you, I would gladly die!!!
That, too, makes me wonderful...!!
...N...
No! What are you saying!?
He's right! Your life is far more important, Sensei!
Heh heh heh! I truly am blessed to be loved by my students so.
I'm so virtuous.
人徳だ

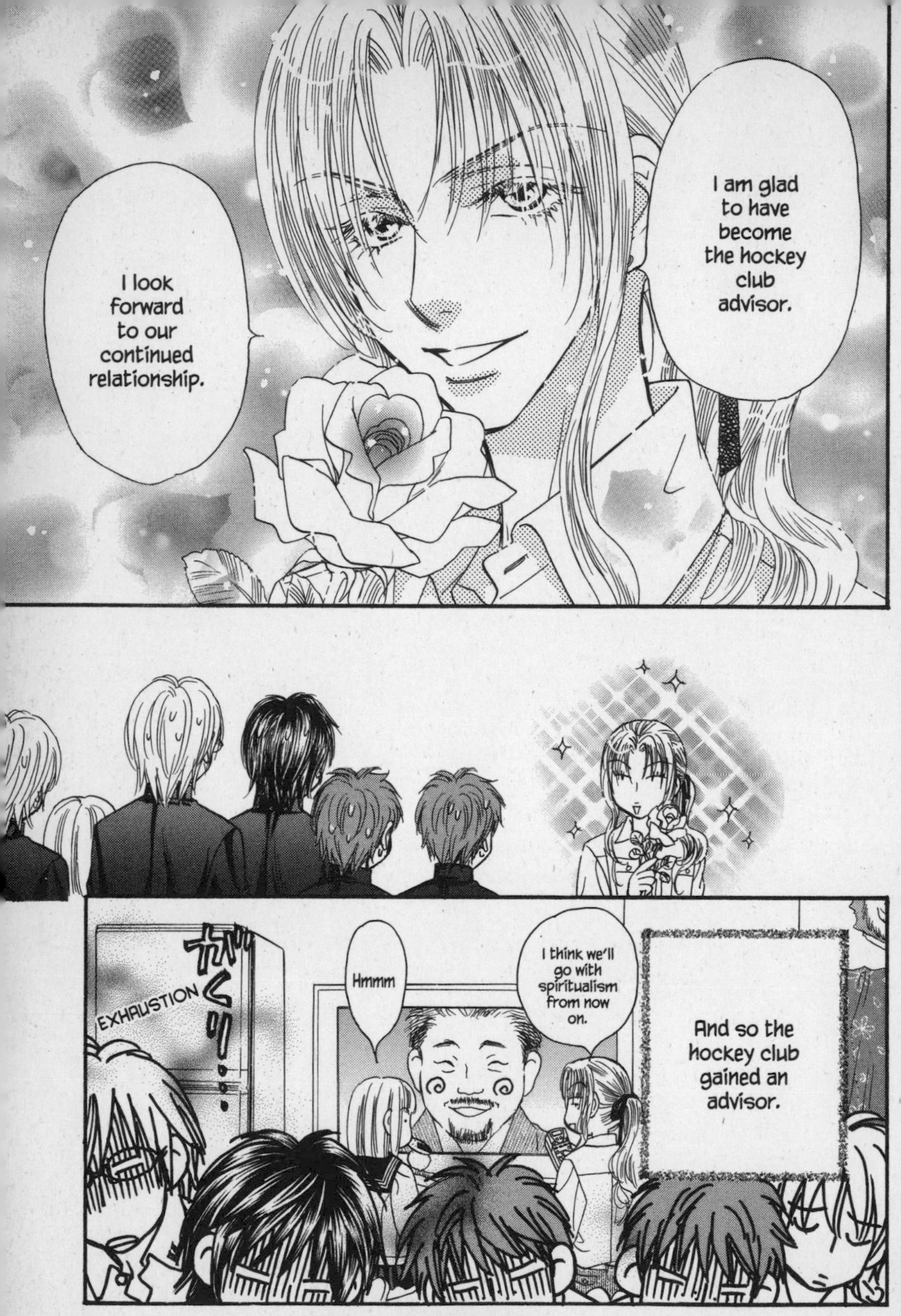
I am glad to have become the hockey club advisor.
I look forward to our continued relationship.
And so the hockey club gained an advisor.
I think we'll go with spiritualism from now on.
Hmmm
EXHAUSTION

The End

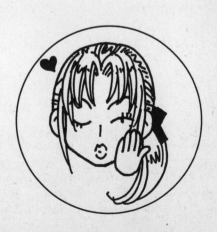

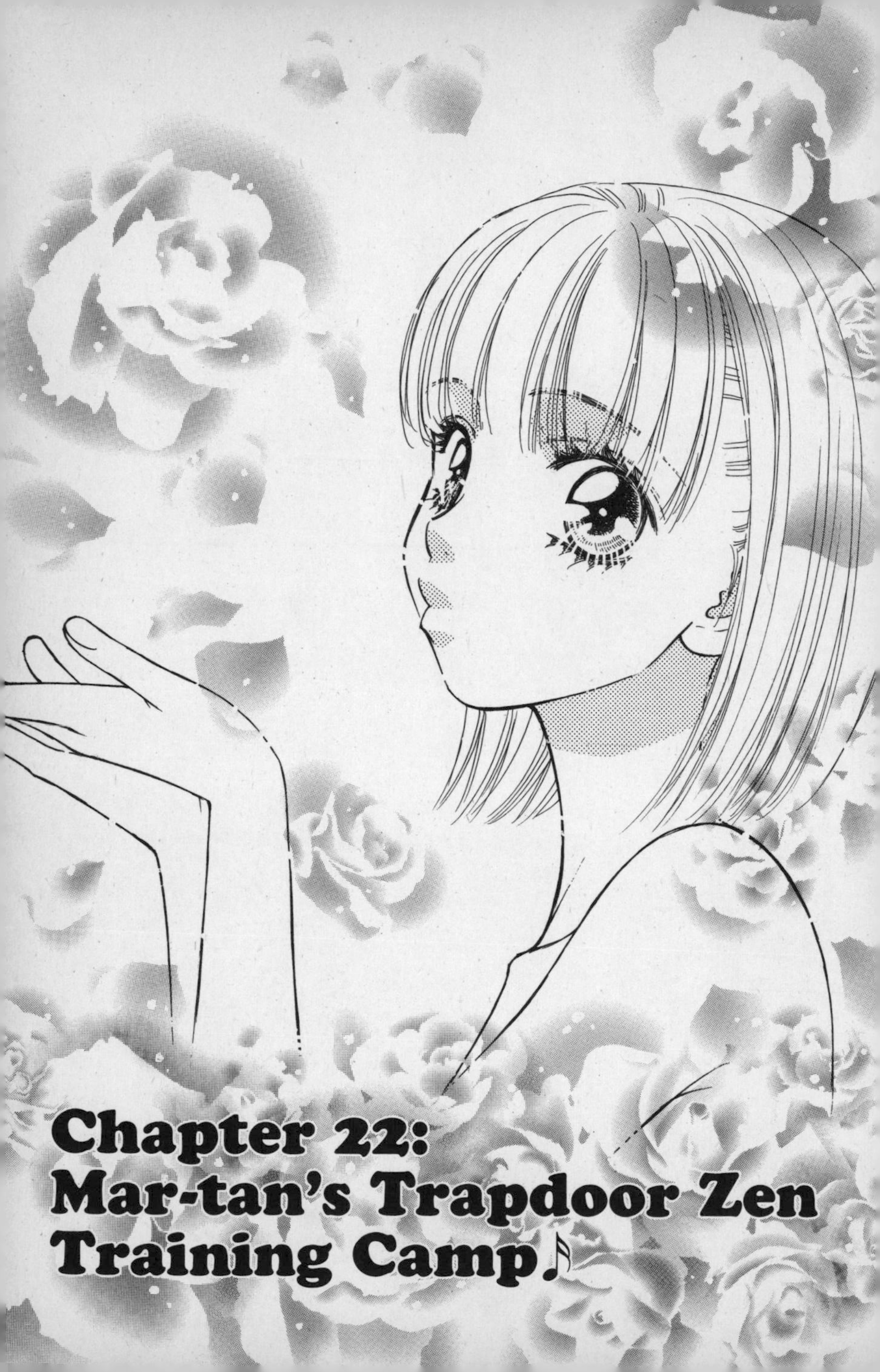

Chapter 22: Mar-tan's Trapdoor Zen Training Camp♪

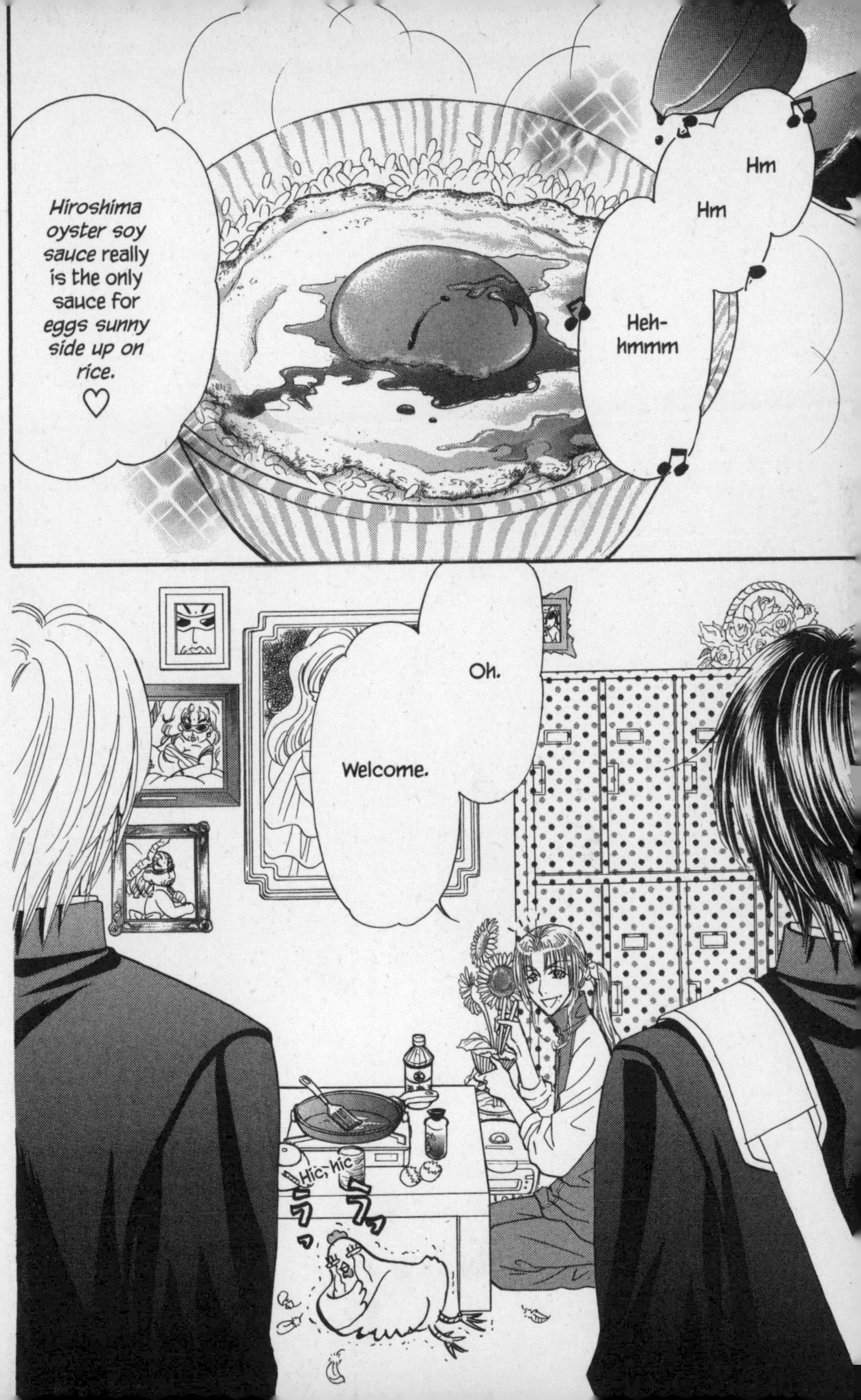
Hm
Hm
Heh-hmmm
Hiroshima oyster soy sauce really is the only sauce for eggs sunny side up on rice. ♡
Oh.
Welcome.
Hic, hic

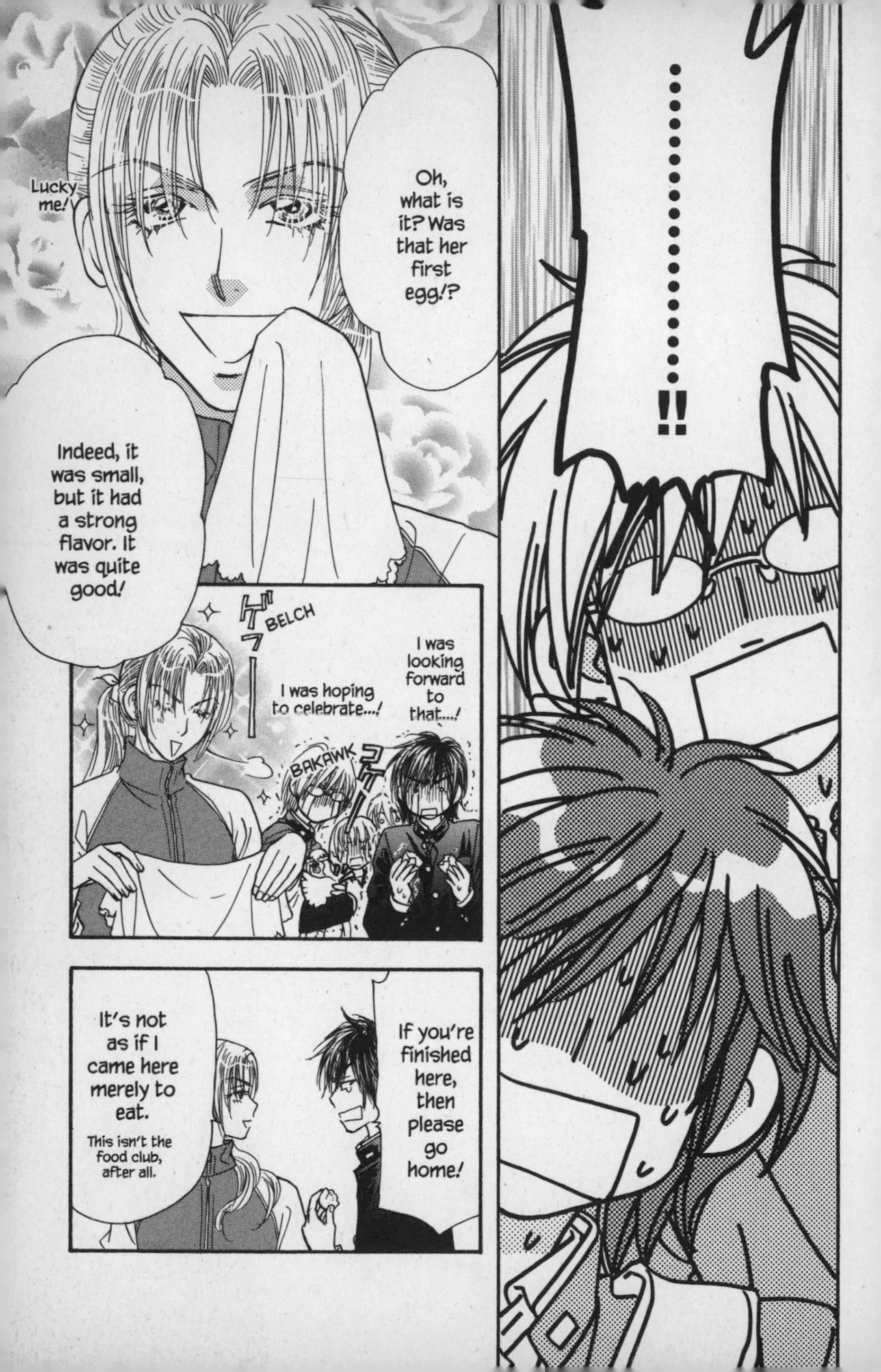
......!!
Oh, what is it? Was that her first egg!?
Lucky me!
Indeed, it was small, but it had a strong flavor. It was quite good!
BELCH
I was looking forward to that...!
I was hoping to celebrate...!
BAKAWK
If you're finished here, then please go home!
It's not as if I came here merely to eat.
This isn't the food club, after all.

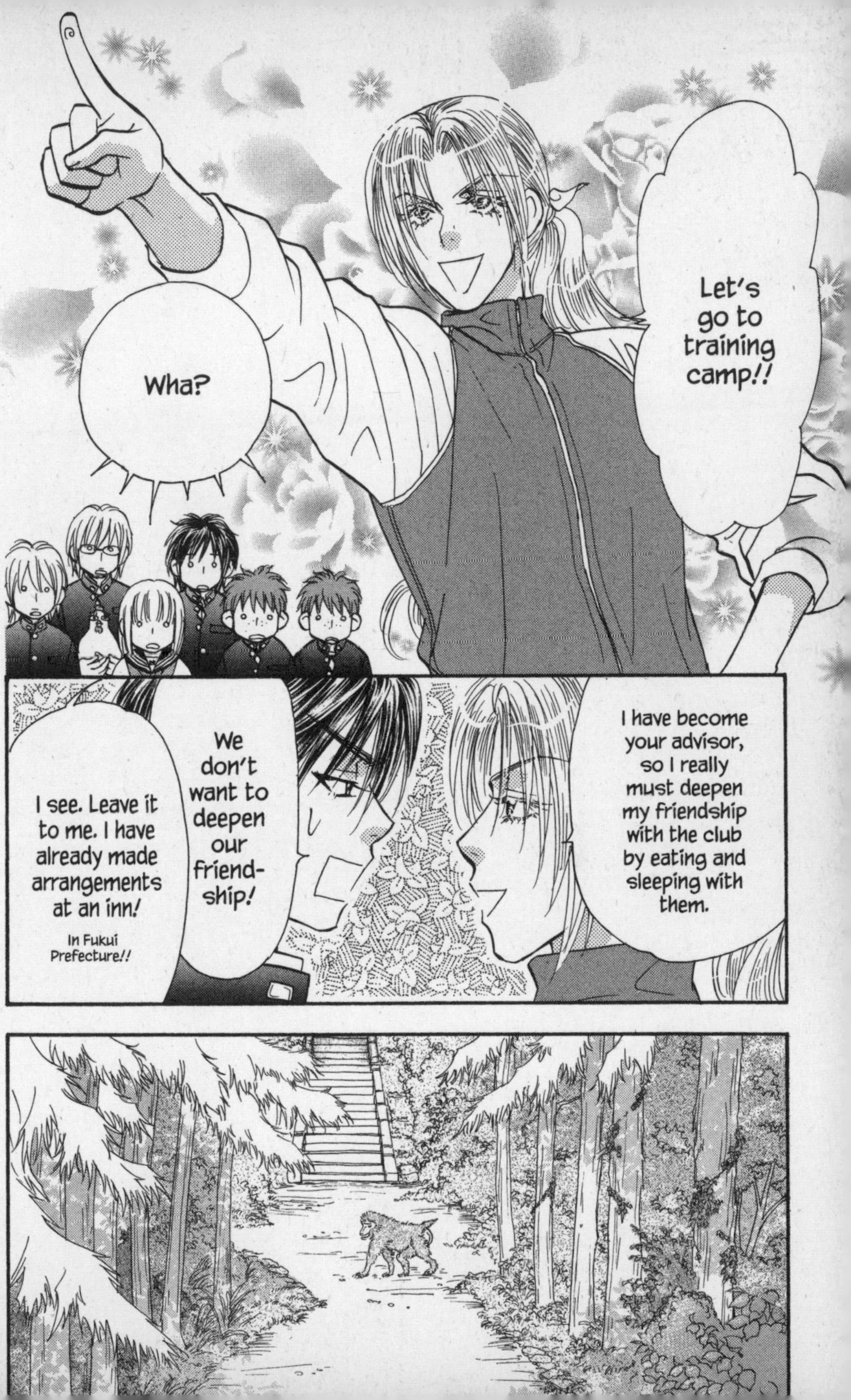
Let's go to training camp!!
Wha?
I have become your advisor, so I really must deepen my friendship with the club by eating and sleeping with them.
We don't want to deepen our friend-ship!
I see. Leave it to me. I have already made arrangements at an inn!
In Fukui Prefecture!!

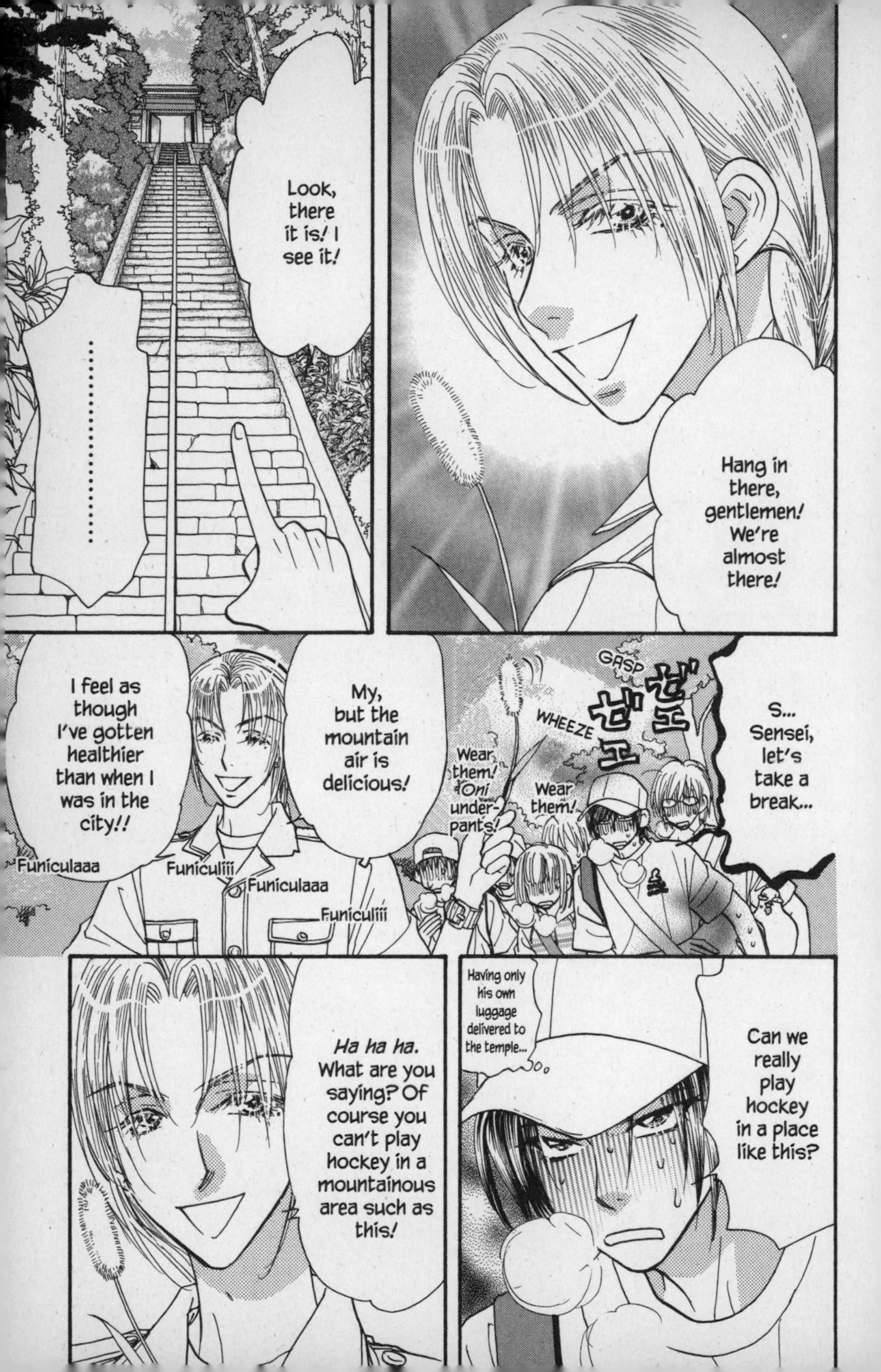
Hang in there, gentlemen! We're almost there!
Look, there it is! I see it!
......
S... Sensei, let's take a break...
GASP
ゼェ
WHEEZE
ゼェ
Wear them!
Wear them! Oni under-pants!
My, but the mountain air is delicious!
I feel as though I've gotten healthier than when I was in the city!!
Funiculiii
Funiculaaa
Funiculaaa
Funiculiii
Can we really play hockey in a place like this?
Having only his own luggage delivered to the temple...
Ha ha ha. What are you saying? Of course you can't play hockey in a mountainous area such as this!

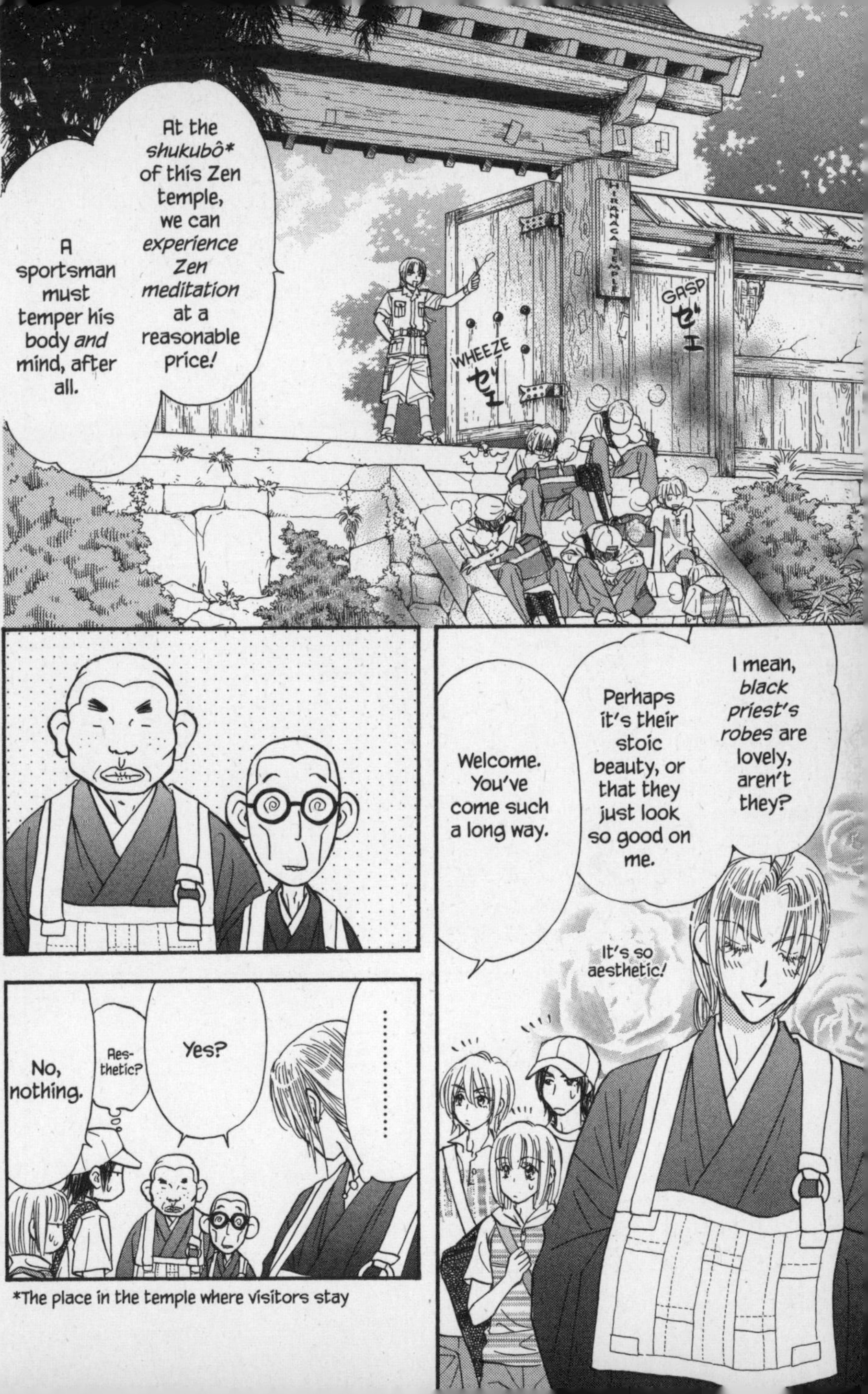
At the *shukubô** of this Zen temple, we can *experience Zen meditation* at a reasonable price!
A sportsman must temper his body *and* mind, after all.
HIRANAGA TEMPLE
GASP
WHEEZE
I mean, *black priest's robes* are lovely, aren't they?
Perhaps it's their stoic beauty, or that they just look so good on me.
Welcome. You've come such a long way.
It's so aesthetic!
......
Yes?
Aes-thetic?
No, nothing.

*The place in the temple where visitors stay

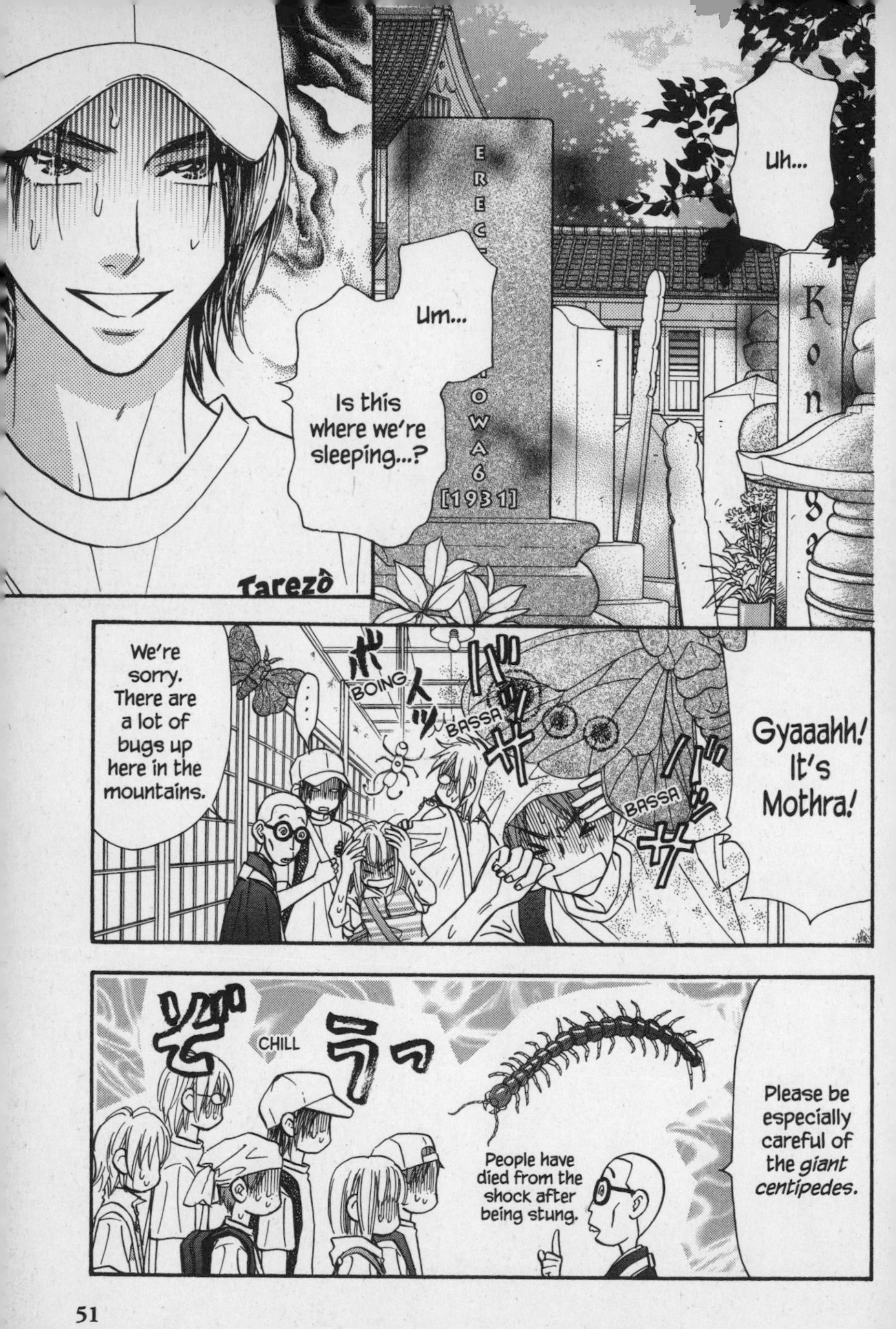
Uh...
Kon
ga
ERECT
OWA 6
[1931]
Um...
Is this where we're sleeping...?
Tarezô
Gyaaahh! It's Mothra!
BASSA
BASSA
BOING
...
We're sorry. There are a lot of bugs up here in the mountains.
Please be especially careful of the *giant centipedes.*
People have died from the shock after being stung.
CHILL

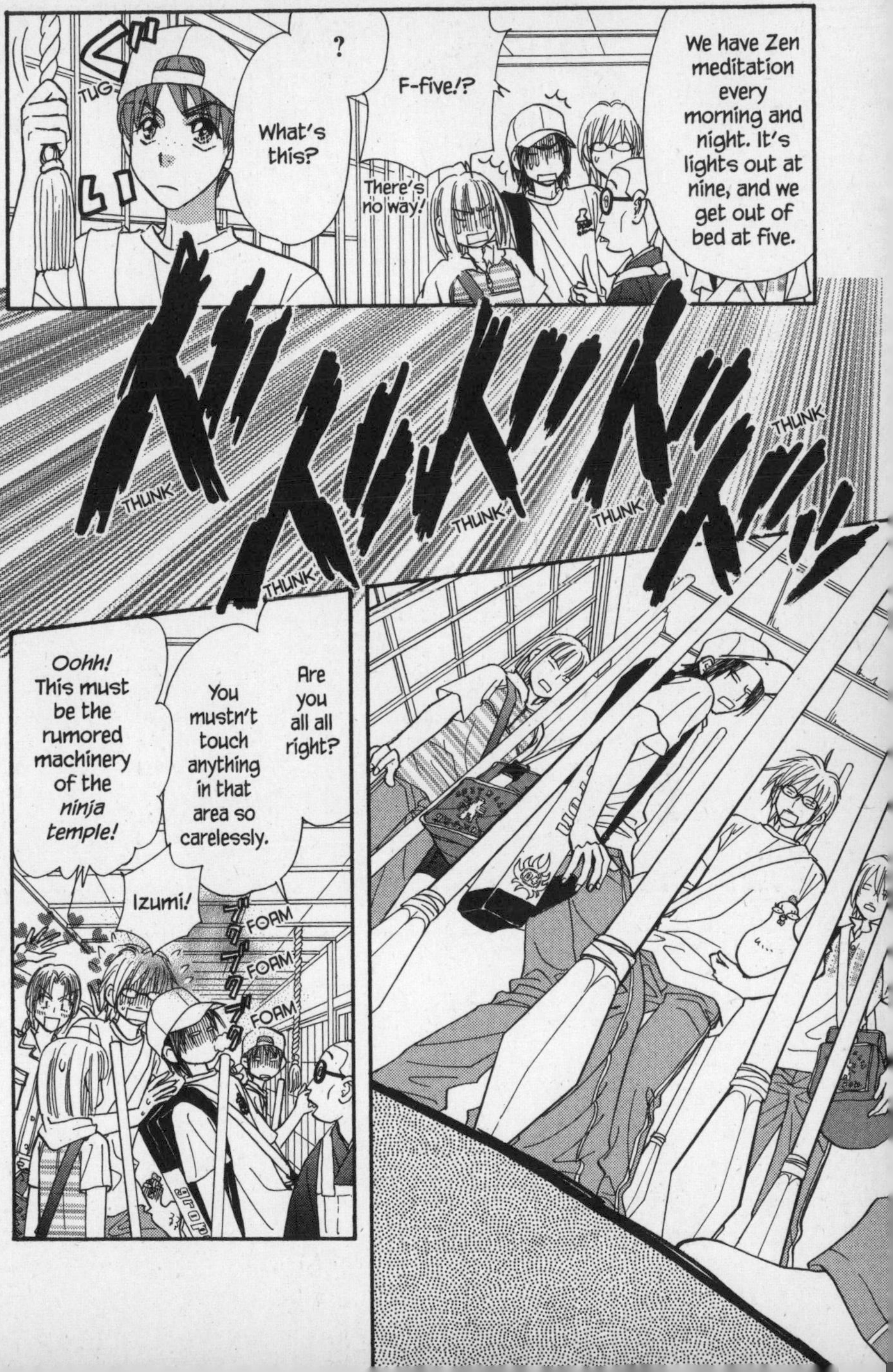
We have Zen meditation every morning and night. It's lights out at nine, and we get out of bed at five.
F-five!?
There's no way!
?
What's this?
TUG
THUNK
THUNK
THUNK
THUNK
THUNK
Are you all all right?
You mustn't touch anything in that area so carelessly.
Oohh! This must be the rumored machinery of the *ninja temple!*
Izumi!
FOAM
FOAM
FOAM

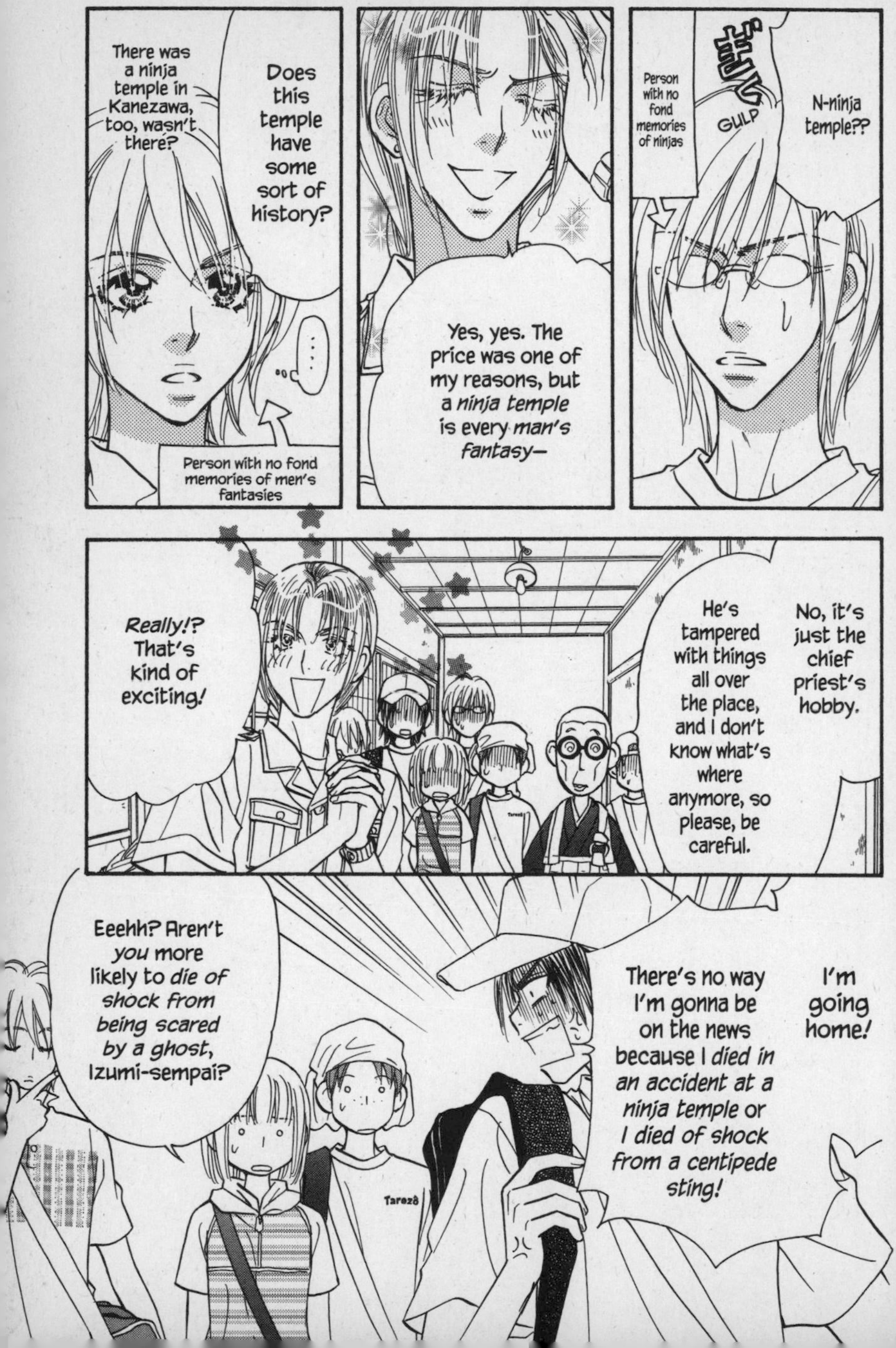
N-ninja temple??
GULP
Person with no fond memories of ninjas
Yes, yes. The price was one of my reasons, but a ninja temple is every man's fantasy—
Does this temple have some sort of history?
There was a ninja temple in Kanezawa, too, wasn't there?
...
Person with no fond memories of men's fantasies
No, it's just the chief priest's hobby.
He's tampered with things all over the place, and I don't know what's where anymore, so please, be careful.
Really!? That's kind of exciting!
I'm going home!
There's no way I'm gonna be on the news because I died in an accident at a ninja temple or I died of shock from a centipede sting!
Eeehh? Aren't you more likely to die of shock from being scared by a ghost, Izumi-sempai?

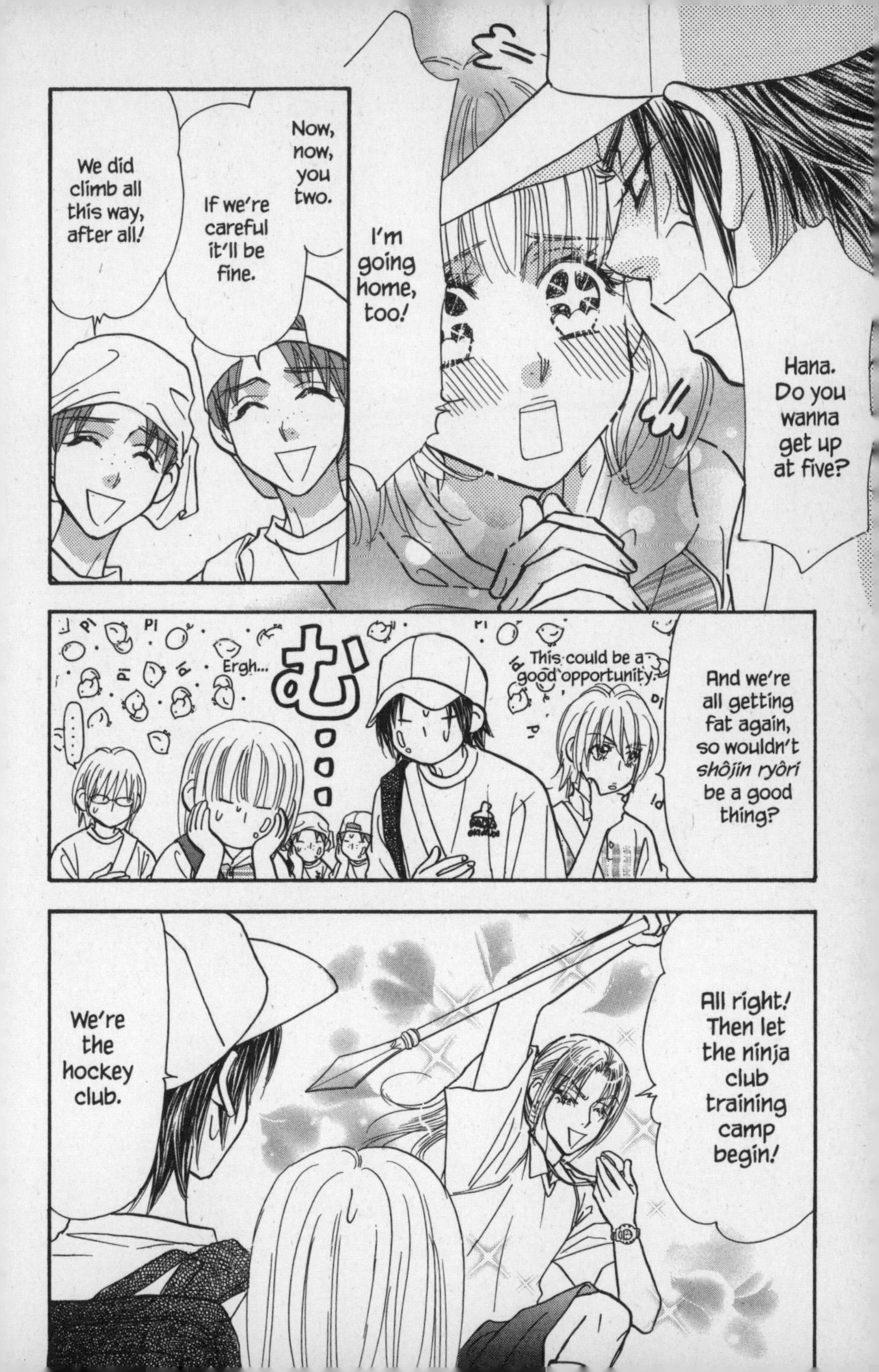
Hana. Do you wanna get up at five?
I'm going home, too!
Now, now, you two.
If we're careful it'll be fine.
We did climb all this way, after all!
And we're all getting fat again, so wouldn't *shôjin ryôri* be a good thing?
This could be a good opportunity.
む
Ergh...
All right! Then let the ninja club training camp begin!
We're the hockey club.

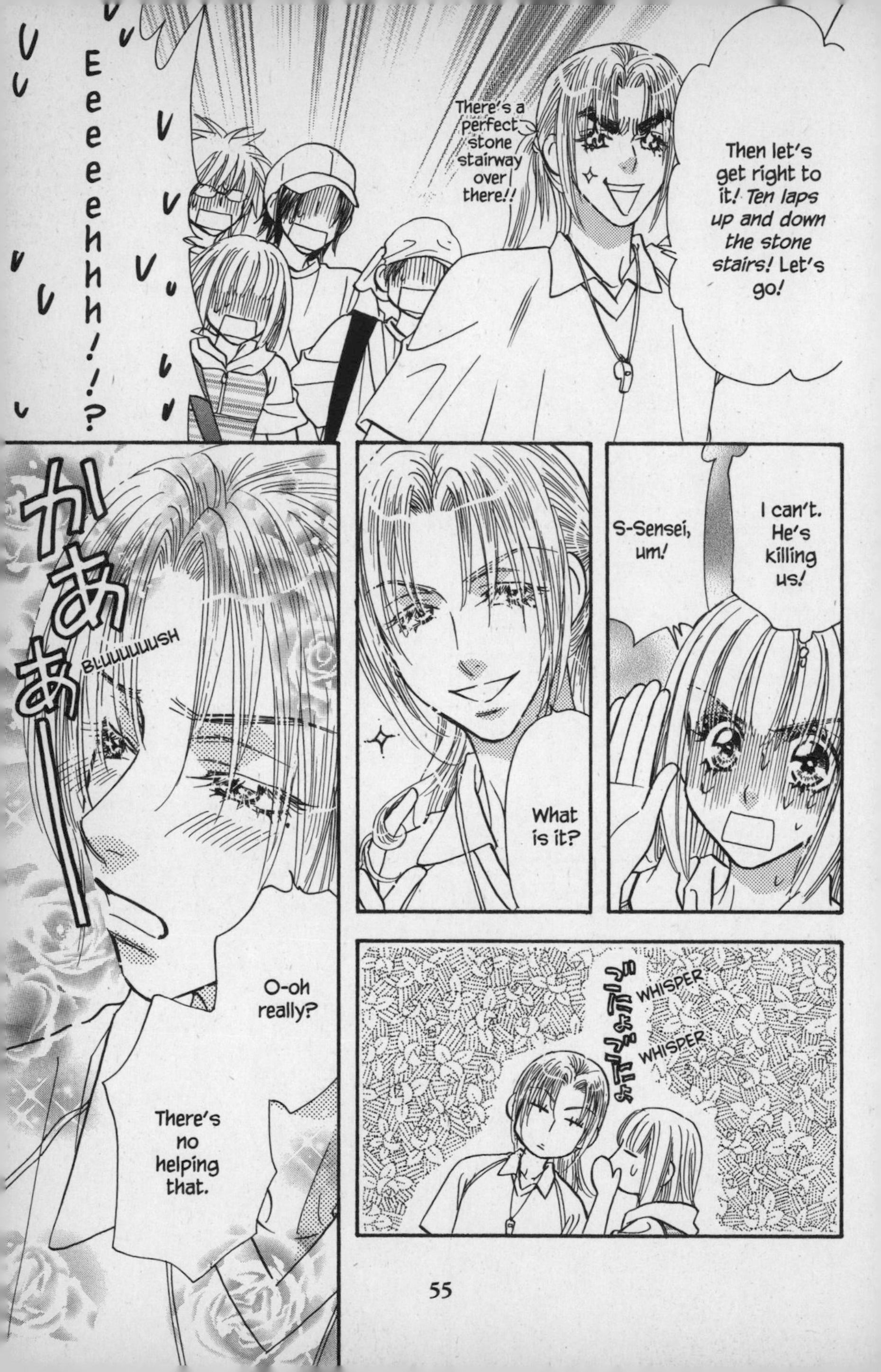
Then let's get right to it! Ten laps up and down the stone stairs! Let's go!
There's a perfect stone stairway over there!!
Eeeeeehhh!!?
I can't. He's killing us!
S-Sensei, um!
What is it?
WHISPER
WHISPER
かあぁ
BLUUUUUUSH
O-oh really?
There's no helping that.

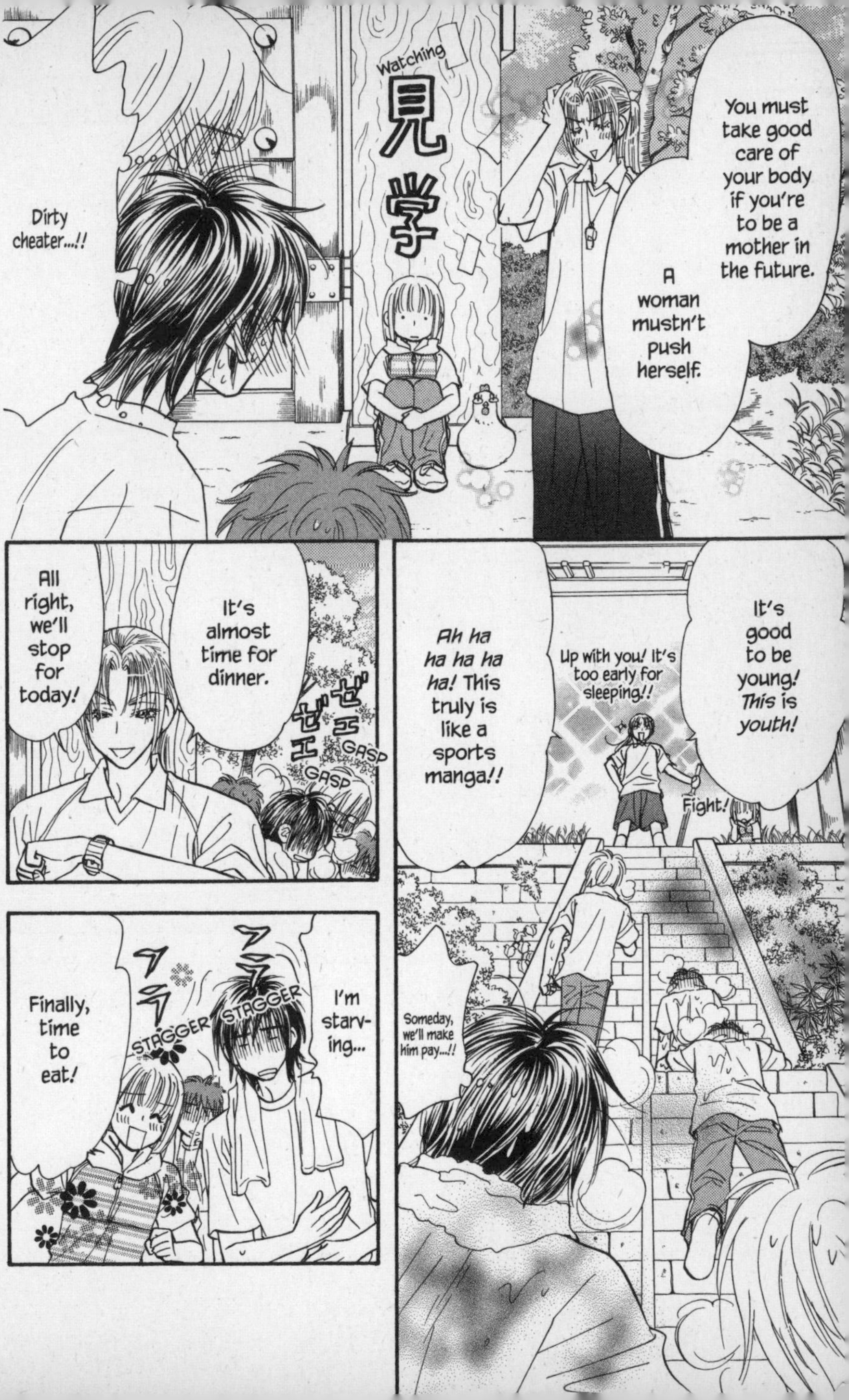

You must take good care of your body if you're to be a mother in the future.
A woman mustn't push herself.
Watching
見学
Dirty cheater...!!
It's good to be young! *This* is *youth!*
Up with you! It's too early for sleeping!!
Fight!
Ah ha ha ha ha! This truly is like a sports manga!!
Someday, we'll make him pay...!!
It's almost time for dinner.
All right, we'll stop for today!
ゼエ ゼエ
GASP GASP
I'm starv-ing...
フラ フラ
STAGGER STAGGER
Finally, time to eat!

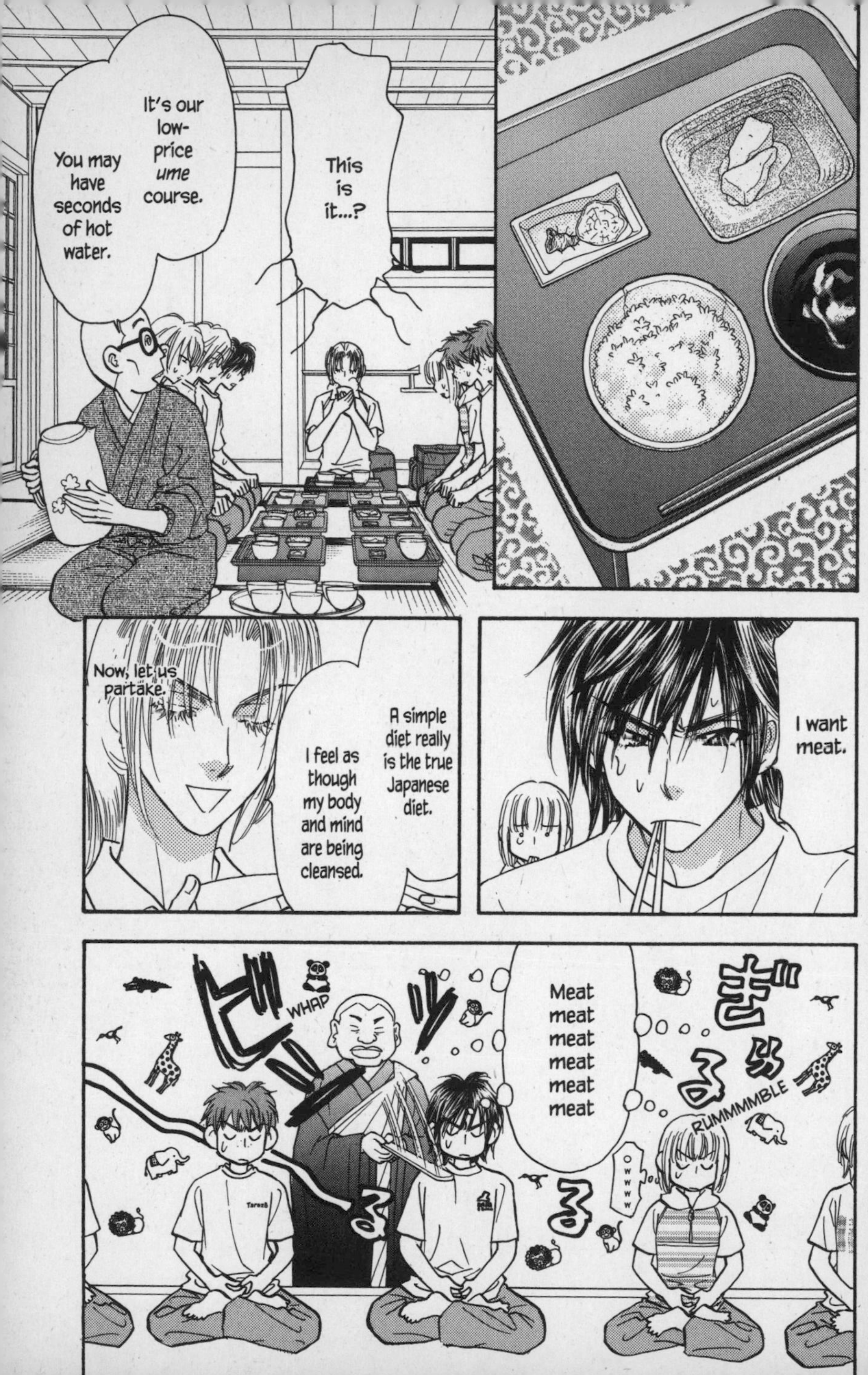
This is it...?
It's our low-price ume course.
You may have seconds of hot water.
I want meat.
A simple diet really is the true Japanese diet.
I feel as though my body and mind are being cleansed.
Now, let us partake.
RUMMMMBLE
Meat meat meat meat meat meat
OWWWW
WHAP

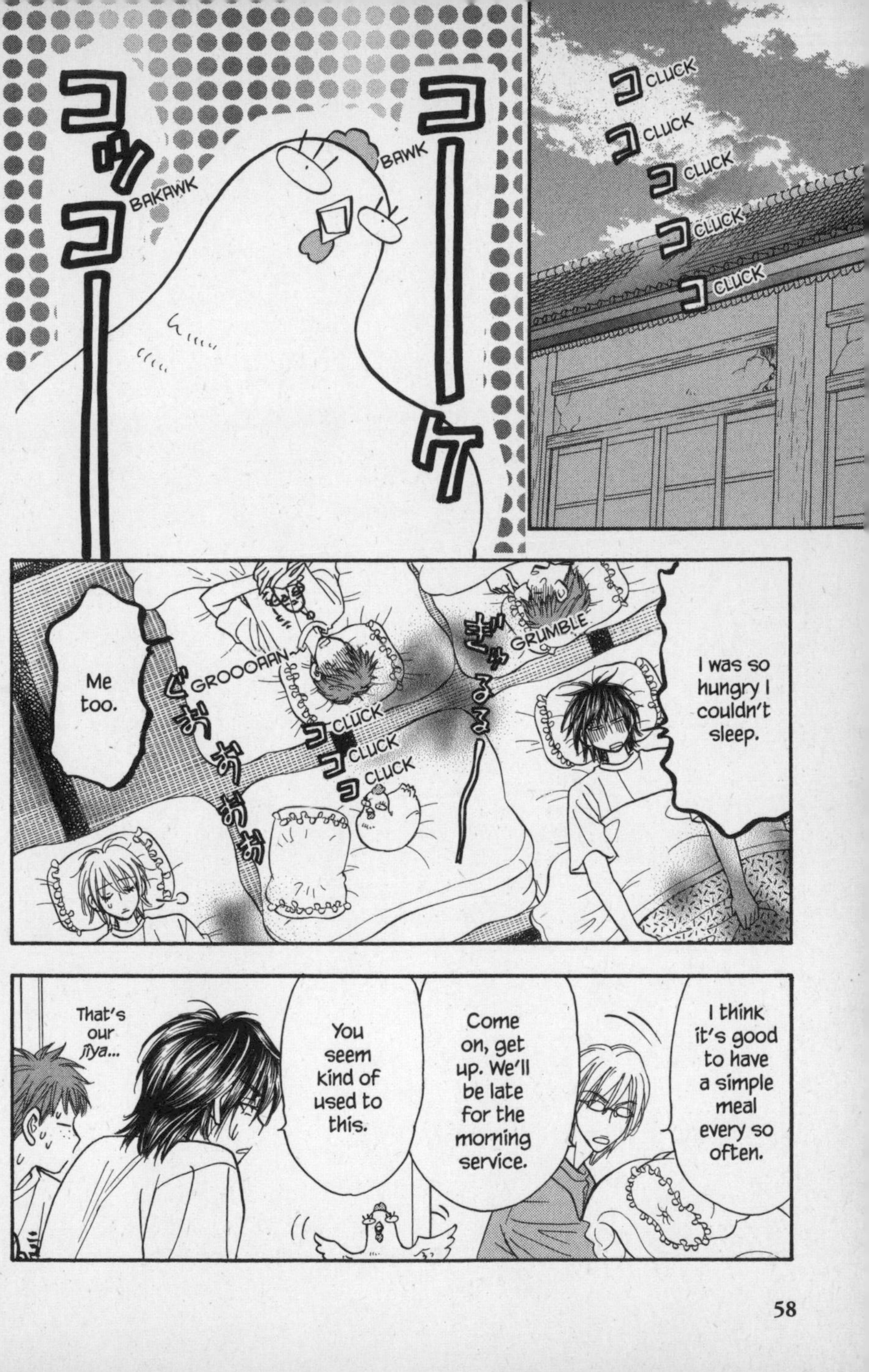
CLUCK
CLUCK
CLUCK
CLUCK
CLUCK
BAWK
BAKAWK
I was so hungry I couldn't sleep.
GRUMBLE
CLUCK
CLUCK
CLUCK
GROOOAAN
Me too.
I think it's good to have a simple meal every so often.
Come on, get up. We'll be late for the morning service.
You seem kind of used to this.
That's our jiya...

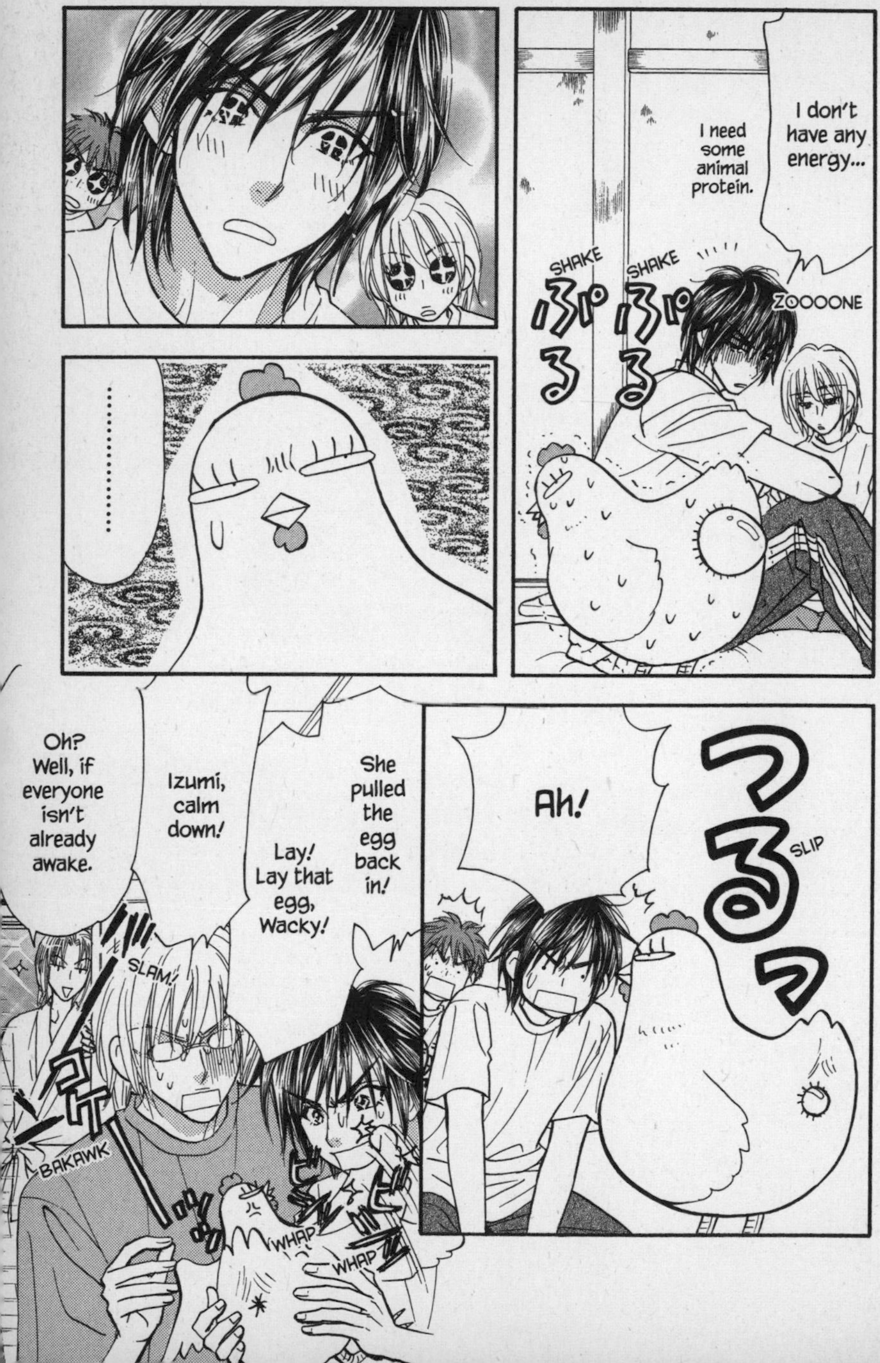
I don't have any energy...
I need some animal protein.
ZOOOONE
SHAKE
ぷる
SHAKE
ぷる
……
つるっ
SLIP
Ah!
She pulled the egg back in!
Lay! Lay that egg, Wacky!
Izumi, calm down!
WHAP
WHAP
Oh? Well, if everyone isn't already awake.
SLAM!
BAKAWK

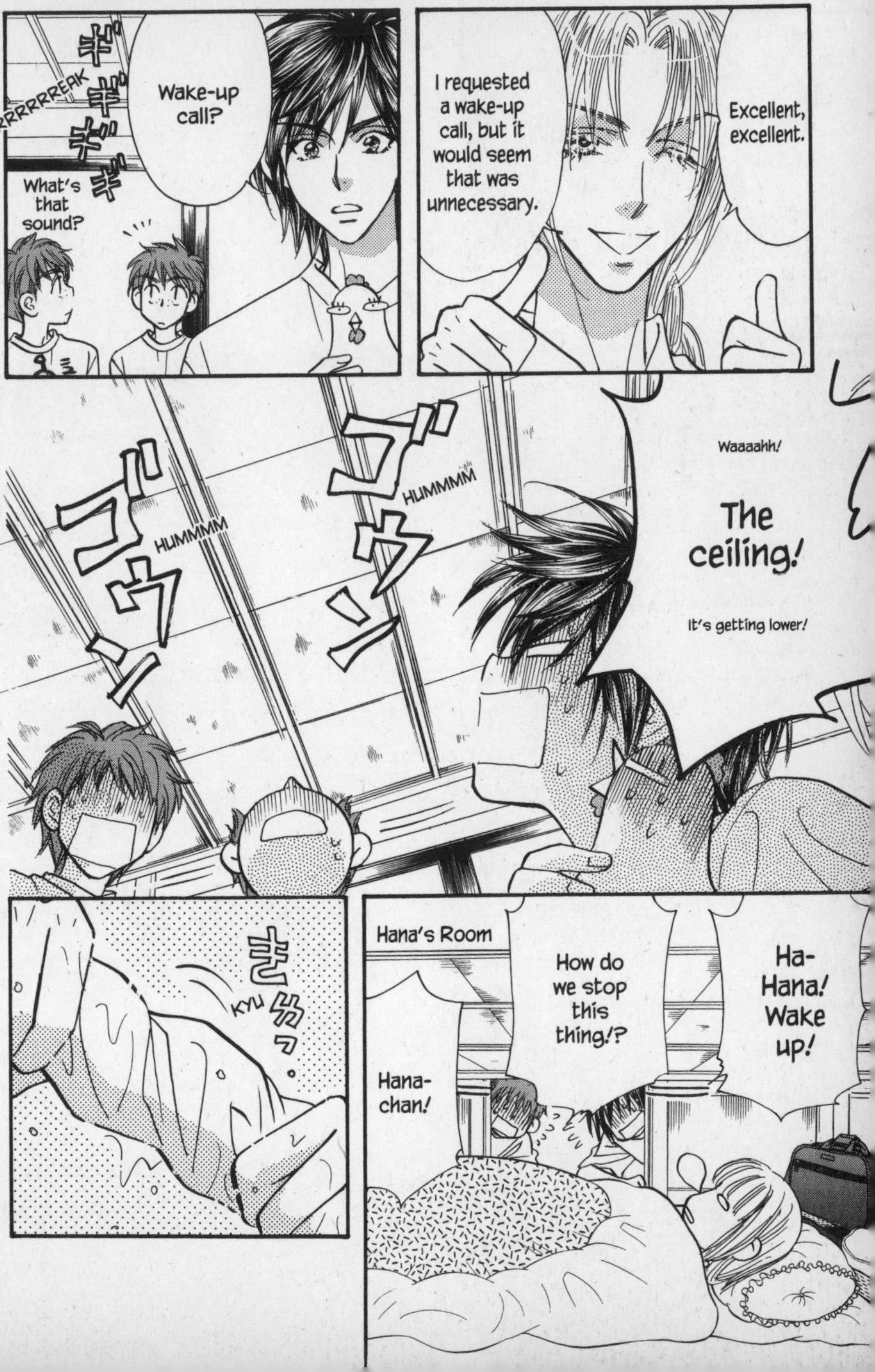
Excellent, excellent.
I requested a wake-up call, but it would seem that was unnecessary.
Wake-up call?
ギギギギ
CRRRRRREAK
What's that sound?
Waaaahh!
The ceiling!
It's getting lower!
ゴウン
HUMMMM
ゴウン
HUMMMM
Hana's Room
Ha-Hana! Wake up!
How do we stop this thing!?
Hana-chan!
きゅっ
KYU

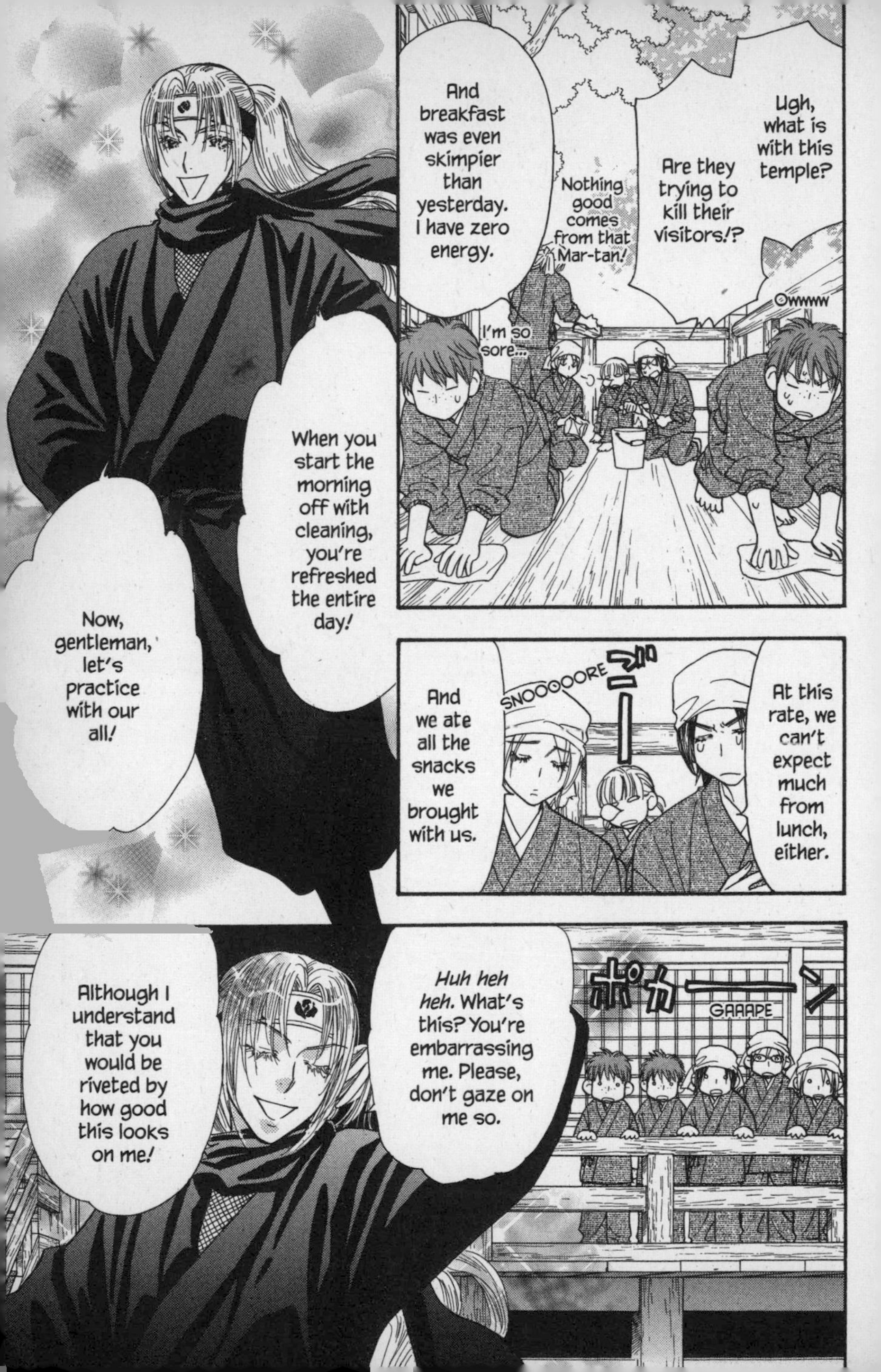
Ugh, what is with this temple?
Are they trying to kill their visitors!?
Owwww
And breakfast was even skimpier than yesterday. I have zero energy.
Nothing good comes from that Mar-tan!
I'm so sore...
At this rate, we can't expect much from lunch, either.
SNOOOOORE
And we ate all the snacks we brought with us.
When you start the morning off with cleaning, you're refreshed the entire day!
Now, gentleman, let's practice with our all!
ポカー
GAAAPE
Huh heh heh. What's this? You're embarrassing me. Please, don't gaze on me so.
Although I understand that you would be riveted by how good this looks on me!

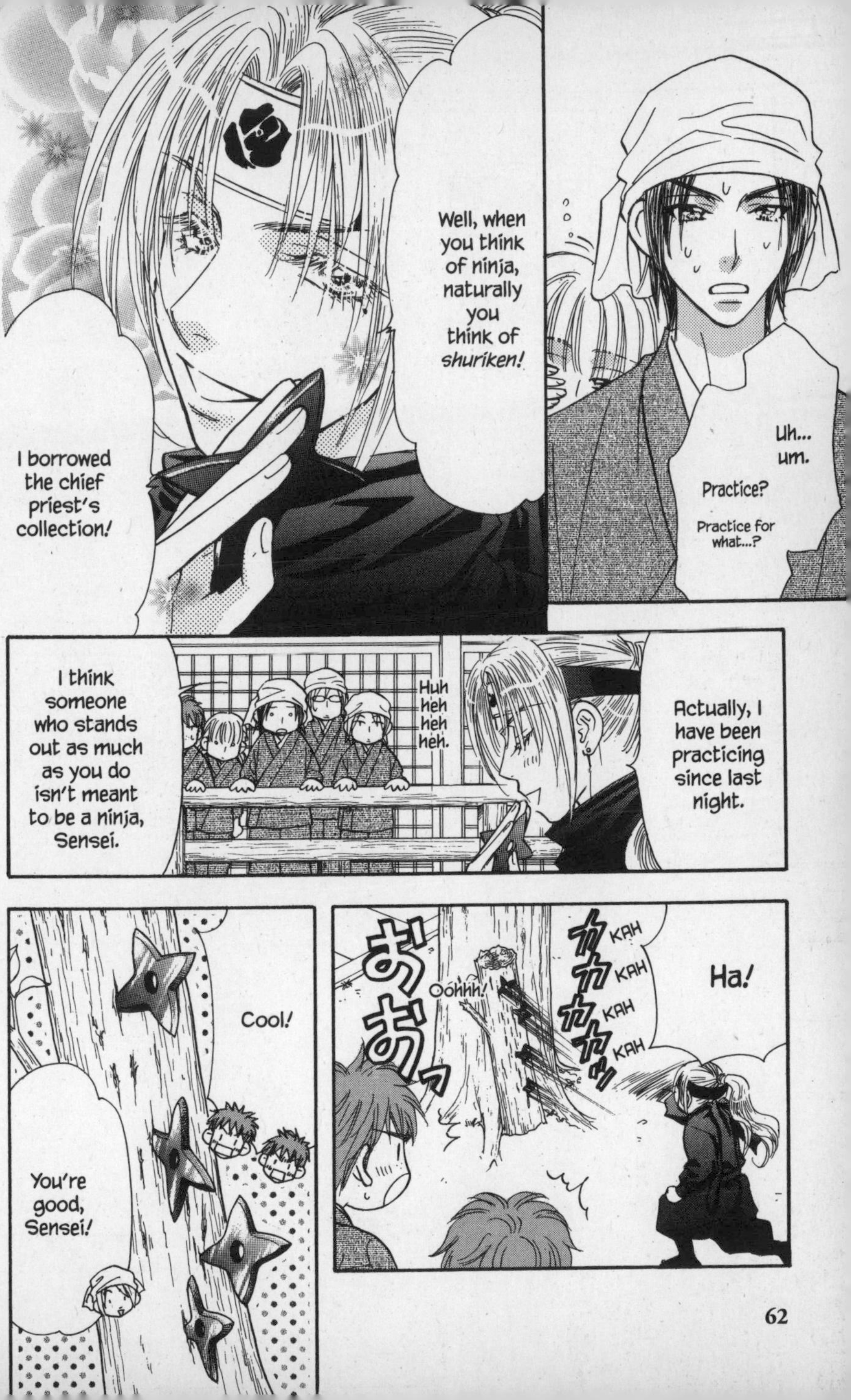
Uh... um.
Practice?
Practice for what...?
Well, when you think of ninja, naturally you think of shuriken!
I borrowed the chief priest's collection!
Actually, I have been practicing since last night.
Huh heh heh heh.
I think someone who stands out as much as you do isn't meant to be a ninja, Sensei.
Ha!
カカカカッ
KAH KAH KAH KAH
おおっ
Oohhh!
Cool!
You're good, Sensei!

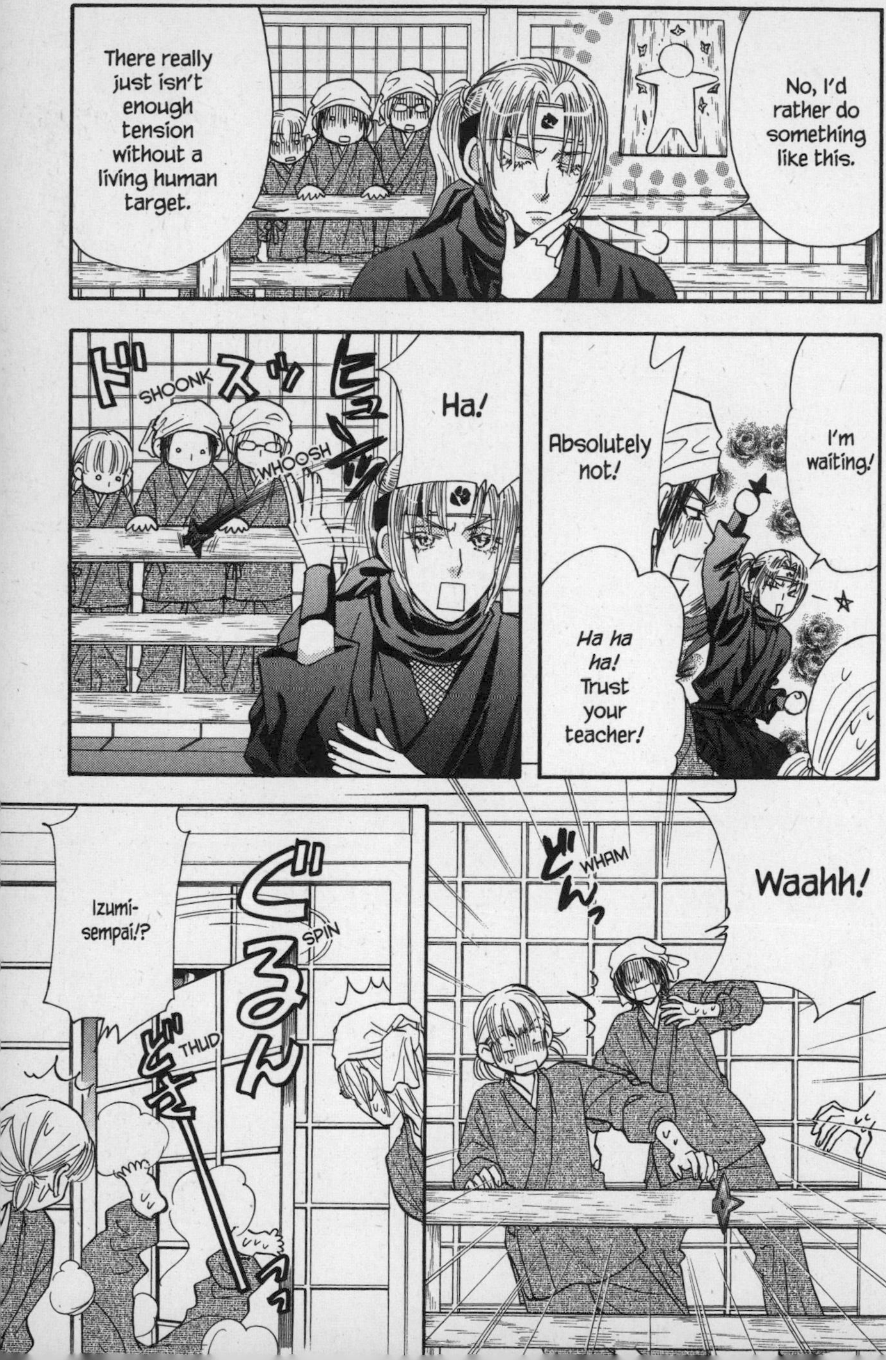
No, I'd rather do something like this.
There really just isn't enough tension without a living human target.
I'm waiting!
Absolutely not!
Ha ha ha! Trust your teacher!
Ha!
WHOOSH
SHOONK
Waahh!
WHAM
SPIN
Izumi-sempai!?
THUD

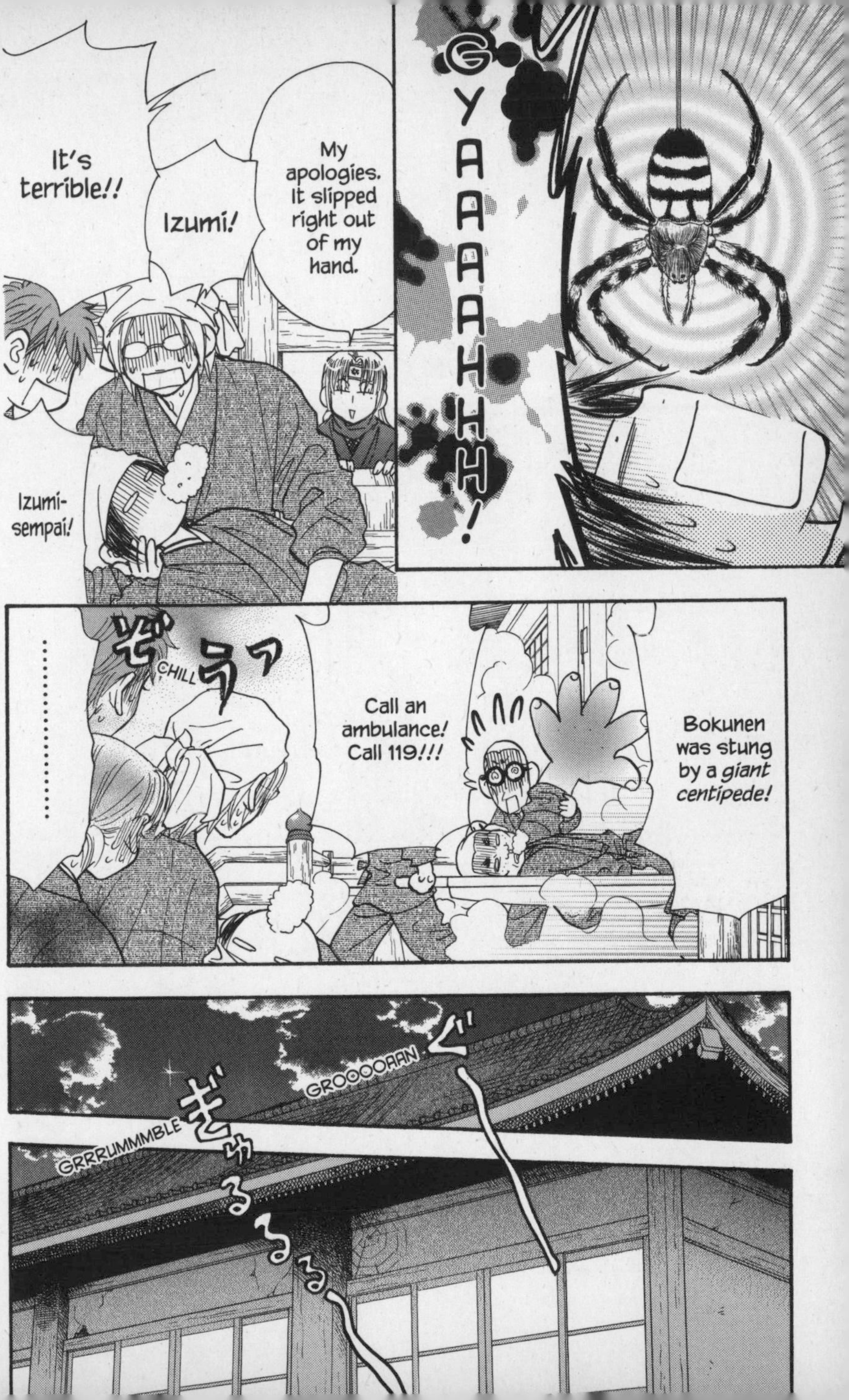
GYAAAAHHH!
My apologies. It slipped right out of my hand.
Izumi!
It's terrible!!
Izumi-sempai!
Bokunen was stung by a *giant* centipede!
Call an ambulance! Call 119!!!
CHILL
....
GROOOOAAN
GRRRUMMMBLE

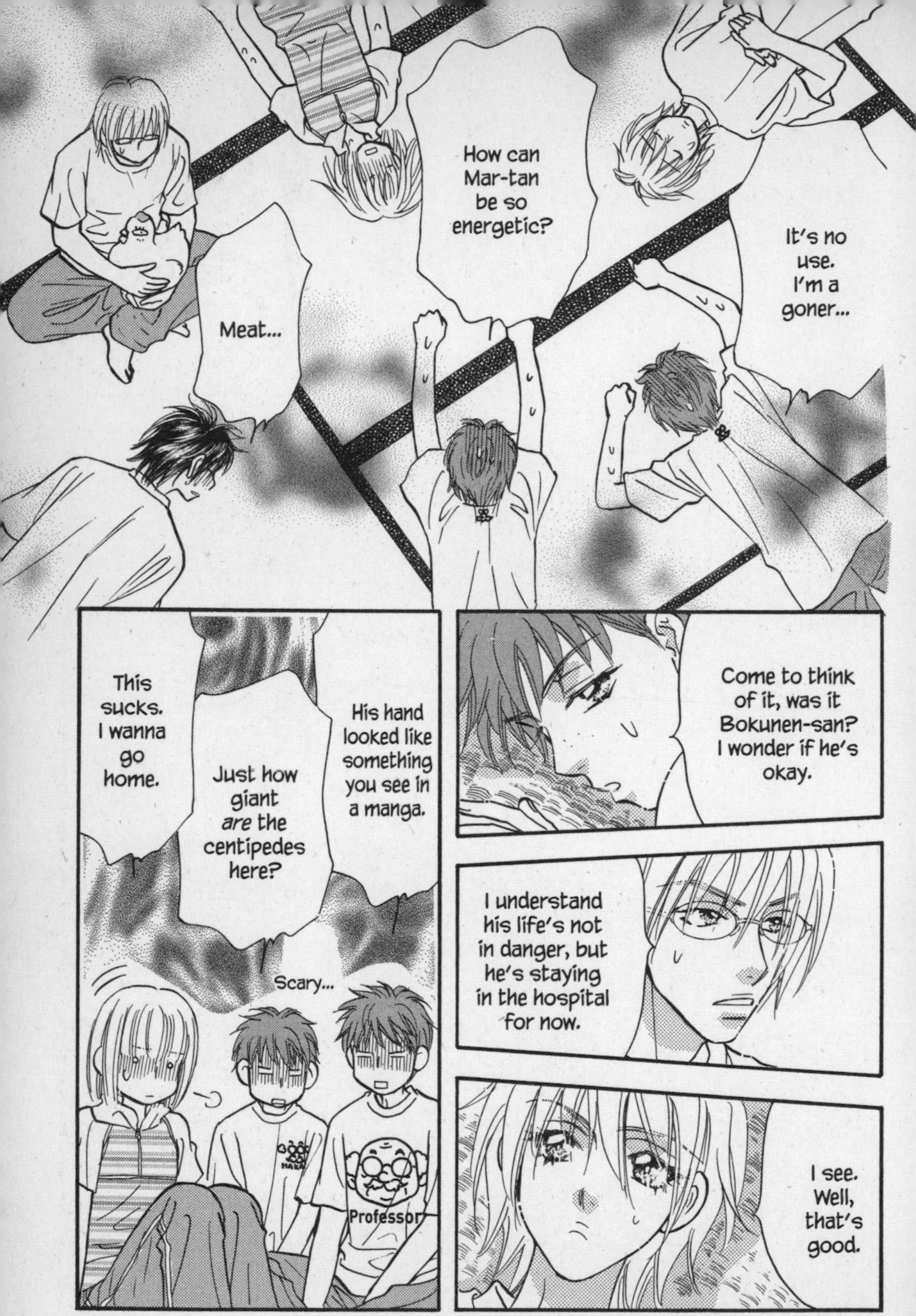

It's no use. I'm a goner...
How can Mar-tan be so energetic?
Meat...
Come to think of it, was it Bokunen-san? I wonder if he's okay.
I understand his life's not in danger, but he's staying in the hospital for now.
I see. Well, that's good.
His hand looked like something you see in a manga.
Just how giant *are* the centipedes here?
This sucks. I wanna go home.
Scary...
Professor

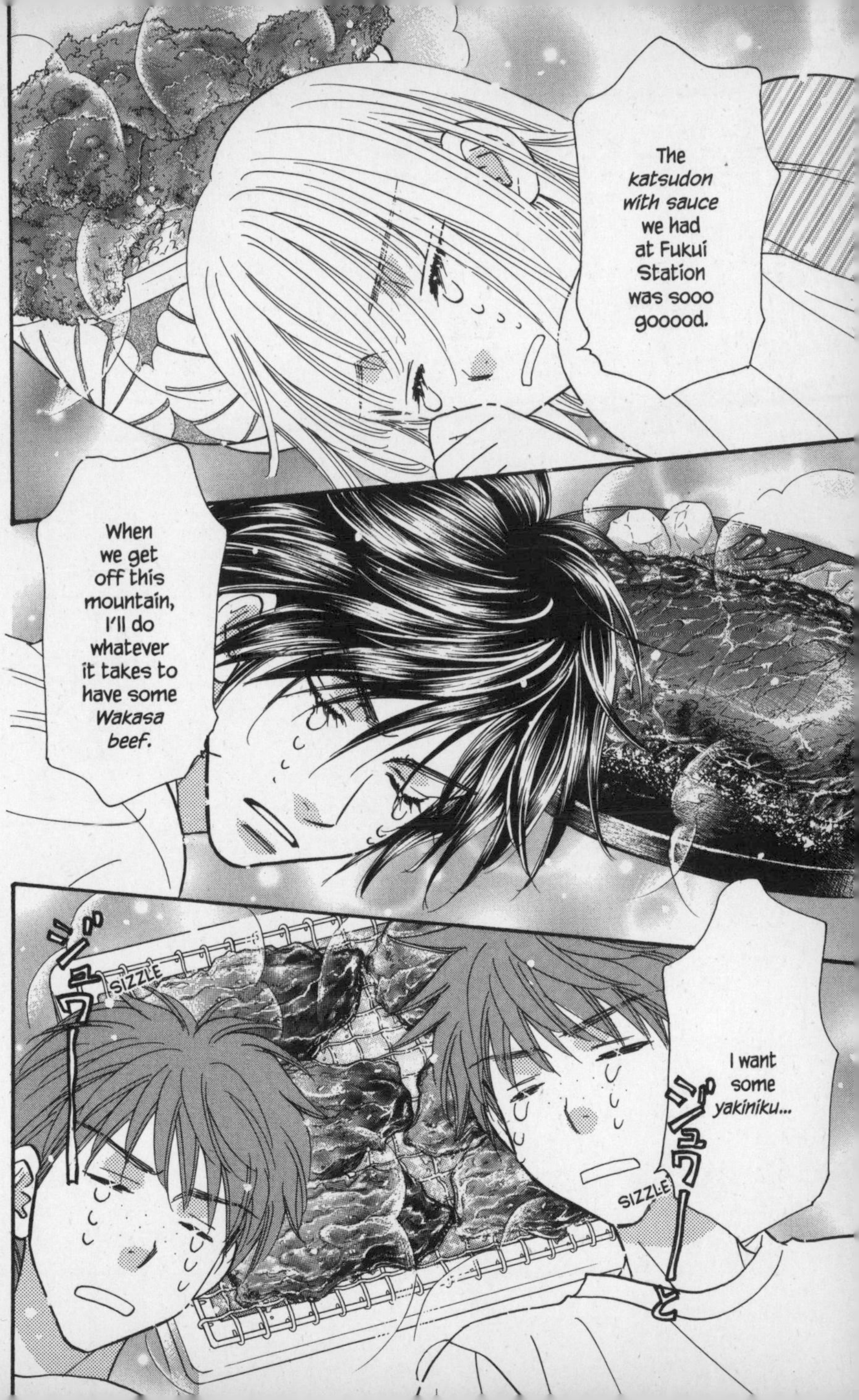
The *katsudon with sauce* we had at Fukui Station was sooo gooood.
When we get off this mountain, I'll do whatever it takes to have some *Wakasa beef.*
I want some *yakiniku...*
SIZZLE
SIZZLE

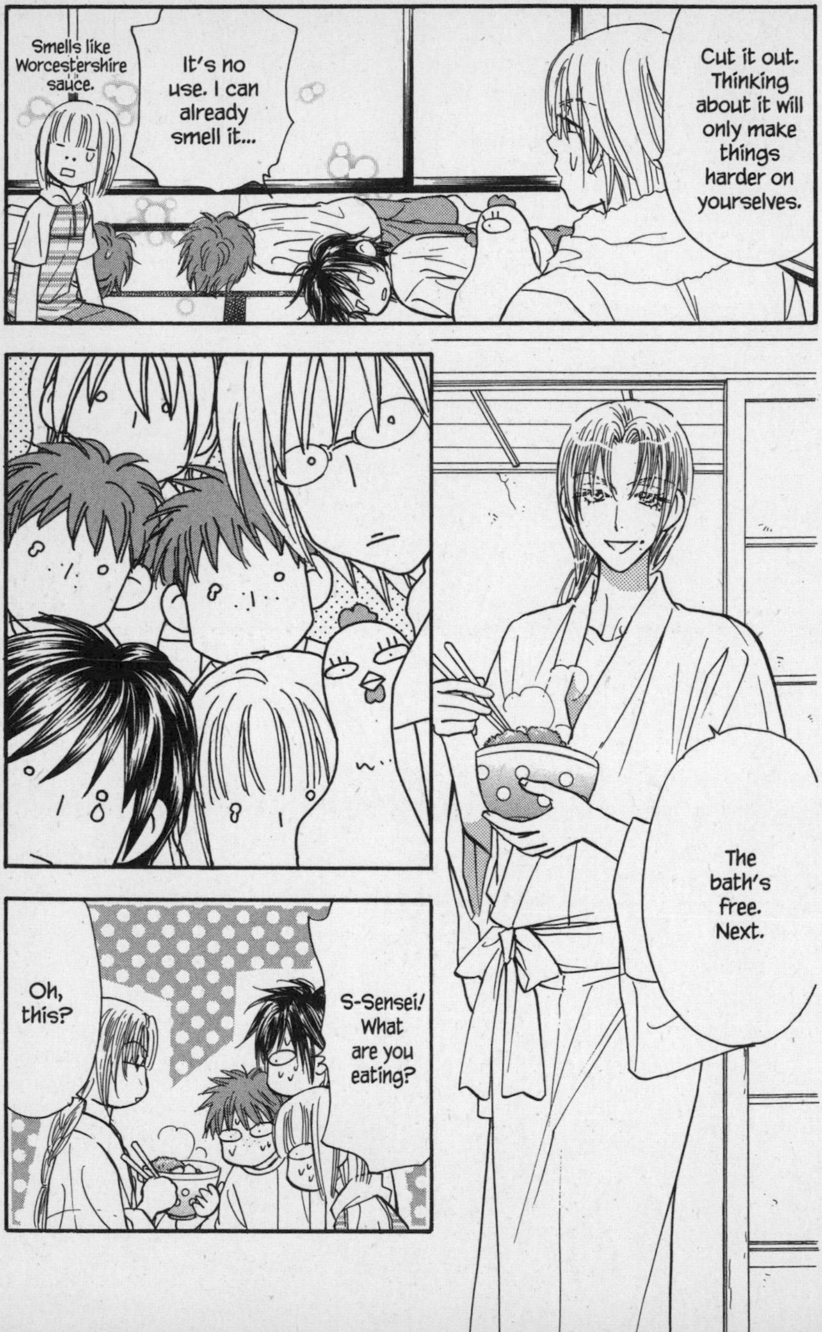
Cut it out. Thinking about it will only make things harder on yourselves.
It's no use. I can already smell it...
Smells like Worcestershire sauce.
The bath's free. Next.
S-Sensei! What are you eating?
Oh, this?

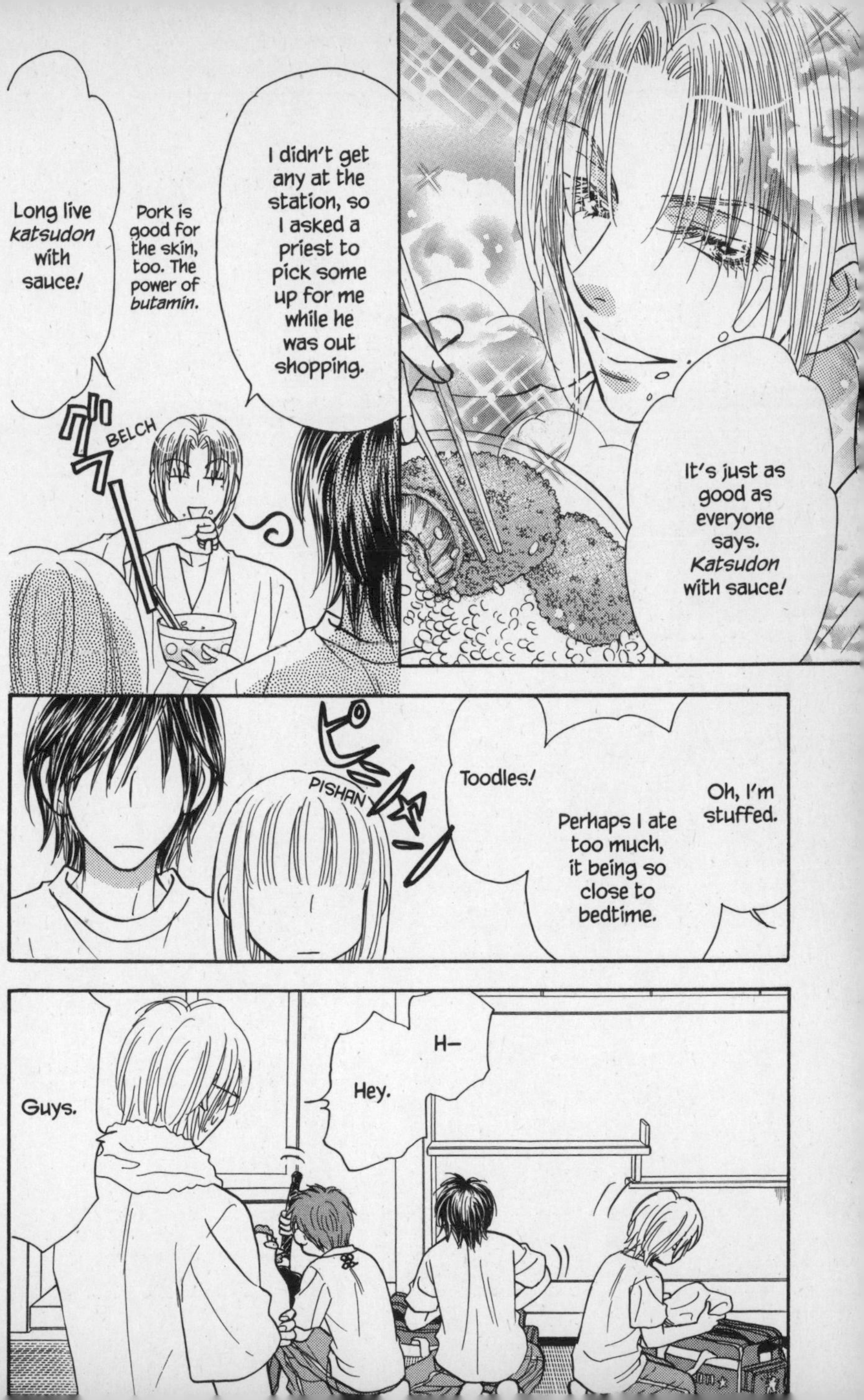
It's just as good as everyone says. *Katsudon* with sauce!
I didn't get any at the station, so I asked a priest to pick some up for me while he was out shopping.
Pork is good for the skin, too. The power of *butamin*.
Long live *katsudon* with sauce!
BELCH
Oh, I'm stuffed.
Perhaps I ate too much, it being so close to bedtime.
Toodles!
PISHAN
H—
Hey.
Guys.

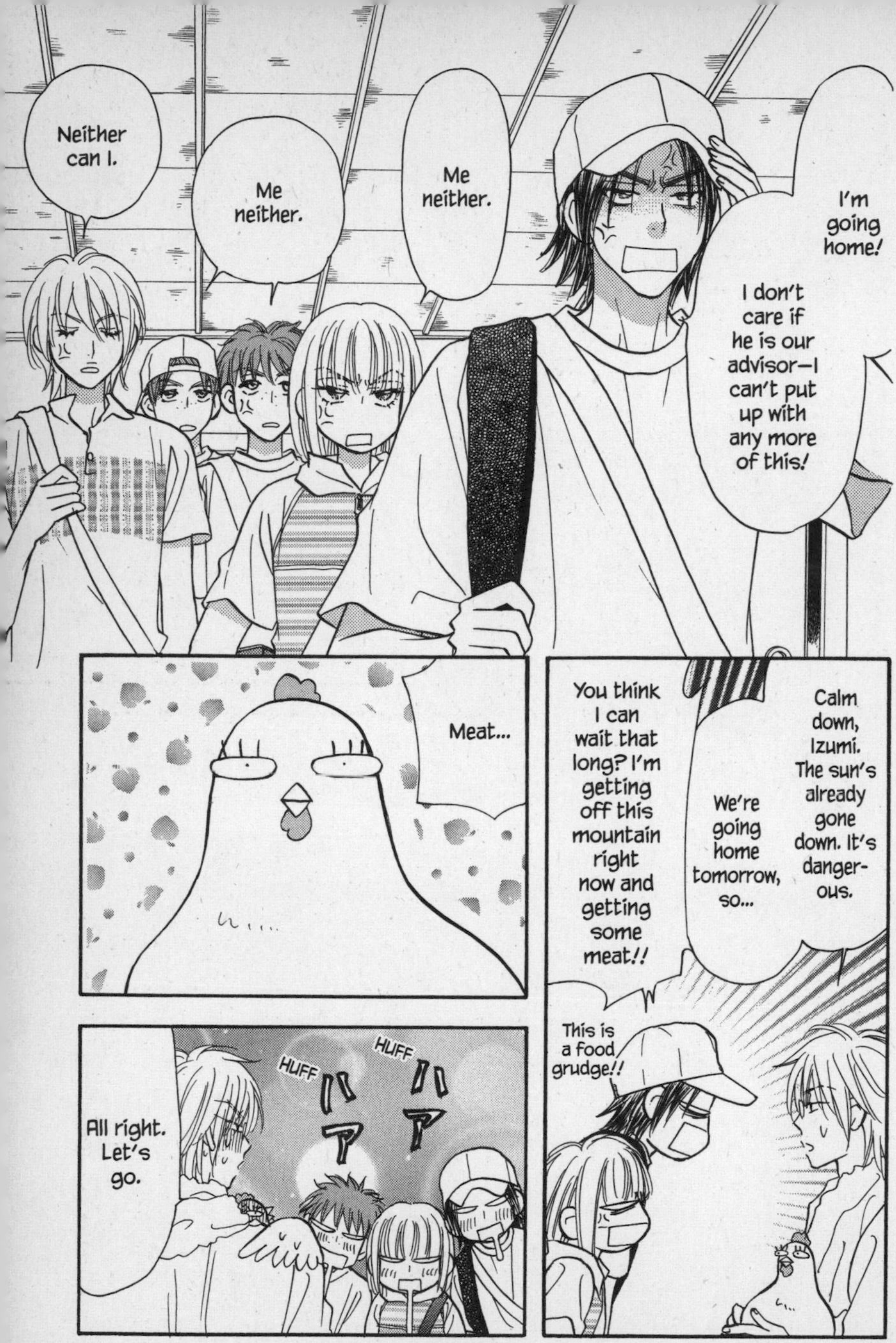
I'm going home!
I don't care if he is our advisor—I can't put up with any more of this!
Me neither.
Me neither.
Neither can I.
Calm down, Izumi. The sun's already gone down. It's danger-ous.
We're going home tomorrow, so...
You think I can wait that long? I'm getting off this mountain right now and getting some meat!!
This is a food grudge!!
Meat...
HUFF
HUFF
All right. Let's go.

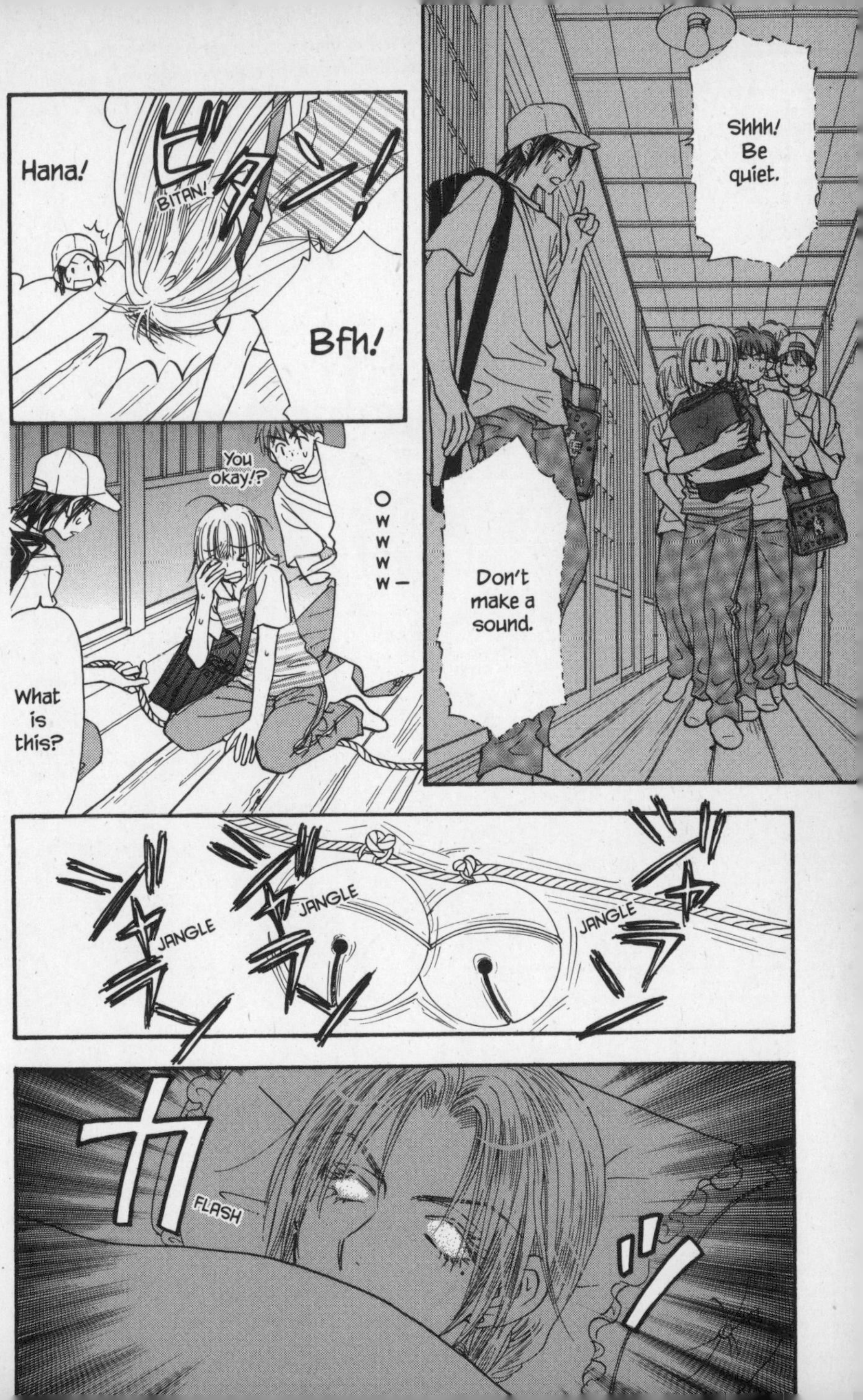
Shhh! Be quiet.
Don't make a sound.
BITAN!
Hana!
Bfh!
Owwww—
You okay!?
What is this?
JANGLE
JANGLE
JANGLE
FLASH

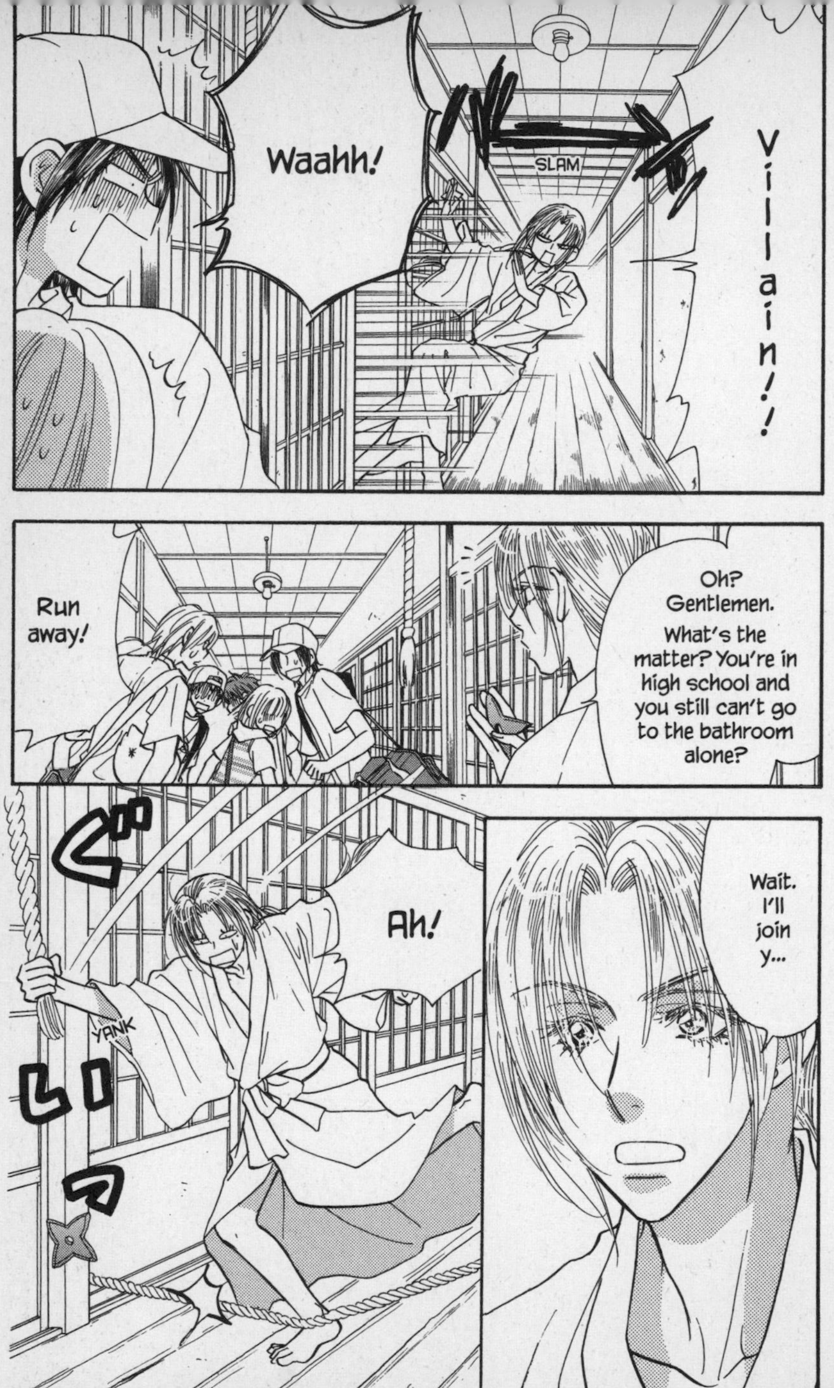
Villain!!
SLAM
Waahh!
Oh? Gentlemen. What's the matter? You're in high school and you still can't go to the bathroom alone?
Run away!
Wait. I'll join y...
Ah!
YANK

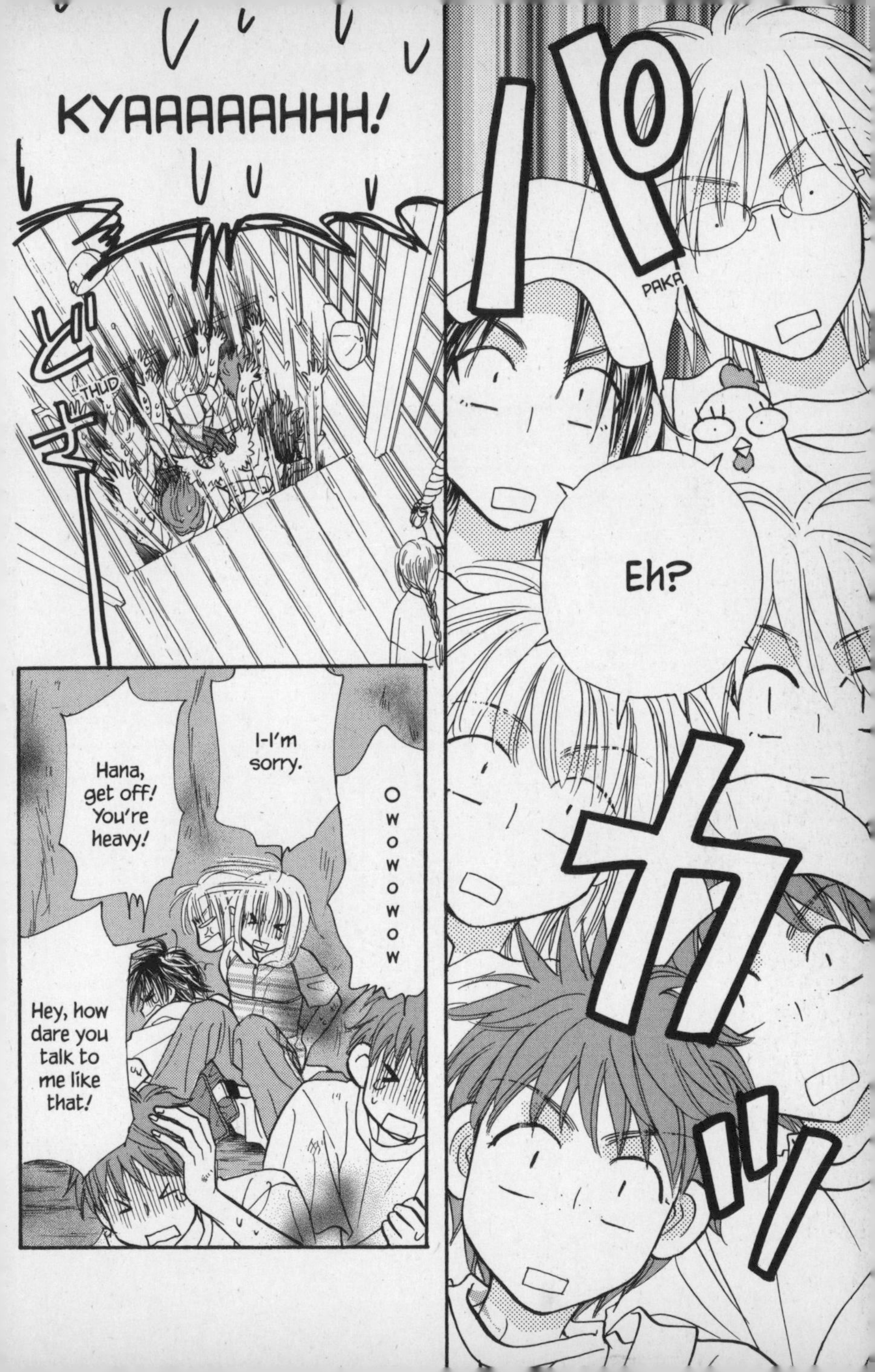
PAKA
Eh?
KYAAAAAAHHH!
THUD
OWOWOWOWOW
I-I'm sorry.
Hana, get off! You're heavy!
Hey, how dare you talk to me like that!

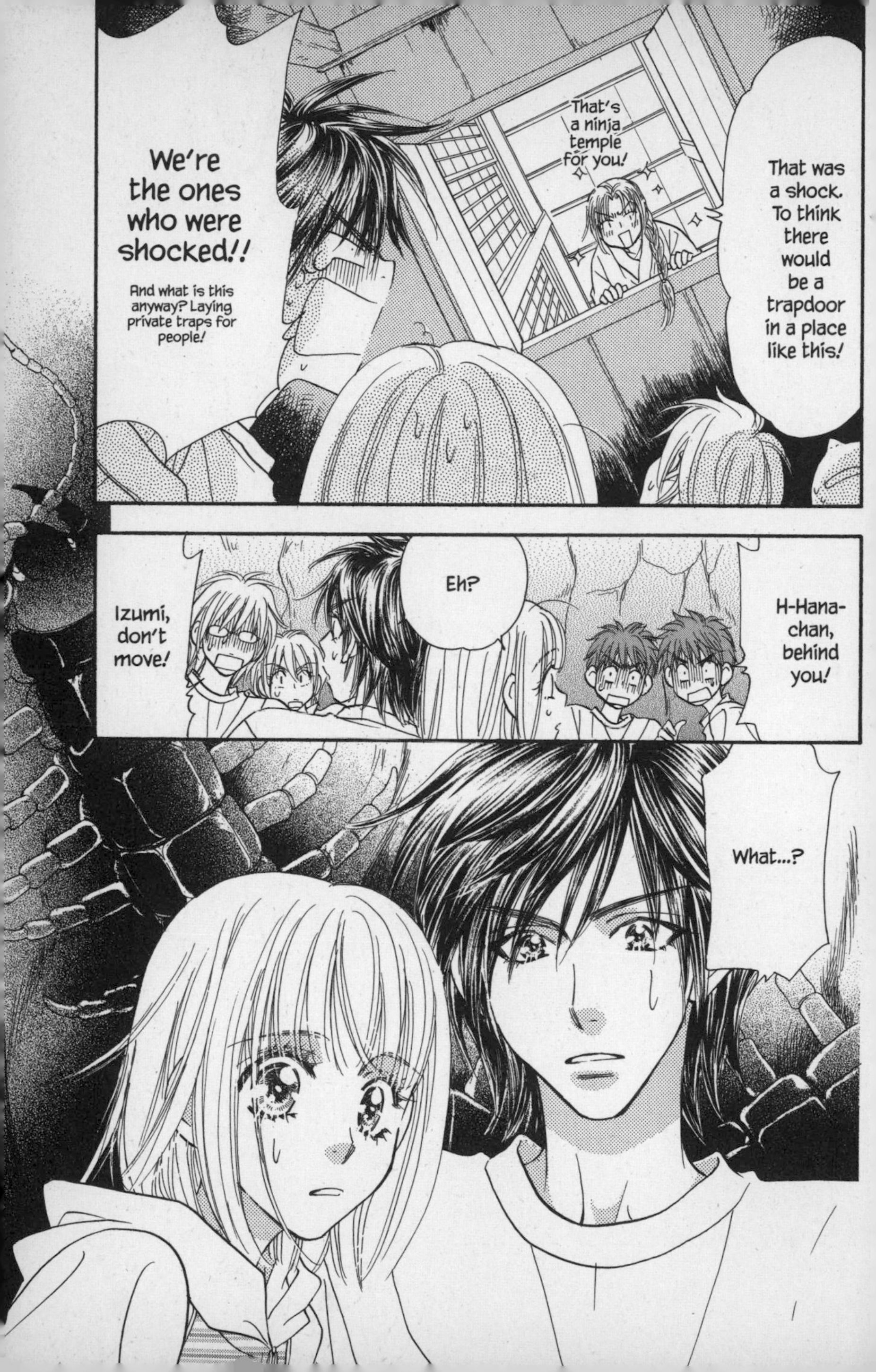
That was a shock. To think there would be a trapdoor in a place like this!
That's a ninja temple for you!
We're the ones who were shocked!!
And what is this anyway? Laying private traps for people!
H-Hana-chan, behind you!
Eh?
Izumi, don't move!
What...?

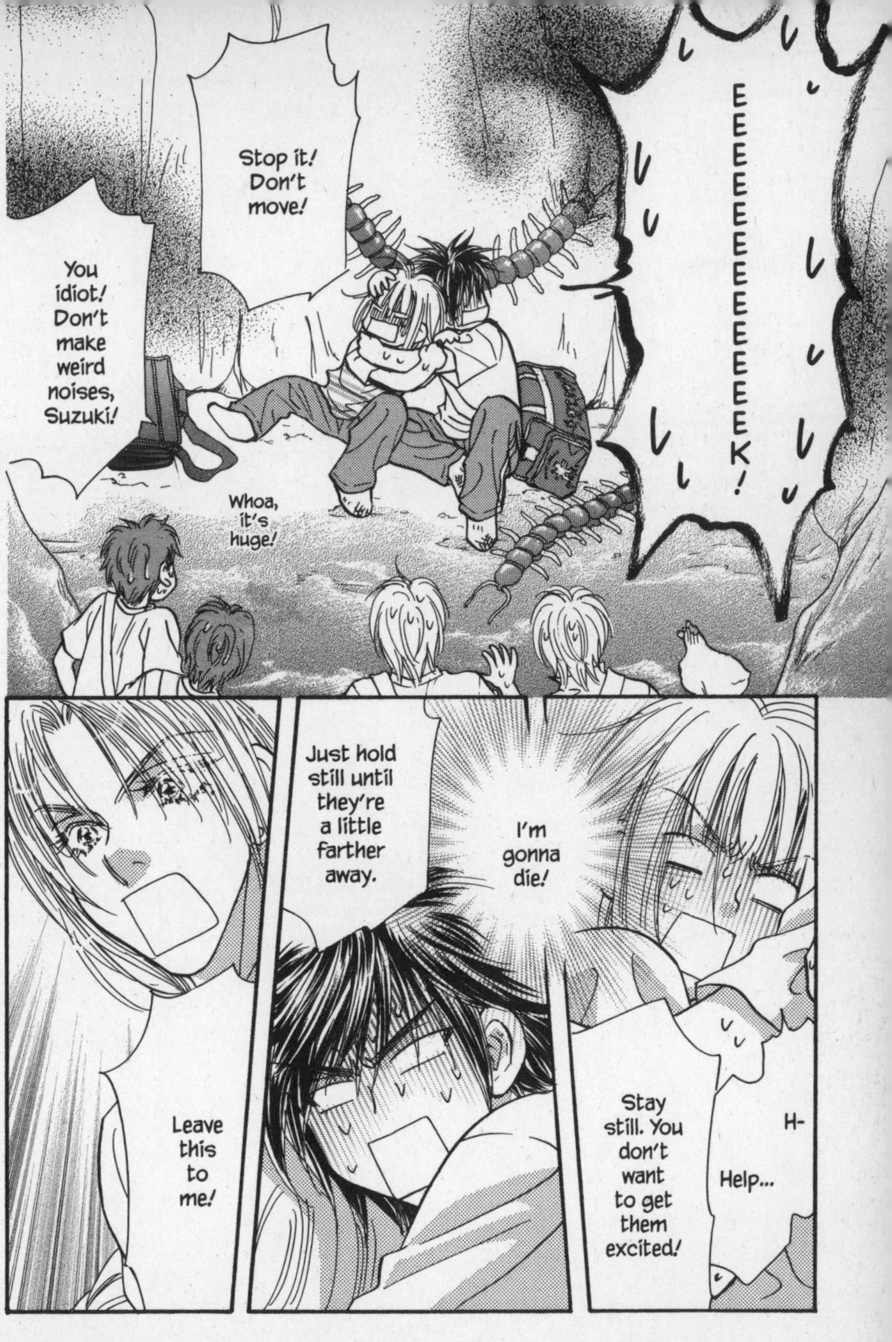
EEEEEEEEEEEEEK!
Stop it! Don't move!
You idiot! Don't make weird noises, Suzuki!
Whoa, it's huge!
H- Help...
Stay still. You don't want to get them excited!
I'm gonna die!
Just hold still until they're a little farther away.
Leave this to me!

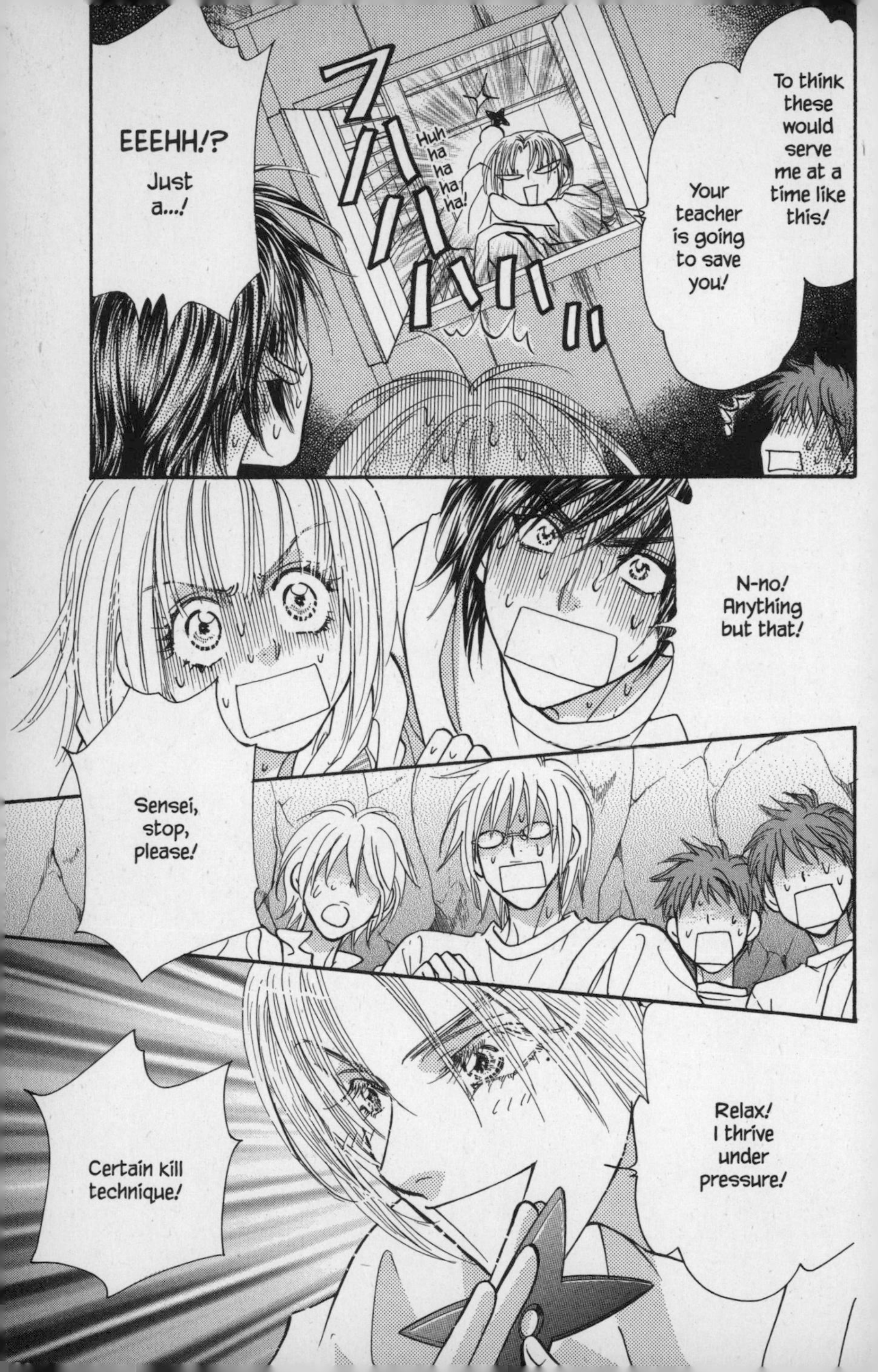
To think these would serve me at a time like this!
Your teacher is going to save you!
Huh ha ha ha ha!
EEEHH!? Just a...!
N-no! Anything but that!
Sensei, stop, please!
Relax! I thrive under pressure!
Certain kill technique!

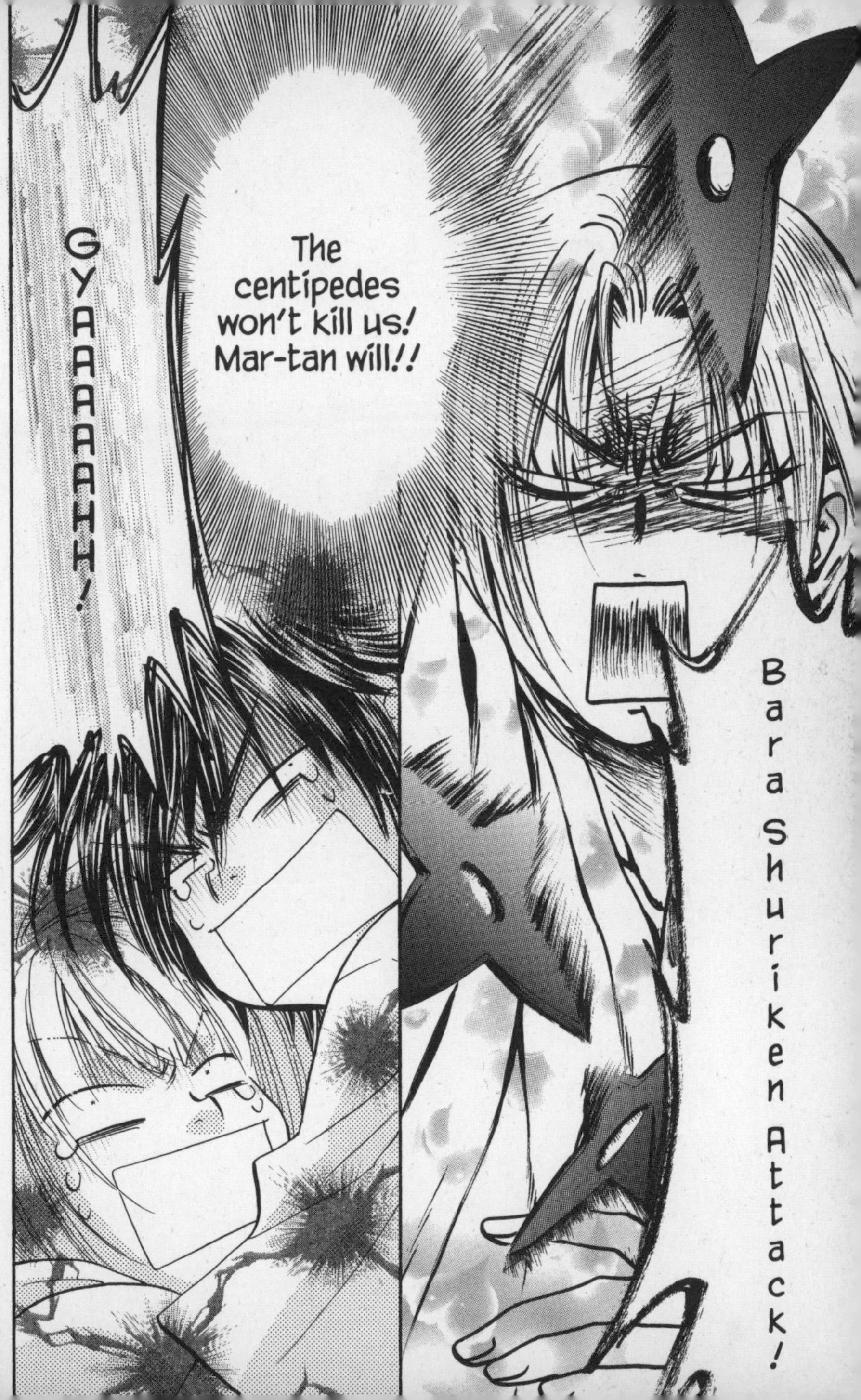
Bara Shuriken Attack!
The centipedes won't kill us! Mar-tan will!!
GYAAAAAHH!

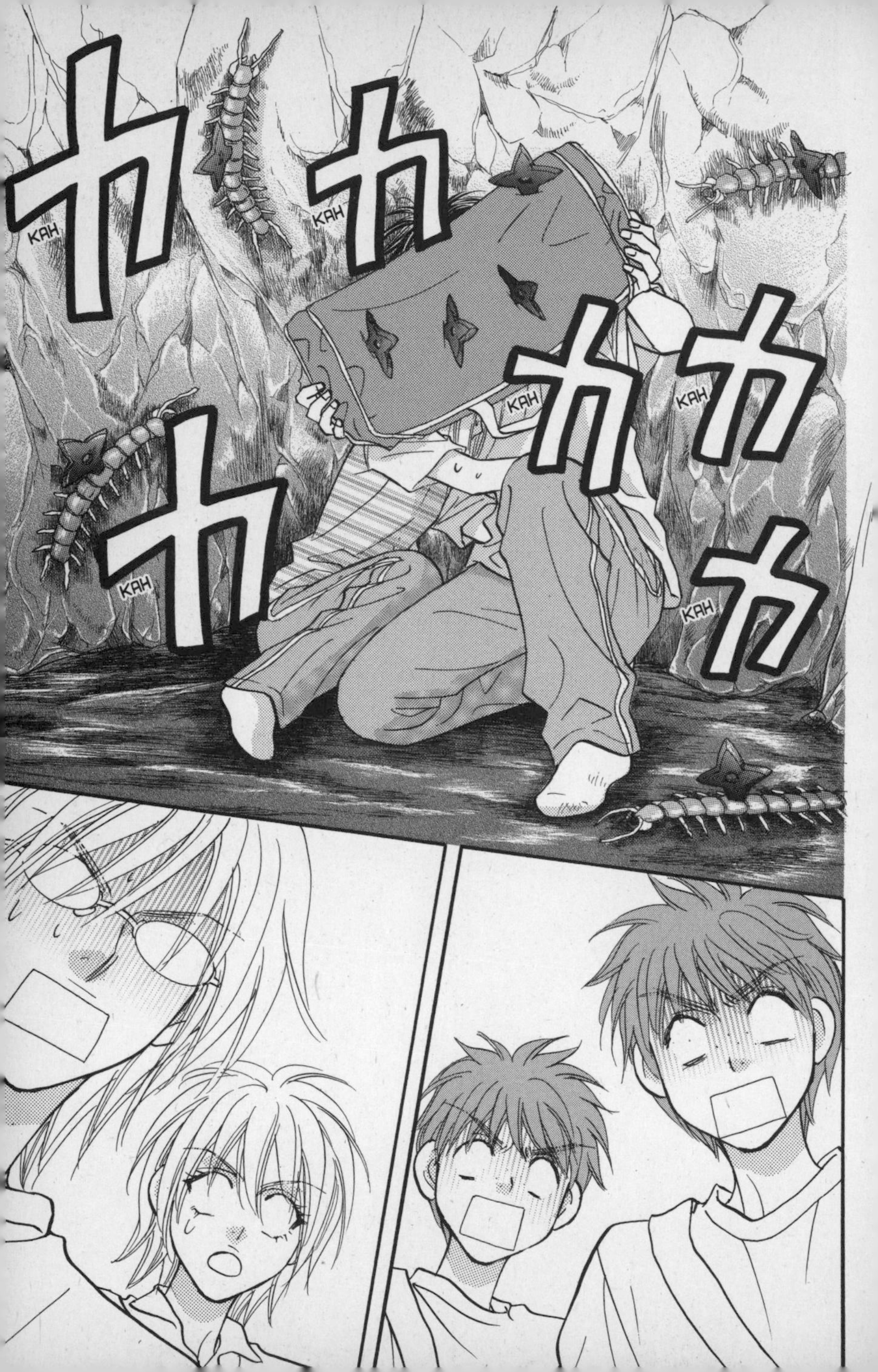
カ KAH
カ KAH
カ KAH
カ KAH
カ KAH
カ KAH

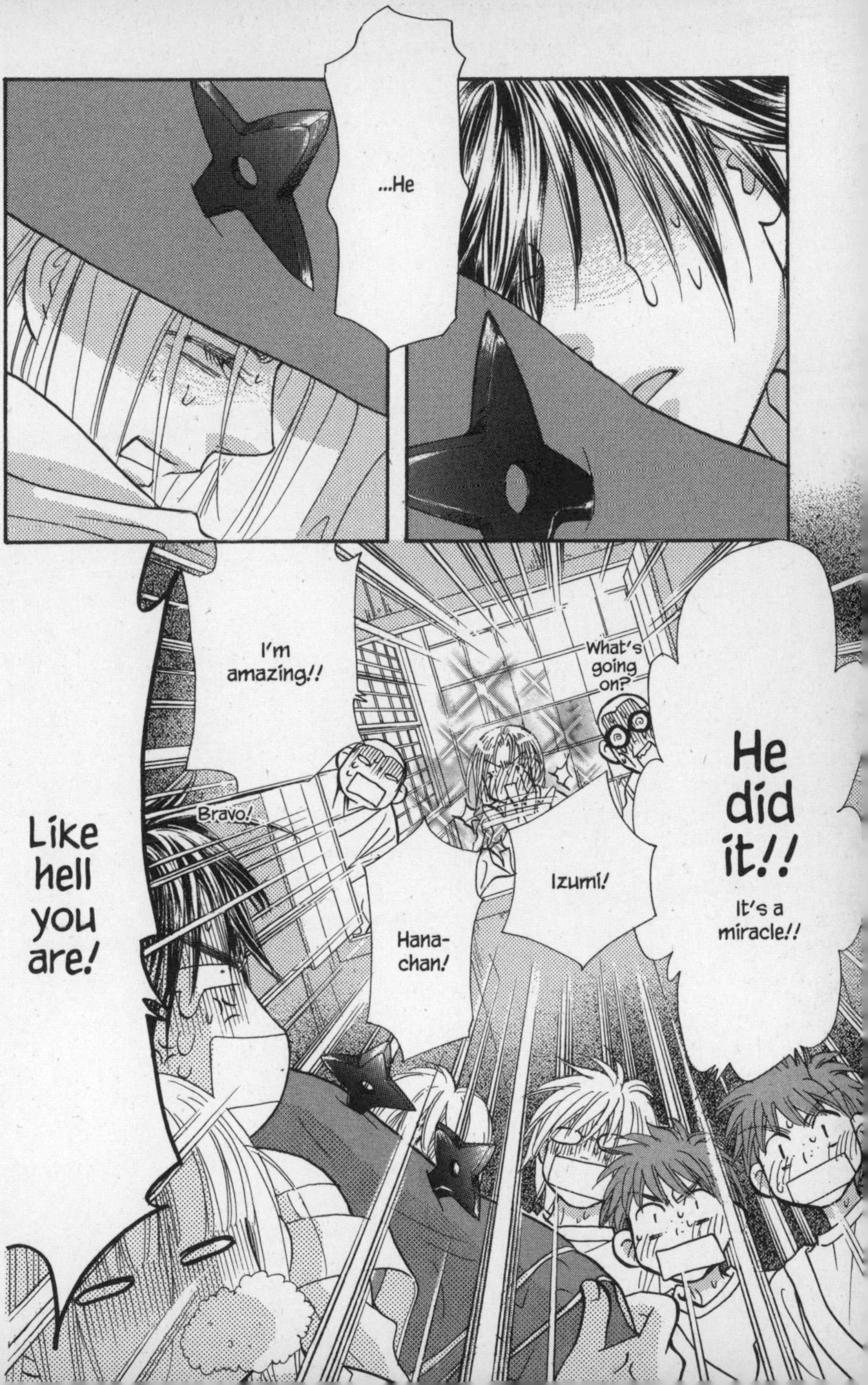
...He
He did it!!
It's a miracle!!
What's going on?
Izumi!
I'm amazing!!
Hana-chan!
Bravo!
Like hell you are!

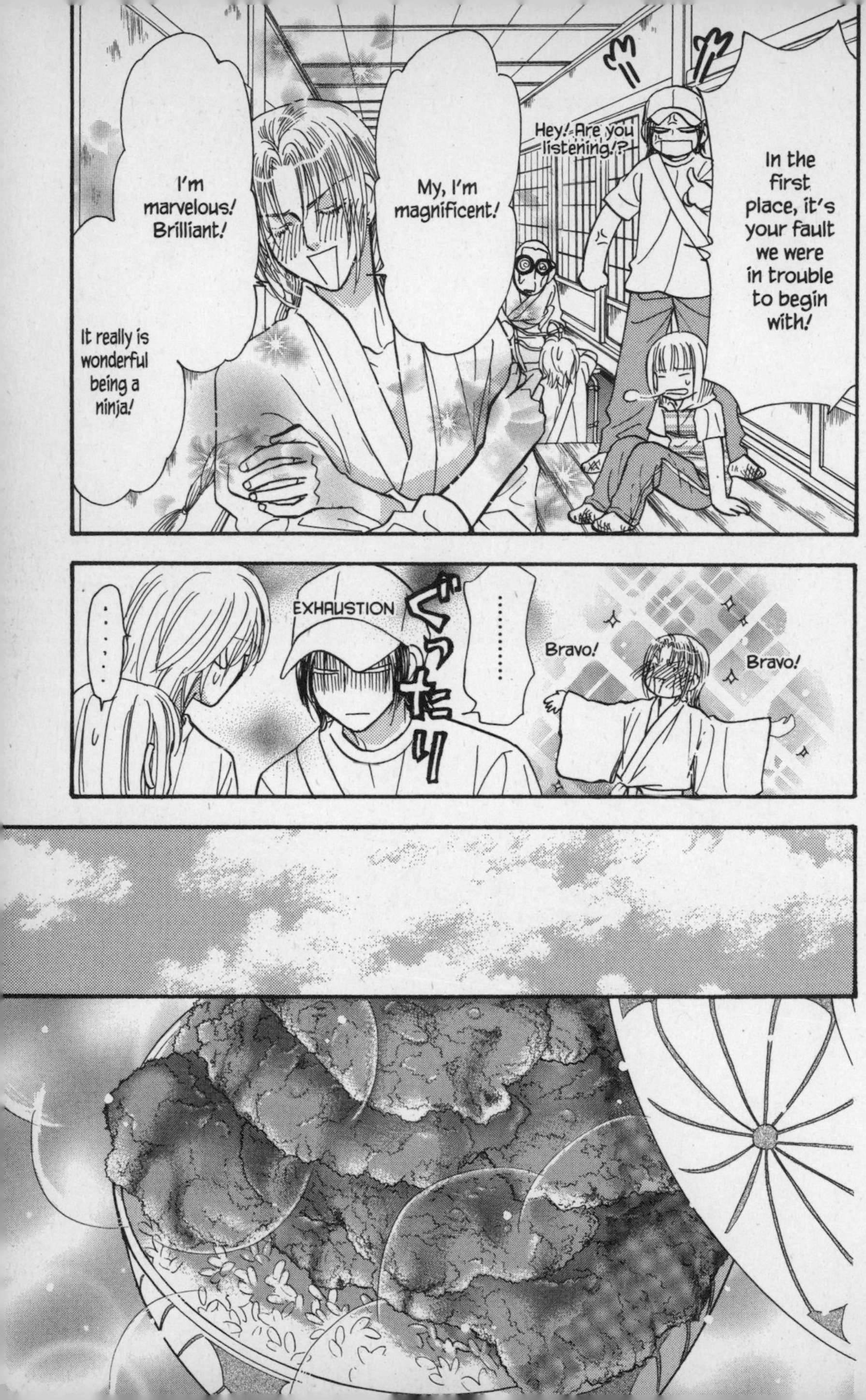
In the first place, it's your fault we were in trouble to begin with!
Hey! Are you listening!?
My, I'm magnificent!
I'm marvelous! Brilliant!
It really is wonderful being a ninja!
Bravo!
Bravo!
......
EXHAUSTION
ぐったり
......

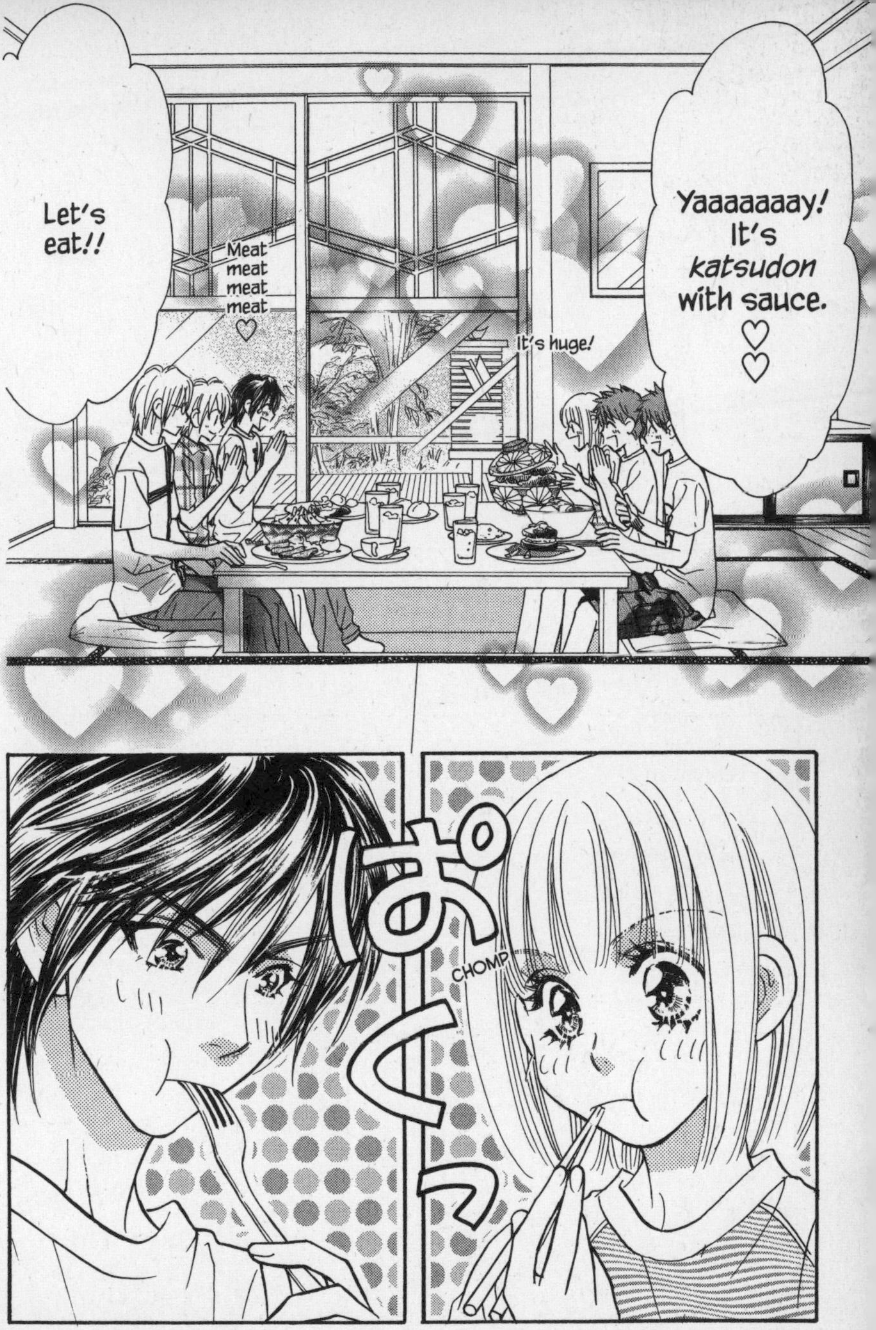
Yaaaaaaay! It's *katsudon* with sauce. ♡ ♡
It's huge!
Meat meat meat meat ♡
Let's eat!!
ぱくっ
CHOMP

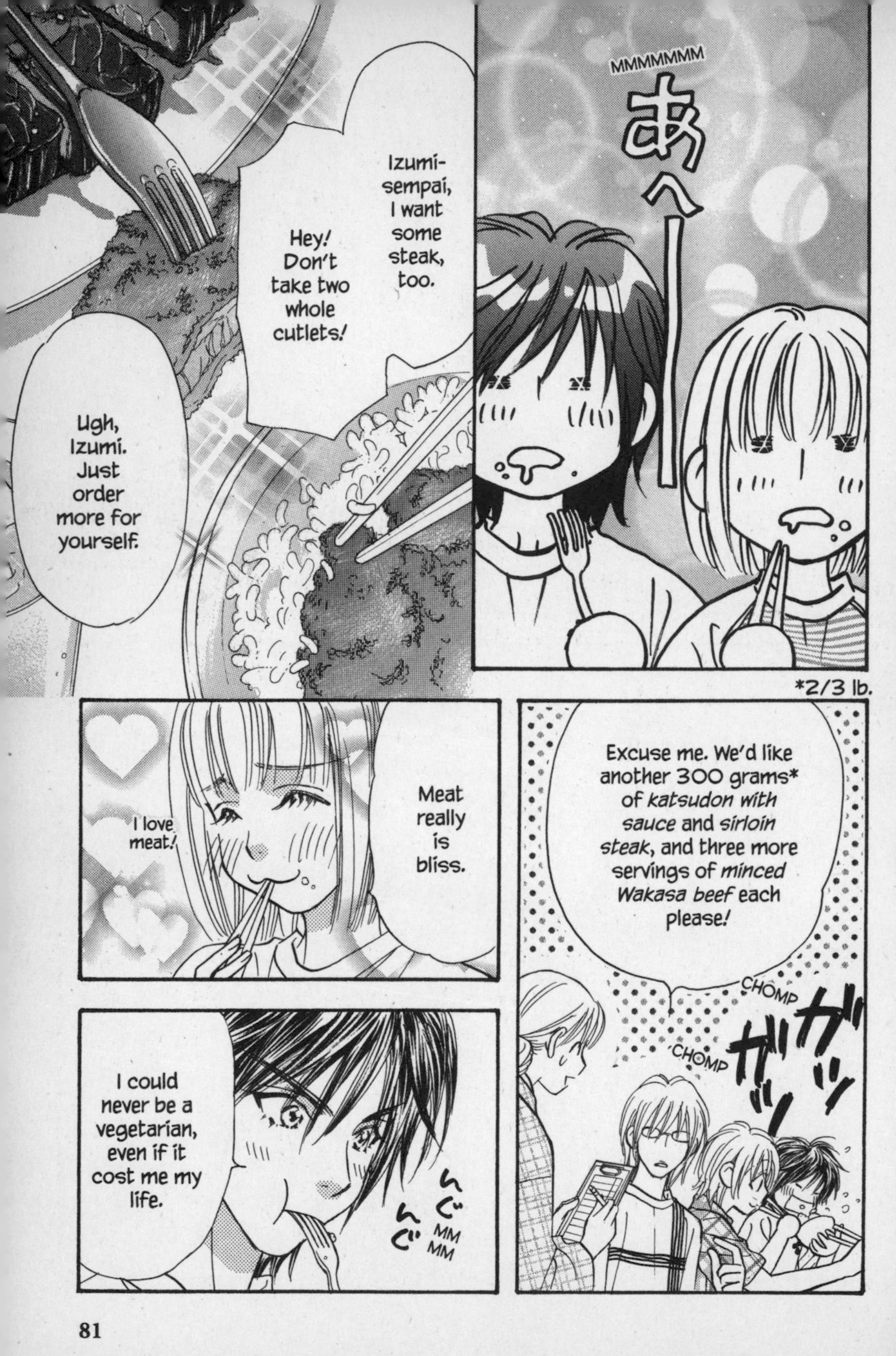
MMMMMMM
あへー
Izumi-sempai, I want some steak, too.
Hey! Don't take two whole cutlets!
Ugh, Izumi. Just order more for yourself.
Excuse me. We'd like another 300 grams* of *katsudon with sauce* and *sirloin steak*, and three more servings of *minced Wakasa beef* each please!
CHOMP
CHOMP
ガツ
ガツ
*2/3 lb.
Meat really is bliss.
I love meat!
I could never be a vegetarian, even if it cost me my life.
んぐ
んぐ
MM
MM

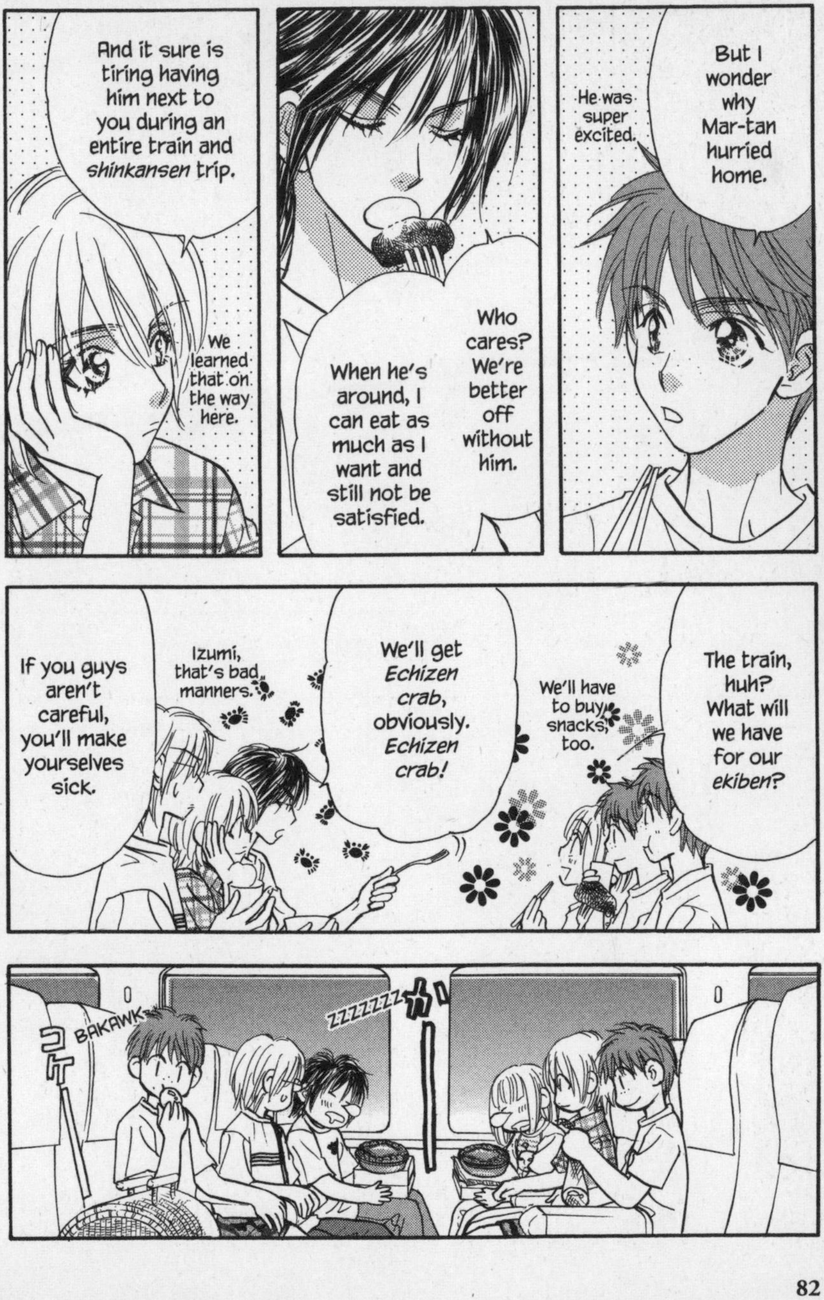

But I wonder why Mar-tan hurried home.
He was super excited.
Who cares? We're better off without him.
When he's around, I can eat as much as I want and still not be satisfied.
And it sure is tiring having him next to you during an entire train and *shinkansen* trip.
We learned that on the way here.
The train, huh? What will we have for our *ekiben*?
We'll have to buy snacks, too.
We'll get *Echizen crab*, obviously. *Echizen crab!*
Izumi, that's bad manners.
If you guys aren't careful, you'll make yourselves sick.
ZZZZZZZ
BAKAWK

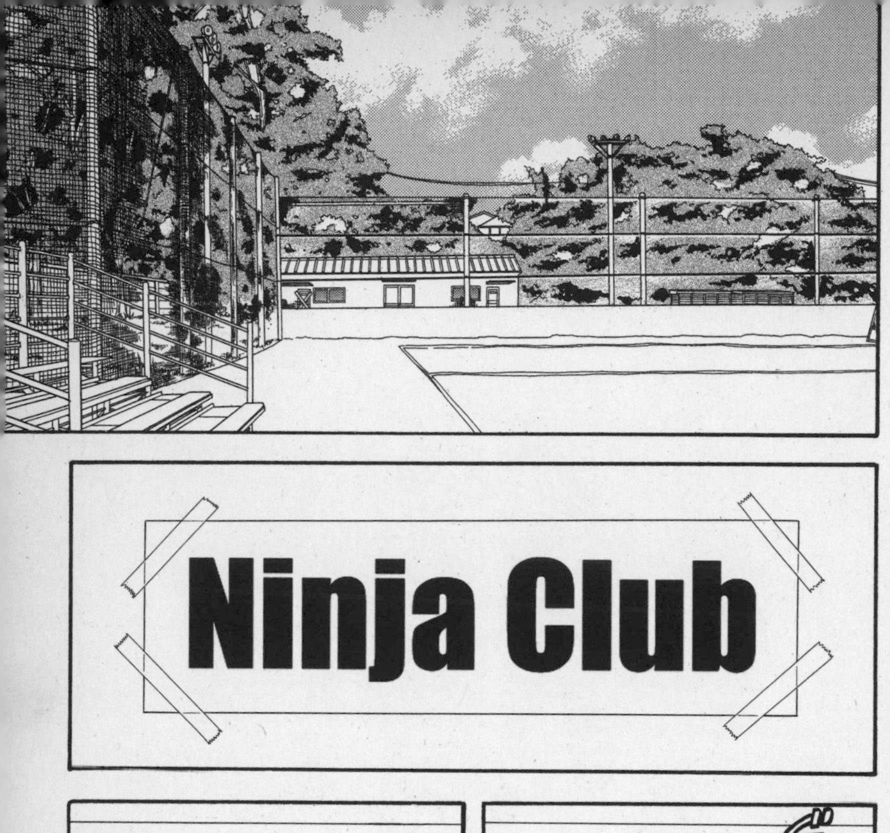
Ninja Club
ぐるん
SPIN
Ninja Club
ぱたん
PATAN
…
Ninja Club

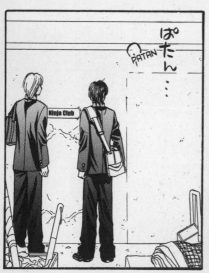

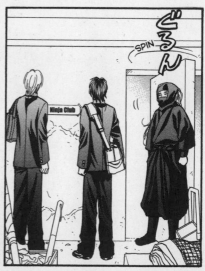

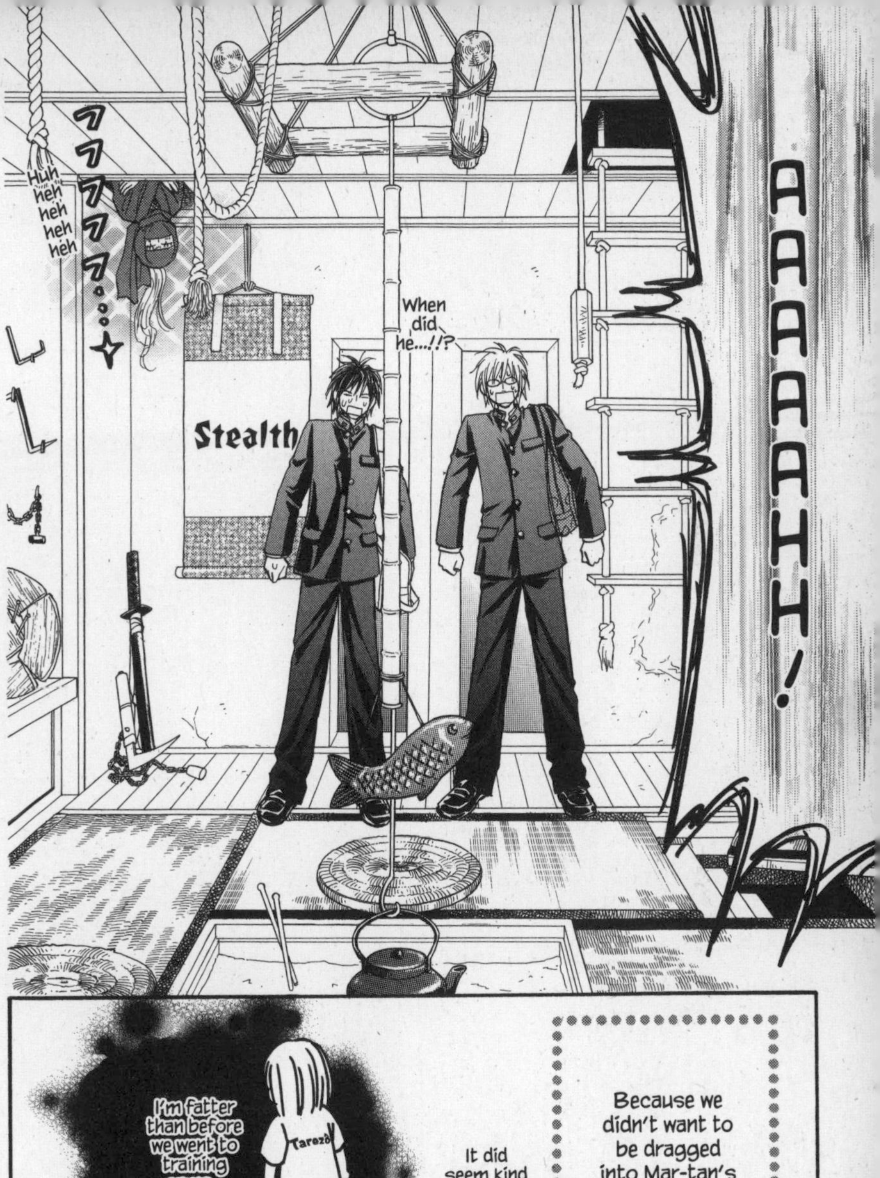
AAAAAAAH!
When did he...!?
Stealth
Huh heh heh heh heh

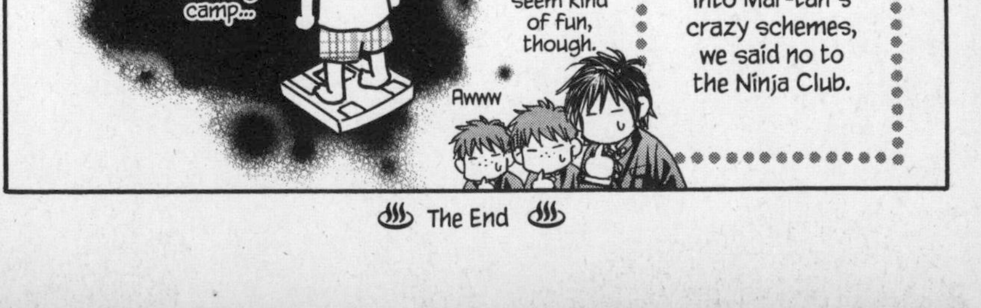
Because we didn't want to be dragged into Mar-tan's crazy schemes, we said no to the Ninja Club.
It did seem kind of fun, though.
Awww
I'm fatter than before we went to training camp...
Tarezo

The End

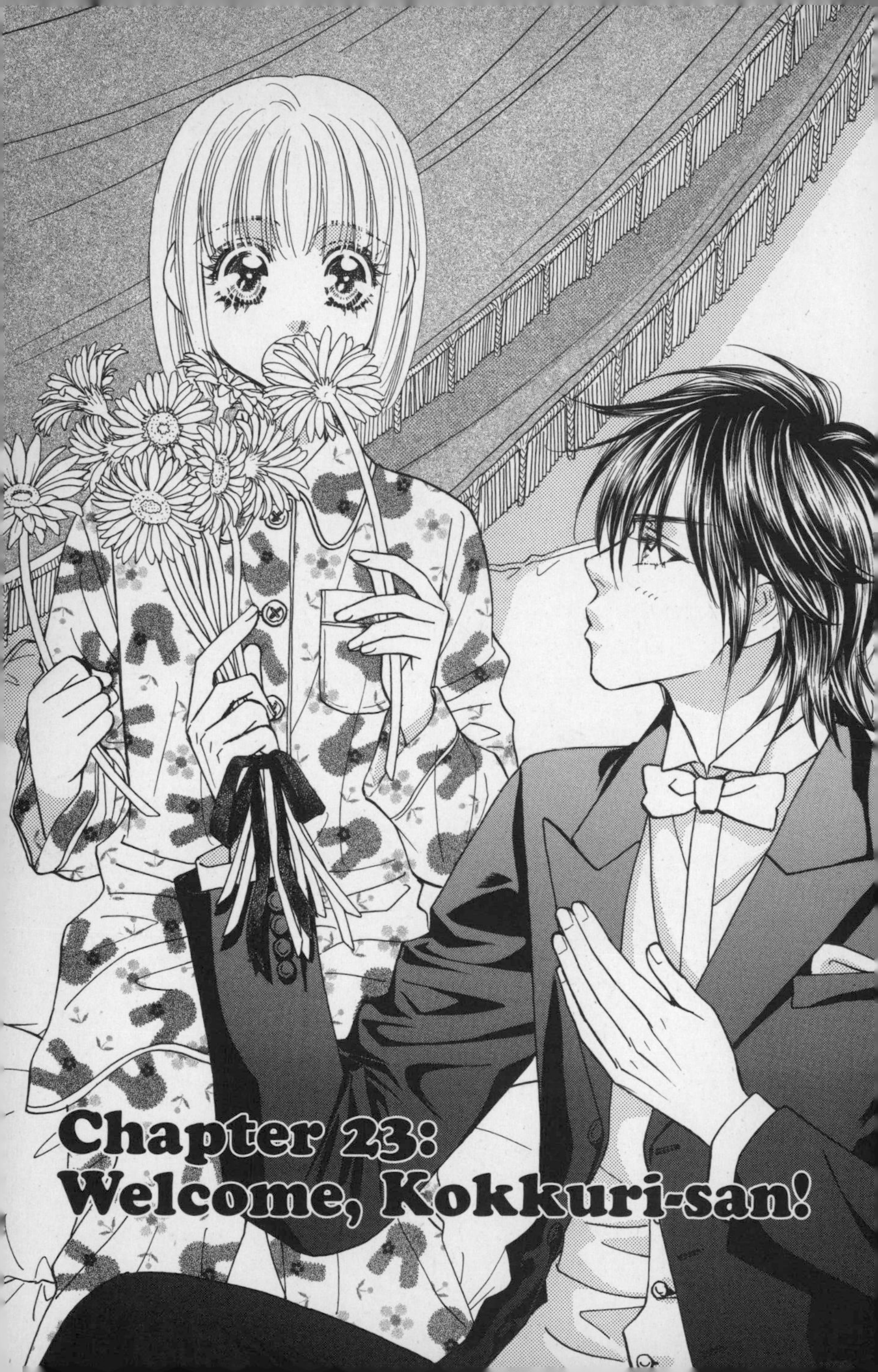

Chapter 23: Welcome, Kokkuri-san!

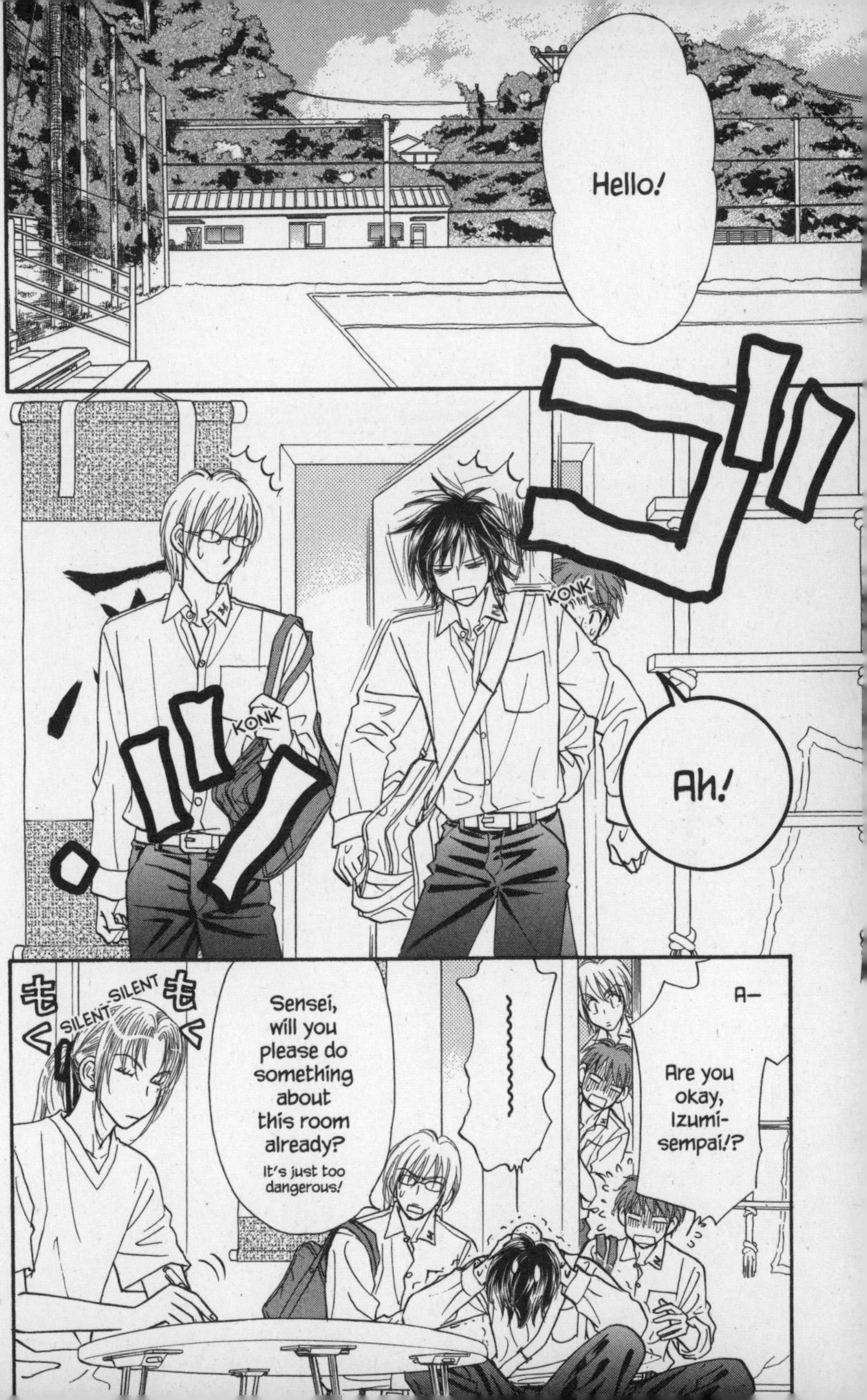
Hello!
Ah!
KONK
KONK
A—
Are you okay, Izumi-sempai!?
Sensei, will you please do something about this room already?
It's just too dangerous!
SILENT SILENT

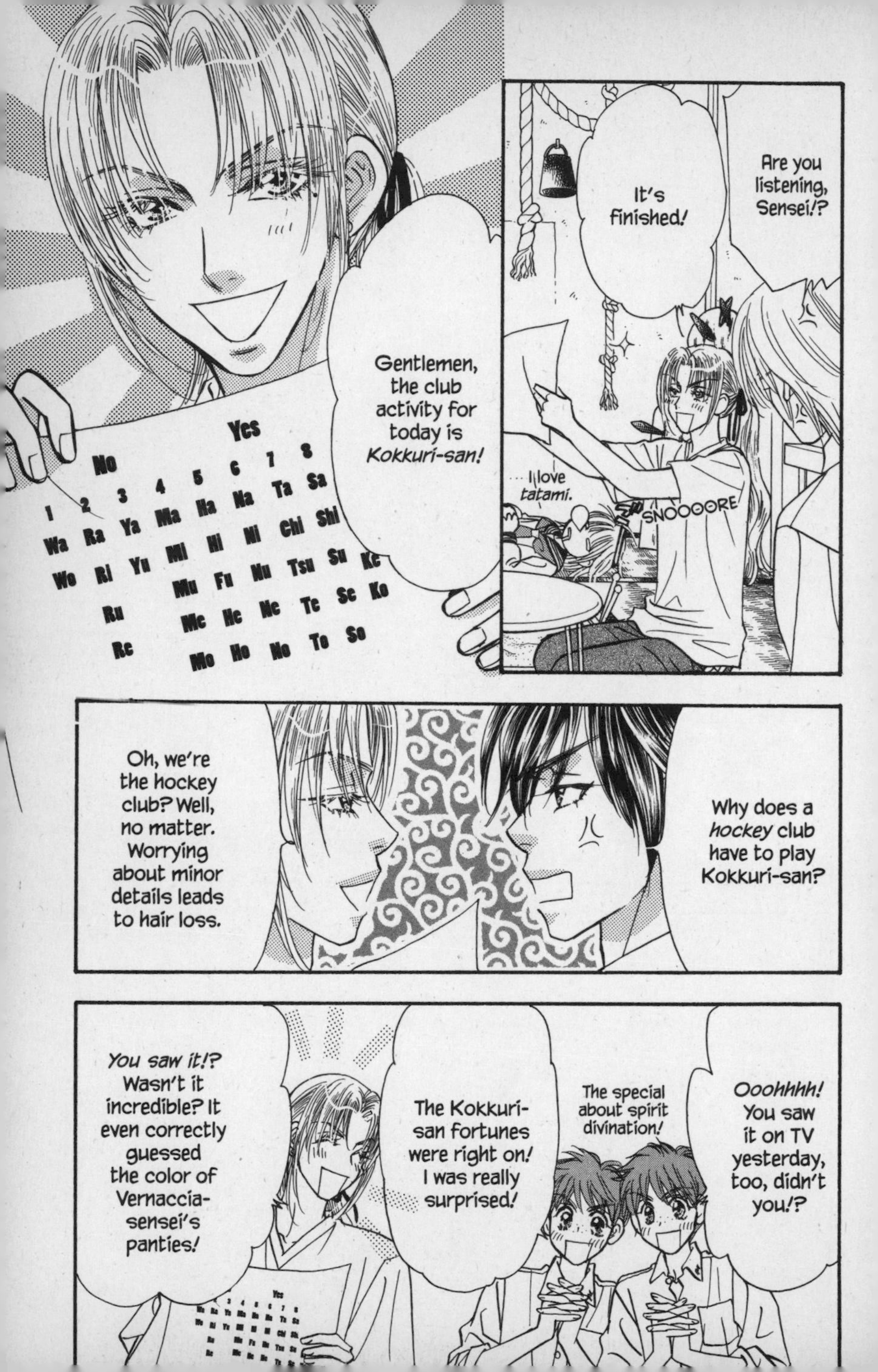
Are you listening, Sensei!?
It's finished!
...I love tatami.
SNOOOORE
Gentlemen, the club activity for today is Kokkuri-san!
Yes
No
1 2 3 4 5 6 7 8
Wa Ra Ya Ma Ha Na Ta Sa
Wo Ri Yu Mi Hi Ni Chi Shi
Ru Mu Fu Nu Tsu Su Ke
Re Me He Ne Te Se Ko
Mo Ho No To So
Why does a *hockey* club have to play Kokkuri-san?
Oh, we're the hockey club? Well, no matter. Worrying about minor details leads to hair loss.
Ooohhhh! You saw it on TV yesterday, too, didn't you!?
The special about spirit divination!
The Kokkuri-san fortunes were right on! I was really surprised!
You saw it!? Wasn't it incredible? It even correctly guessed the color of Vernaccia-sensei's panties!

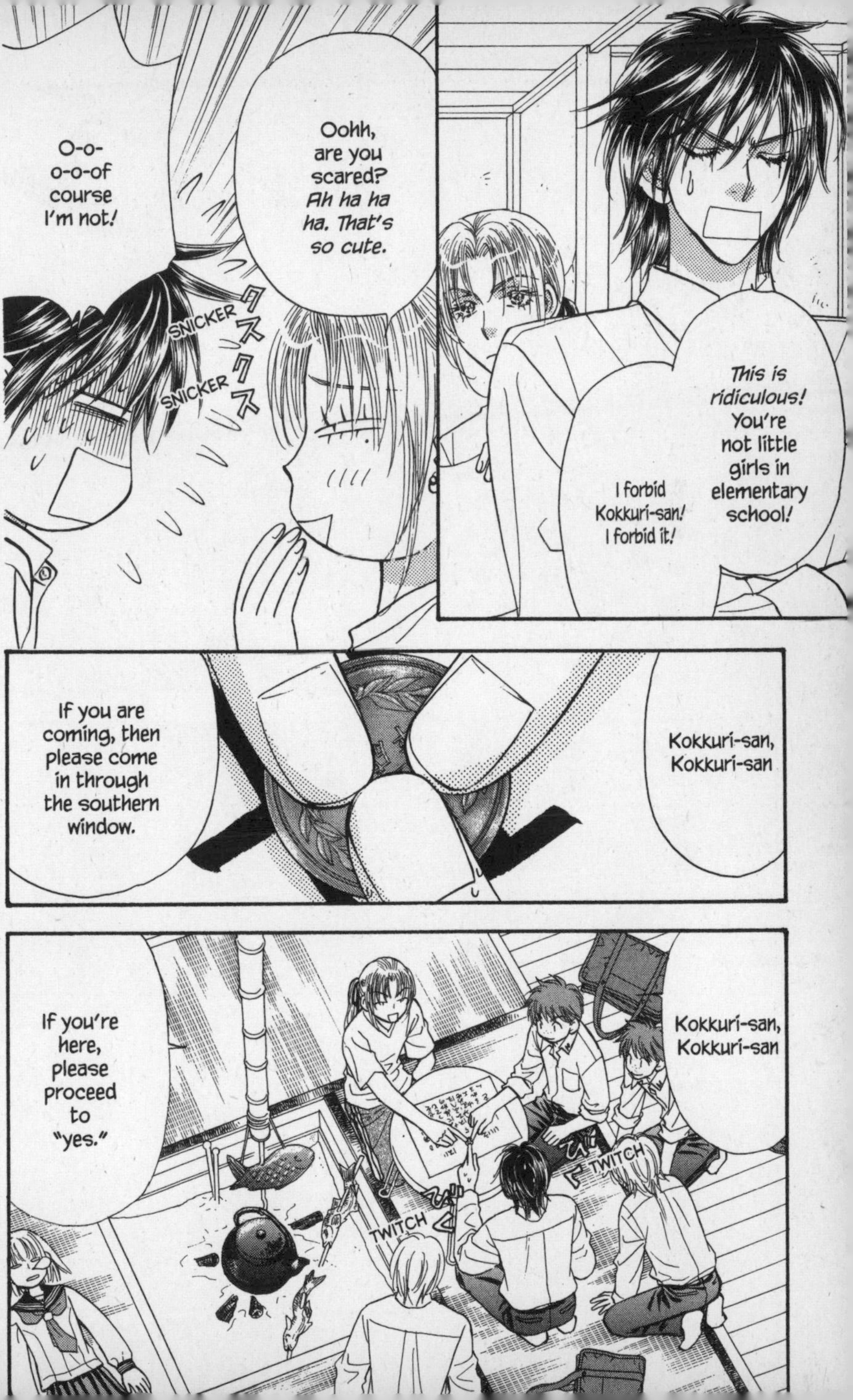
This is ridiculous! You're not little girls in elementary school!
I forbid Kokkuri-san! I forbid it!
Oohh, are you scared? Ah ha ha. That's so cute.
SNICKER
SNICKER
O-o-o-o-of course I'm not!
Kokkuri-san, Kokkuri-san
If you are coming, then please come in through the southern window.
Kokkuri-san, Kokkuri-san
TWITCH
TWITCH
If you're here, please proceed to "yes."

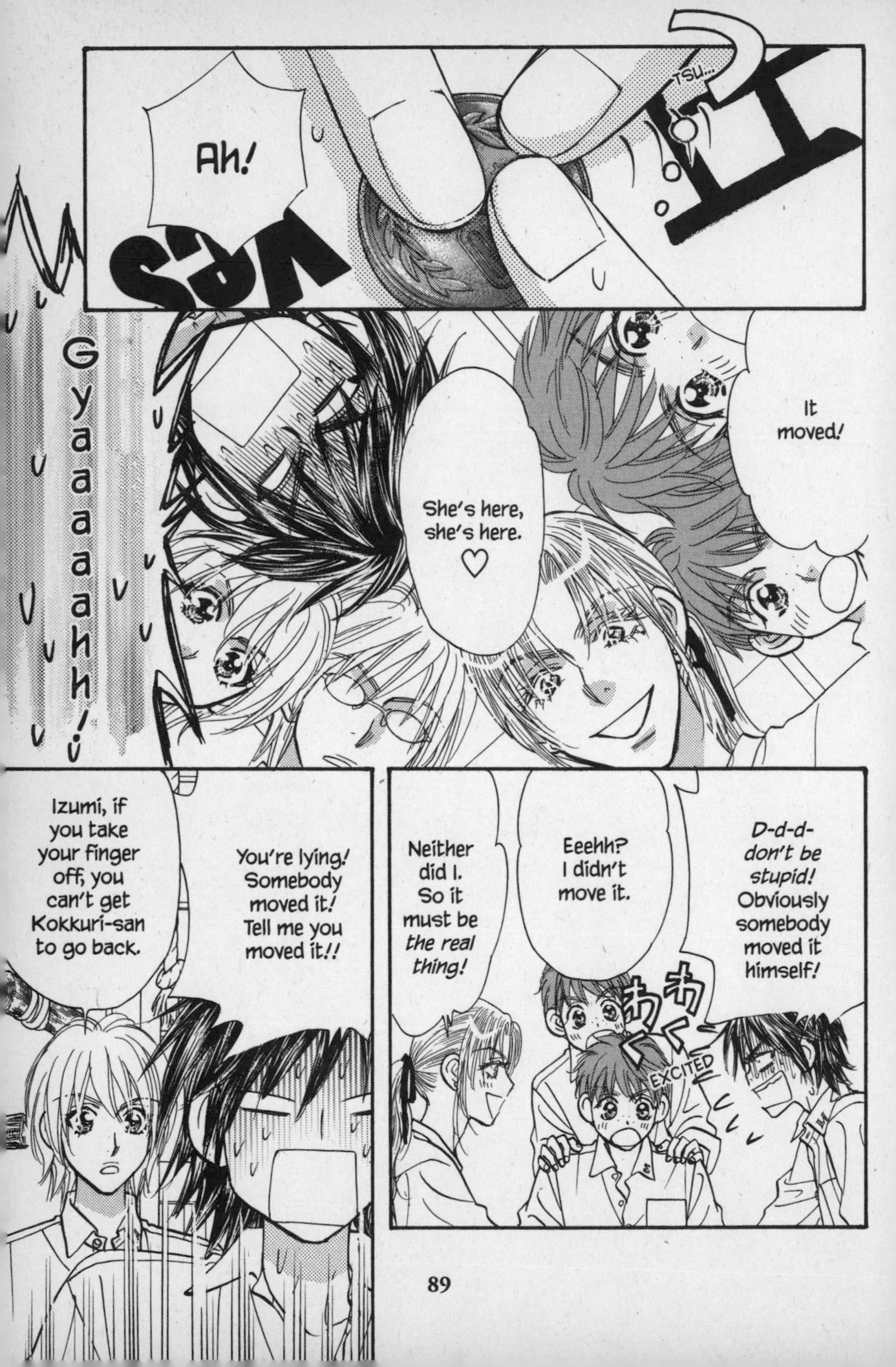

TSU...
Ah!
It moved!
She's here, she's here. ♡
Gyaaaaaahh!!
D-d-d-don't be stupid! Obviously somebody moved it himself!
わくわく
EXCITED
Eeehh? I didn't move it.
Neither did I. So it must be *the real thing!*
You're lying! Somebody moved it! Tell me you moved it!!
Izumi, if you take your finger off, you can't get Kokkuri-san to go back.

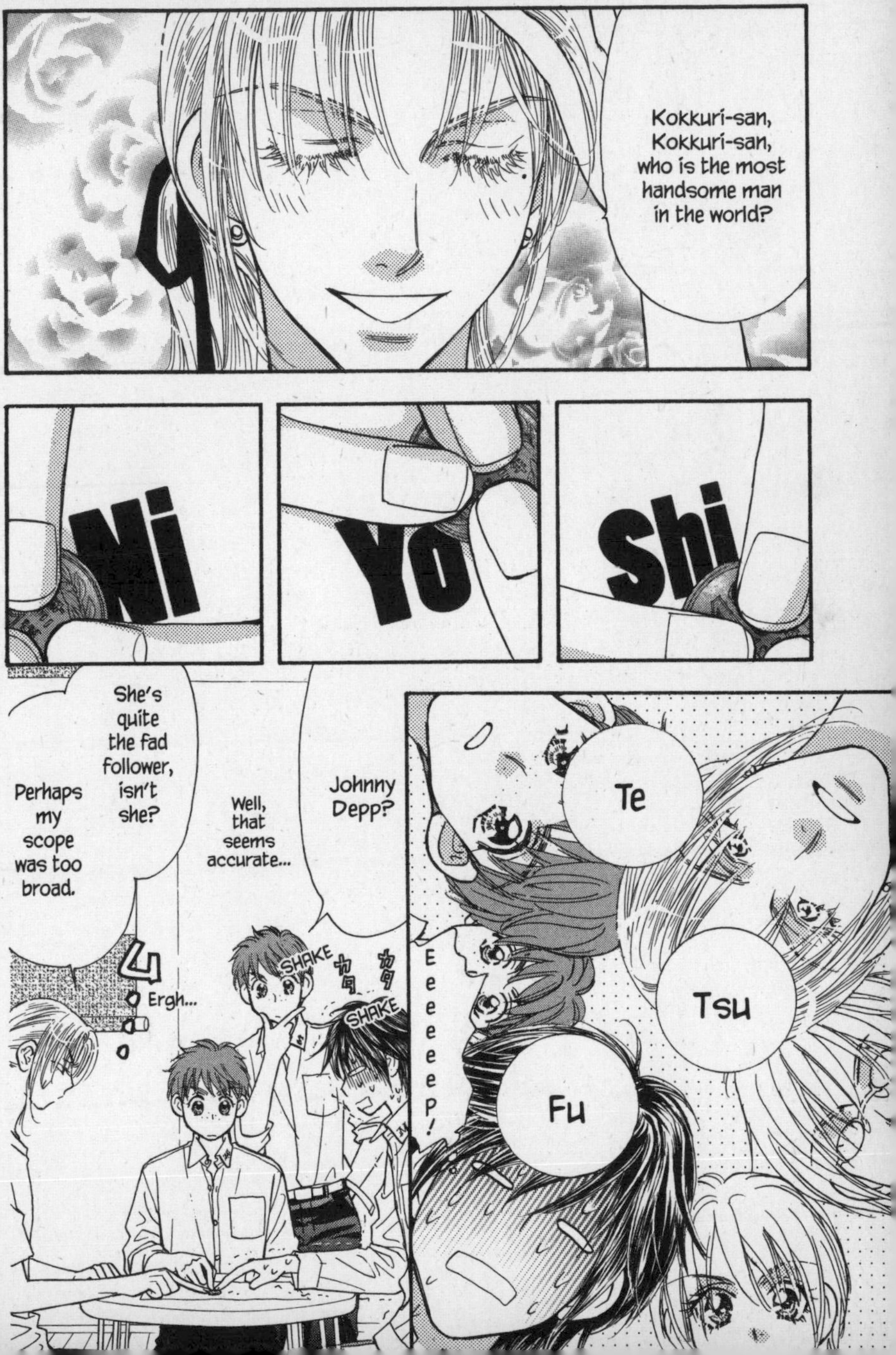
Kokkuri-san, Kokkuri-san, who is the most handsome man in the world?
Shi
Yo
Ni
Te
Tsu
Fu
Eeeeeeep!
Johnny Depp?
Well, that seems accurate...
She's quite the fad follower, isn't she?
Perhaps my scope was too broad.
SHAKE
カタ
カタ
SHAKE
Ergh...

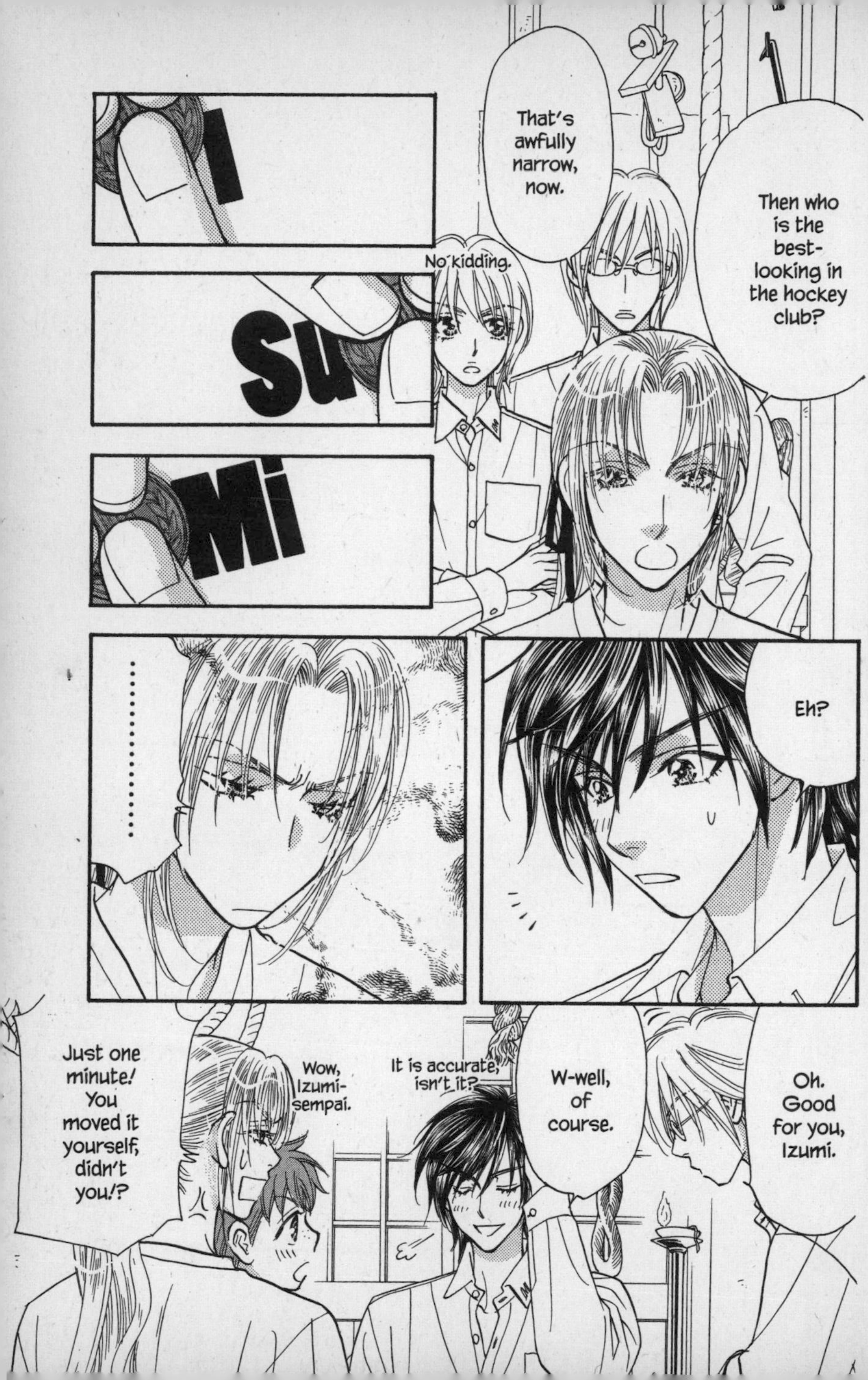
That's awfully narrow, now.
No kidding.
Then who is the best-looking in the hockey club?
I
Su
Mi
Eh?
......
Oh. Good for you, Izumi.
W-well, of course.
It is accurate, isn't it?
Wow, Izumi-sempai.
Just one minute! You moved it yourself, didn't you!?

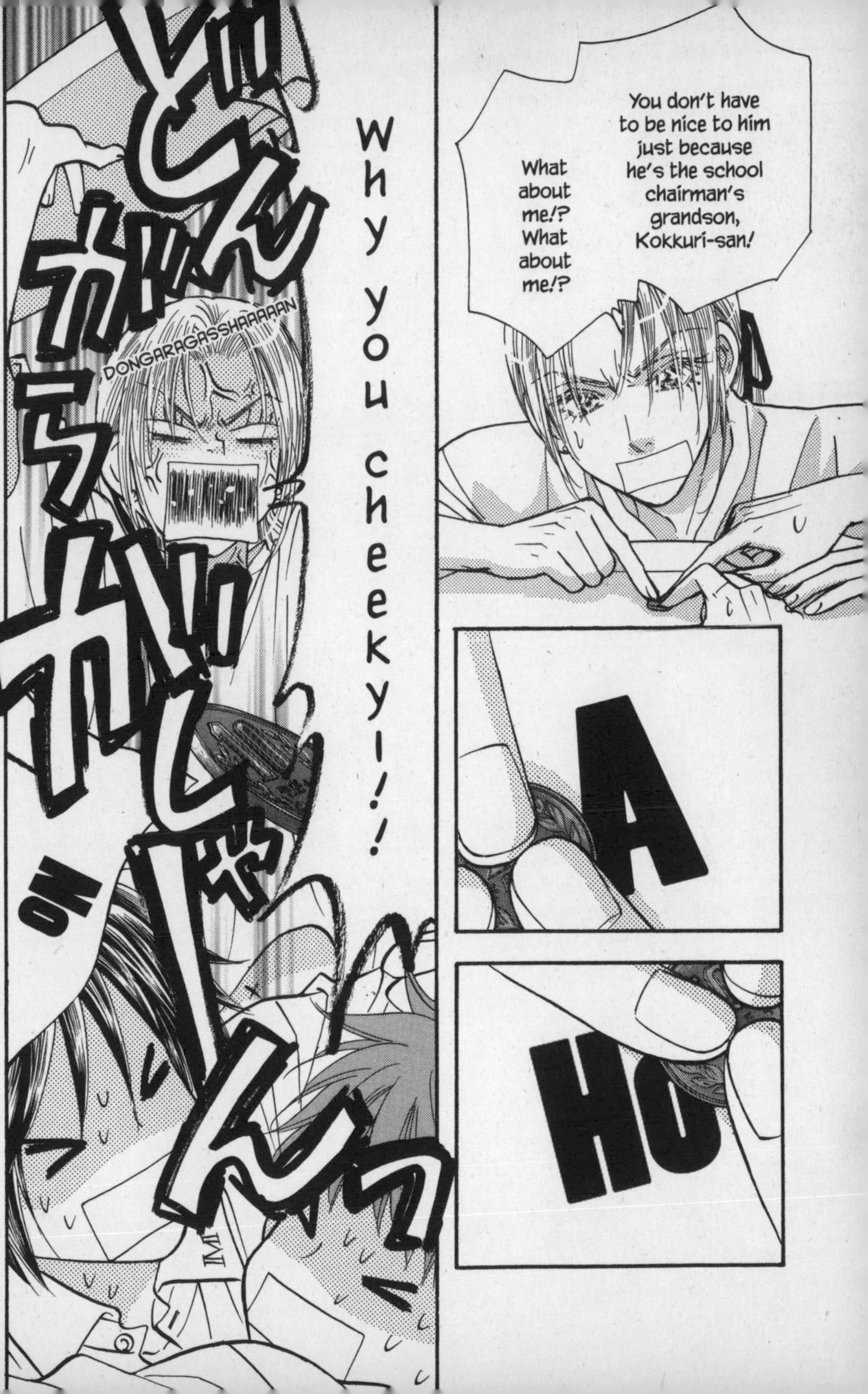
You don't have to be nice to him just because he's the school chairman's grandson, Kokkuri-san!
What about me!? What about me!?
A
HO
Why you cheeky!!!
DONGARAGASSHAAAAAN

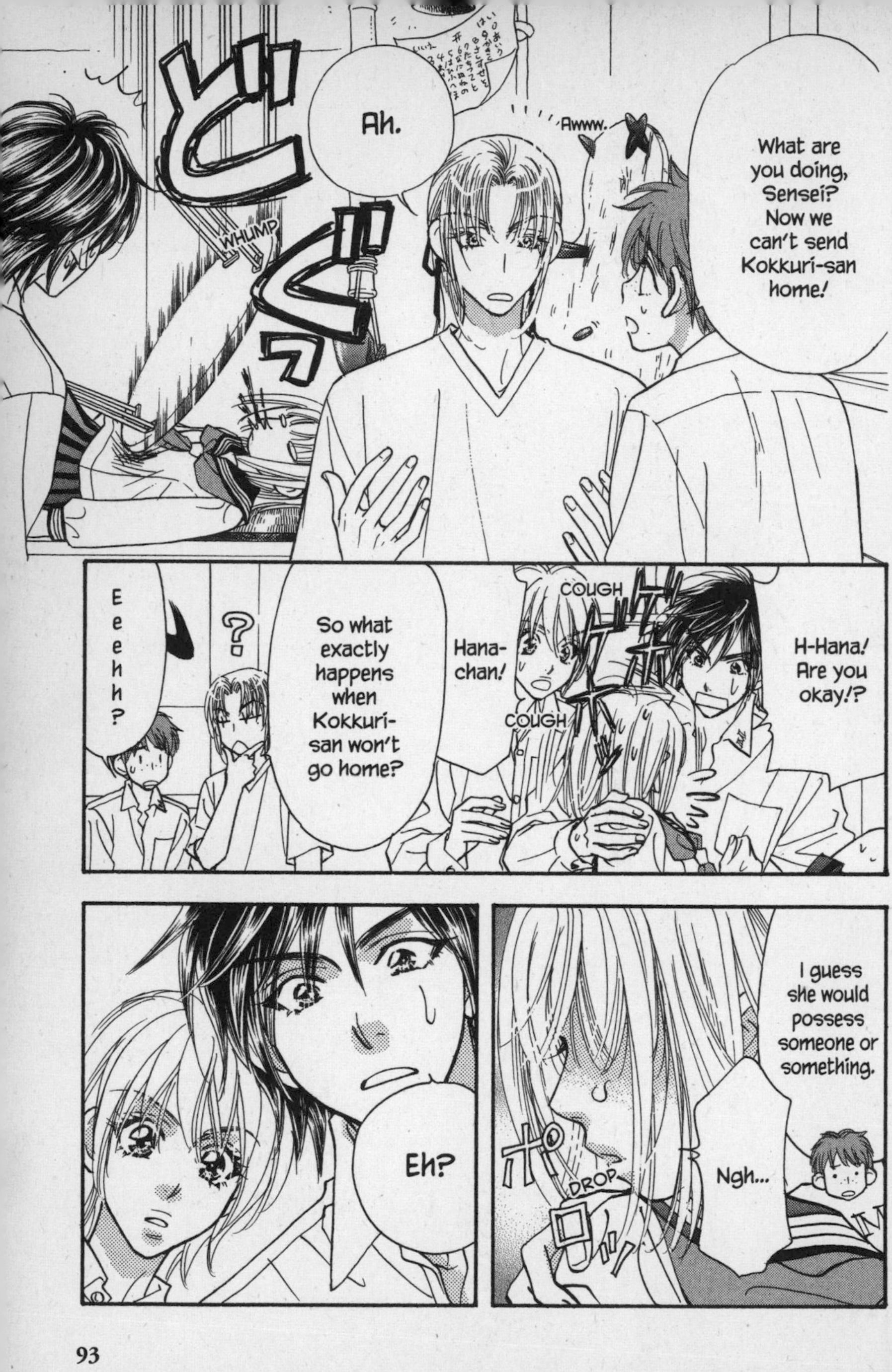
What are you doing, Sensei? Now we can't send Kokkuri-san home!
Awww.
Ah.
WHUMP
H-Hana! Are you okay!?
COUGH
Hana-chan!
COUGH
So what exactly happens when Kokkuri-san won't go home?
?
Eeehh?
I guess she would possess someone or something.
Ngh...
DROP
Eh?

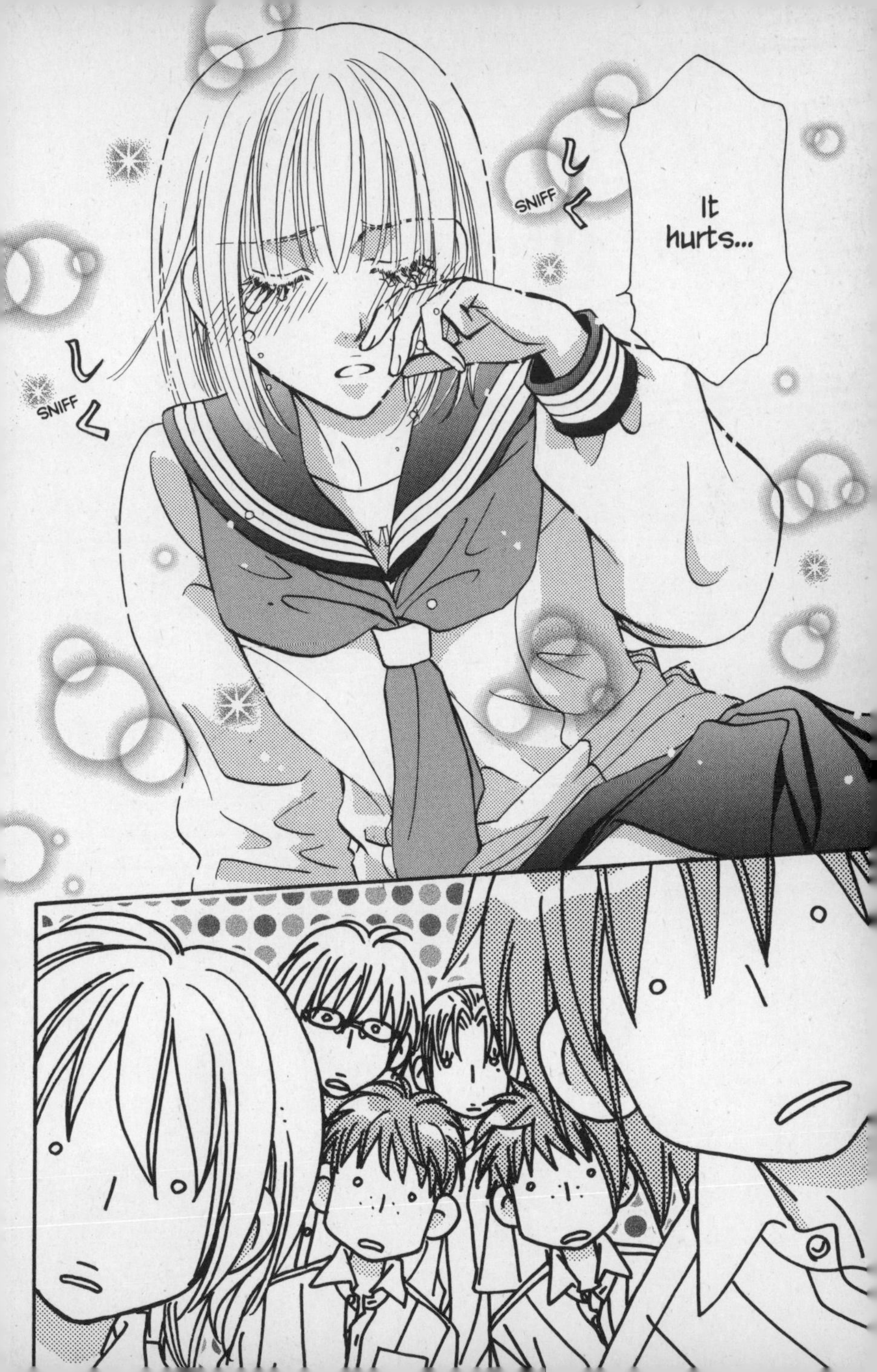

It hurts...
SNIFF
SNIFF

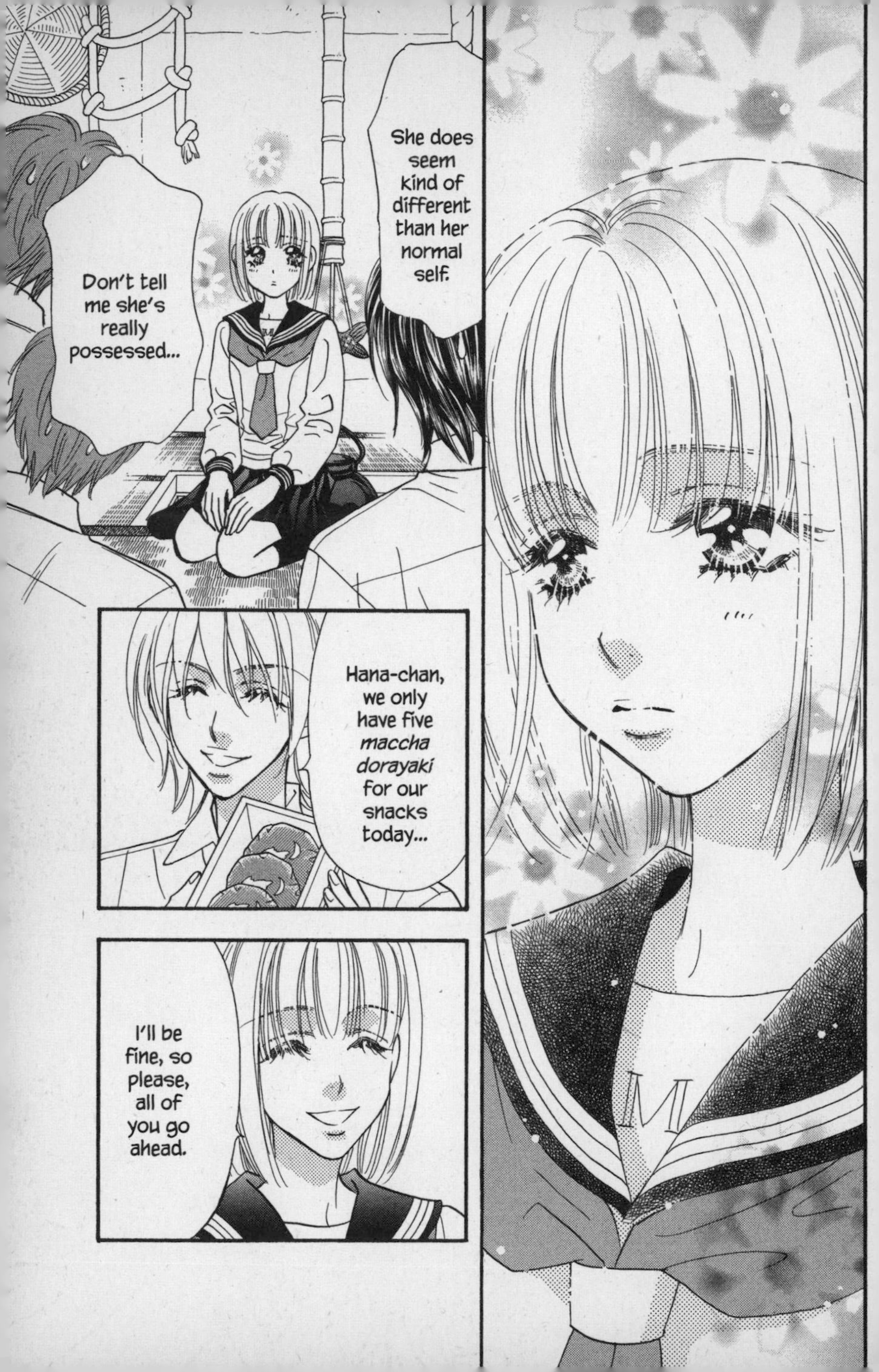
She does seem kind of different than her normal self.
Don't tell me she's really possessed...
Hana-chan, we only have five *maccha dorayaki* for our snacks today...
I'll be fine, so please, all of you go ahead.

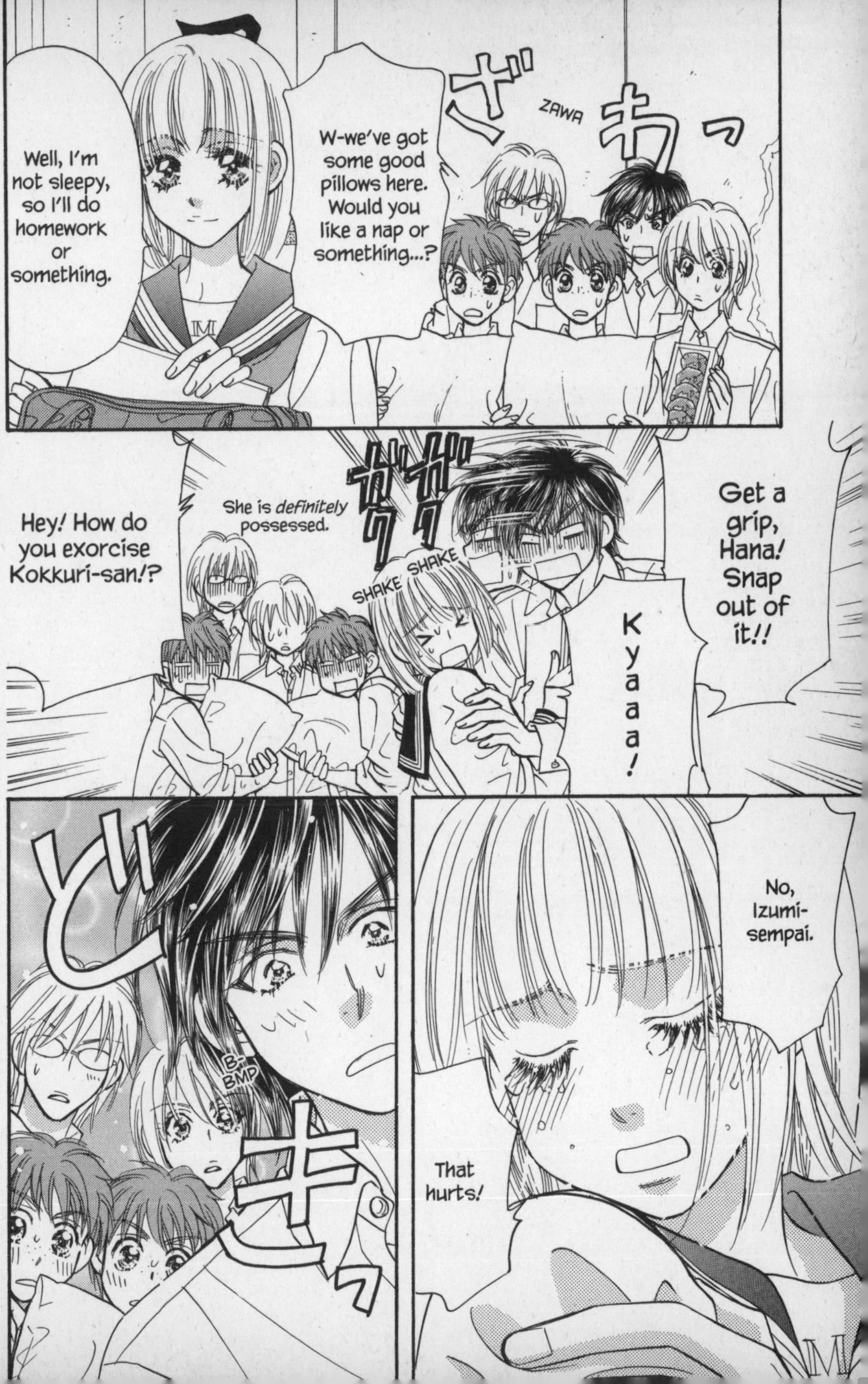
ZAWA
W-we've got some good pillows here. Would you like a nap or something...?
Well, I'm not sleepy, so I'll do homework or something.
Get a grip, Hana! Snap out of it!!
Kyaaa!
SHAKE SHAKE
She is *definitely* possessed.
Hey! How do you exorcise Kokkuri-san!?
No, Izumi-sempai.
That hurts!
B-BMP

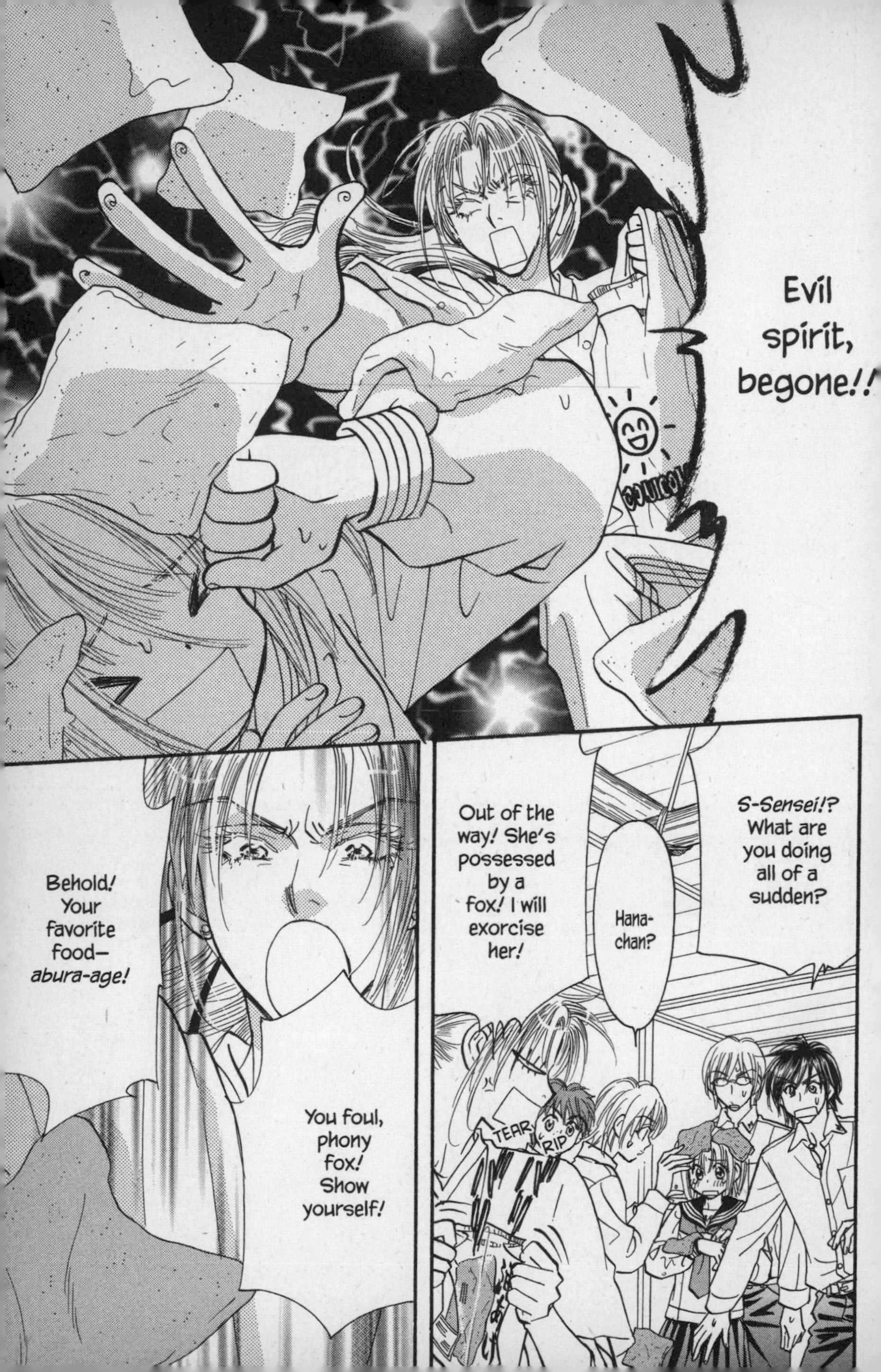
Evil spirit, begone!!
S-Sensei!? What are you doing all of a sudden?
Hana-chan?
Out of the way! She's possessed by a fox! I will exorcise her!
TEAR
RIP
Behold! Your favorite food—abura-age!
You foul, phony fox! Show yourself!

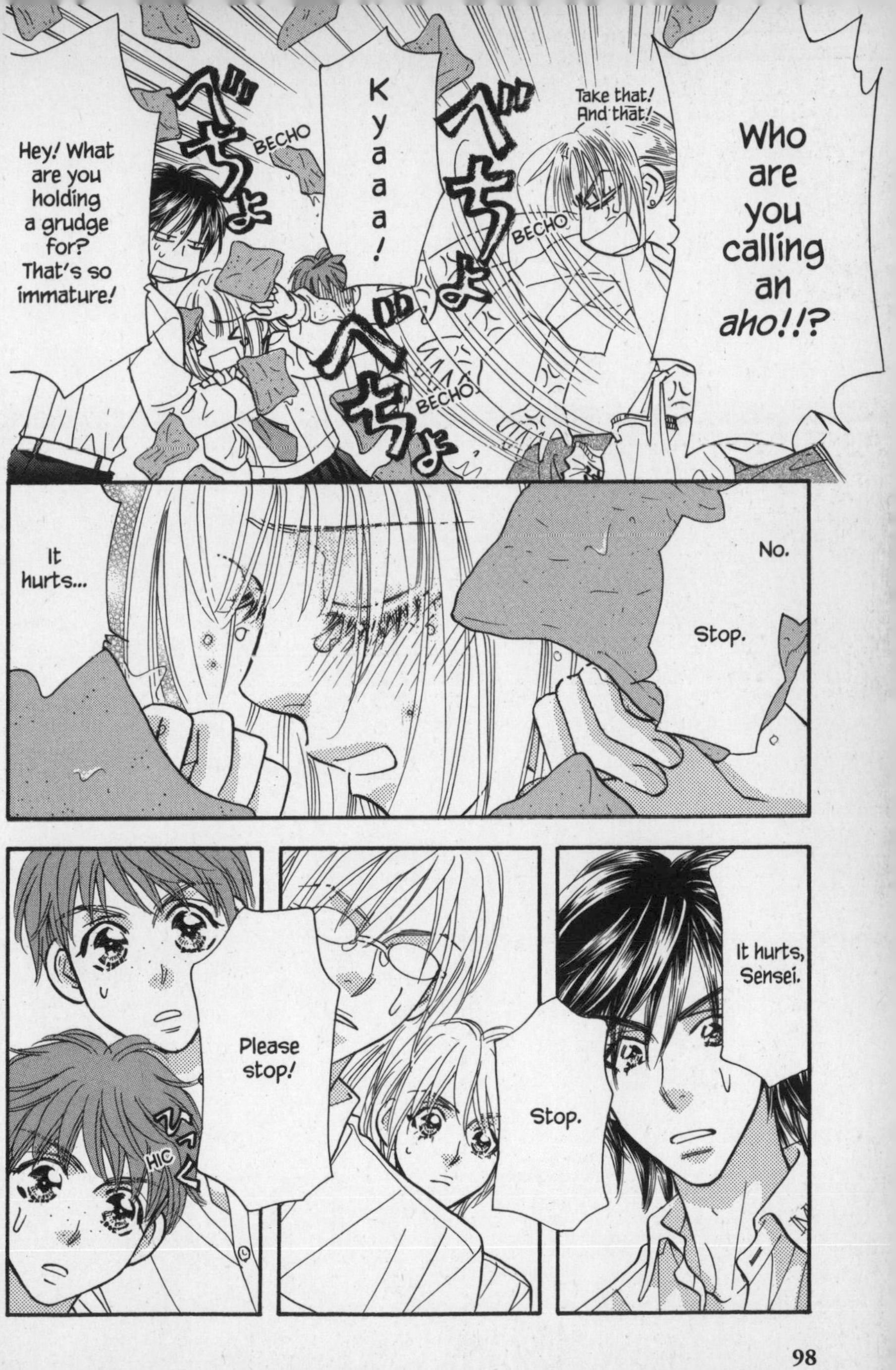
Who are you calling an aho!!?
Take that! And that!
BECHO
BECHO
Kyaaa!
BECHO
Hey! What are you holding a grudge for? That's so immature!
No.
Stop.
It hurts...
It hurts, Sensei.
Stop.
Please stop!
HIC

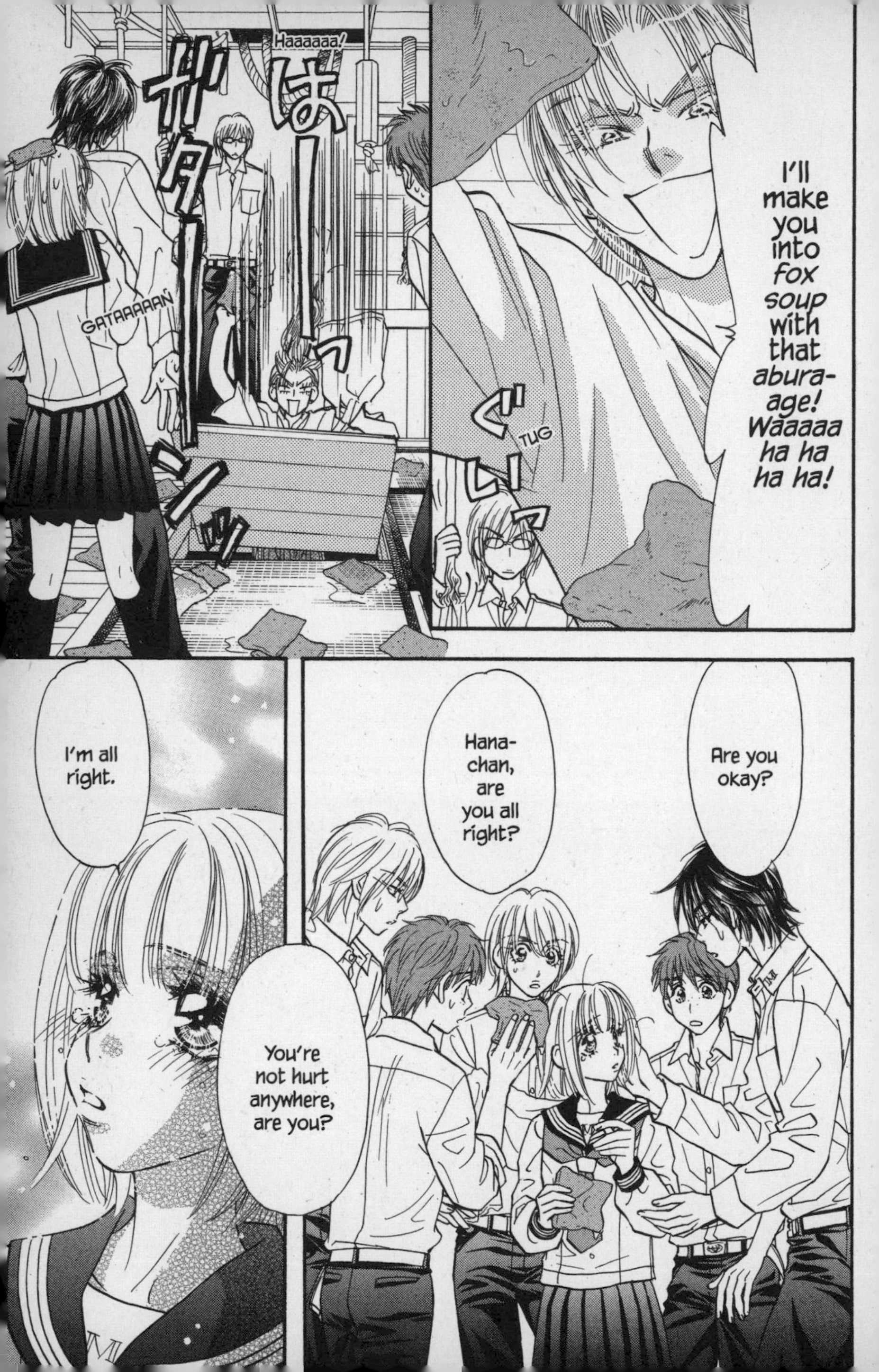
I'll make you into fox soup with that abura-age! Waaaaa ha ha ha ha!
TUG
Haaaaaa!
GATAAAAAN
Are you okay?
Hana-chan, are you all right?
You're not hurt anywhere, are you?
I'm all right.

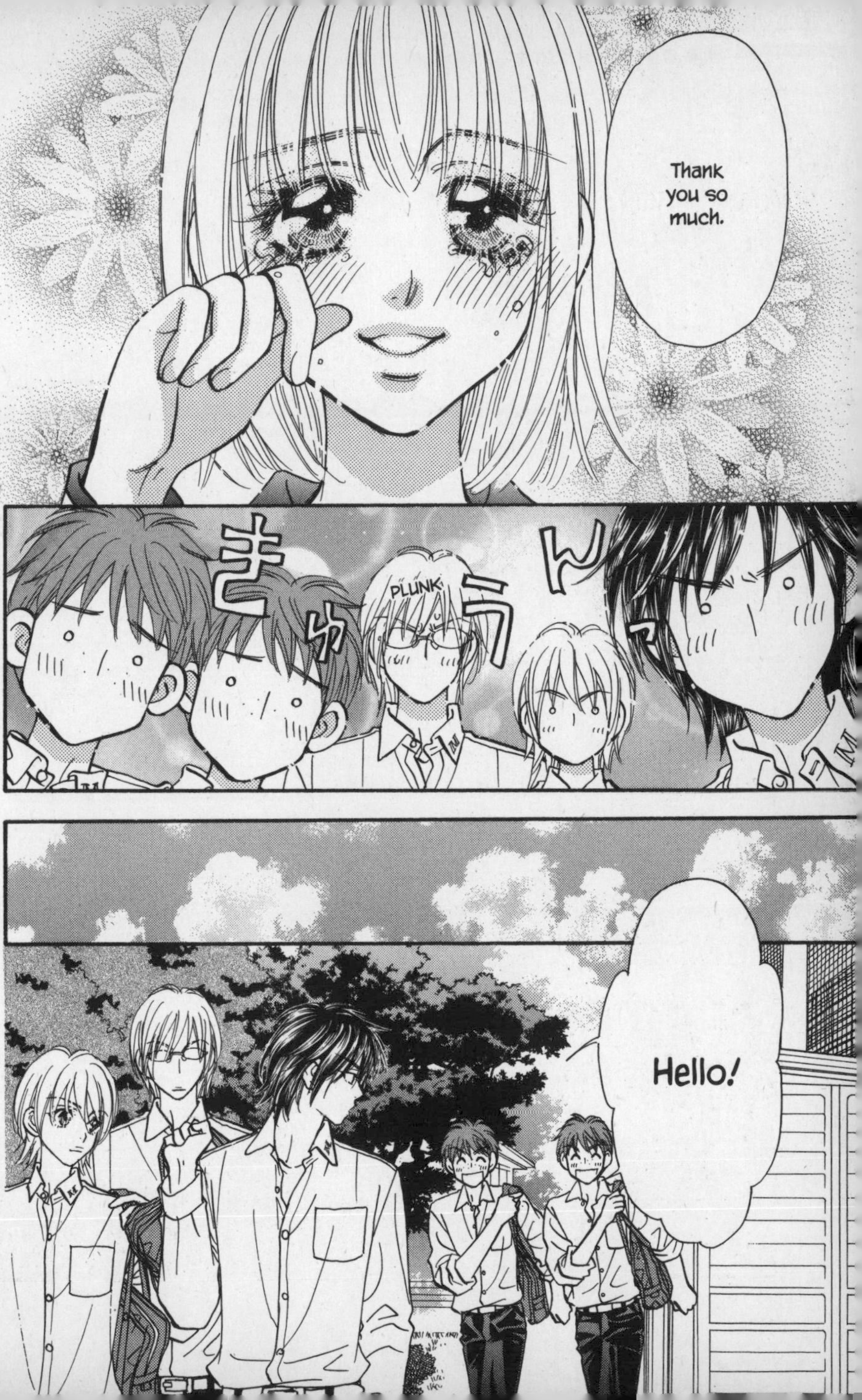
Thank you so much.
きゅうんっ
PLUNK
Hello!

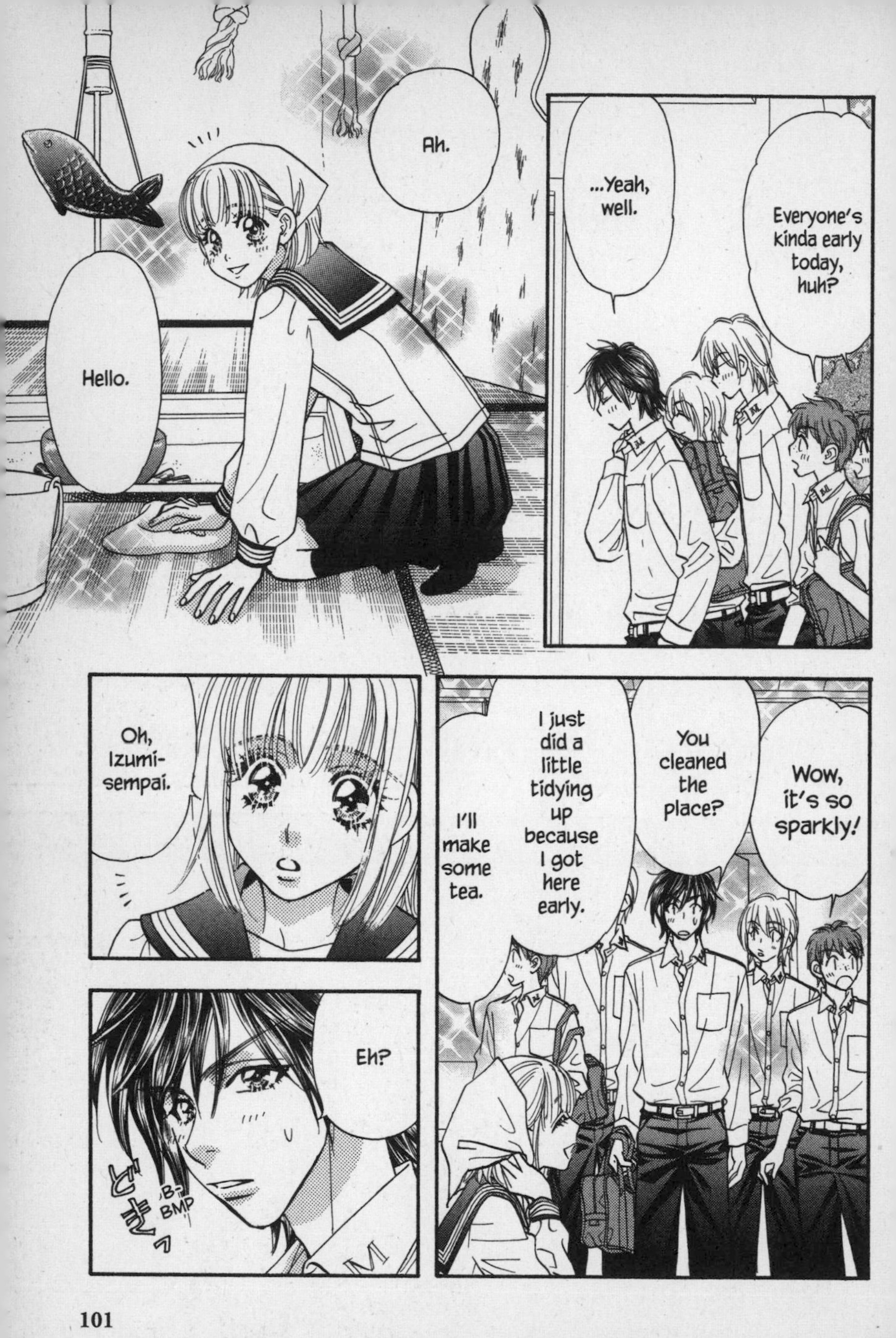
Everyone's kinda early today, huh?
...Yeah, well.
Ah.
Hello.
Wow, it's so sparkly!
You cleaned the place?
I just did a little tidying up because I got here early.
I'll make some tea.
Oh, Izumi-sempai.
Eh?
B-BMP

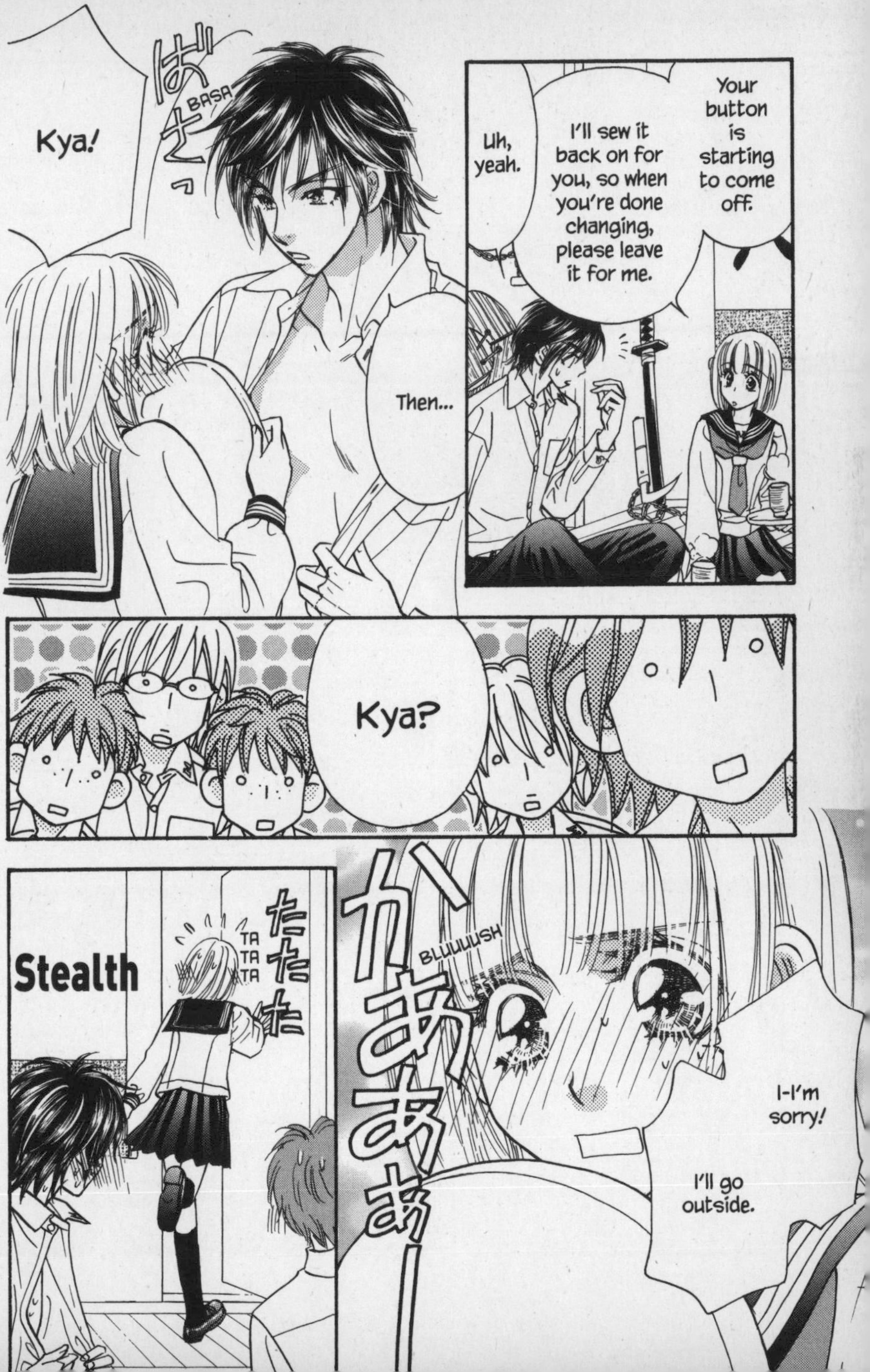
Your button is starting to come off.
I'll sew it back on for you, so when you're done changing, please leave it for me.
Uh, yeah.
ばさっ
BASA
Kya!
Then...
Kya?
かあああ
BLUUUUSH
I-I'm sorry!
I'll go outside.
たたた
TA TA TA
Stealth

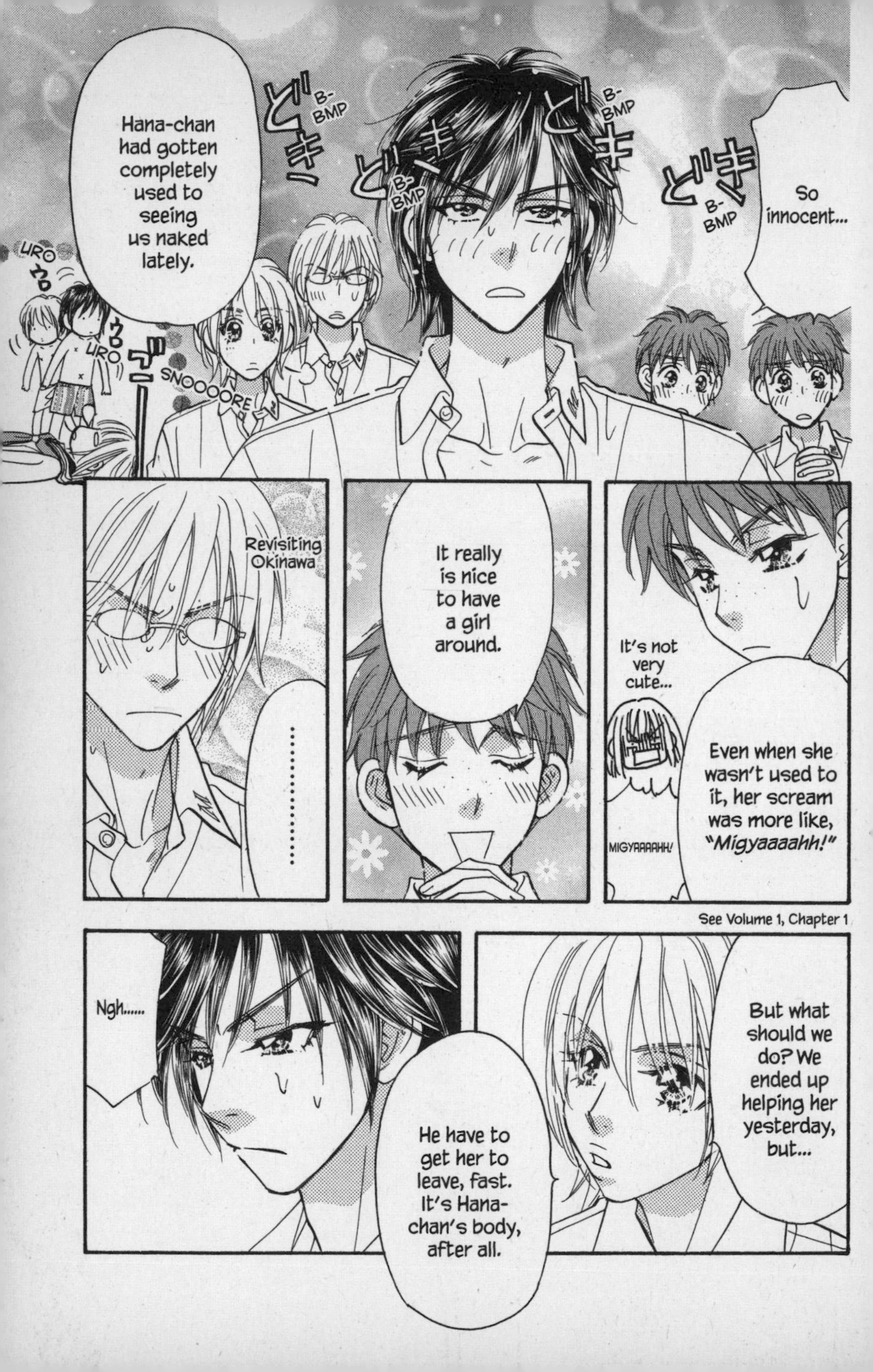
So innocent...
B-BMP
B-BMP
B-BMP
B-BMP
Hana-chan had gotten completely used to seeing us naked lately.
URO
URO
SNOOOORE
Even when she wasn't used to it, her scream was more like, "Migyaaaahh!"
It's not very cute...
MIGYAAAAHH!
See Volume 1, Chapter 1
It really is nice to have a girl around.
Revisiting Okinawa
......
But what should we do? We ended up helping her yesterday, but...
He have to get her to leave, fast. It's Hana-chan's body, after all.
Ngh......

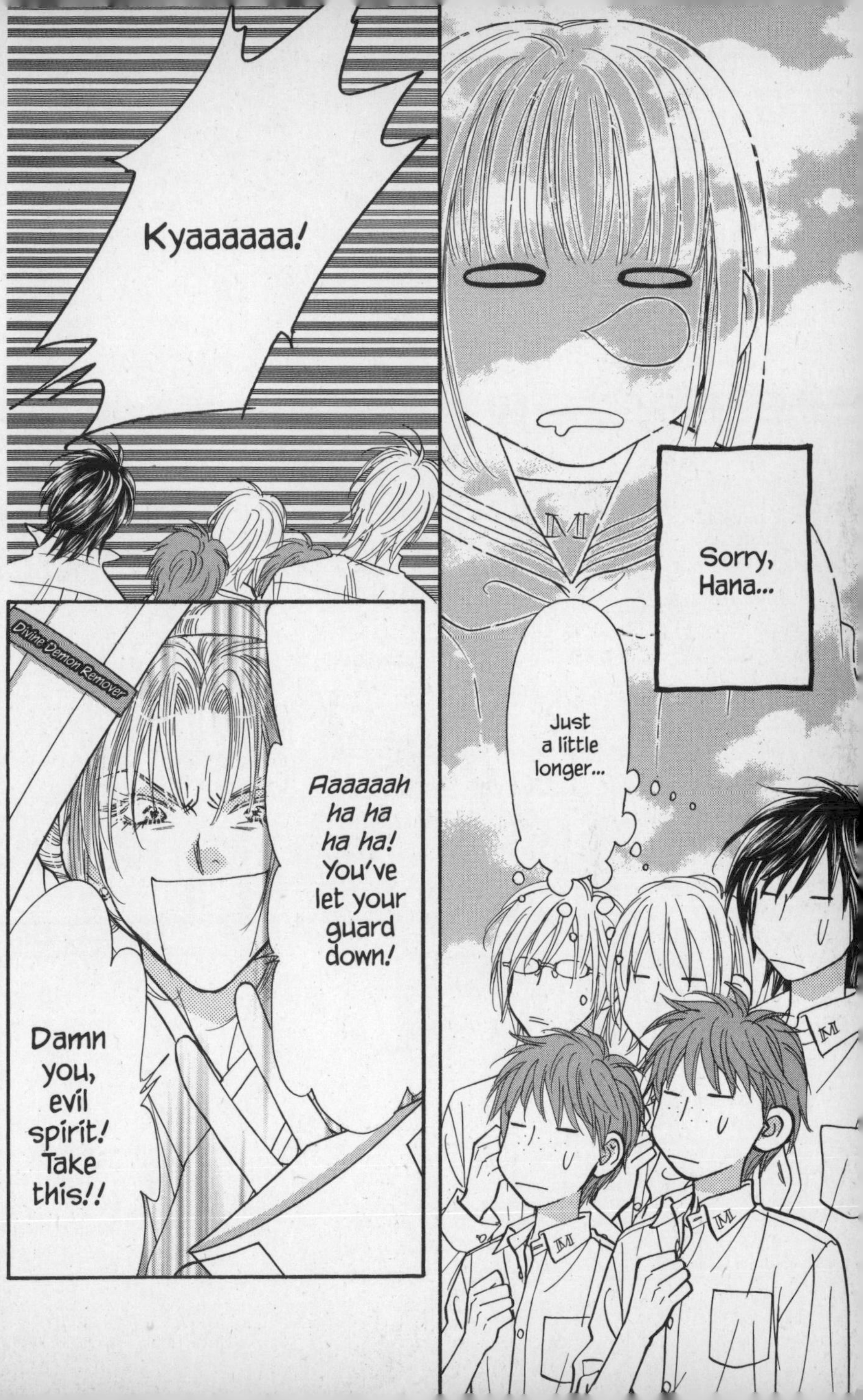
Sorry, Hana...
Just a little longer...
Kyaaaaaa!
Divine Demon Remover
Aaaaaah ha ha ha ha! You've let your guard down!
Damn you, evil spirit! Take this!!

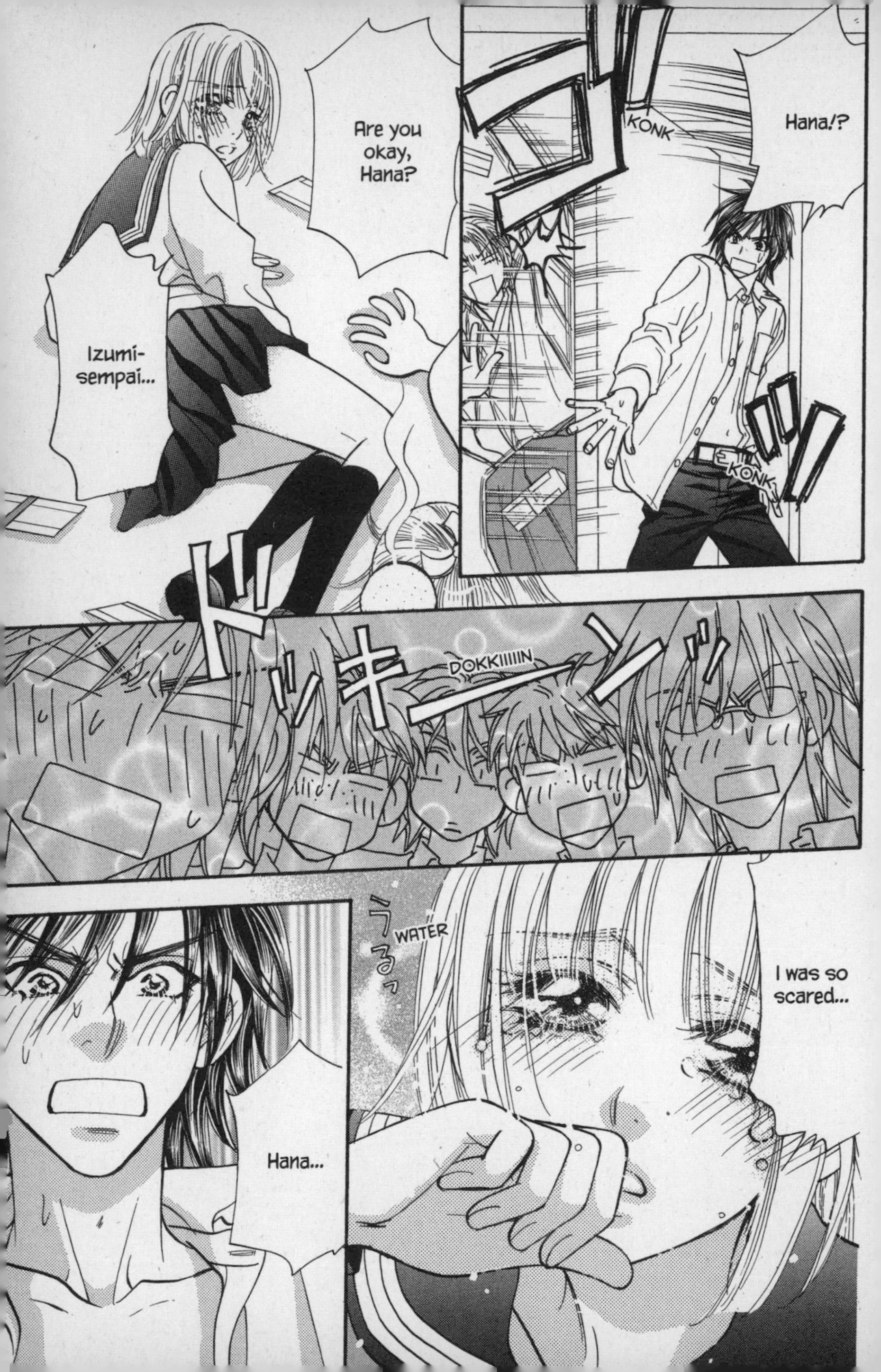
Hana!?
KONK
KONK
Are you okay, Hana?
Izumi-sempai...
DOKKIIIIIN
WATER
I was so scared...
Hana...

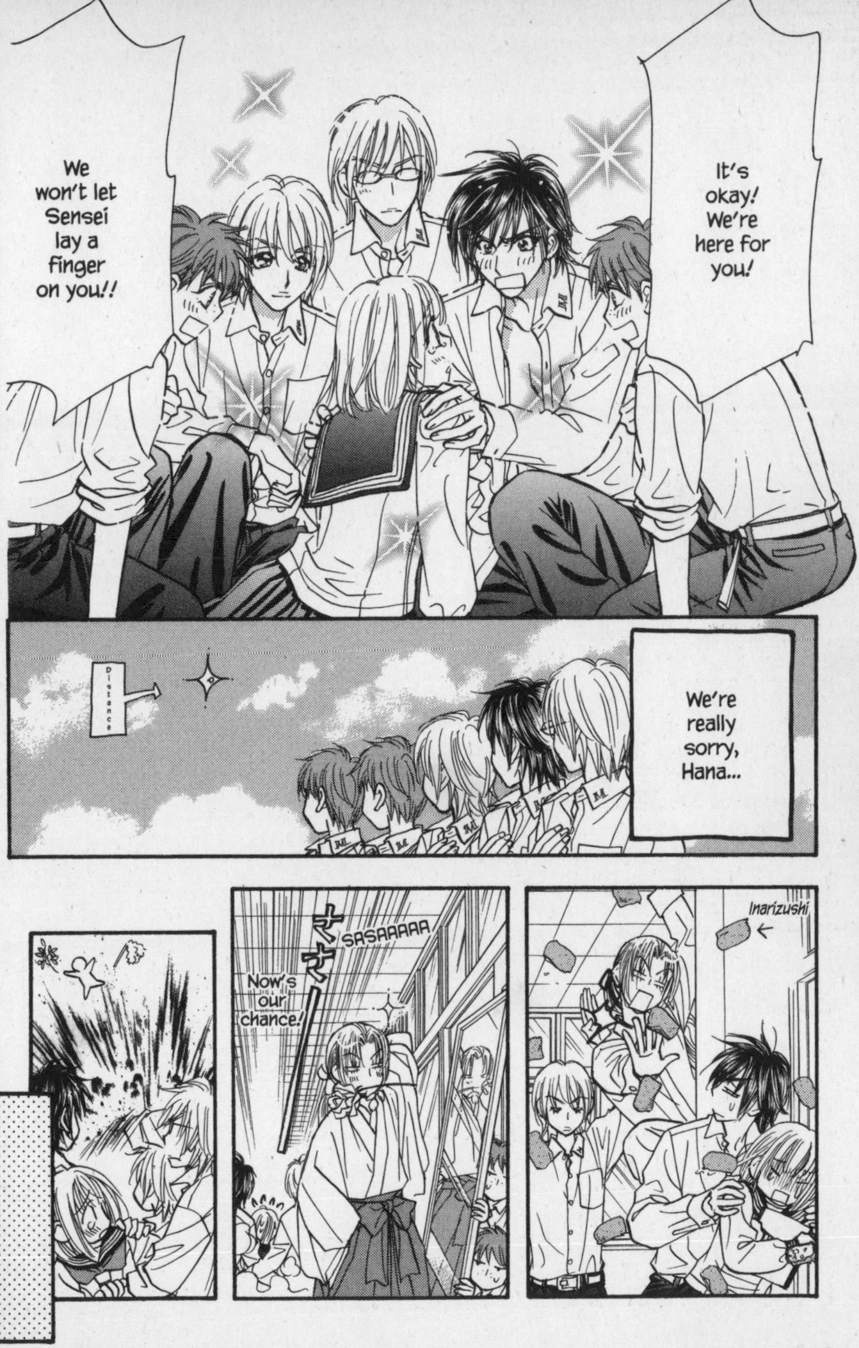
It's okay! We're here for you!
We won't let Sensei lay a finger on you!!
We're really sorry, Hana...
Distance
Inarizushi
SASAAAAA
Now's our chance!

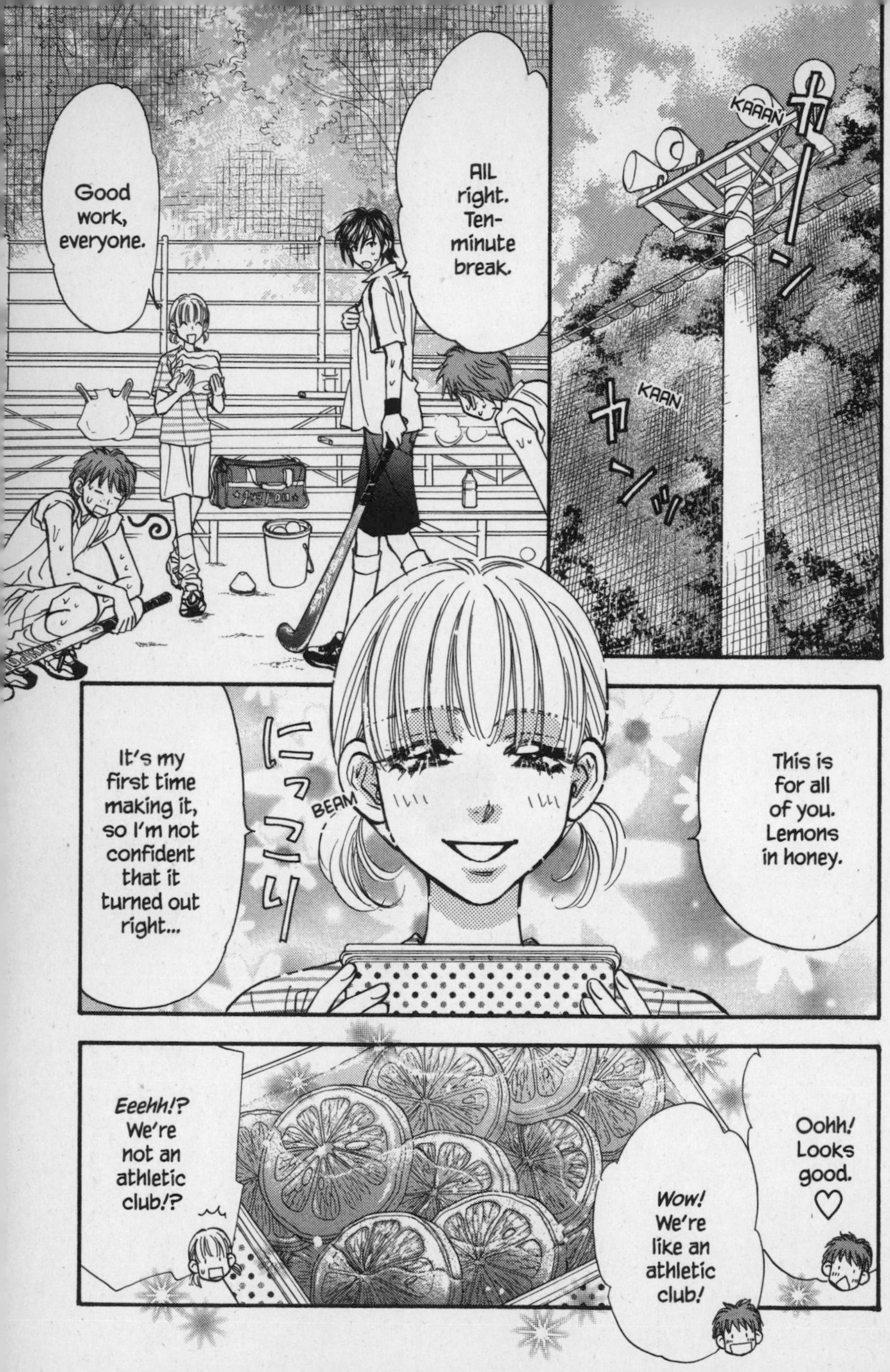
KAAAN
KAAN
All right. Ten-minute break.
Good work, everyone.
This is for all of you. Lemons in honey.
BEAM
It's my first time making it, so I'm not confident that it turned out right...
Oohh! Looks good. ♡
Wow! We're like an athletic club!
Eeehh!? We're not an athletic club!?

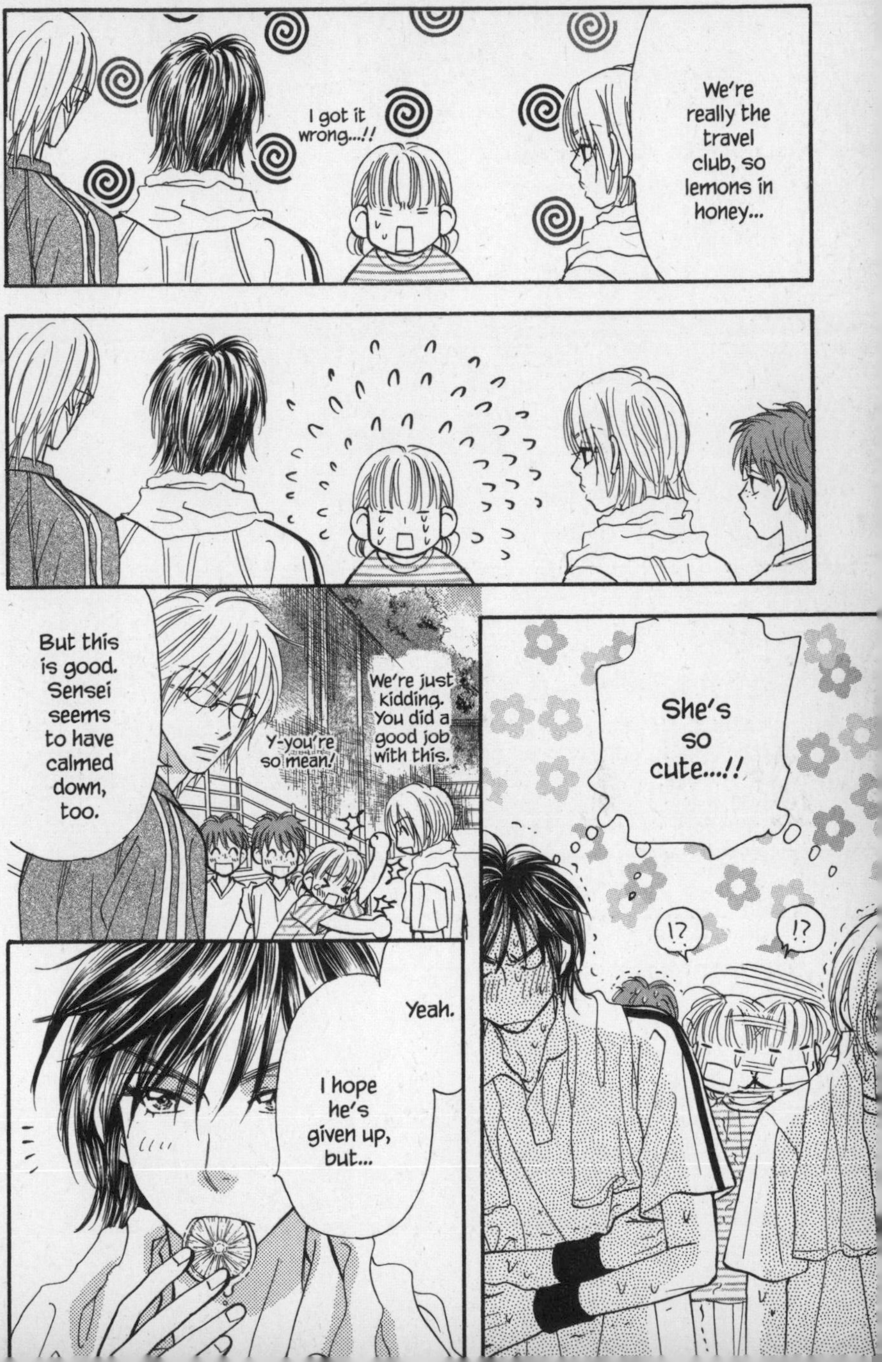
We're really the travel club, so lemons in honey...
I got it wrong...!!
She's so cute...!!
!?
!?
We're just kidding. You did a good job with this.
Y-you're so mean!
But this is good. Sensei seems to have calmed down, too.
Yeah.
I hope he's given up, but...

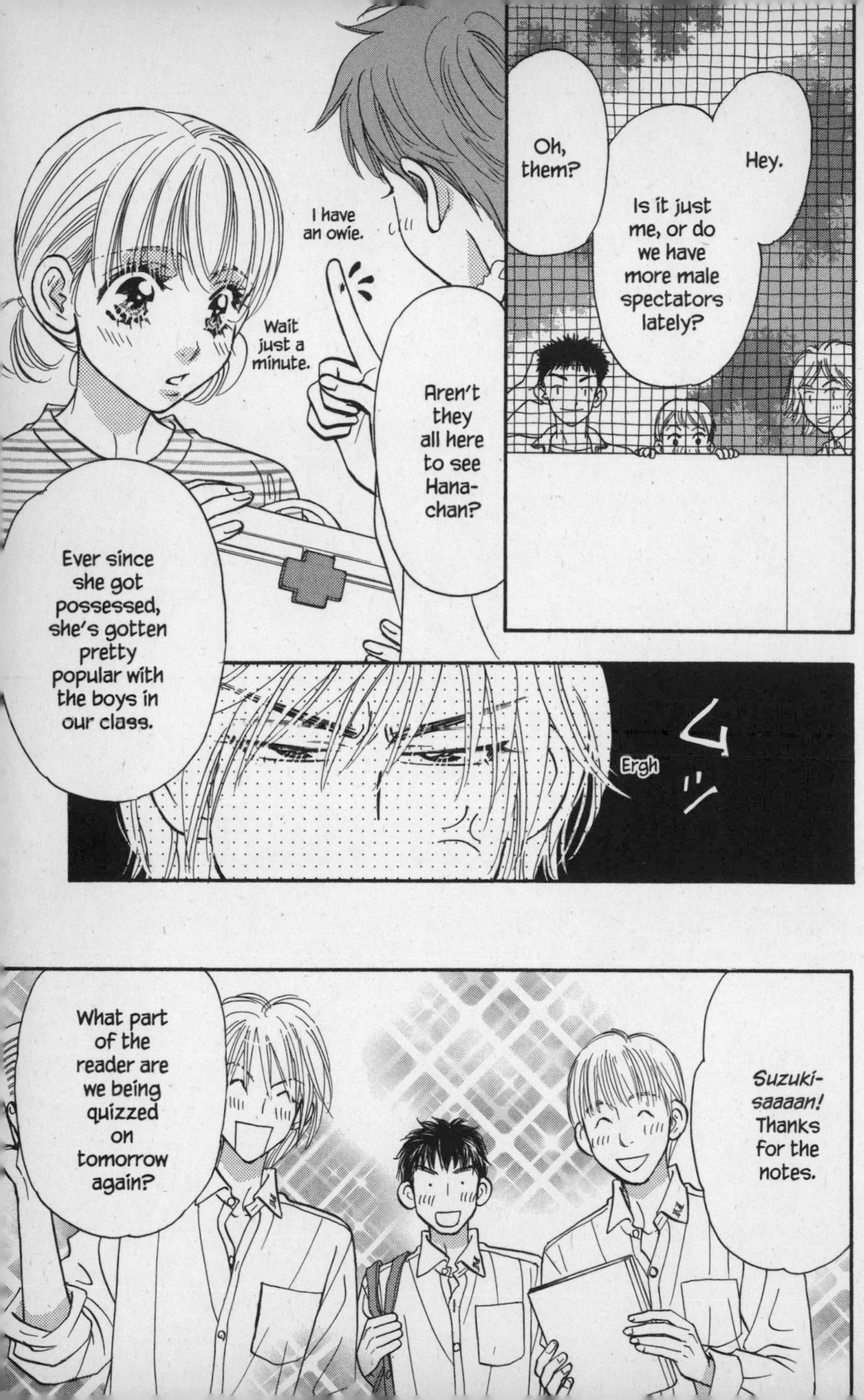
Hey.
Is it just me, or do we have more male spectators lately?
Oh, them?
Aren't they all here to see Hana-chan?
I have an owie.
Wait just a minute.
Ever since she got possessed, she's gotten pretty popular with the boys in our class.
ムッ
Ergh
Suzuki-saaaan! Thanks for the notes.
What part of the reader are we being quizzed on tomorrow again?

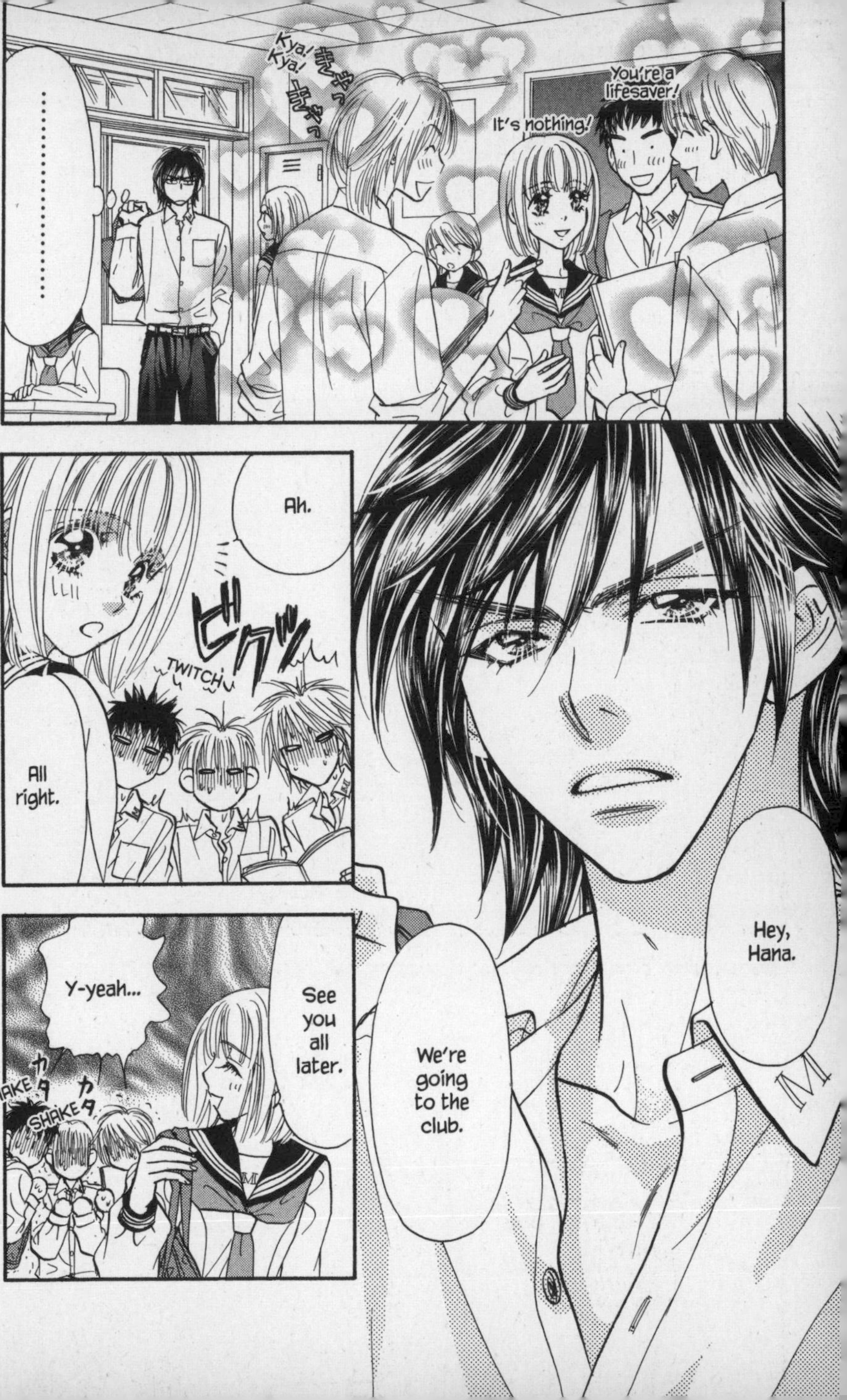
You're a lifesaver!
It's nothing!
Kya! Kya!
......
Hey, Hana.
We're going to the club.
Ah.
ビクッ
TWITCH
All right.
See you all later.
Y-yeah...
カタ カタ
SHAKE SHAKE

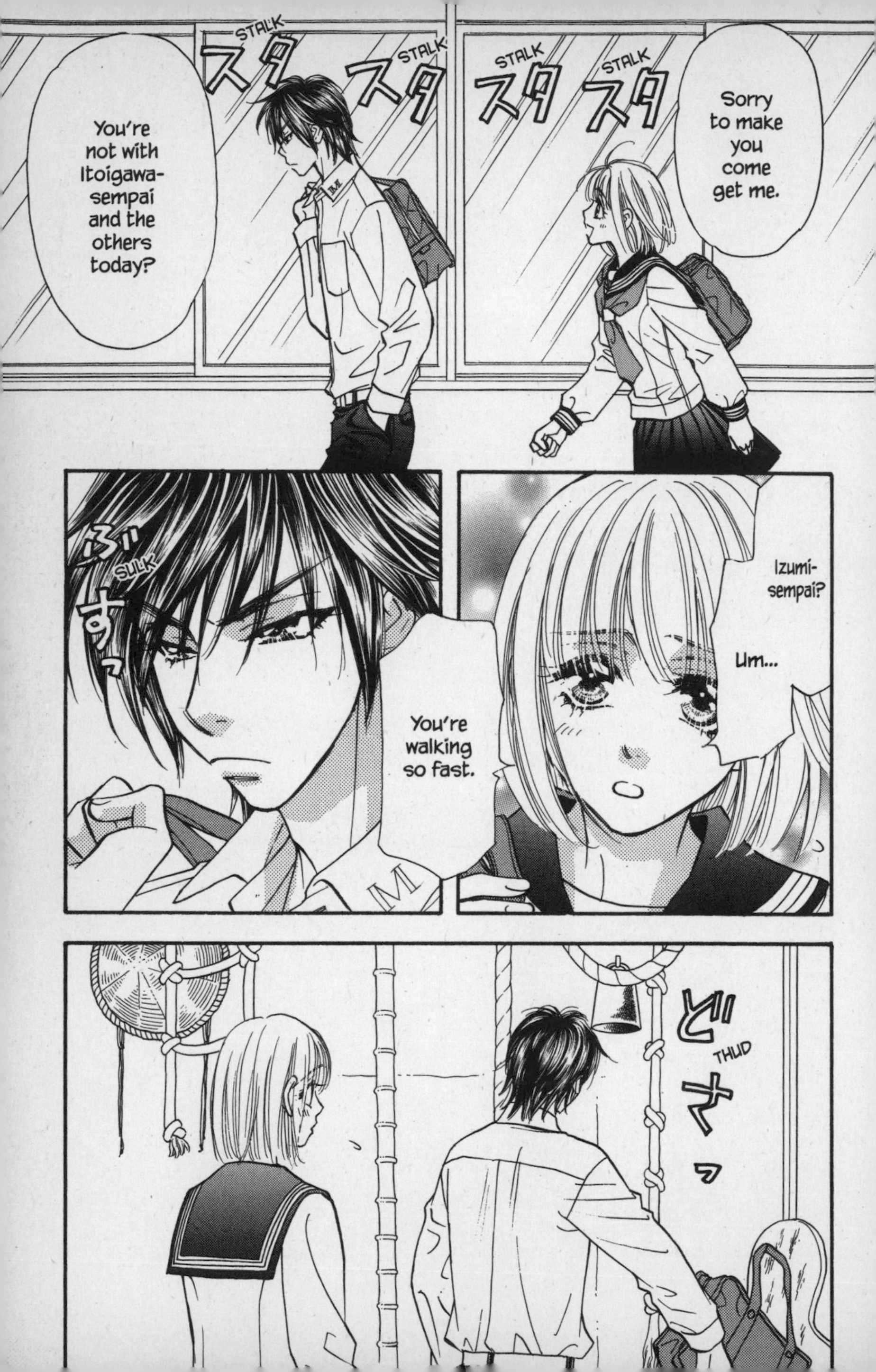
Sorry to make you come get me.
スタ
STALK
スタ
STALK
スタ
STALK
スタ
STALK
You're not with Itoigawa-sempai and the others today?
Izumi-sempai?
Um...
You're walking so fast.
ぶすっ
SULK
どさっ
THUD

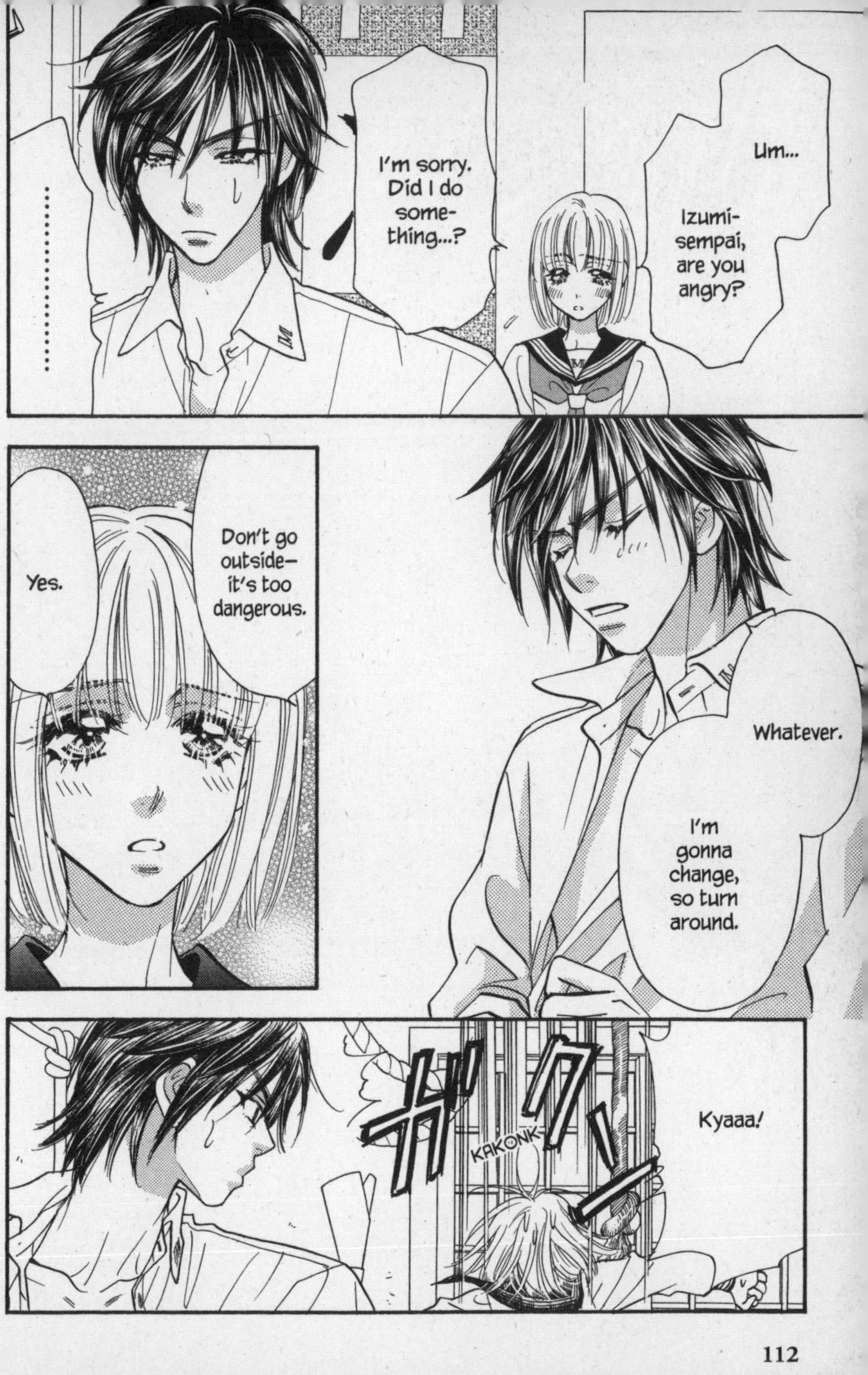
Um...
Izumi-sempai, are you angry?
I'm sorry. Did I do some-thing...?
....
Whatever.
I'm gonna change, so turn around.
Don't go outside—it's too dangerous.
Yes.
Kyaaa!
KAKONK

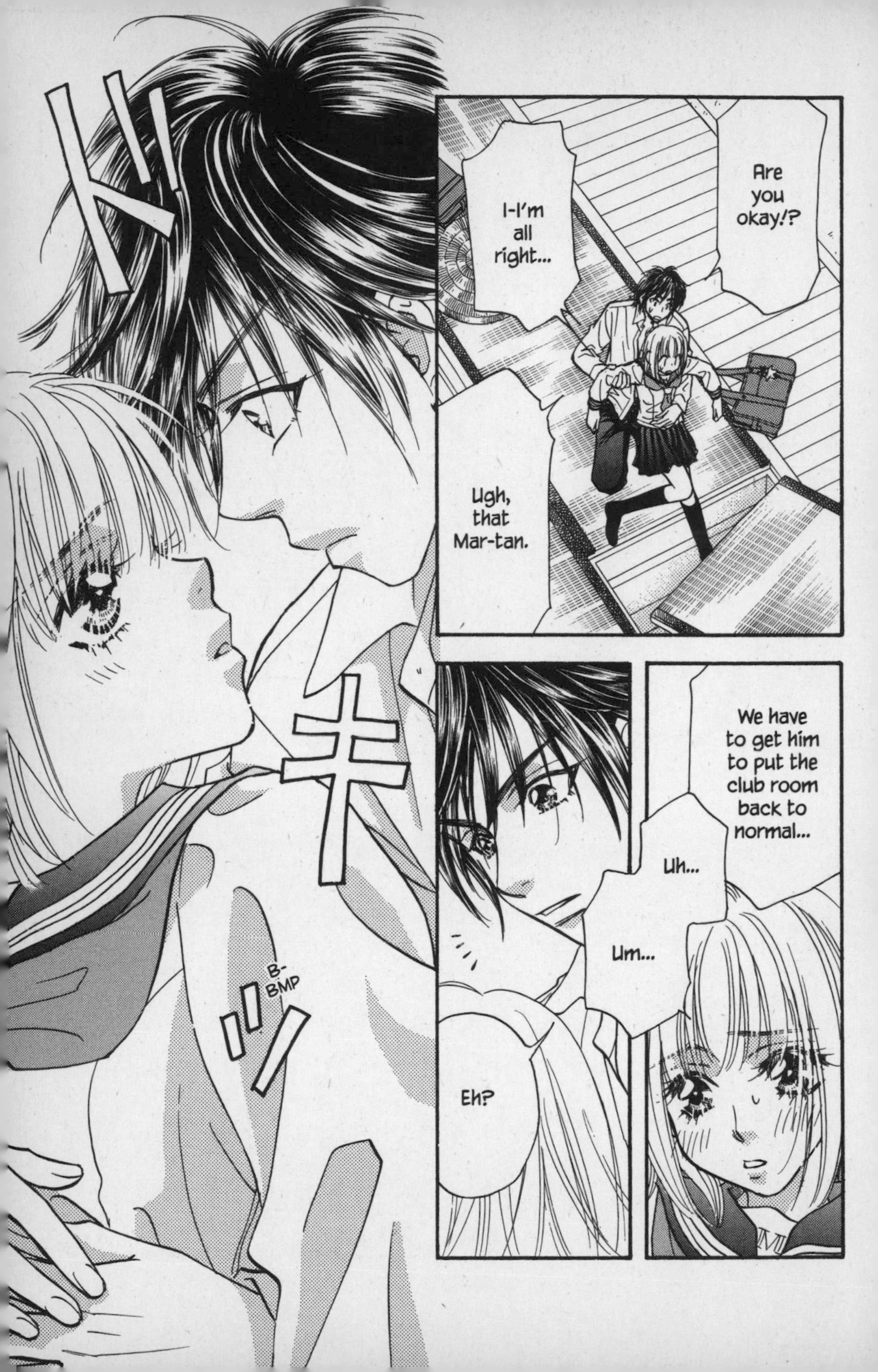
Are you okay!?
I-I'm all right...
Ugh, that Mar-tan.
We have to get him to put the club room back to normal...
Uh...
Um...
Eh?
B-BMP

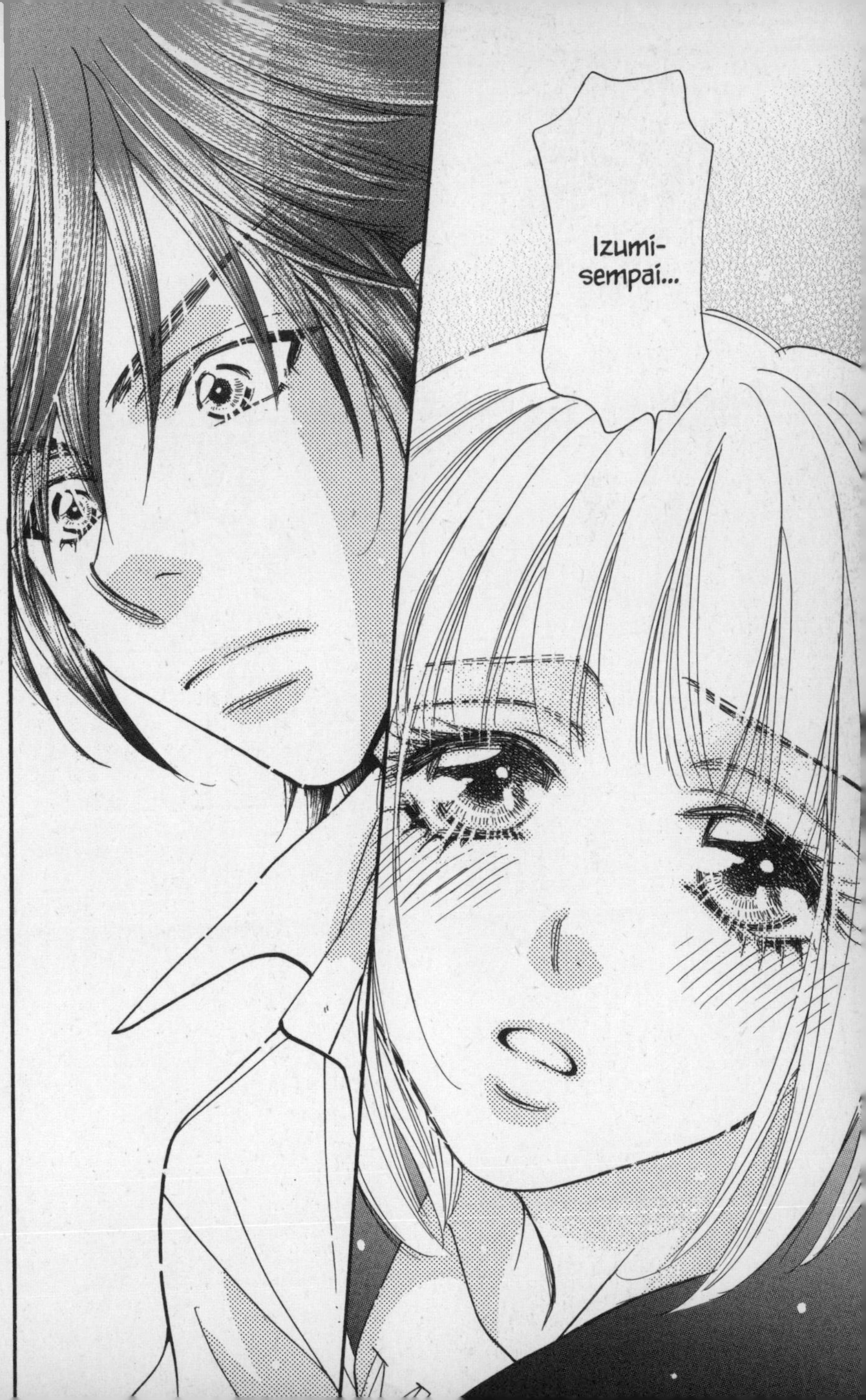
Izumi-
sempai...

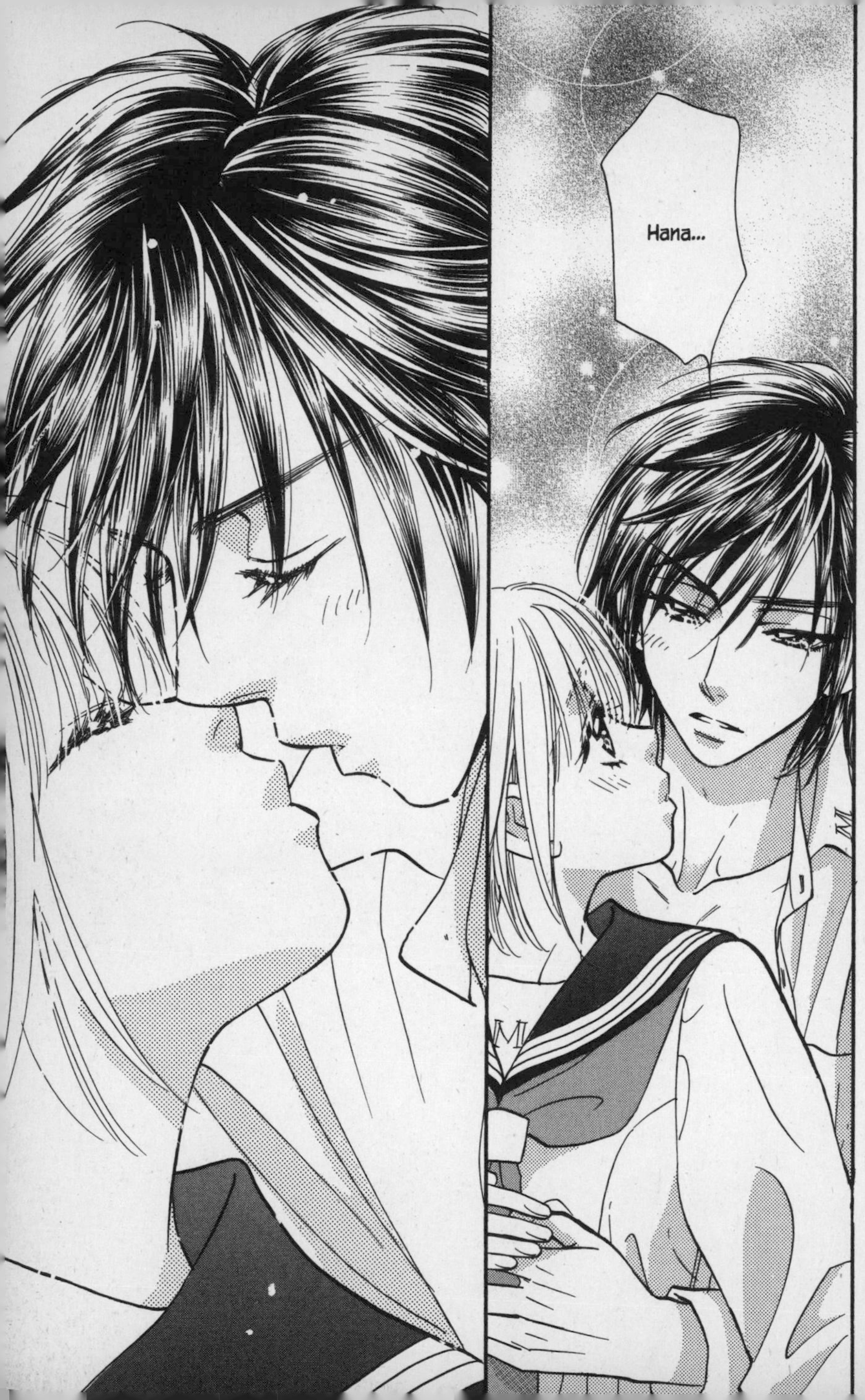
Hana...

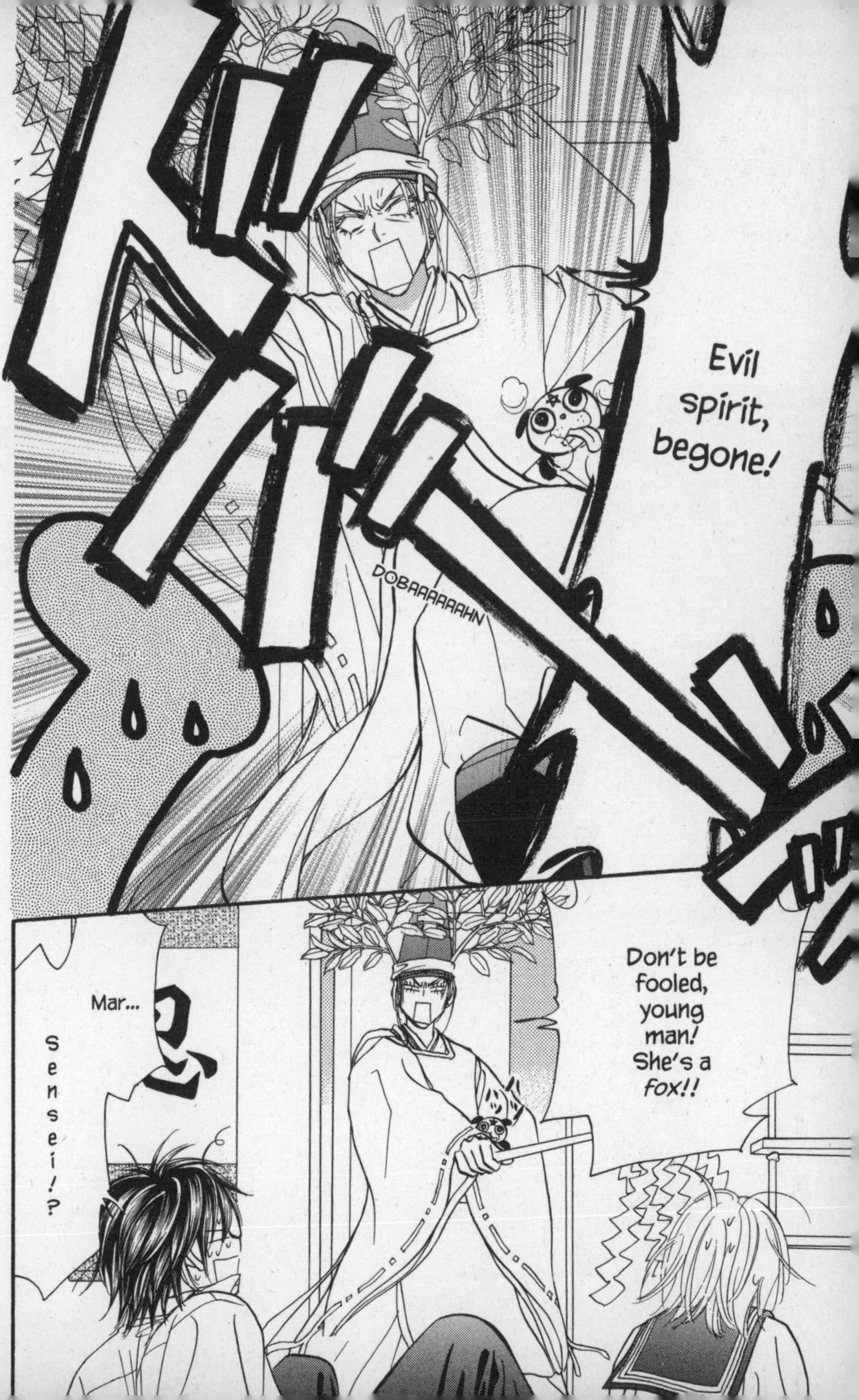
Evil spirit, begone!
DOBAAAAAAAHN
Don't be fooled, young man! She's a fox!!
Mar...
Sensei!?

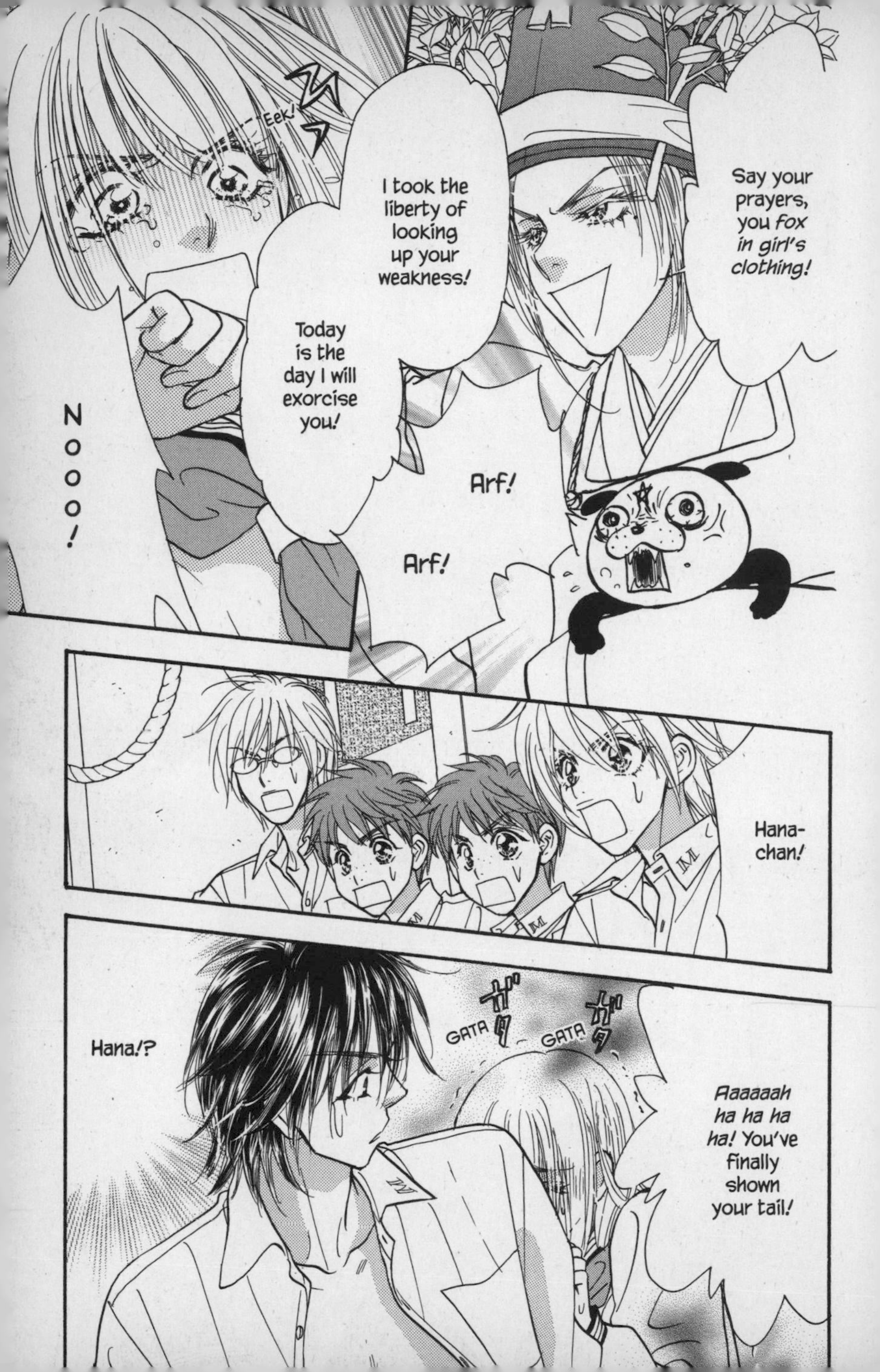
Say your prayers, you *fox in girl's clothing!*
I took the liberty of looking up your weakness!
Eek!
Today is the day I will exorcise you!
Arf!
Arf!
Noooo!
Hana-chan!
Aaaaaah ha ha ha! You've finally shown your tail!
GATA
GATA
Hana!?

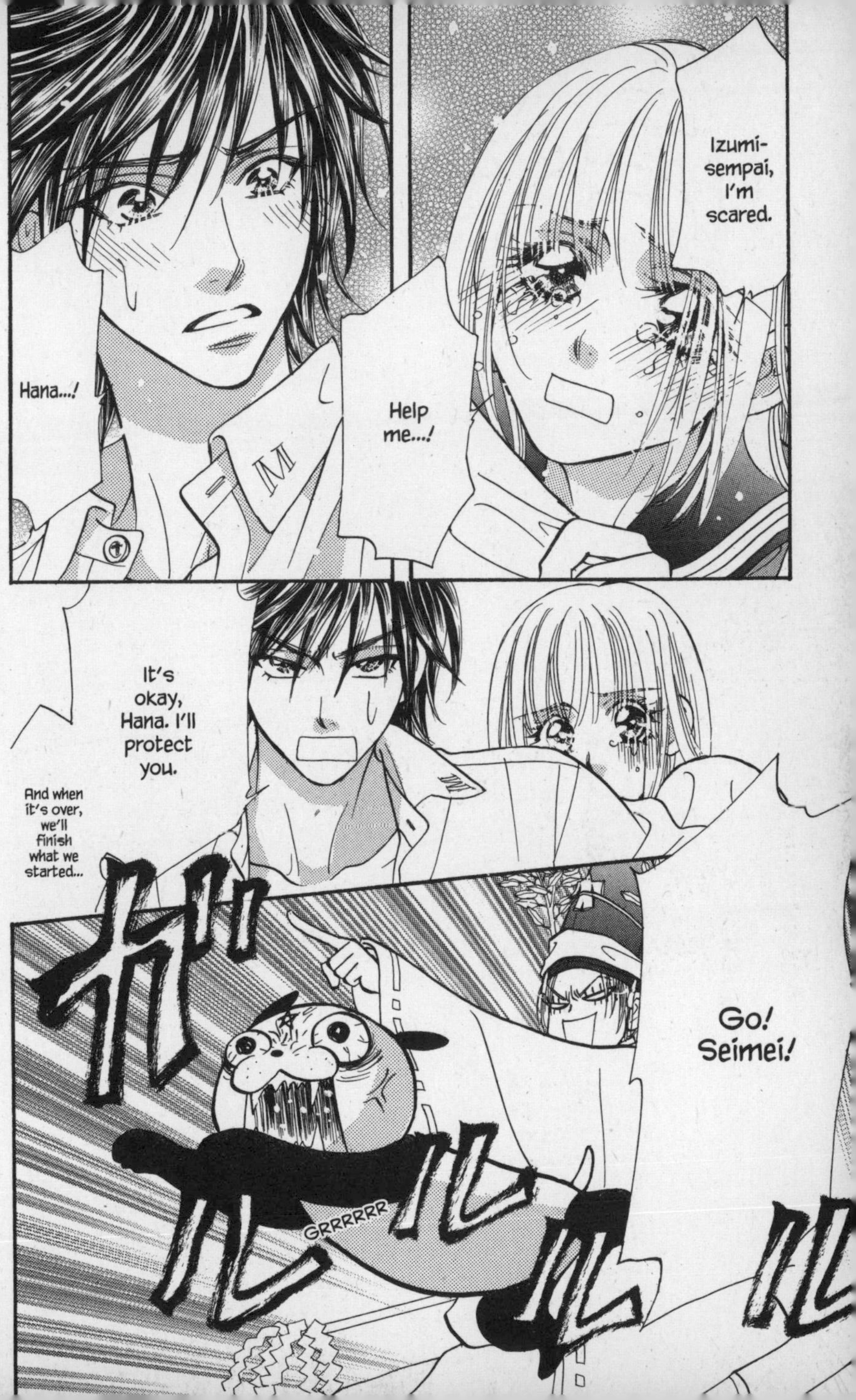
Izumi-sempai, I'm scared.
Help me...!
Hana...!
It's okay, Hana. I'll protect you.
And when it's over, we'll finish what we started...
Go! Seimei!
GRRRRRR

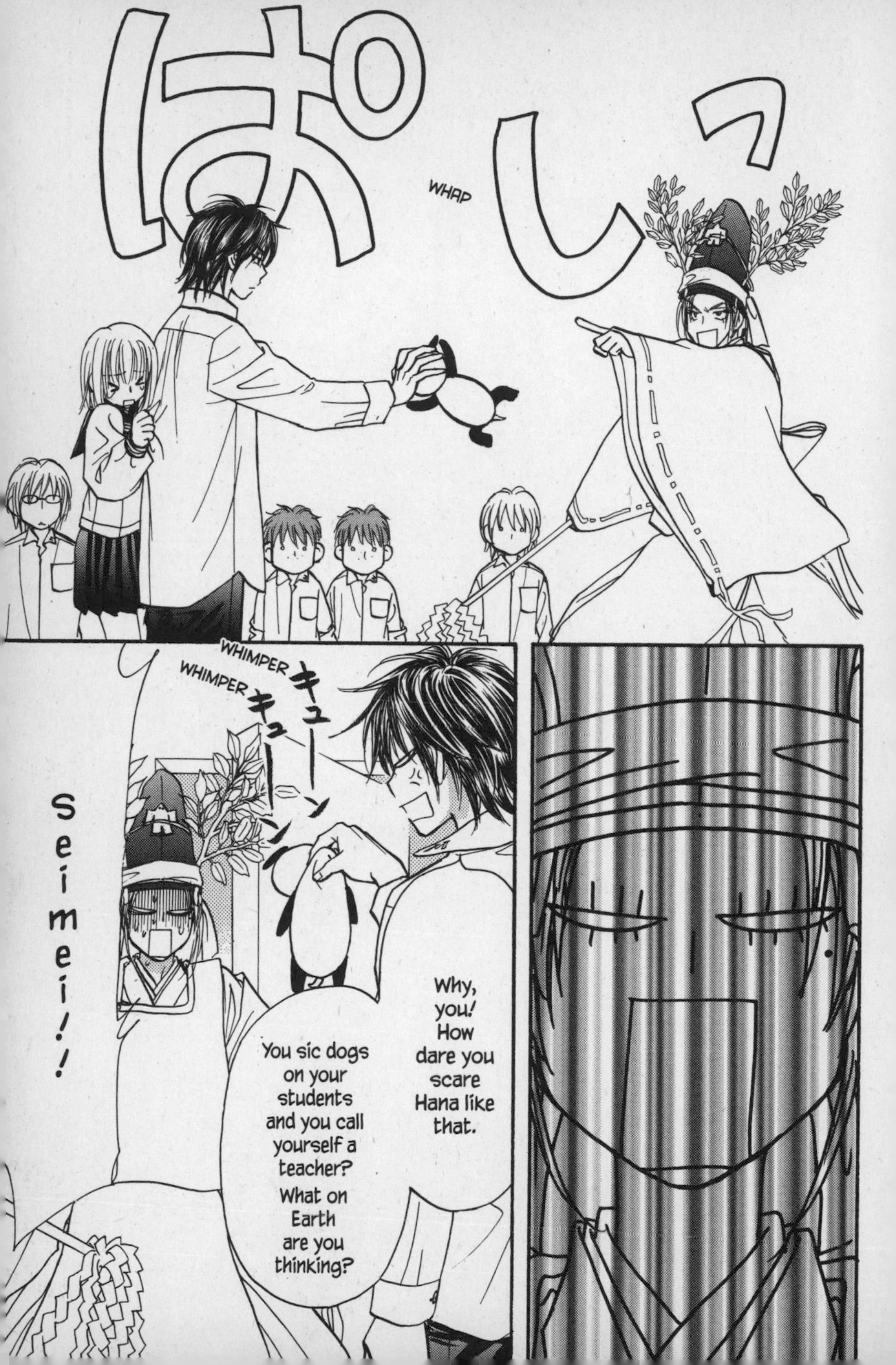
ぱしっ
WHAP
WHIMPER キューン
WHIMPER キューン
Why, you! How dare you scare Hana like that.
You sic dogs on your students and you call yourself a teacher? What on Earth are you thinking?
Seimei!!

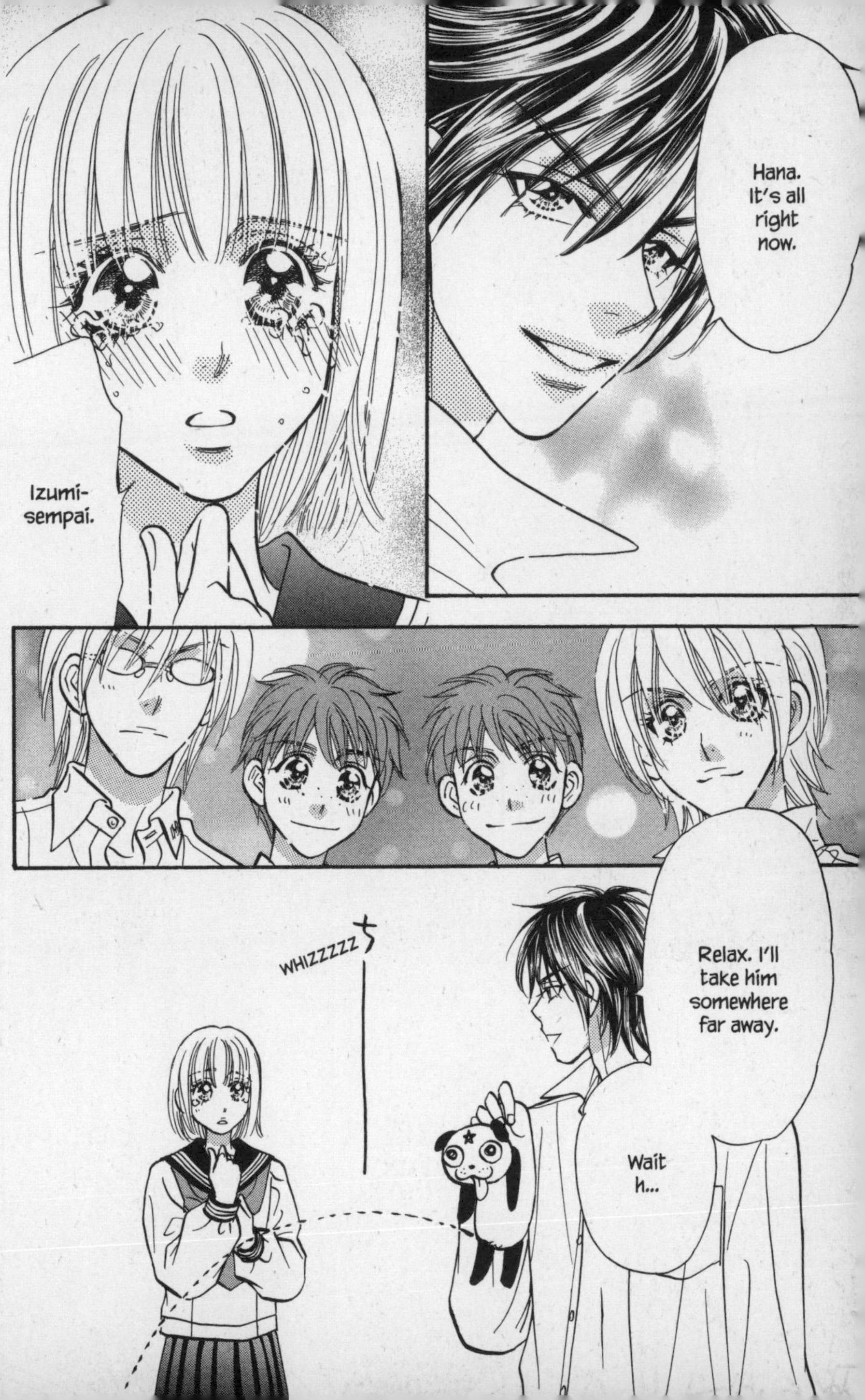
Hana. It's all right now.
Izumi-sempai.
Relax. I'll take him somewhere far away.
WHIZZZZZ
Wait h...

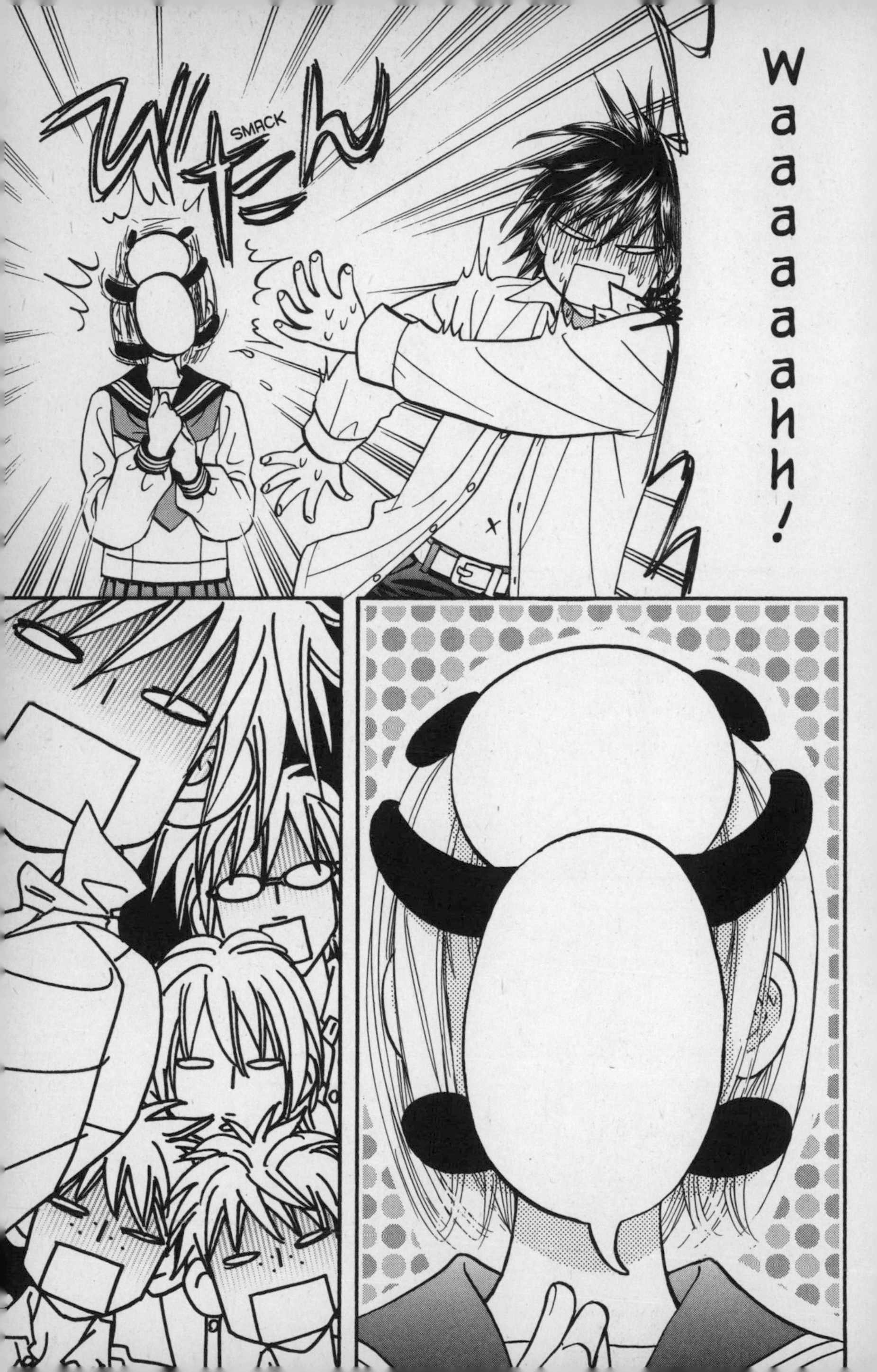
Waaaaaahh!
SMACK

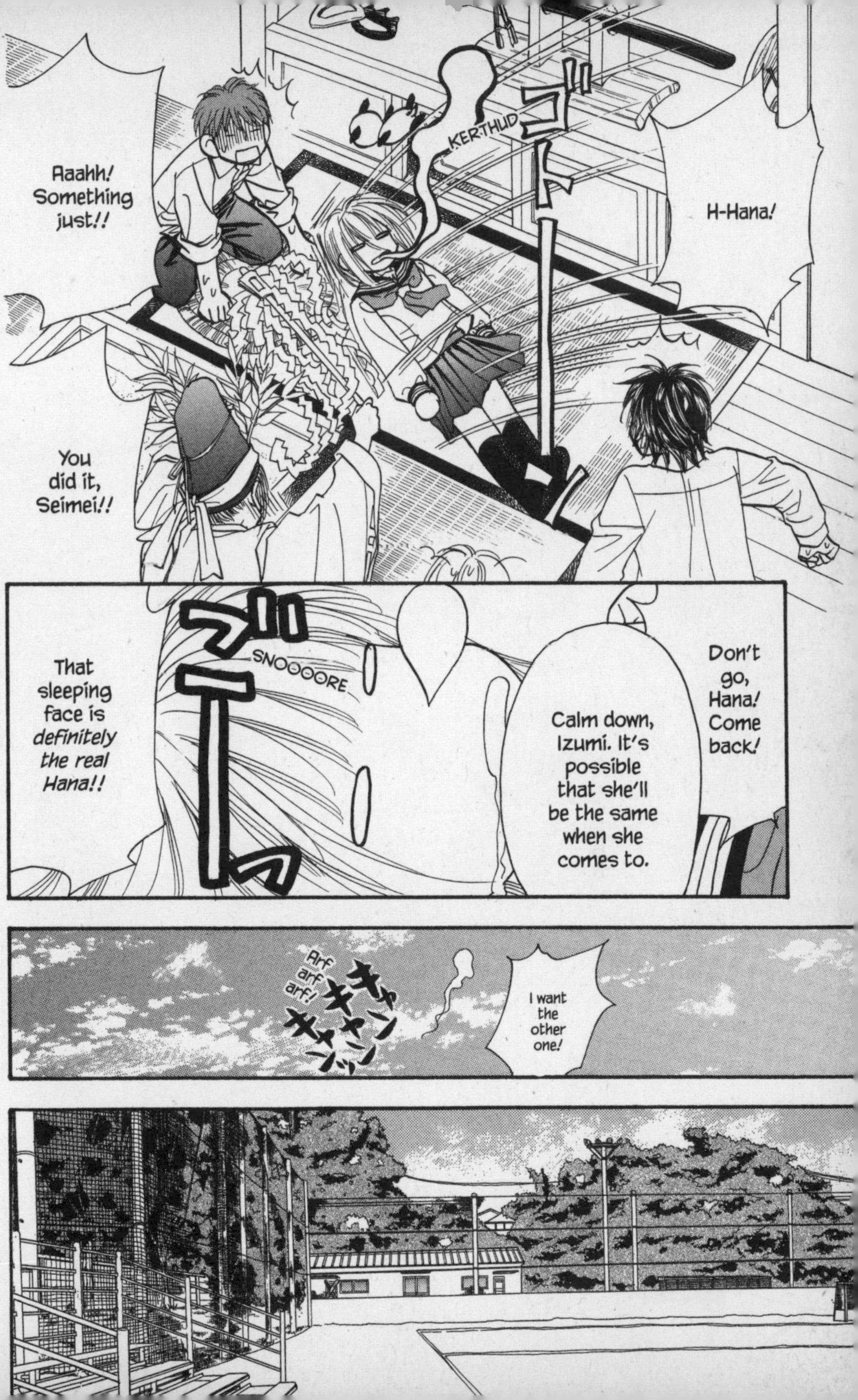
H-Hana!
KERTHUD
Aaahh! Something just!!
You did it, Seimei!!
Don't go, Hana! Come back!
Calm down, Izumi. It's possible that she'll be the same when she comes to.
SNOOOORE
That sleeping face is *definitely* the real Hana!!
I want the other one!
Arf arf arf!

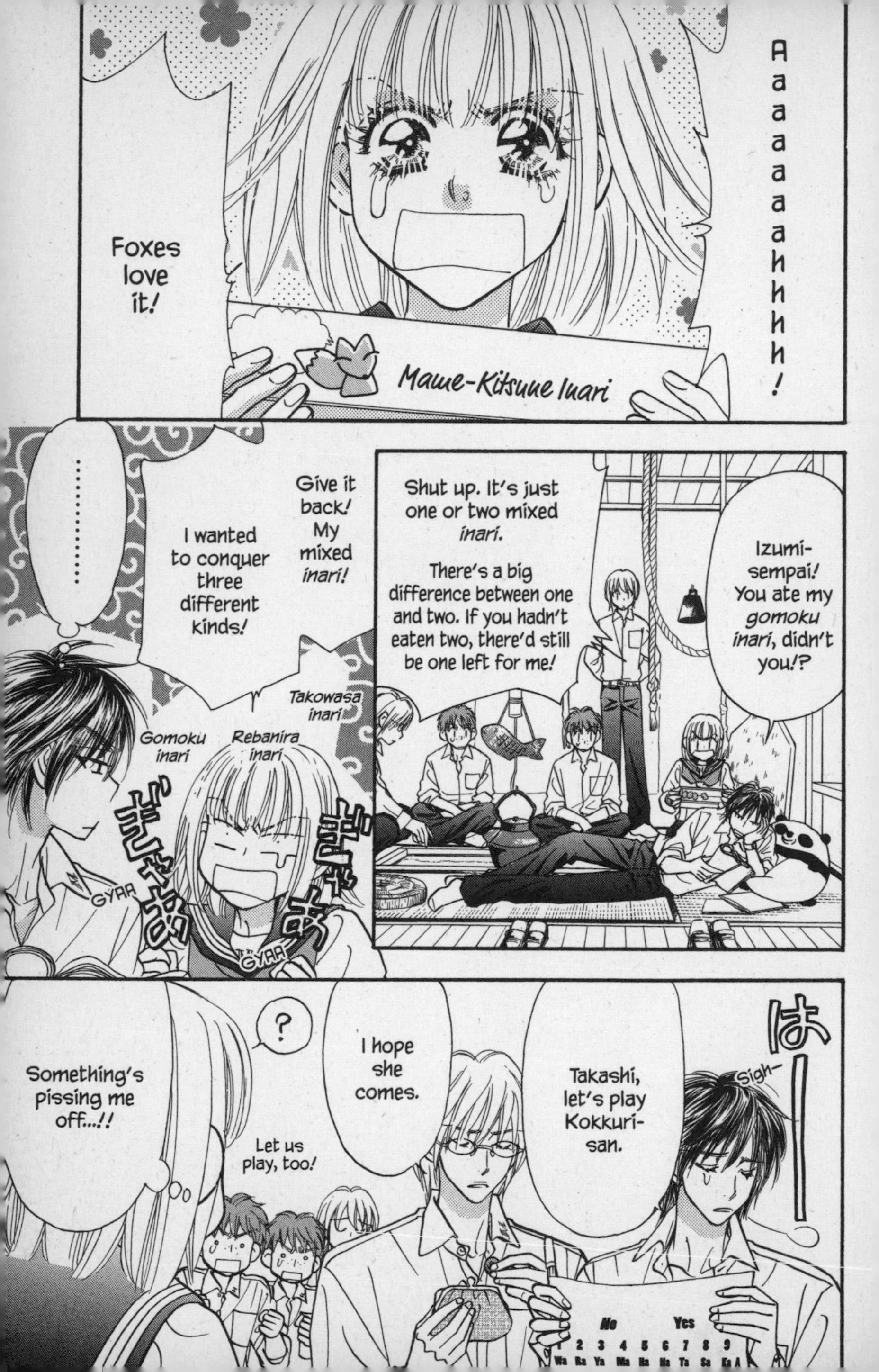
Aaaaaaaahhhh!
Foxes love it!
Mame-Kitsune Inari
Izumi-sempai! You ate my gomoku inari, didn't you!?
Shut up. It's just one or two mixed inari.
There's a big difference between one and two. If you hadn't eaten two, there'd still be one left for me!
Give it back! My mixed inari!
I wanted to conquer three different kinds!
......
Takowasa inari
Rebanira inari
Gomoku inari
GYAA
GYAA
Sigh-
Takashi, let's play Kokkuri-san.
I hope she comes.
?
Let us play, too!
Something's pissing me off...!!
No Yes
1 2 3 4 5 6 7 8 9
Wa Ra Ya Ma Ha Na Ta Sa Ka A

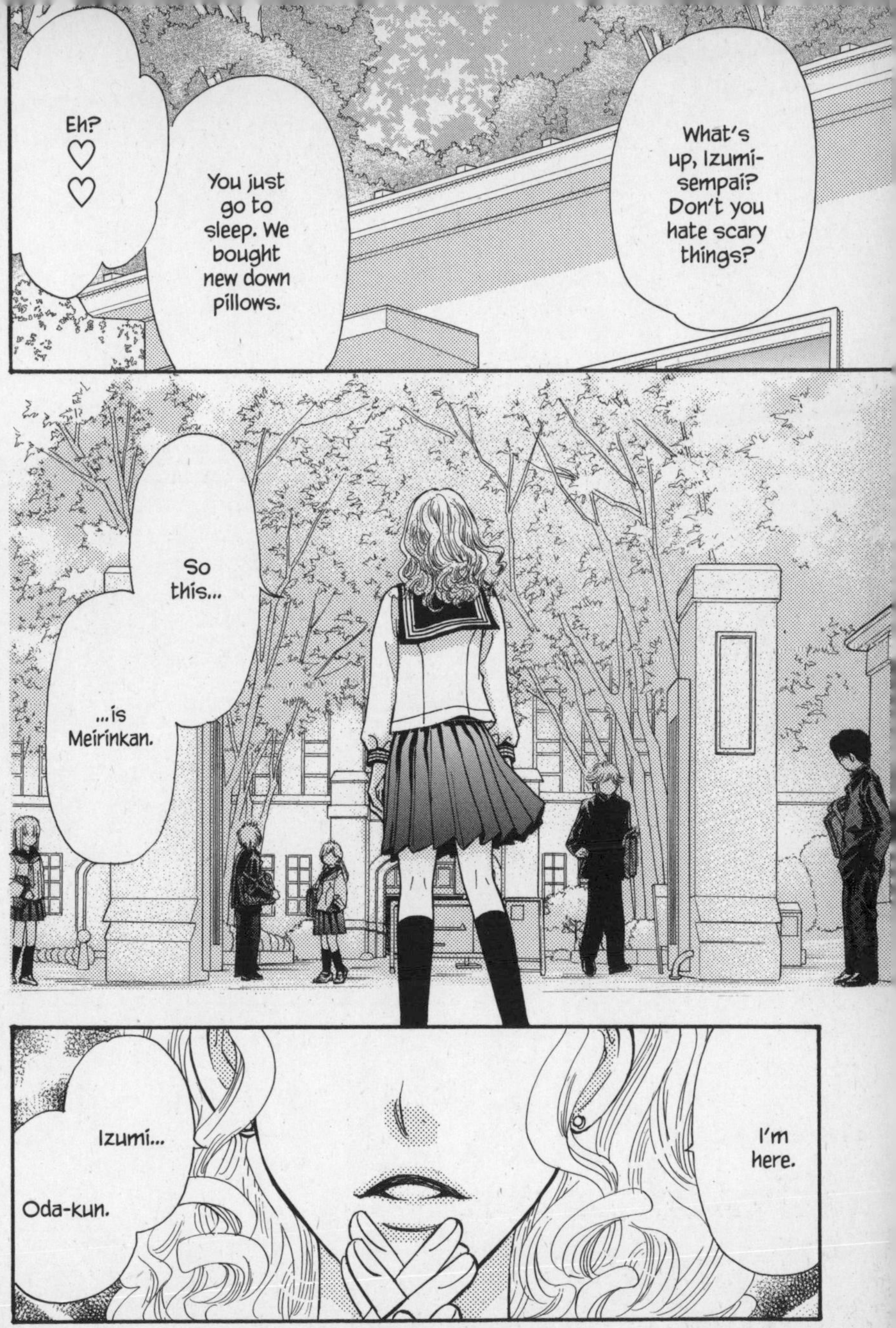
What's up, Izumi-sempai? Don't you hate scary things?
You just go to sleep. We bought new down pillows.
Eh? ♡ ♡
So this...
...is Meirinkan.
I'm here.
Izumi...
Oda-kun.

The End

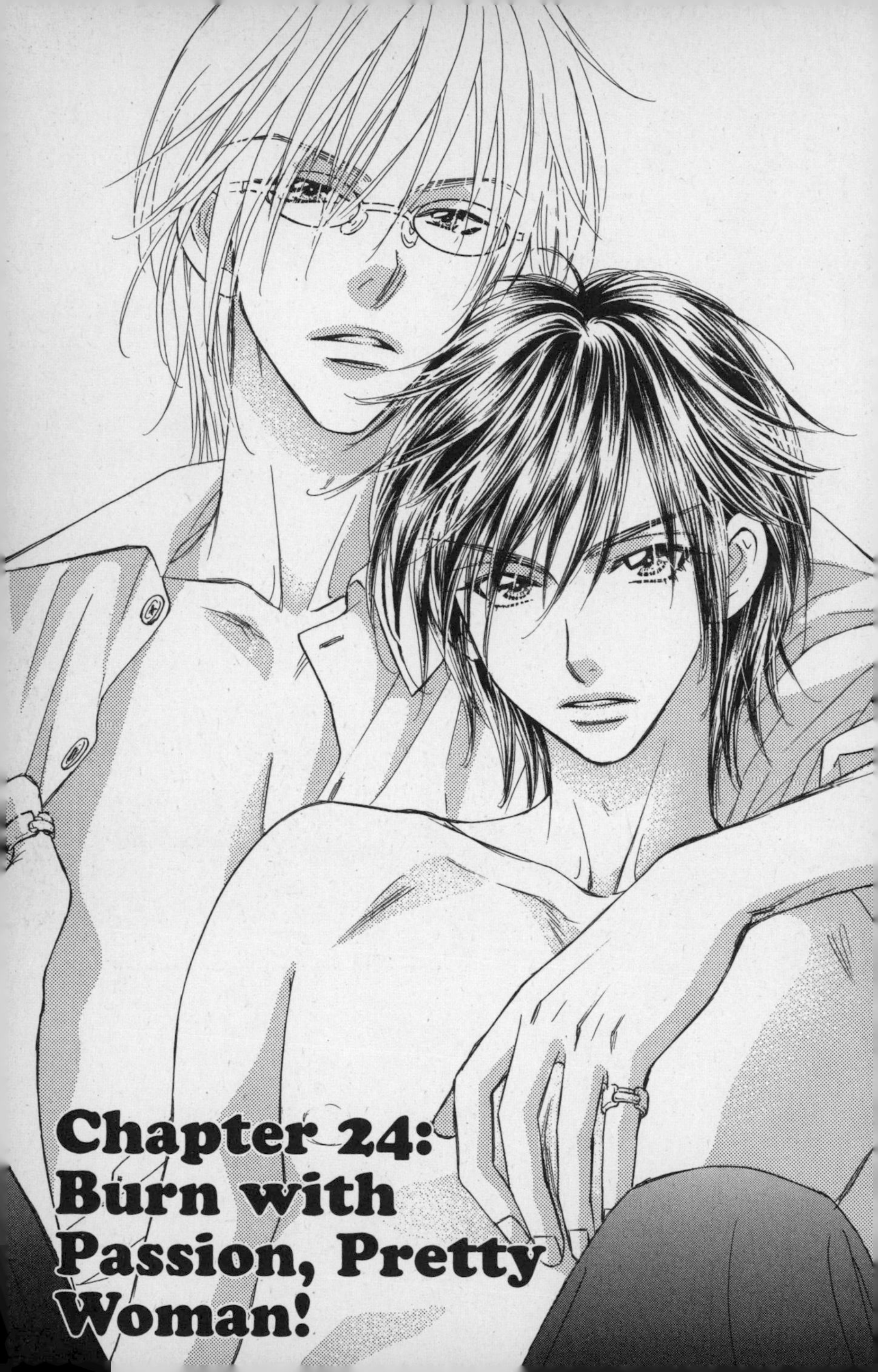
Chapter 24:
Burn with
Passion, Pretty
Woman!

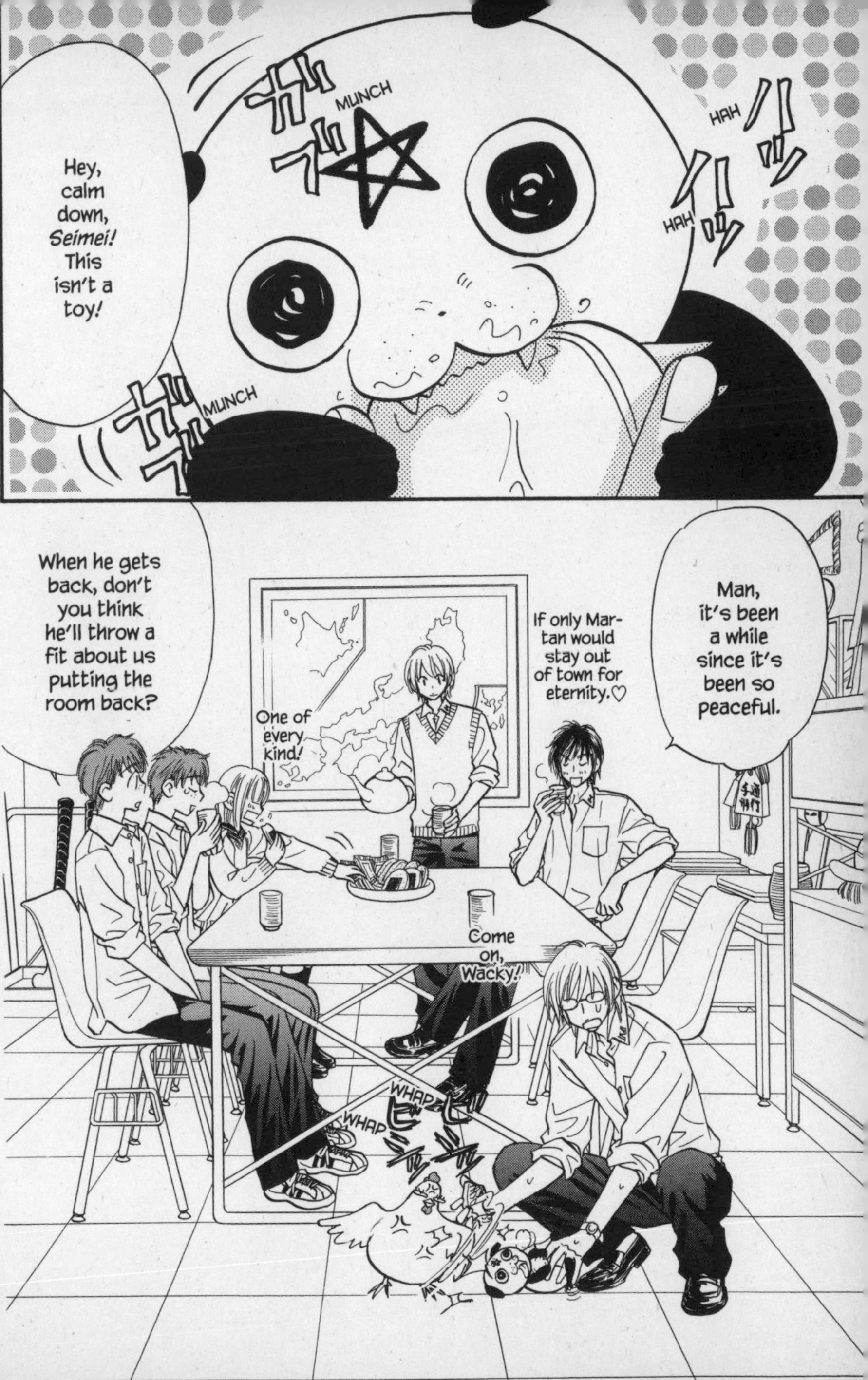
HAH
HAH
MUNCH
Hey, calm down, Seimei! This isn't a toy!
MUNCH
Man, it's been a while since it's been so peaceful.
If only Mar-tan would stay out of town for eternity.♡
One of every kind!
When he gets back, don't you think he'll throw a fit about us putting the room back?
Come on, Wacky!
WHAP
WHAP

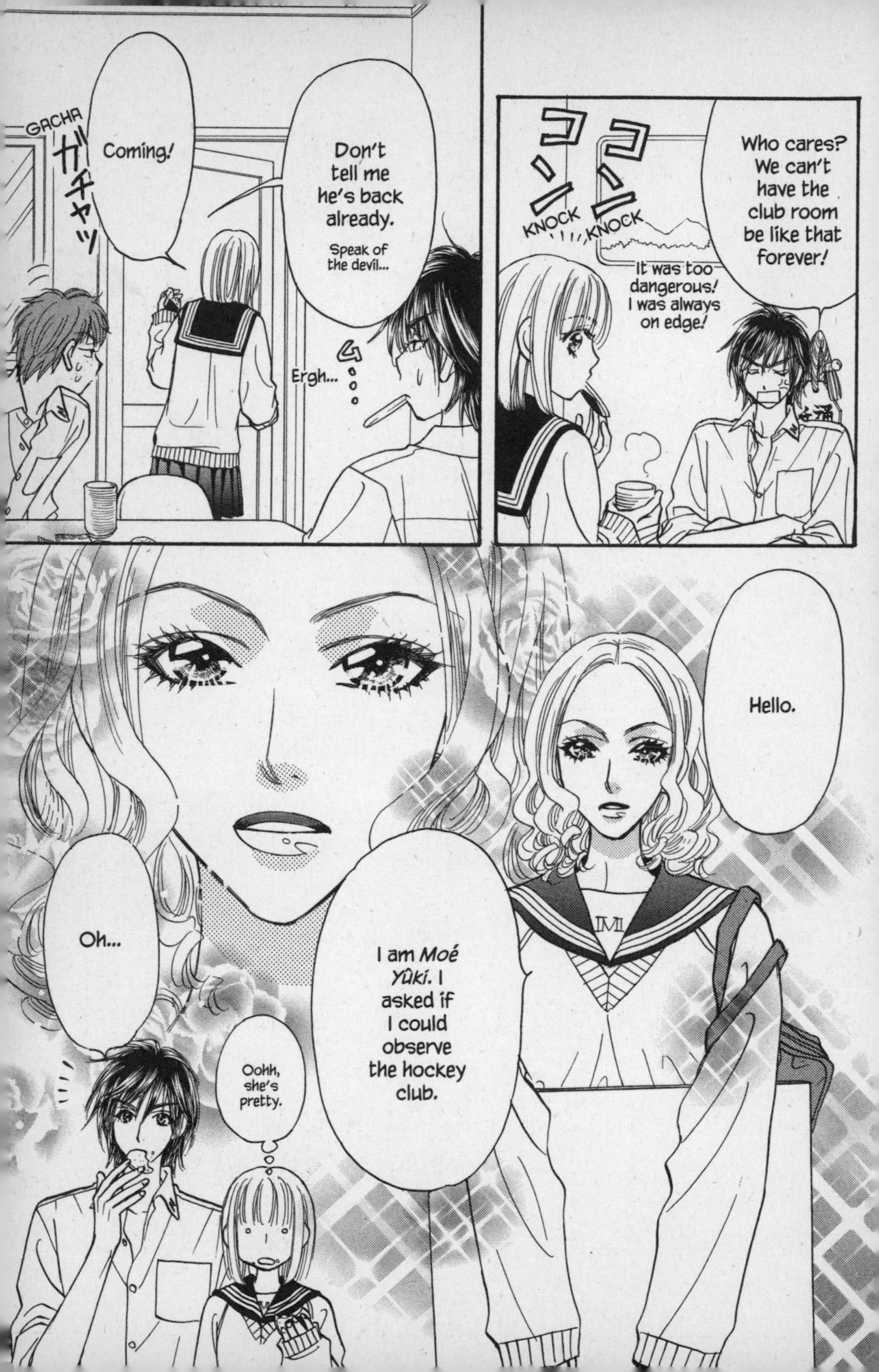
Who cares? We can't have the club room be like that forever!
KNOCK KNOCK
It was too dangerous! I was always on edge!
Don't tell me he's back already.
Speak of the devil...
Coming!
GACHA
Ergh...
Hello.
I am *Moé Yûki*. I asked if I could observe the hockey club.
Oh...
Oohh, she's pretty.

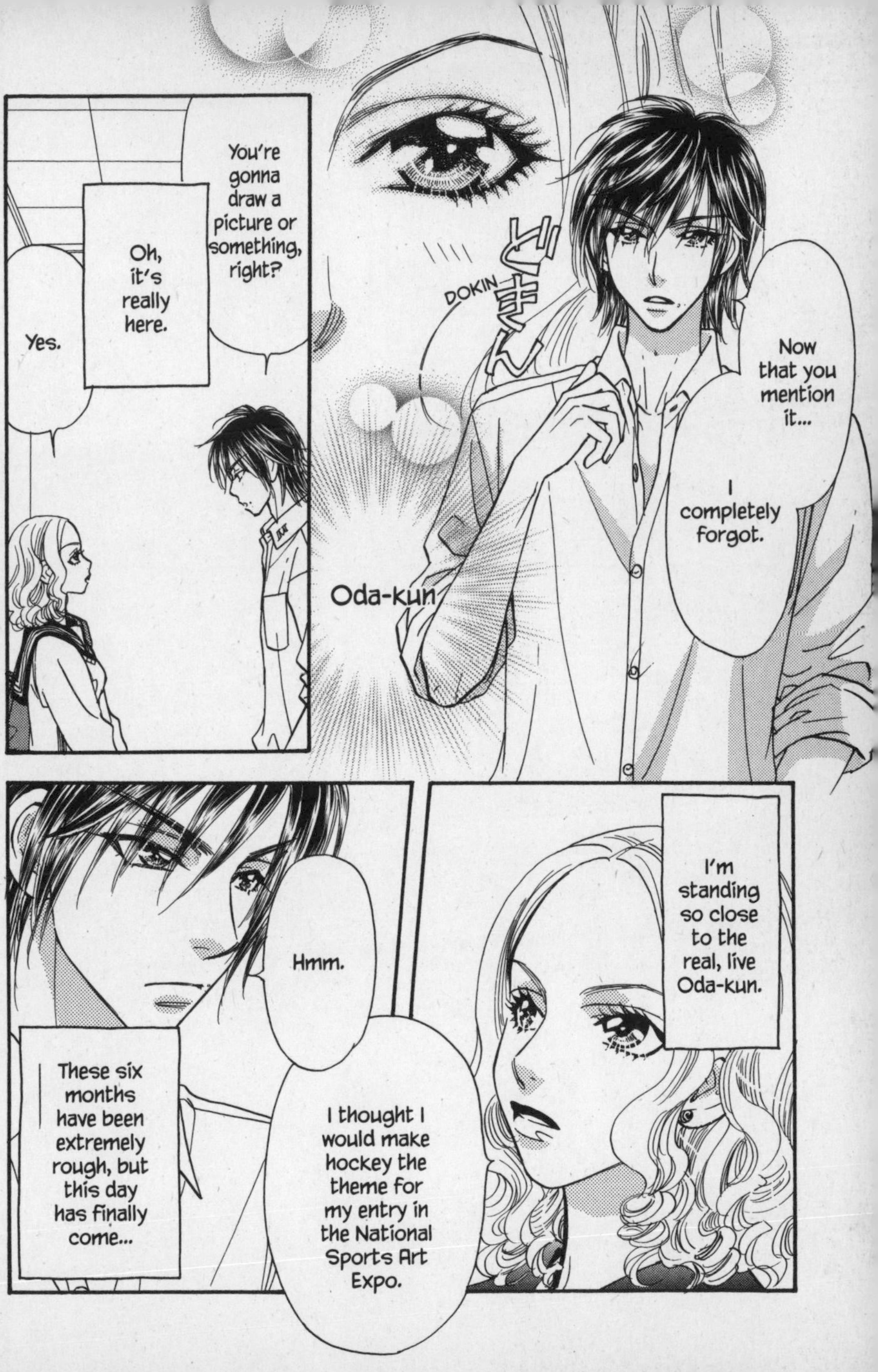
Now that you mention it...
I completely forgot.
DOKIN
Oda-kun
You're gonna draw a picture or something, right?
Oh, it's really here.
Yes.
I'm standing so close to the real, live Oda-kun.
Hmm.
I thought I would make hockey the theme for my entry in the National Sports Art Expo.
These six months have been extremely rough, but this day has finally come...

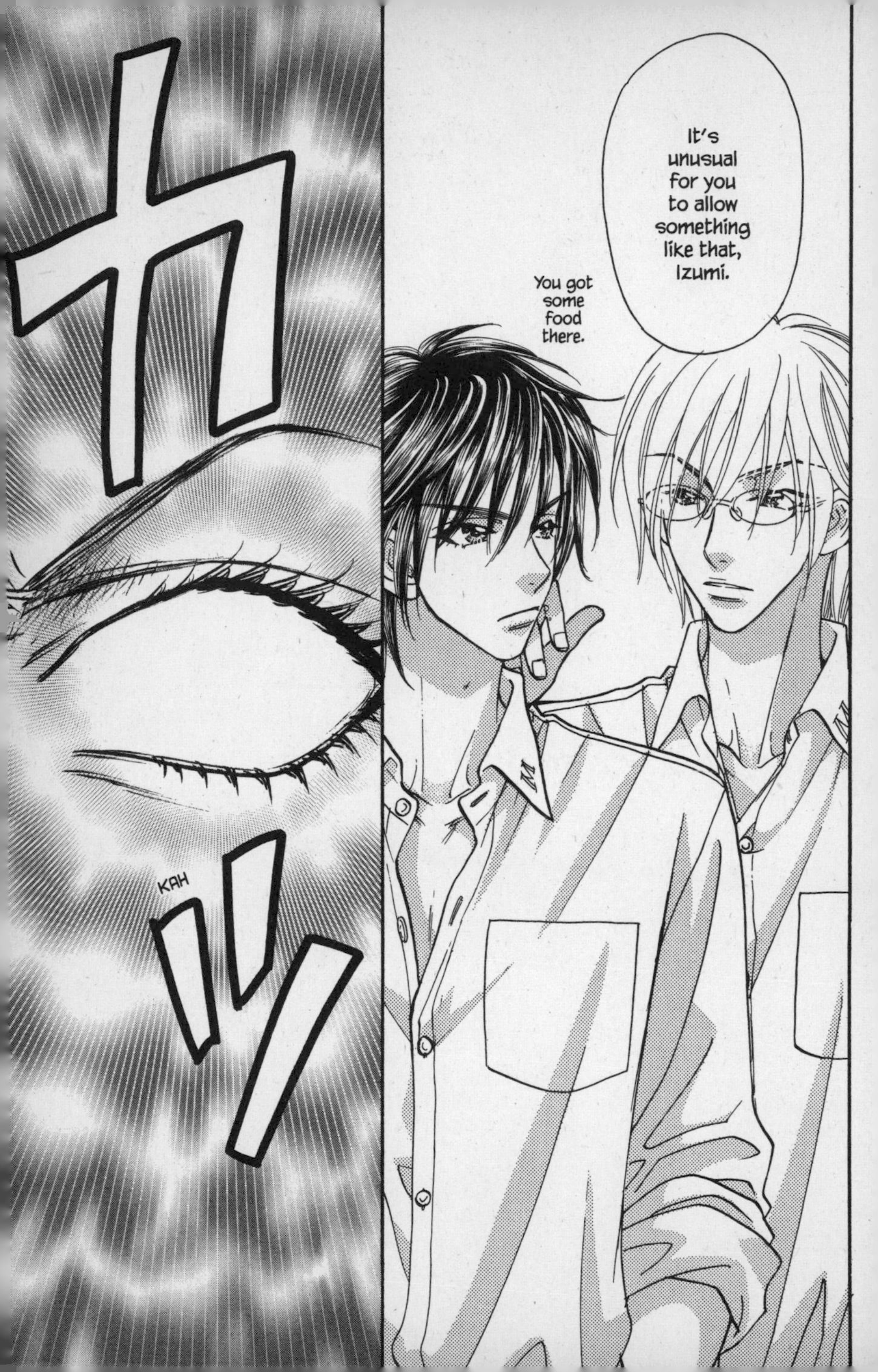
It's unusual for you to allow something like that, Izumi.
You got some food there.
KAH

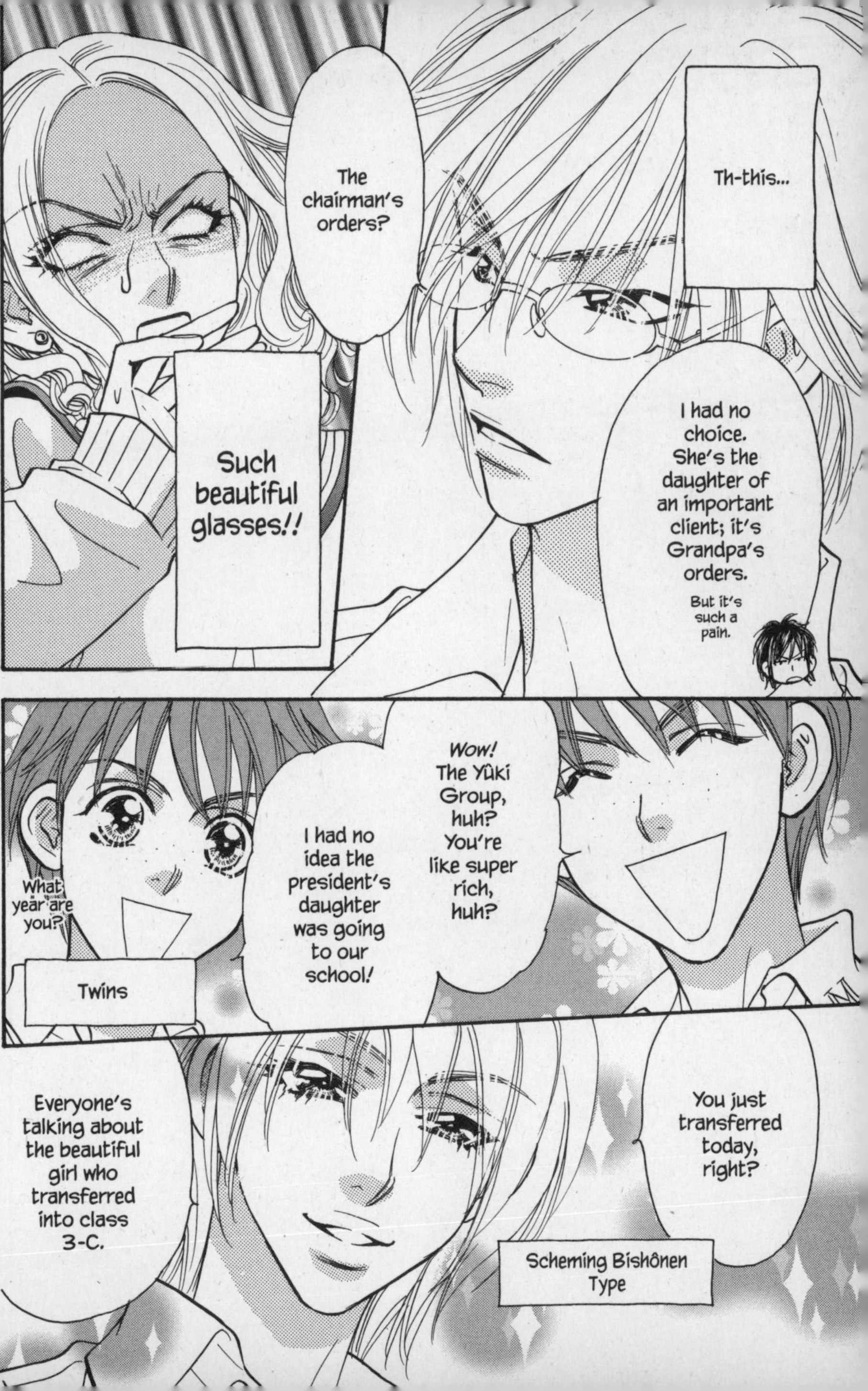
Th-this...
The chairman's orders?
I had no choice. She's the daughter of an important client; it's Grandpa's orders.
But it's such a pain.
Such beautiful glasses!!
Wow! The Yûki Group, huh? You're like super rich, huh?
I had no idea the president's daughter was going to our school!
What year are you?
Twins
You just transferred today, right?
Everyone's talking about the beautiful girl who transferred into class 3-C.
Scheming Bishônen Type

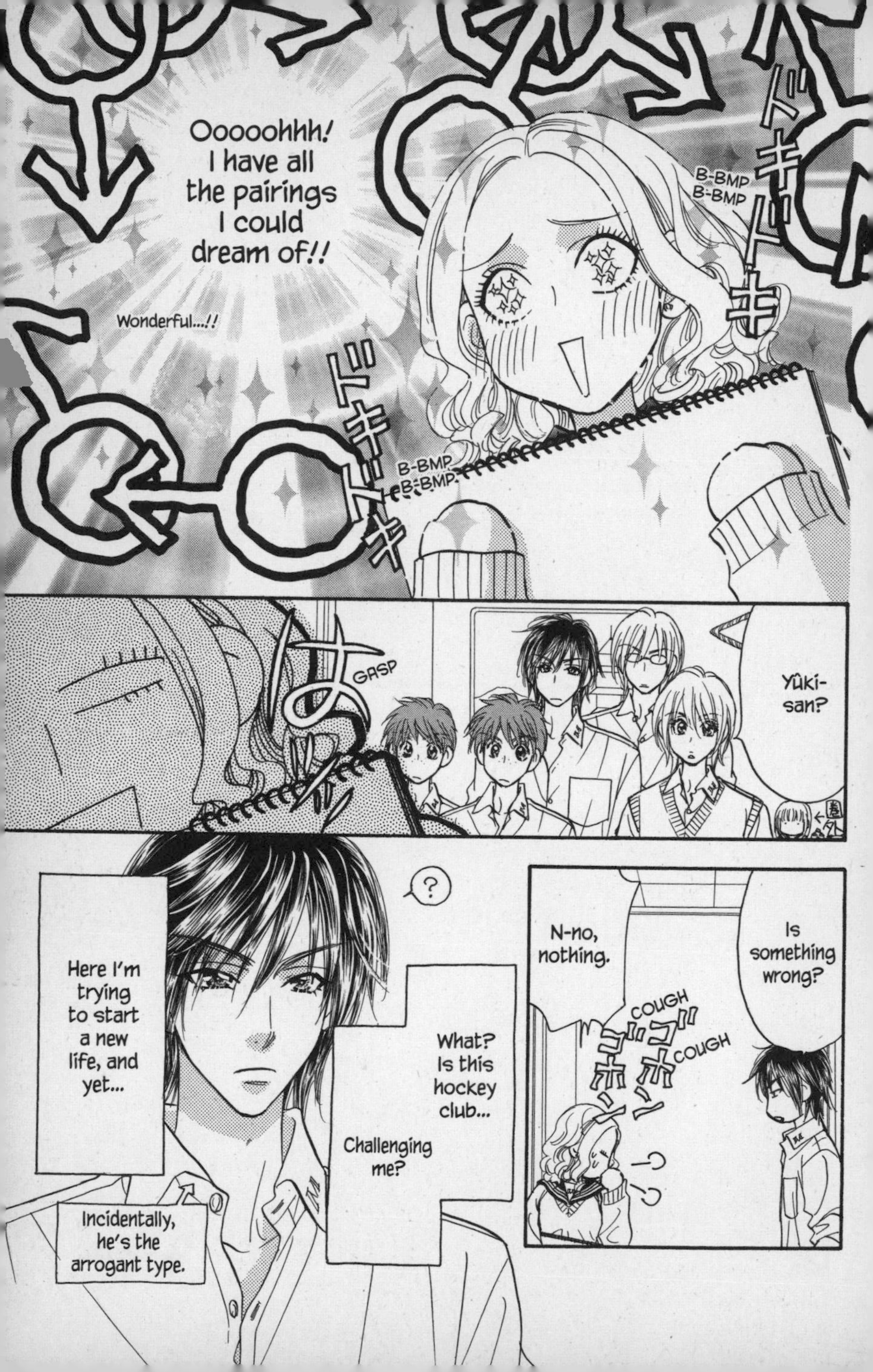
B-BMP B-BMP
Ooooohhh! I have all the pairings I could dream of!!
Wonderful...!!
B-BMP B-BMP
Yûki-san?
GASP
Is something wrong?
N-no, nothing.
COUGH
COUGH
?
What? Is this hockey club...
Challenging me?
Here I'm trying to start a new life, and yet...
Incidentally, he's the arrogant type.

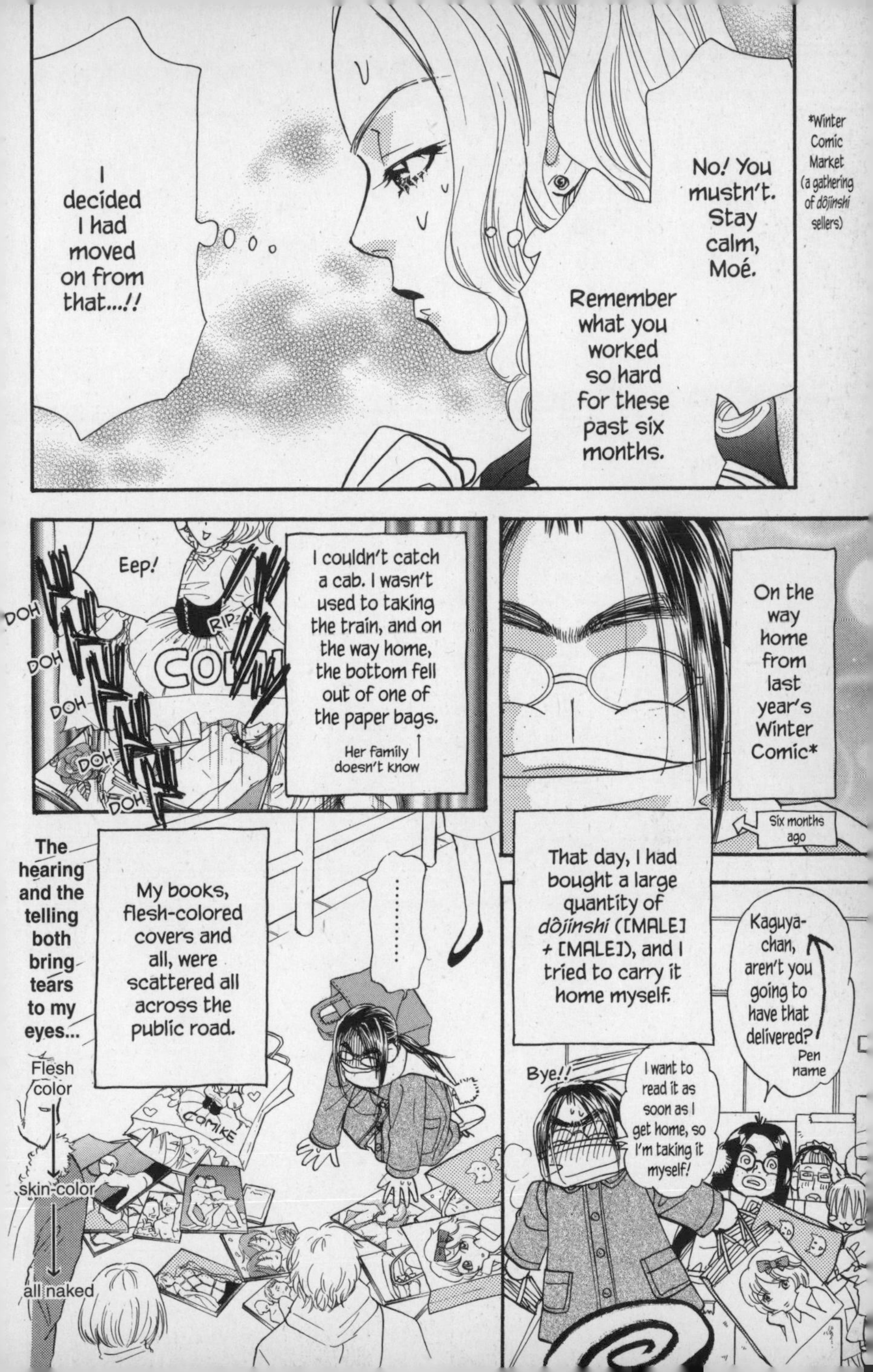
*Winter Comic Market (a gathering of *dôjinshi* sellers)
No! You mustn't. Stay calm, Moé.
Remember what you worked so hard for these past six months.
I decided I had moved on from that...!!
On the way home from last year's Winter Comic*
Six months ago
I couldn't catch a cab. I wasn't used to taking the train, and on the way home, the bottom fell out of one of the paper bags.
Her family doesn't know
Eep!
RIP
COM
DOH
DOH
DOH
DOH
DOH
That day, I had bought a large quantity of *dôjinshi* ([MALE] + [MALE]), and I tried to carry it home myself.
Kaguya-chan, aren't you going to have that delivered?
Pen name
I want to read it as soon as I get home, so I'm taking it myself!
Bye!!
My books, flesh-colored covers and all, were scattered all across the public road.
......
The hearing and the telling both bring tears to my eyes...
Flesh color
skin-color
all naked
COMIKE

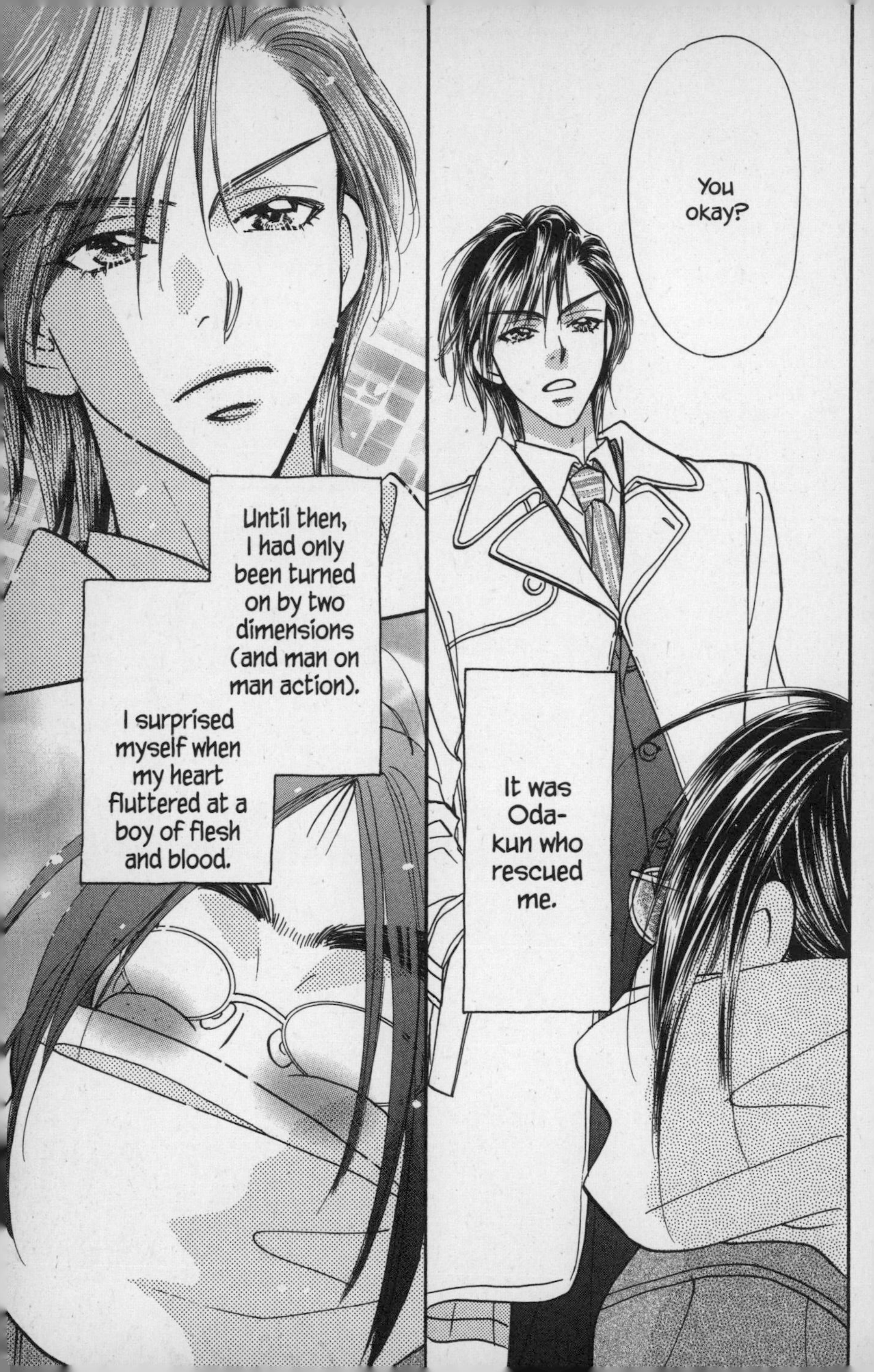
You okay?
It was Oda-kun who rescued me.
Until then, I had only been turned on by two dimensions (and man on man action).
I surprised myself when my heart fluttered at a boy of flesh and blood.

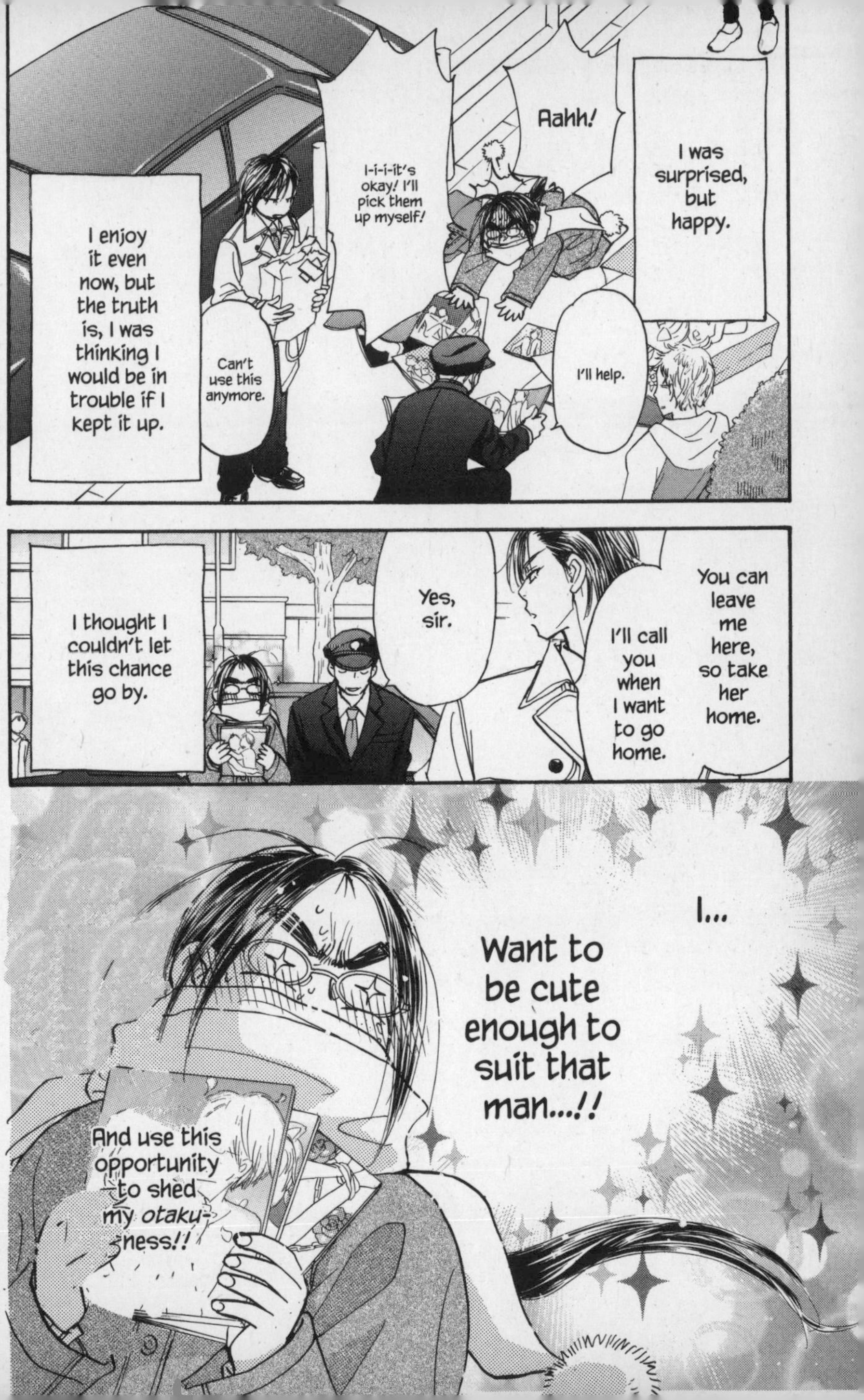
I was surprised, but happy.
Aahh!
I-i-i-it's okay! I'll pick them up myself!
I'll help.
Can't use this anymore.
I enjoy it even now, but the truth is, I was thinking I would be in trouble if I kept it up.
You can leave me here, so take her home.
I'll call you when I want to go home.
Yes, sir.
I thought I couldn't let this chance go by.
I...
Want to be cute enough to suit that man...!!
And use this opportunity to shed my *otaku*-ness!!

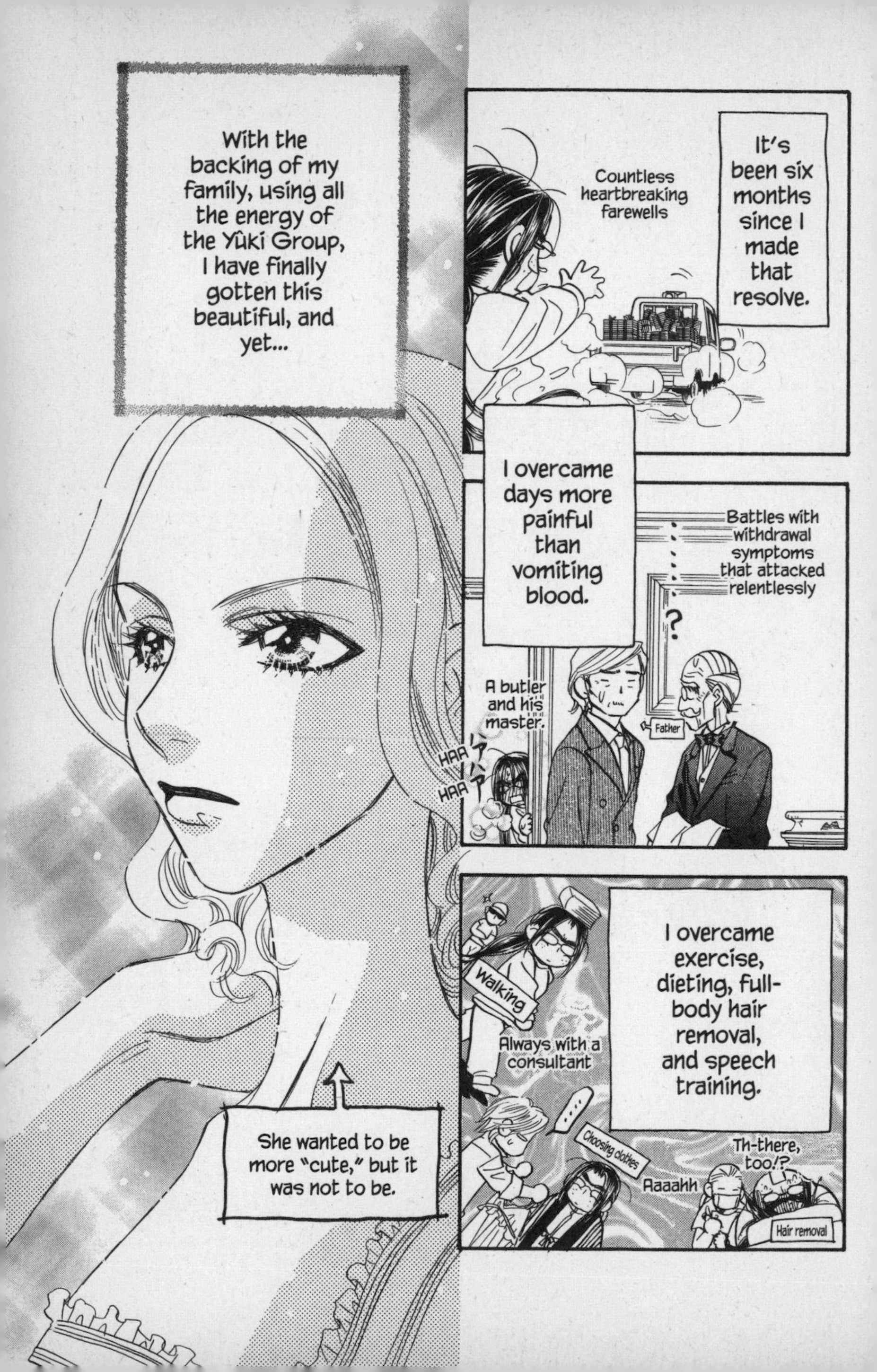
It's been six months since I made that resolve.
Countless heartbreaking farewells
I overcame days more painful than vomiting blood.
Battles with withdrawal symptoms that attacked relentlessly
?
Father
A butler and his master.
HAA HAA
I overcame exercise, dieting, full-body hair removal, and speech training.
Walking
Always with a consultant
Th-there, too!?
Hair removal
Aaaahh
Choosing clothes
....
With the backing of my family, using all the energy of the Yûki Group, I have finally gotten this beautiful, and yet...
She wanted to be more "cute," but it was not to be.

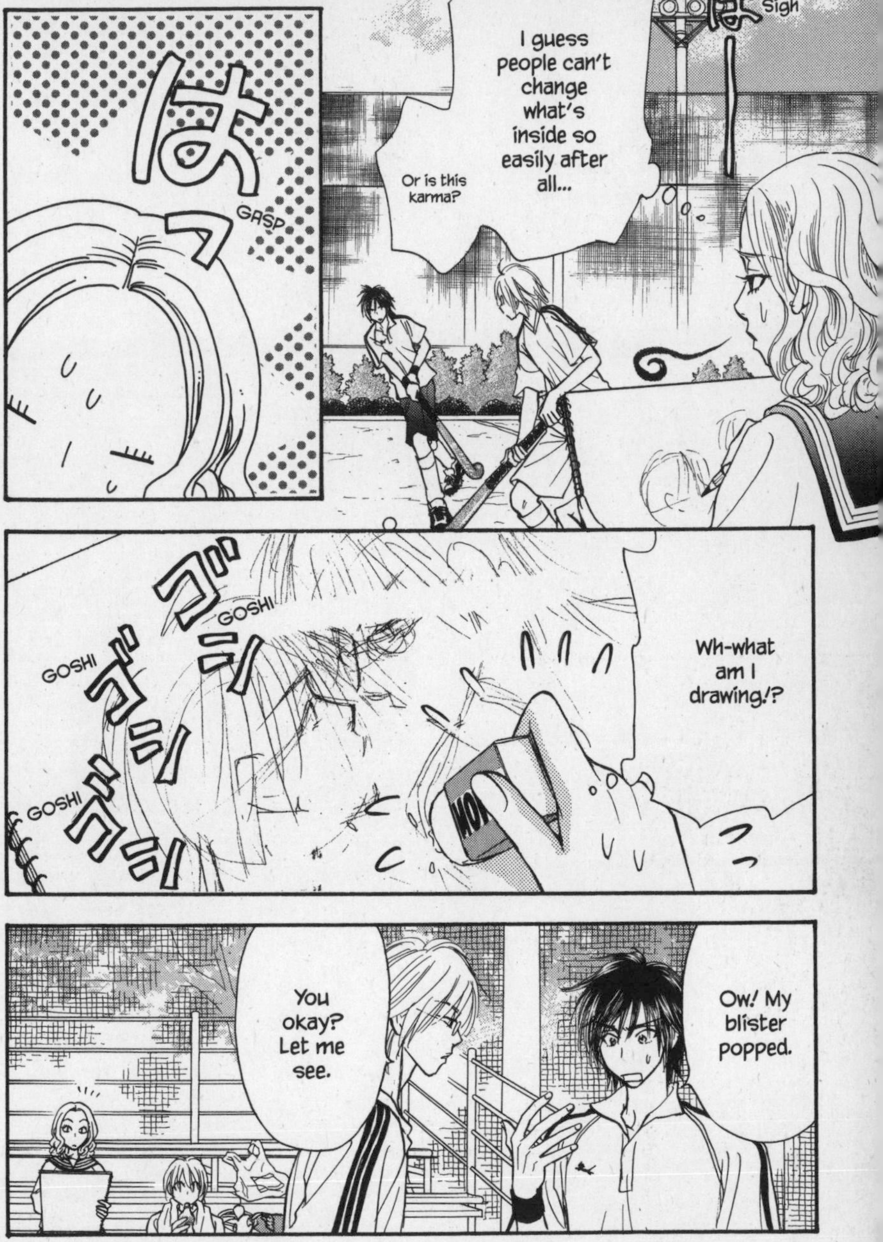
はー
Sigh
I guess people can't change what's inside so easily after all...
Or is this karma?
はっ
GASP
Wh-what am I drawing!?
ゴシ
GOSHI
ゴシ
GOSHI
ゴシ
GOSHI
Ow! My blister popped.
You okay? Let me see.

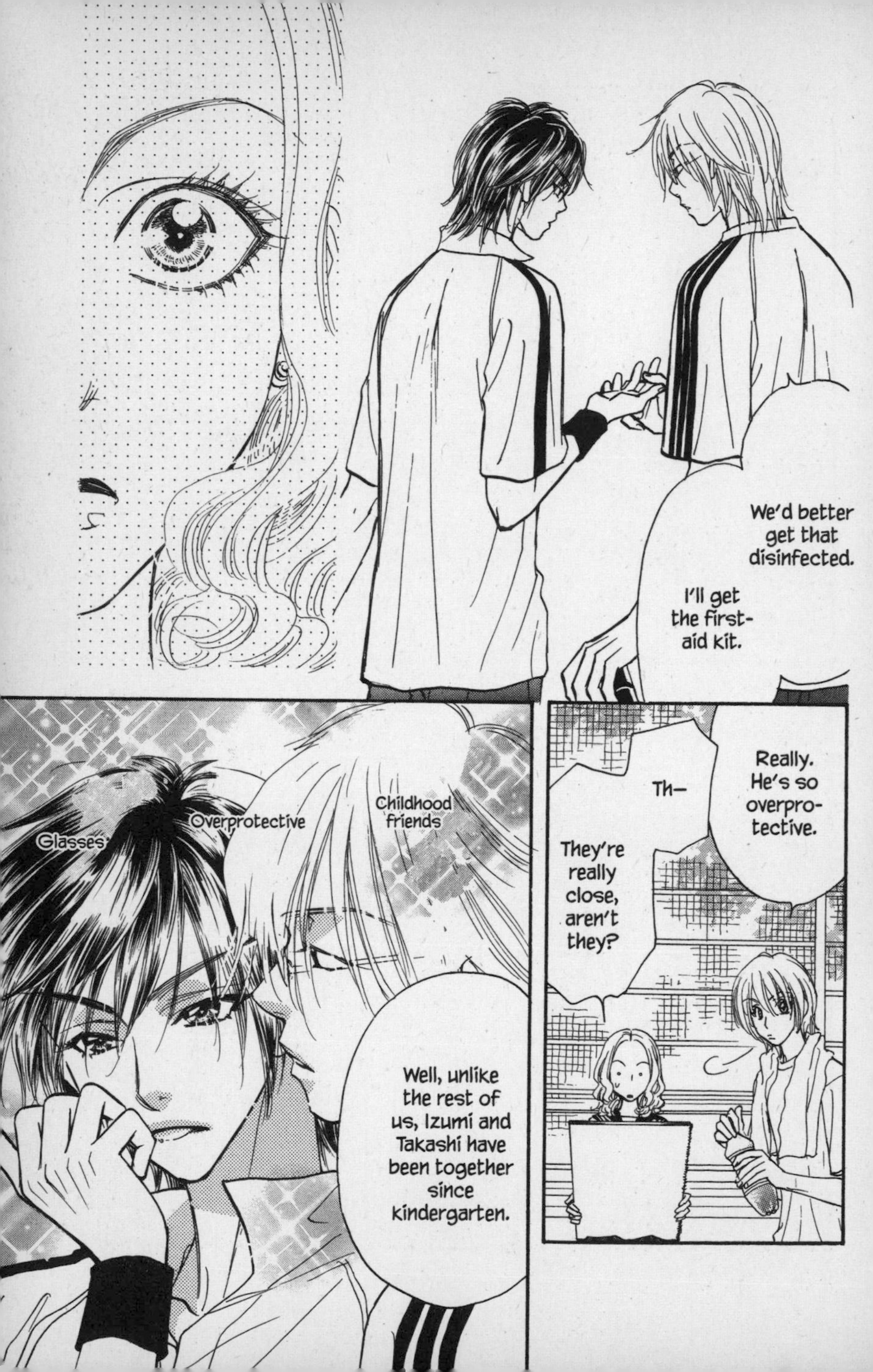
We'd better get that disinfected.
I'll get the first-aid kit.
Really. He's so overpro-tective.
Th—
They're really close, aren't they?
Childhood friends
Overprotective
Glasses
Well, unlike the rest of us, Izumi and Takashi have been together since kindergarten.

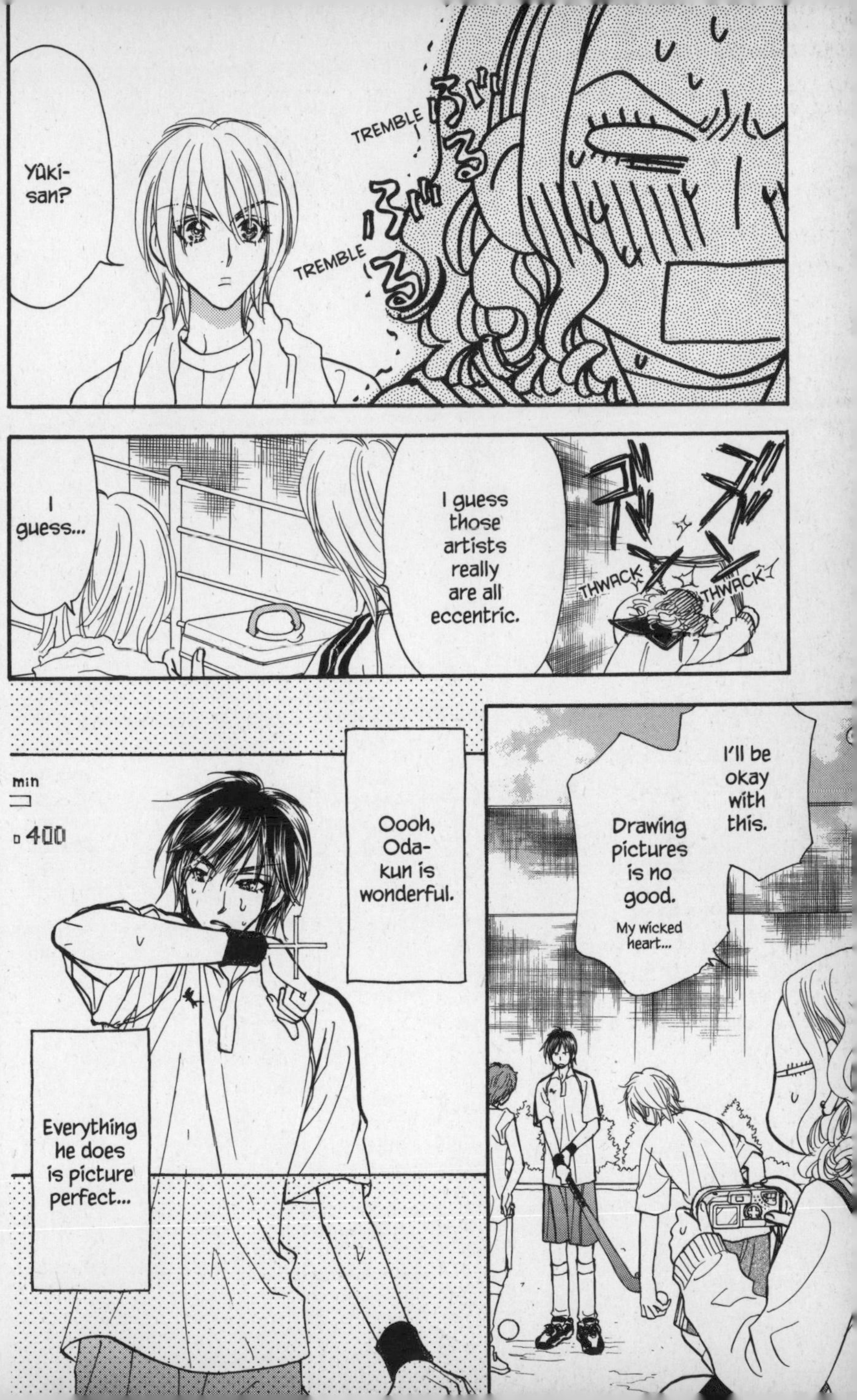
TREMBLE
TREMBLE
Yûki-san?
THWACK
THWACK
I guess those artists really are all eccentric.
I guess...
I'll be okay with this.
Drawing pictures is no good.
My wicked heart...
Oooh, Oda-kun is wonderful.
min
400
Everything he does is picture perfect...

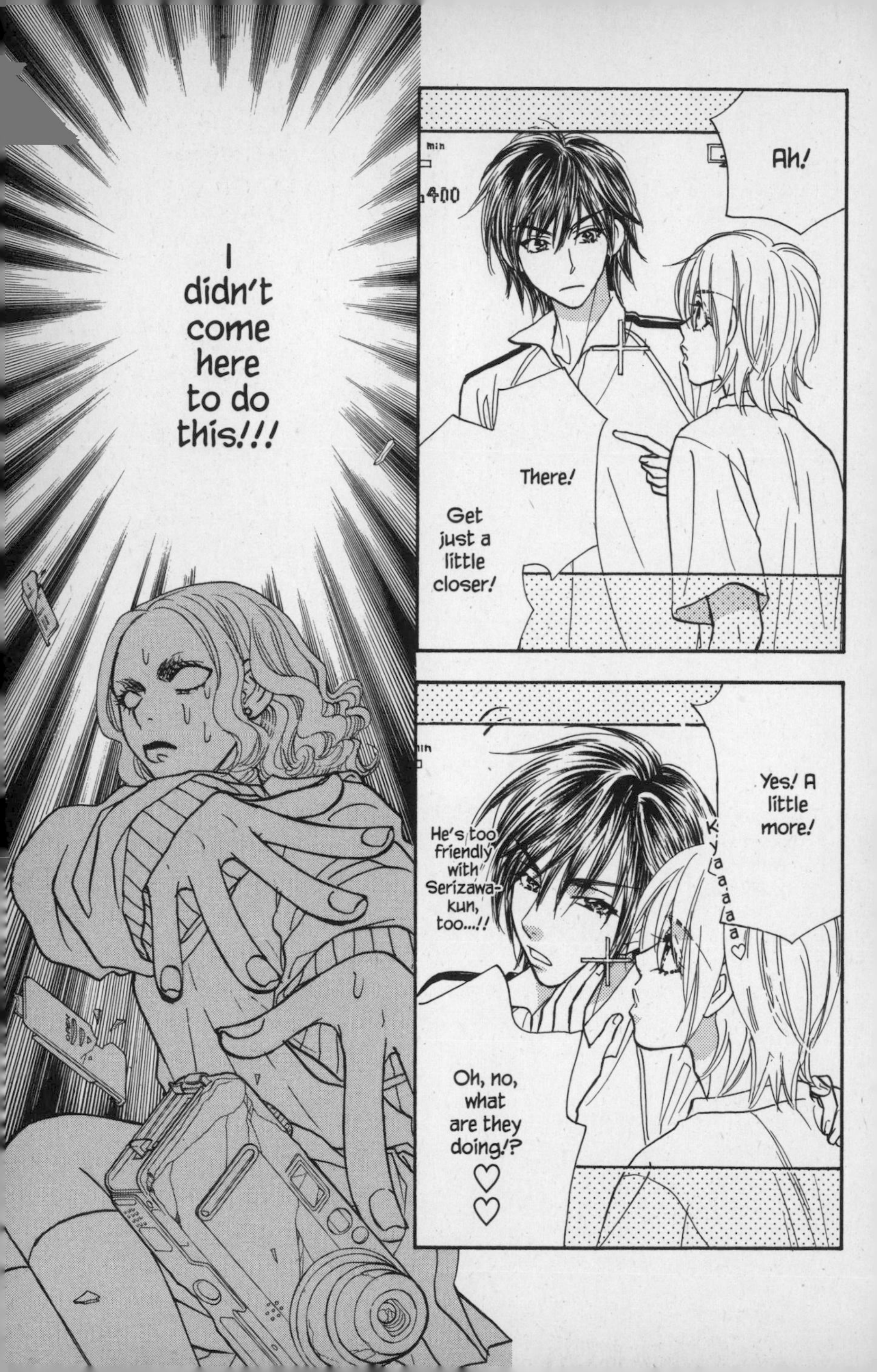
Ah!
There!
Get just a little closer!
Yes! A little more!
Kyaaaaaa♡
He's too friendly with Serizawa-kun, too...!!
Oh, no, what are they doing!? ♡♡
I didn't come here to do this!!!

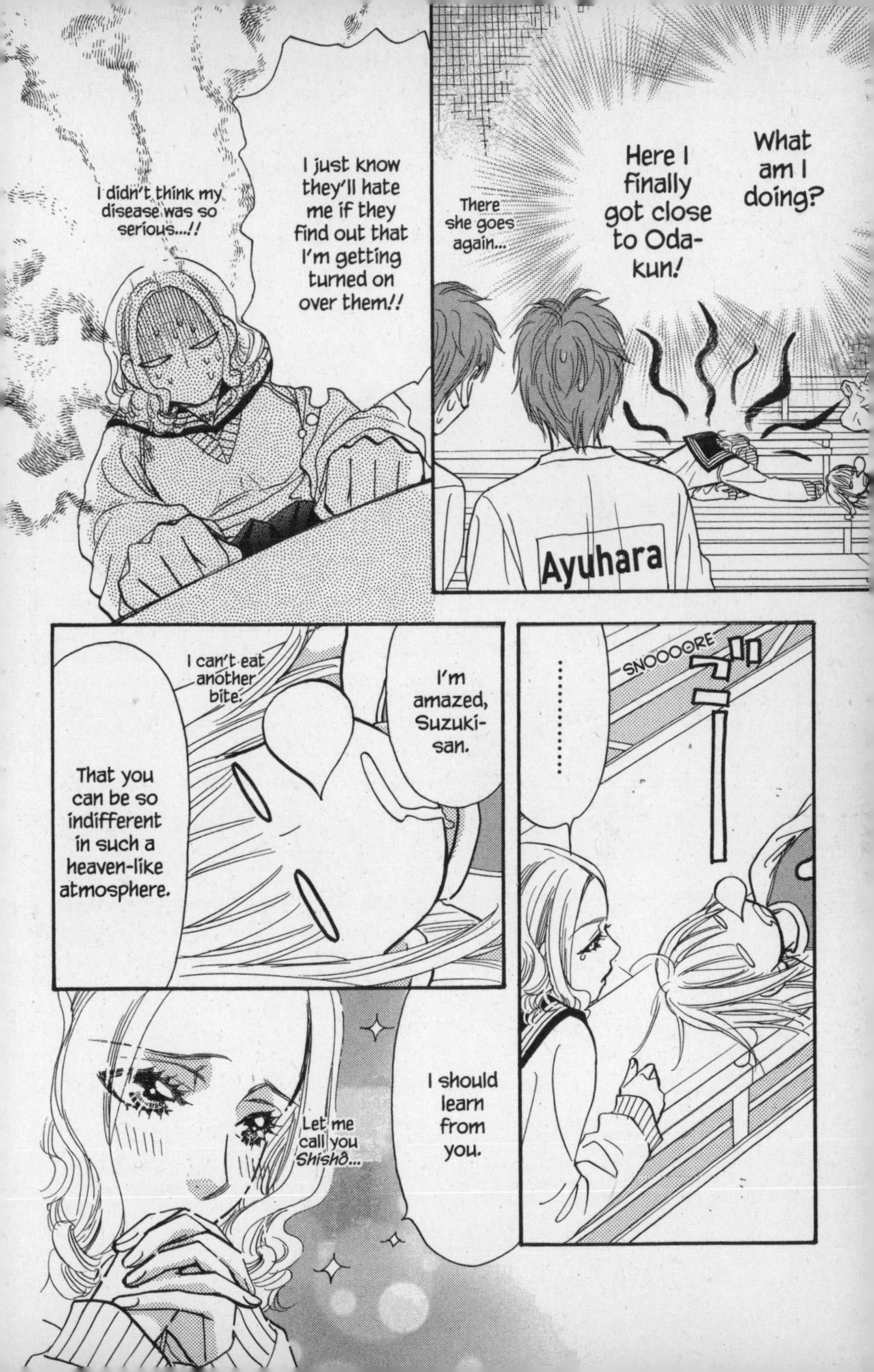
What am I doing?
Here I finally got close to Oda-kun!
There she goes again...
Ayuhara
I just know they'll hate me if they find out that I'm getting turned on over them!!
I didn't think my disease was so serious...!!
......
SNOOOORE
I'm amazed, Suzuki-san.
I can't eat another bite.
That you can be so indifferent in such a heaven-like atmosphere.
I should learn from you.
Let me call you Shishō...

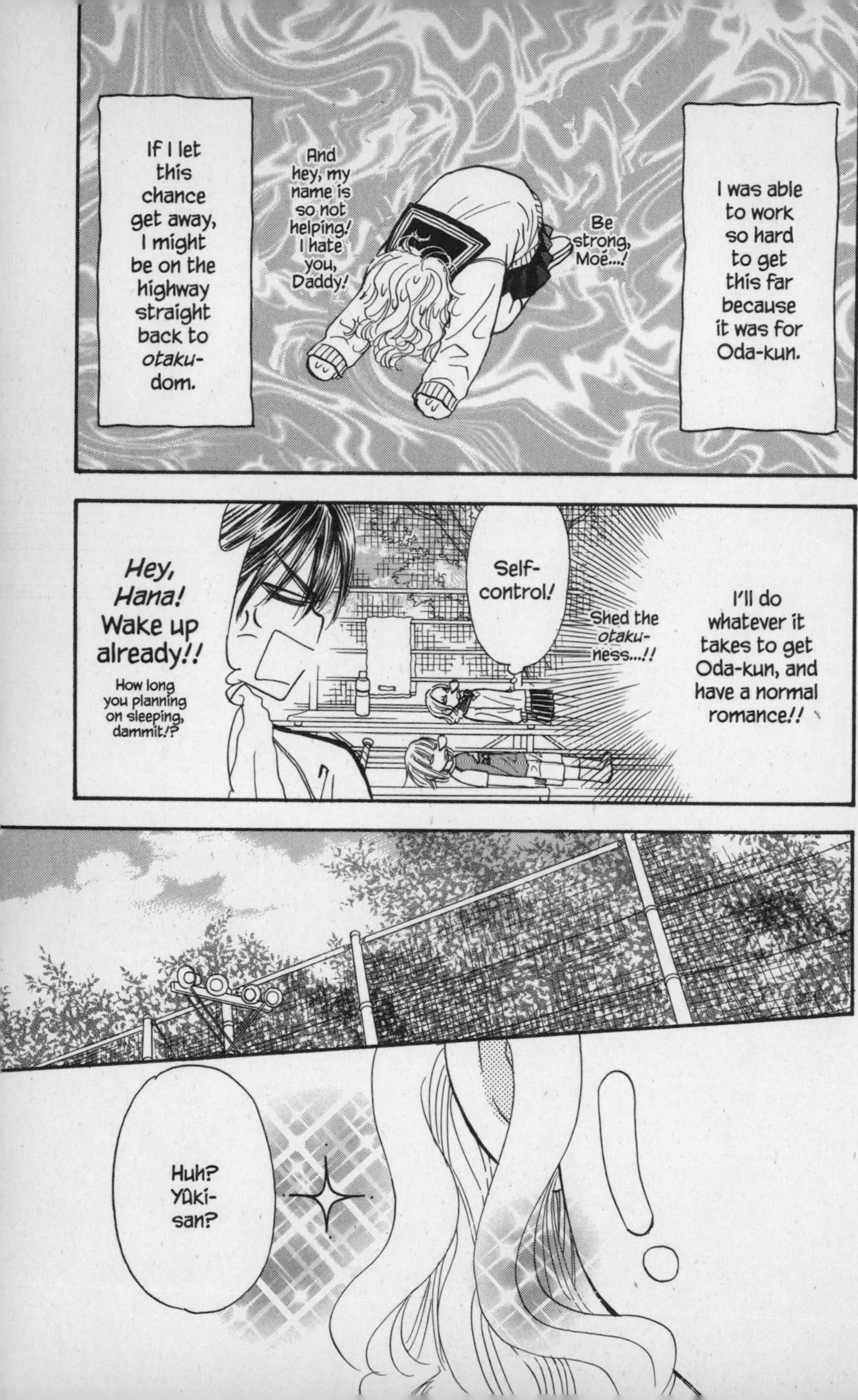
I was able to work so hard to get this far because it was for Oda-kun.
Be strong, Moe...!
And hey, my name is so not helping! I hate you, Daddy!
If I let this chance get away, I might be on the highway straight back to *otaku*-dom.
I'll do whatever it takes to get Oda-kun, and have a normal romance!!
Shed the *otaku*-ness...!!
Self-control!
Hey, Hana! Wake up already!!
How long you planning on sleeping, dammit!?
!
Huh? Yûki-san?

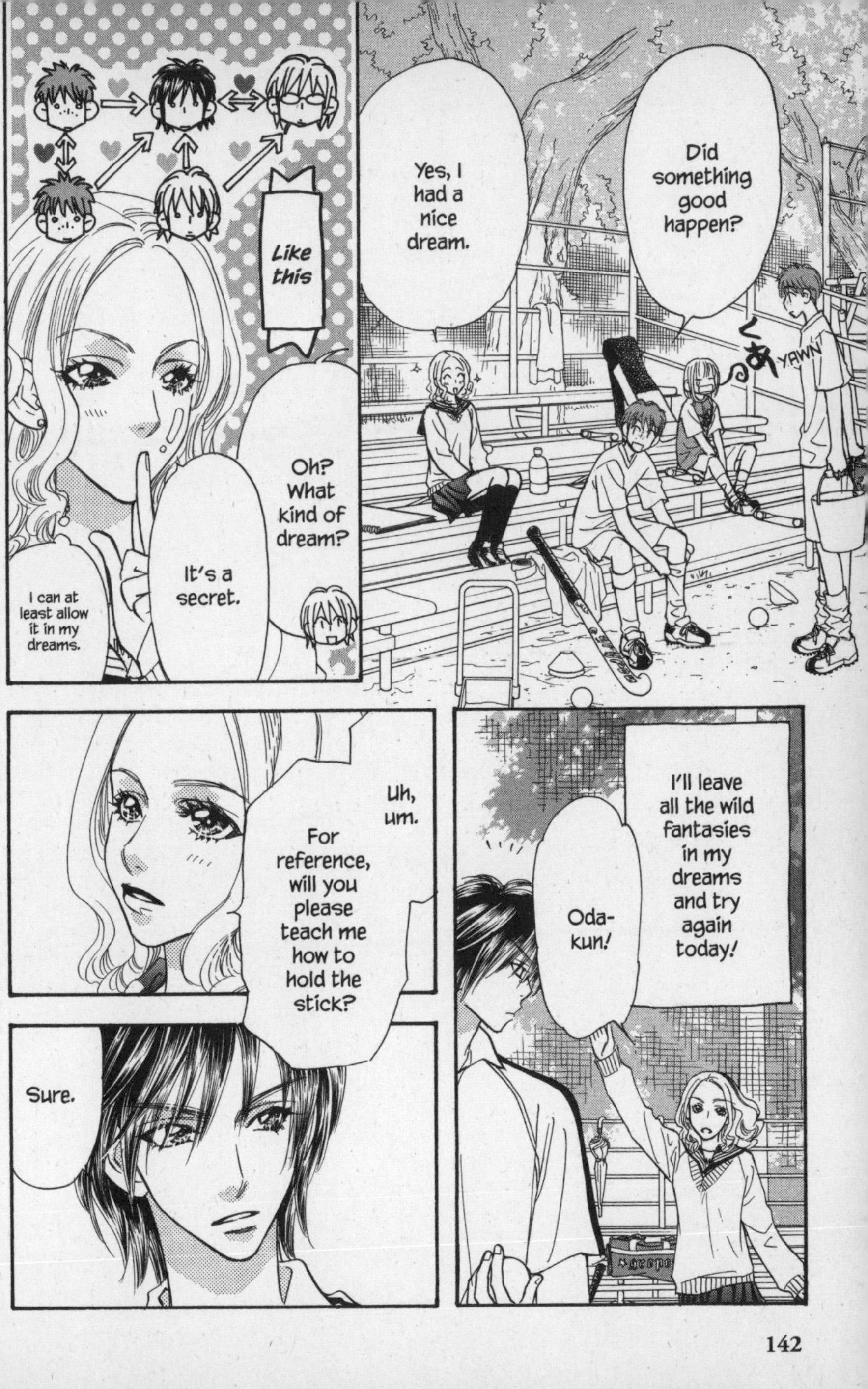
Did something good happen?
Yes, I had a nice dream.
くあ YAWN
Like this
Oh? What kind of dream?
It's a secret.
I can at least allow it in my dreams.
I'll leave all the wild fantasies in my dreams and try again today!
Oda-kun!
Uh, um.
For reference, will you please teach me how to hold the stick?
Sure.

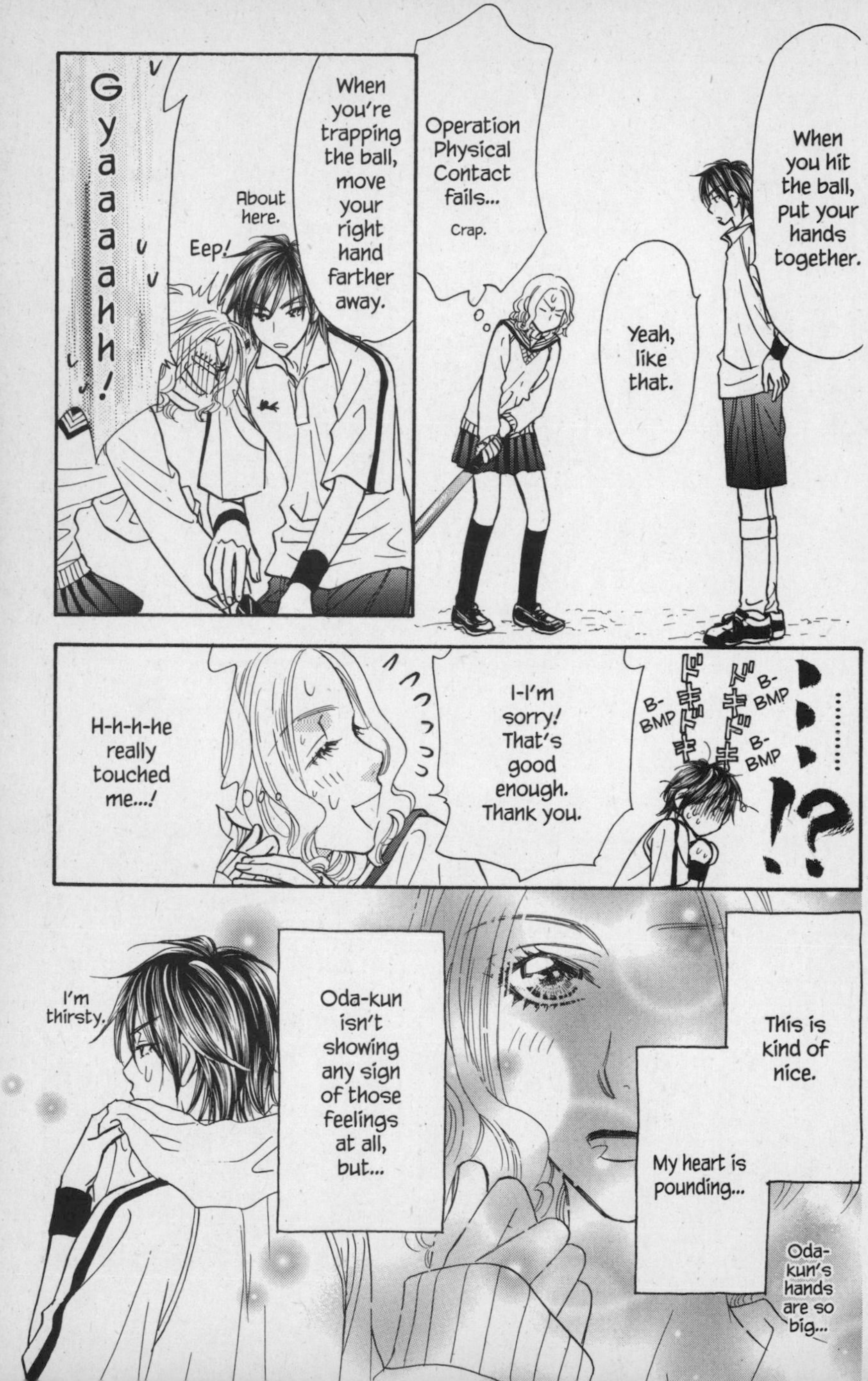
When you hit the ball, put your hands together.
Yeah, like that.
Operation Physical Contact fails...
Crap.
When you're trapping the ball, move your right hand farther away.
About here.
Eep!
Gyaaaahh!
......!?
ドキドキ
B-BMP
ドキドキ
B-BMP
B-BMP
I-I'm sorry! That's good enough. Thank you.
H-h-h-he really touched me...!
This is kind of nice.
My heart is pounding...
Oda-kun's hands are so big...
Oda-kun isn't showing any sign of those feelings at all, but...
I'm thirsty.

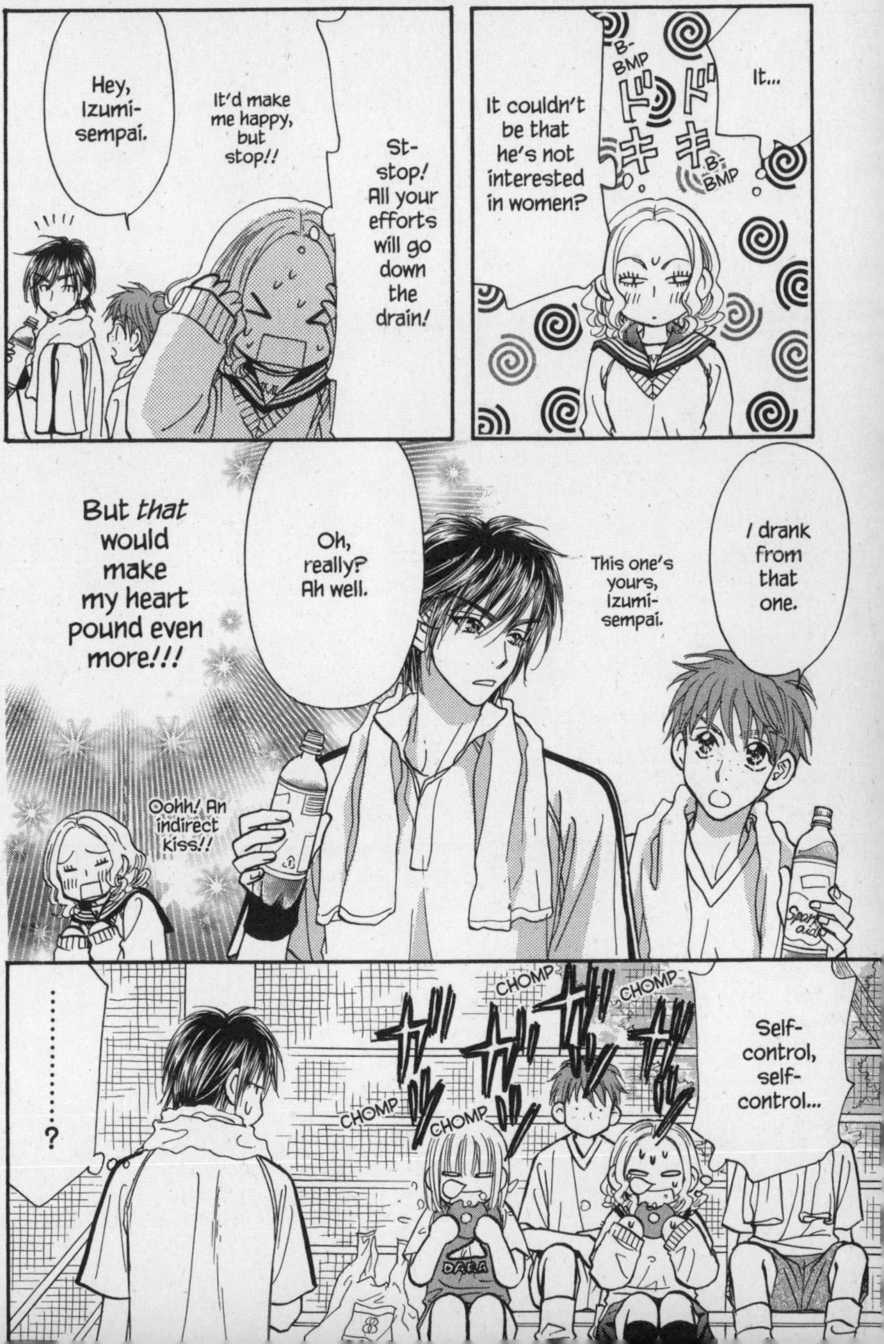
It...
B-BMP
B-BMP
It couldn't be that he's not interested in women?
St-stop! All your efforts will go down the drain!
It'd make me happy, but stop!!
Hey, Izumi-sempai.
I drank from that one.
This one's yours, Izumi-sempai.
Oh, really? Ah well.
But *that* would make my heart pound even more!!!
Oohh! An indirect kiss!!
Self-control, self-control...
CHOMP
CHOMP
CHOMP
CHOMP
......?

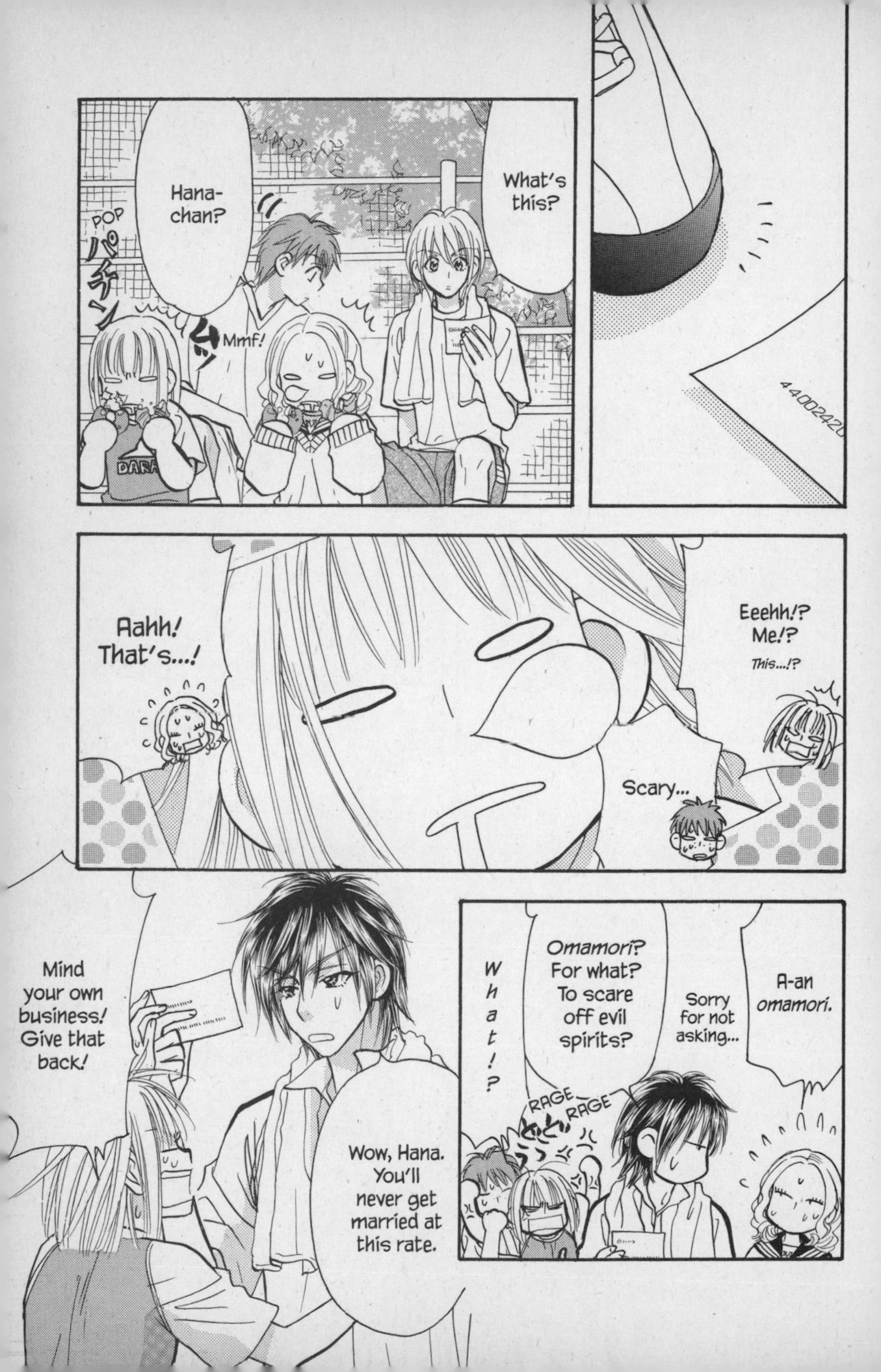

4400242
What's this?
Hana-chan?
POP
パチン
Mmf!
ムッ
Eeehh!? Me!?
This...!?
Aahh! That's...!
Scary...
A-an omamori.
Sorry for not asking...
Omamori? For what? To scare off evil spirits?
What!?
RAGE RAGE
Wow, Hana. You'll never get married at this rate.
Mind your own business! Give that back!

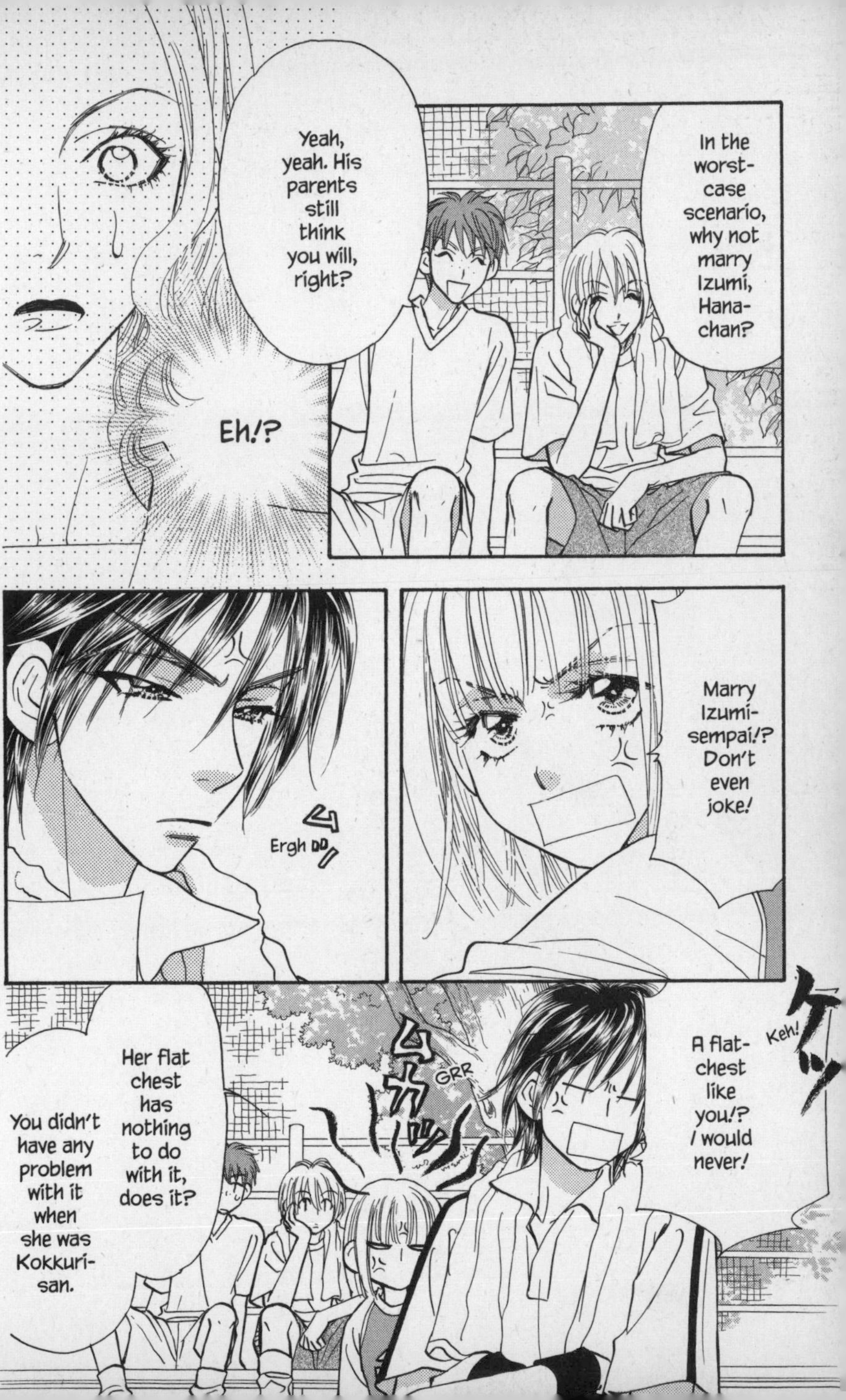
In the worst-case scenario, why not marry Izumi, Hana-chan?
Yeah, yeah. His parents still think you will, right?
Eh!?
Marry Izumi-sempai!? Don't even joke!
Ergh
ケッ
Keh!
A flat-chest like you!? I would never!
ムカッ
GRR
Her flat chest has nothing to do with it, does it?
You didn't have any problem with it when she was Kokkuri-san.

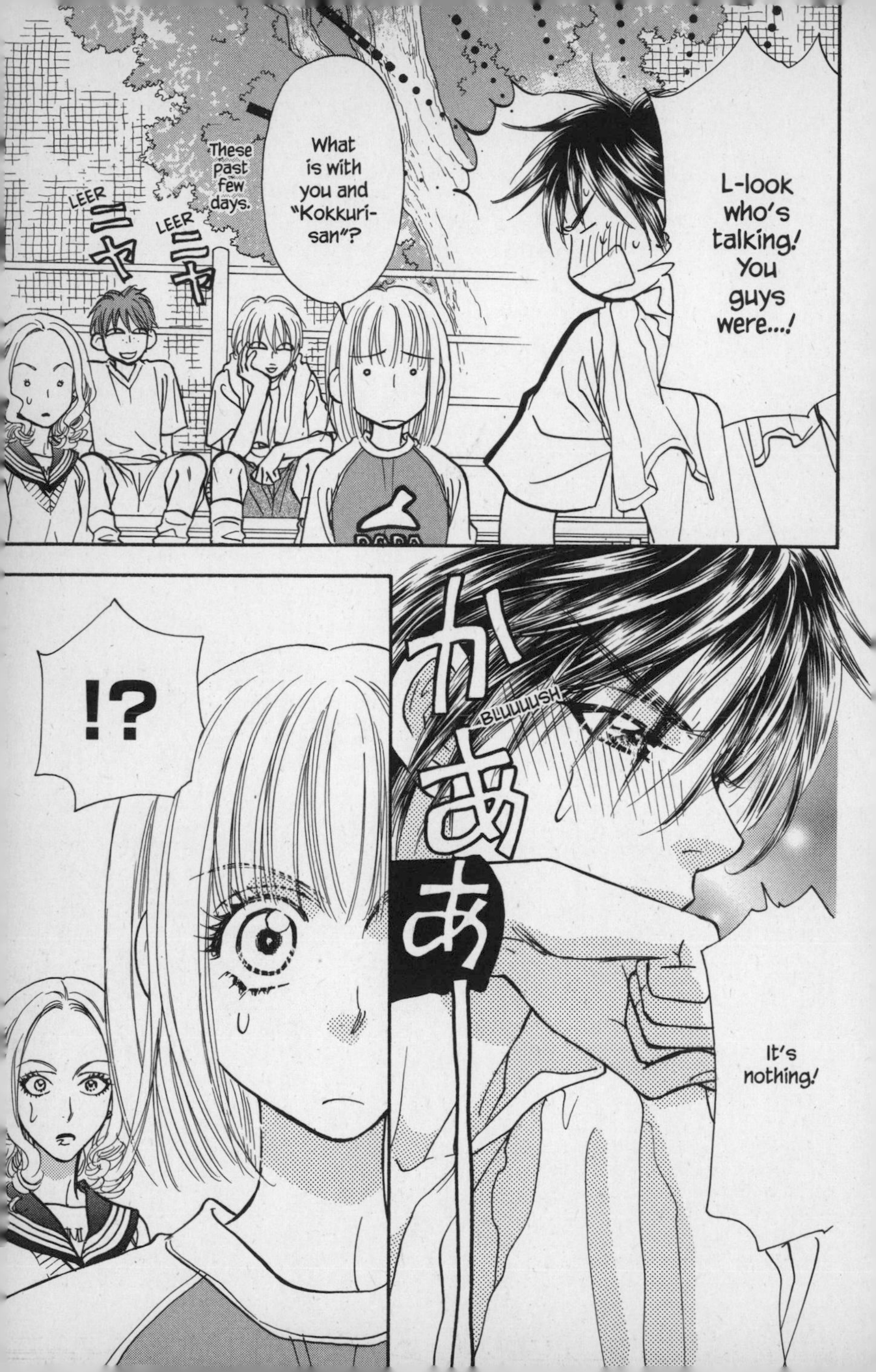
L-look who's talking! You guys were...!
What is with you and "Kokkuri-san"?
These past few days.
LEER
ニヤ
LEER
ニヤ
かあぁ
BLUUUUSH
It's nothing!
!?

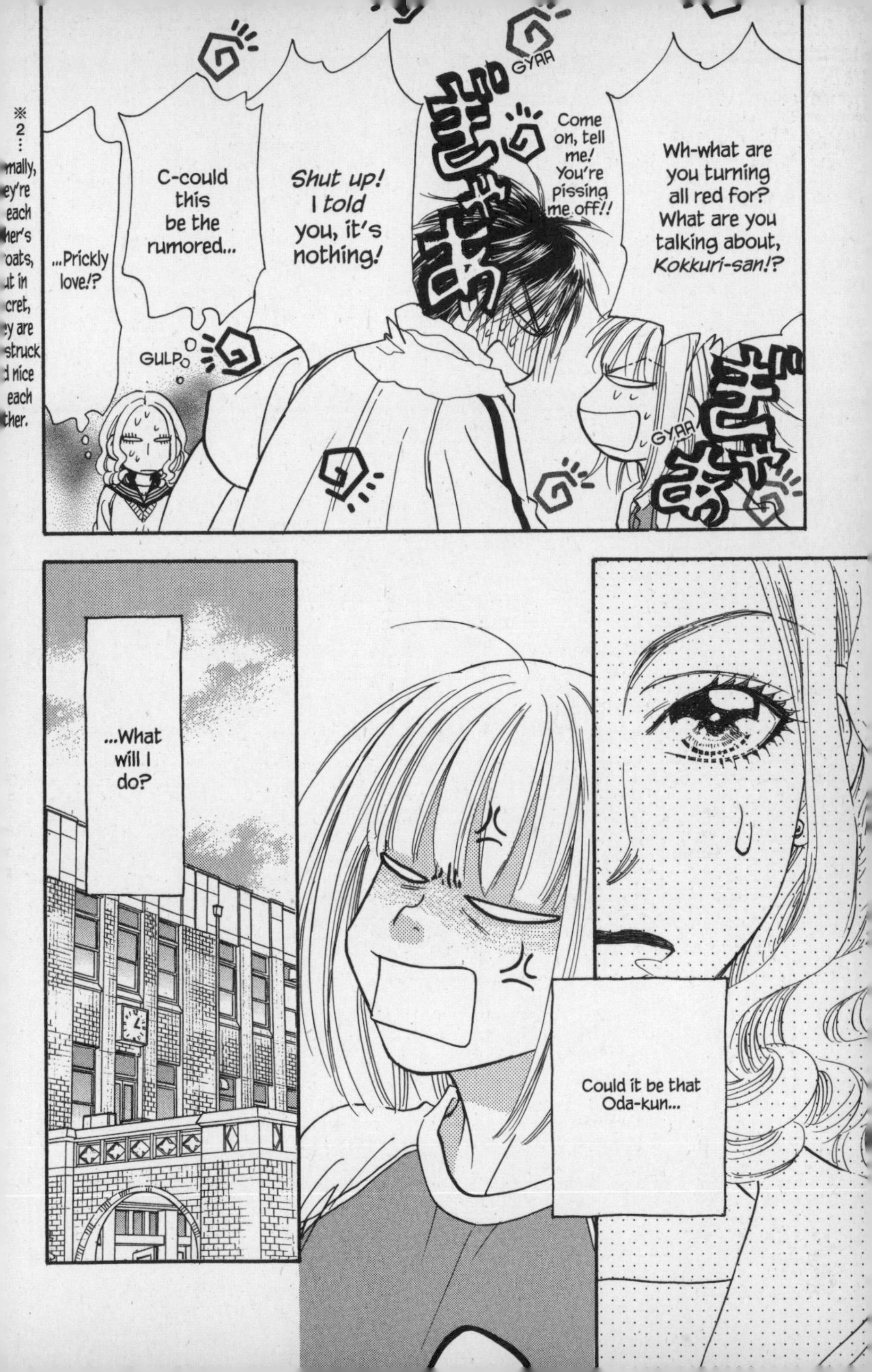
Wh-what are you turning all red for? What are you talking about, Kokkuri-san!?
GYAA
Come on, tell me! You're pissing me off!!
GYAA
Shut up! I told you, it's nothing!
C-could this be the rumored...
...Prickly love!?
GULP
Could it be that Oda-kun...
...What will I do?

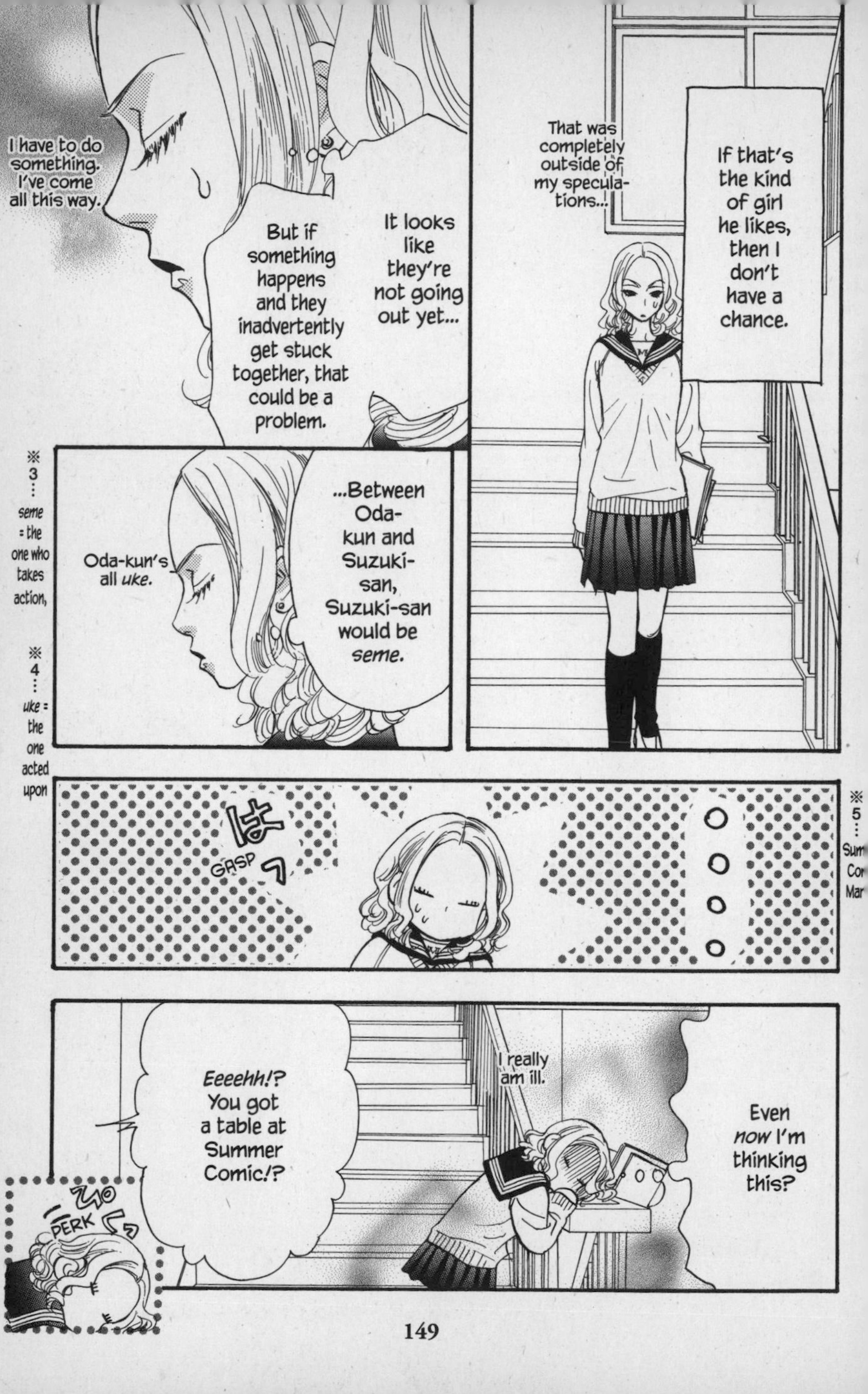

If that's the kind of girl he likes, then I don't have a chance.
That was completely outside of my specula-tions...
It looks like they're not going out yet...
But if something happens and they inadvertently get stuck together, that could be a problem.
I have to do something. I've come all this way.
...Between Oda-kun and Suzuki-san, Suzuki-san would be *seme*.
Oda-kun's all *uke*.
※3 … *seme* = the one who takes action,
※4 … *uke* = the one acted upon
○○○○
は
GASP
Even *now* I'm thinking this?
I really am ill.
Eeeehh!? You got a table at Summer Comic!?
PERK

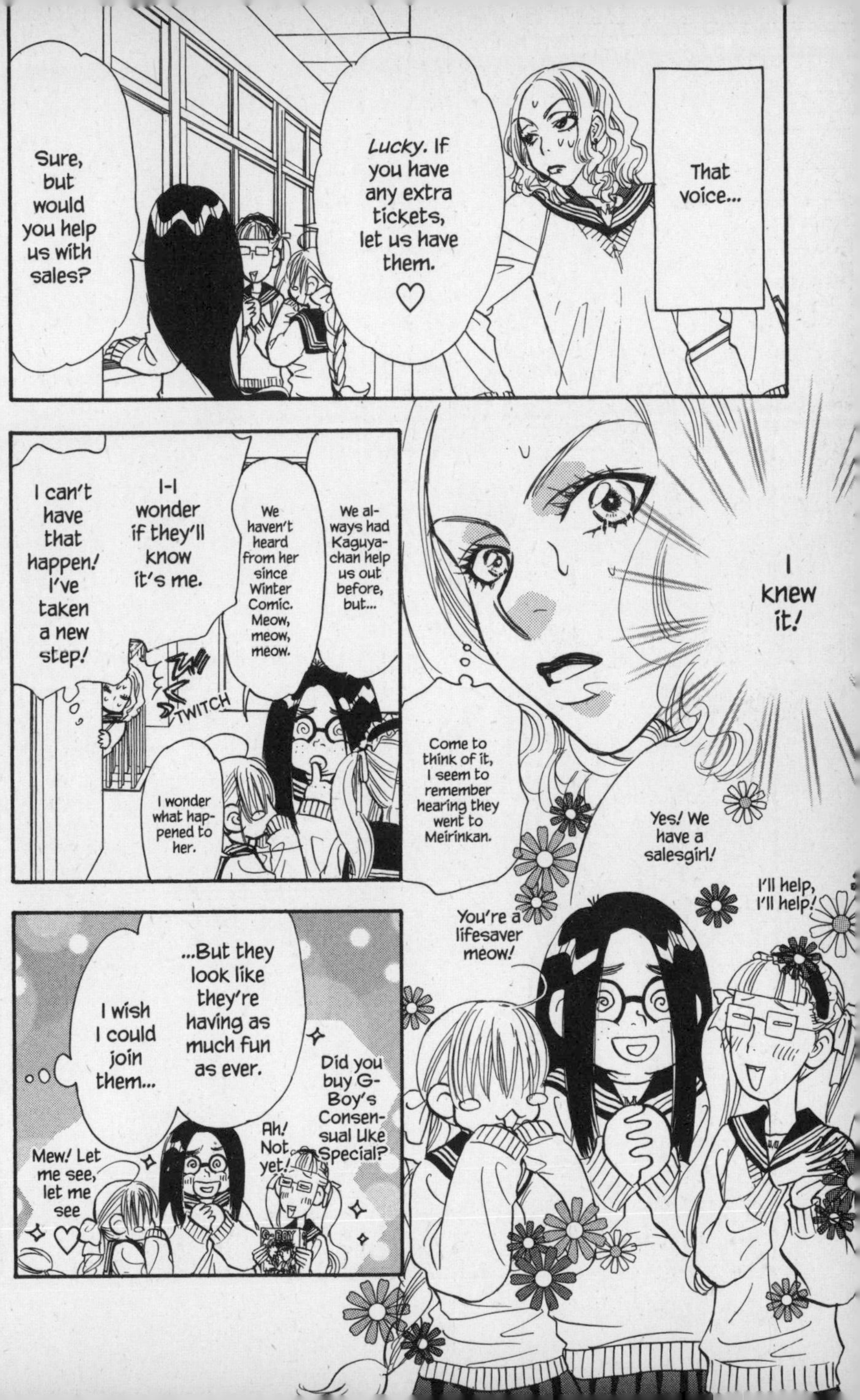

That voice...
Lucky. If you have any extra tickets, let us have them. ♡
Sure, but would you help us with sales?
I knew it!
Come to think of it, I seem to remember hearing they went to Meirinkan.
Yes! We have a salesgirl!
I'll help, I'll help!
You're a lifesaver meow!
We always had Kaguya-chan help us out before, but...
We haven't heard from her since Winter Comic. Meow, meow, meow.
I-I wonder if they'll know it's me.
I can't have that happen! I've taken a new step!
TWITCH
I wonder what happened to her.
...But they look like they're having as much fun as ever.
I wish I could join them...
Did you buy G-Boy's Consensual Uke Special?
Ah! Not yet!
Mew! Let me see, let me see ♡
G-BOY

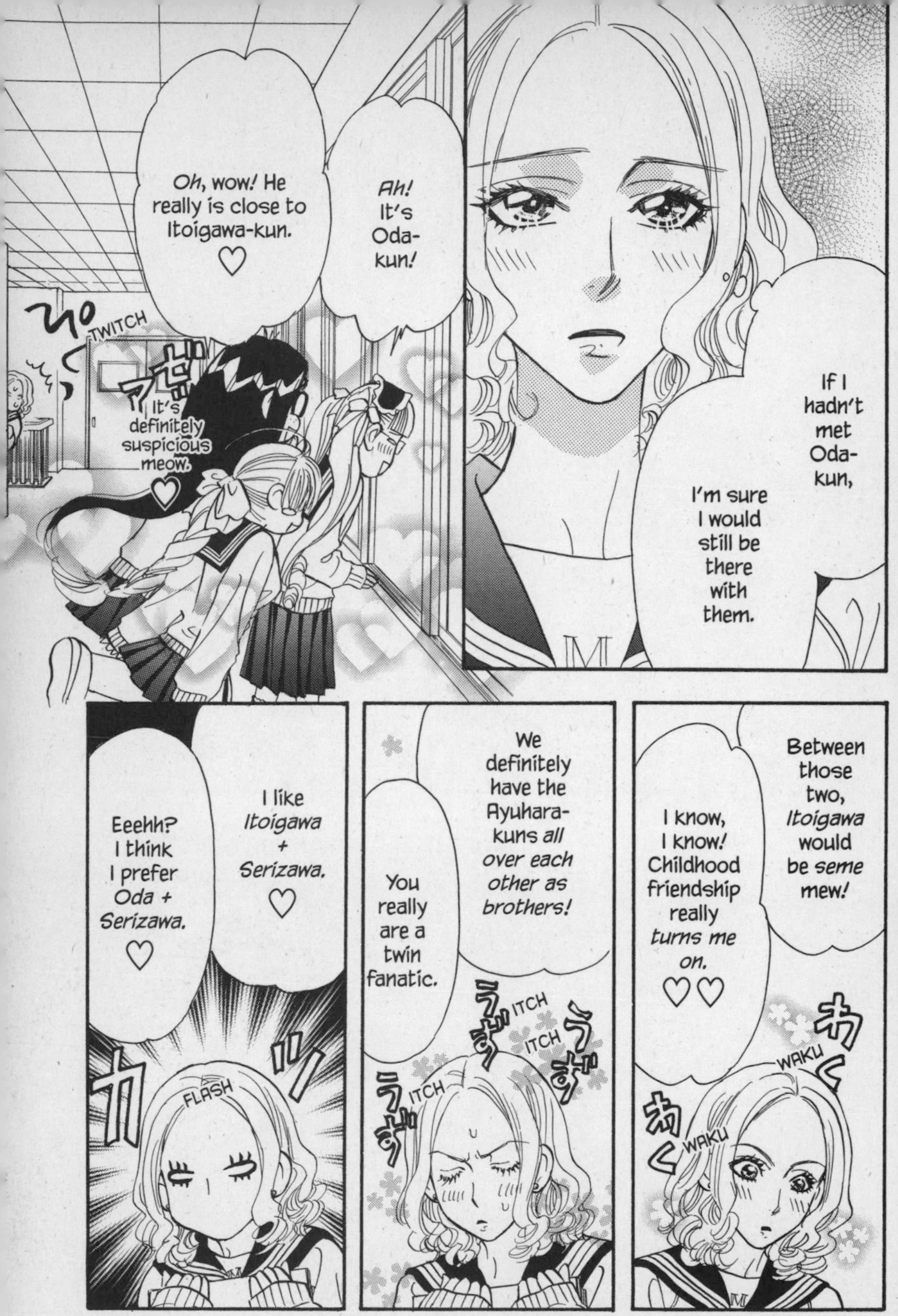
If I hadn't met Oda-kun,
I'm sure I would still be there with them.
Ah! It's Oda-kun!
Oh, wow! He really is close to Itoigawa-kun. ♡
TWITCH
It's definitely suspicious meow. ♡
Between those two, *Itoigawa* would be *seme mew!*
I know, I know! Childhood friendship really *turns me on.* ♡♡
WAKU
WAKU
We definitely have the Ayuhara-kuns *all over each other as brothers!*
You really are a twin fanatic.
ITCH
ITCH
ITCH
I like *Itoigawa + Serizawa.* ♡
Eeehh? I think I prefer *Oda + Serizawa.* ♡
FLASH

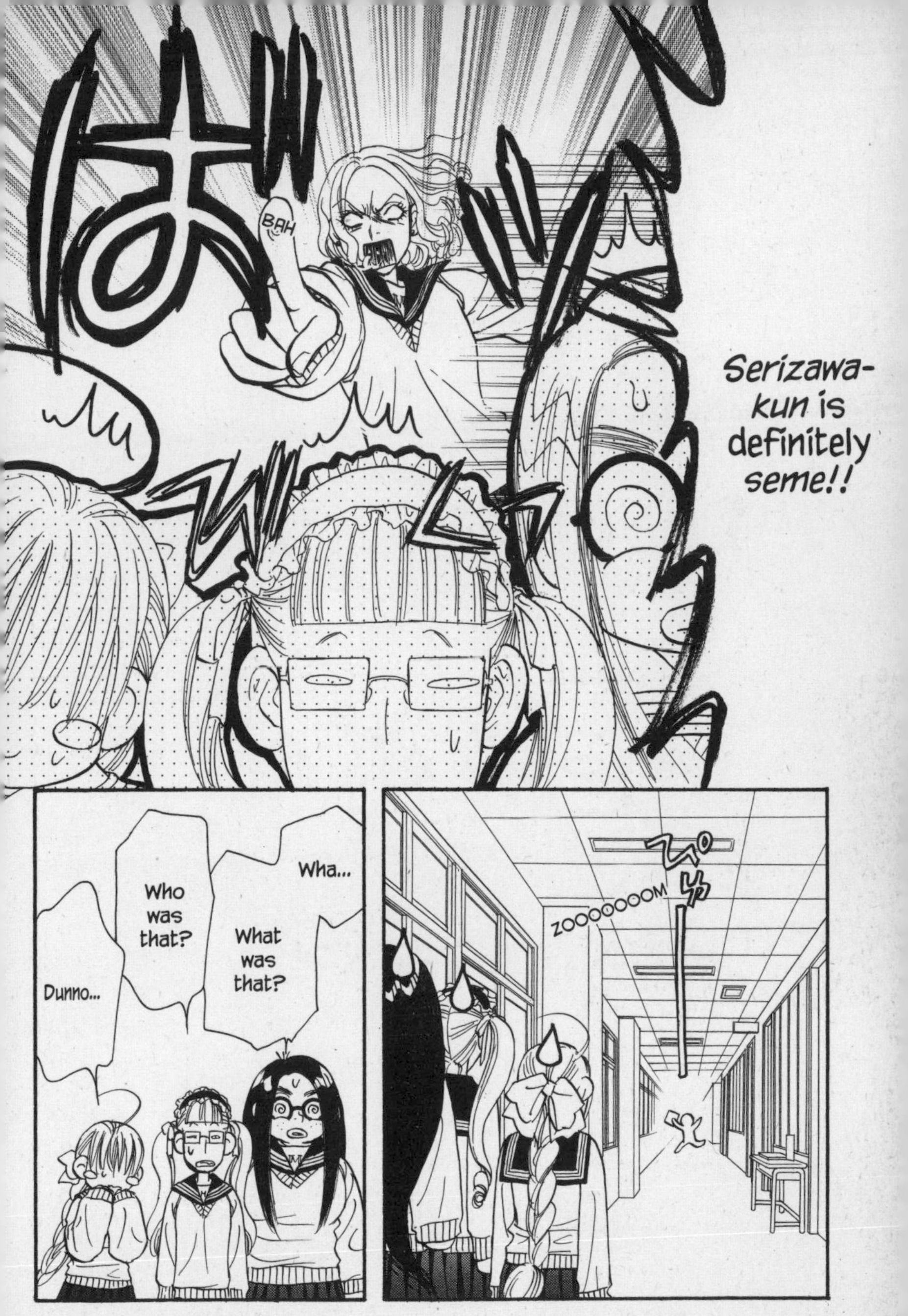
BAH
Serizawa-kun is definitely seme!!
ZOOOOOOOM
Wha...
What was that?
Who was that?
Dunno...

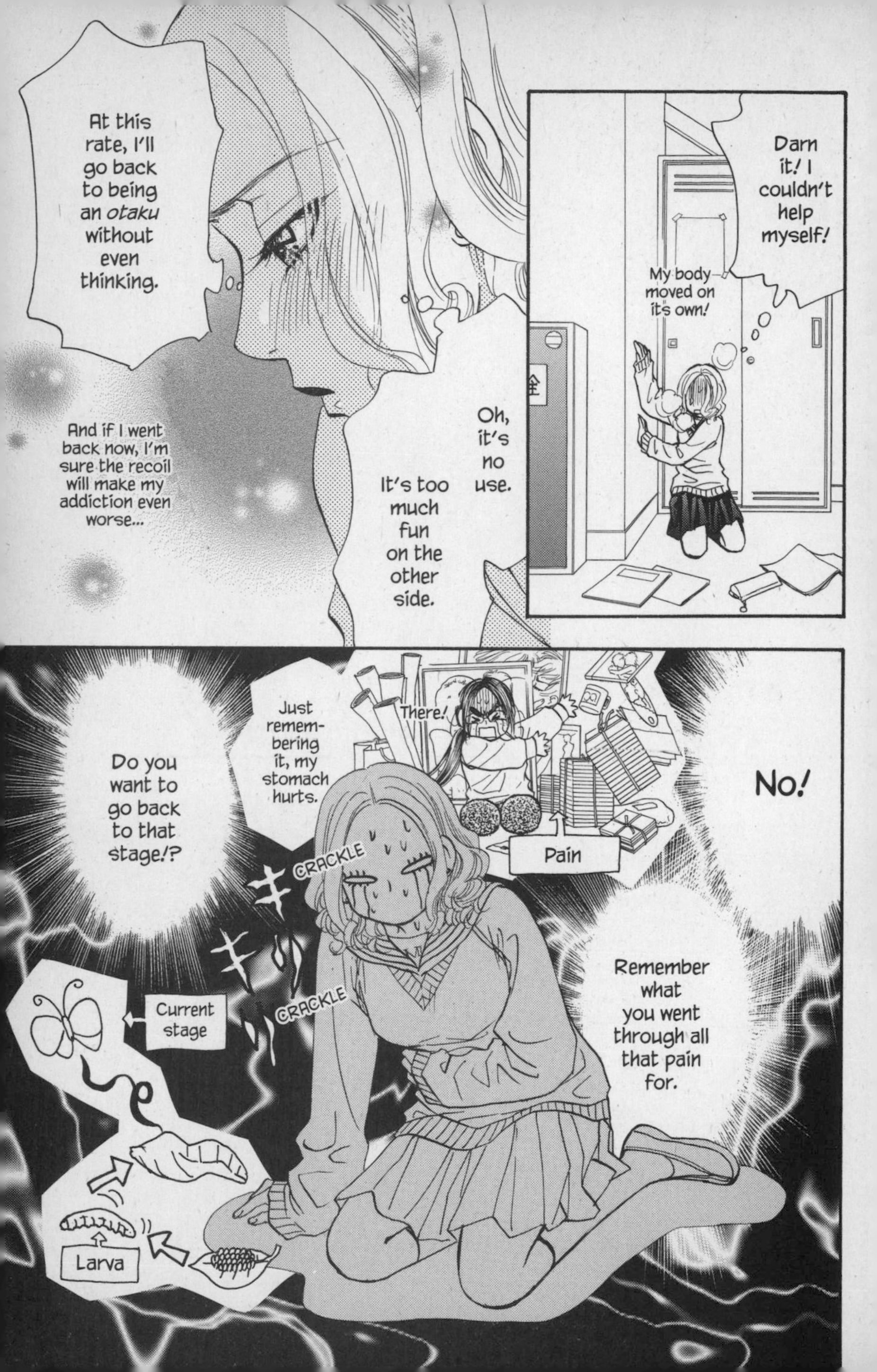
Darn it! I couldn't help myself!
My body moved on its own!
Oh, it's no use.
It's too much fun on the other side.
At this rate, I'll go back to being an *otaku* without even thinking.
And if I went back now, I'm sure the recoil will make my addiction even worse...
No!
Remember what you went through all that pain for.
There!
Pain
Just remembering it, my stomach hurts.
Do you want to go back to that stage!?
CRACKLE
CRACKLE
Current stage
Larva

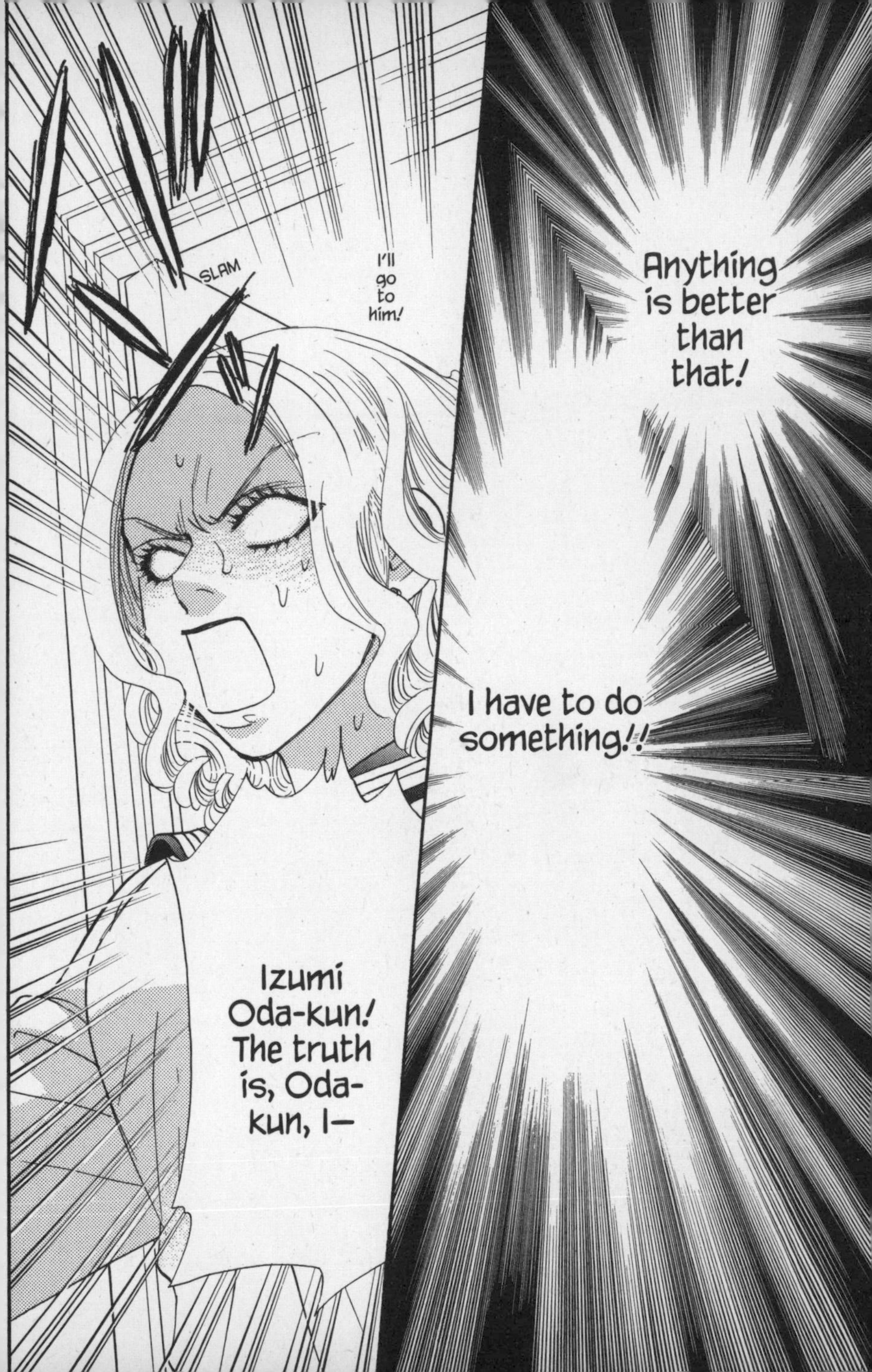
Anything is better than that!
I have to do something!!
I'll go to him!
SLAM
Izumi Oda-kun! The truth is, Oda-kun, I—

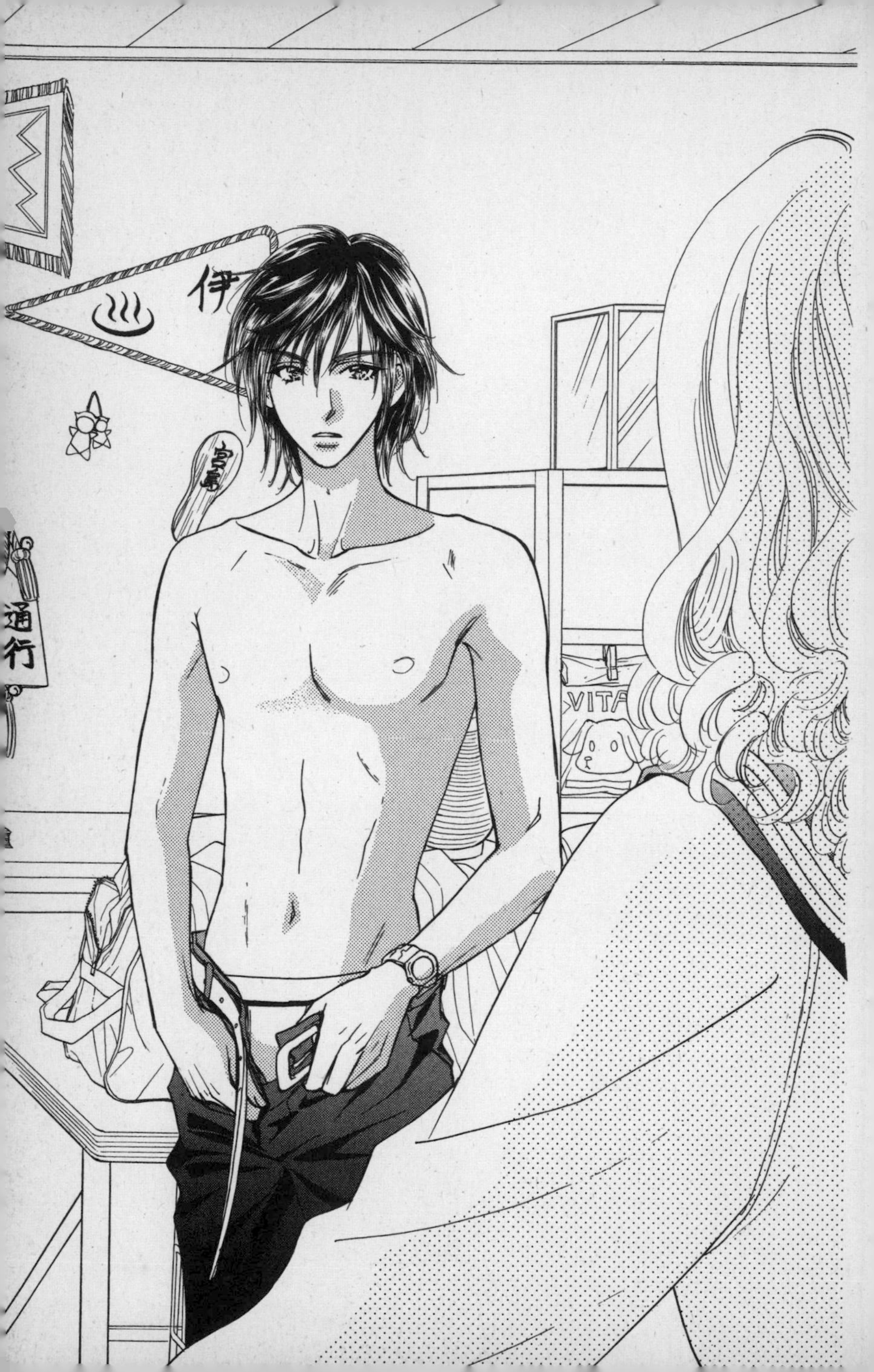
伊
通行
VITA

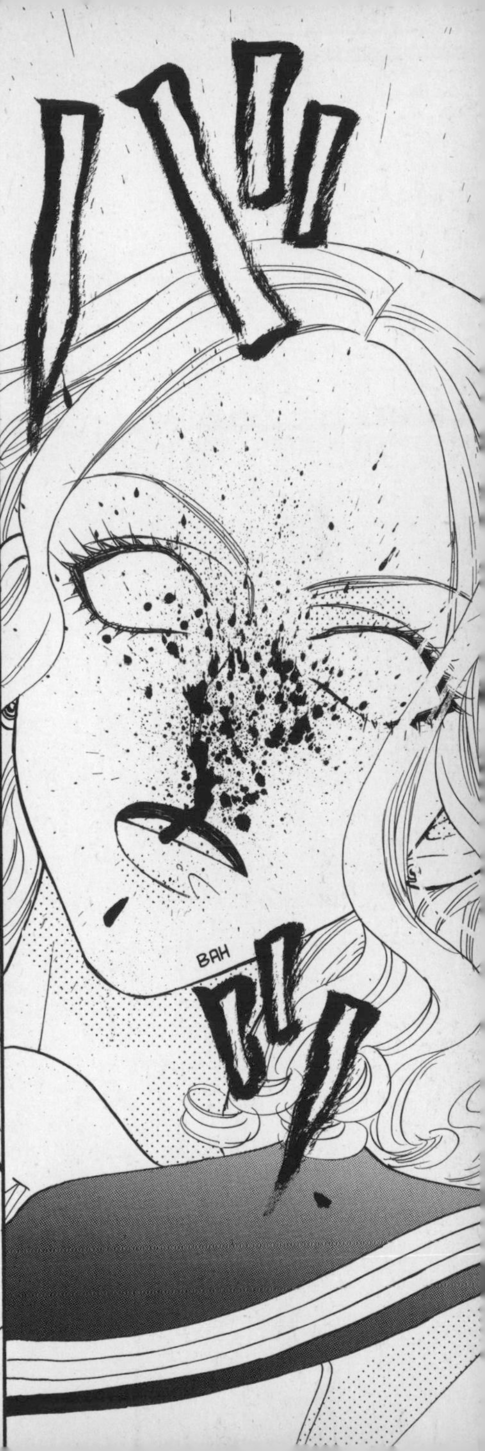
BAH
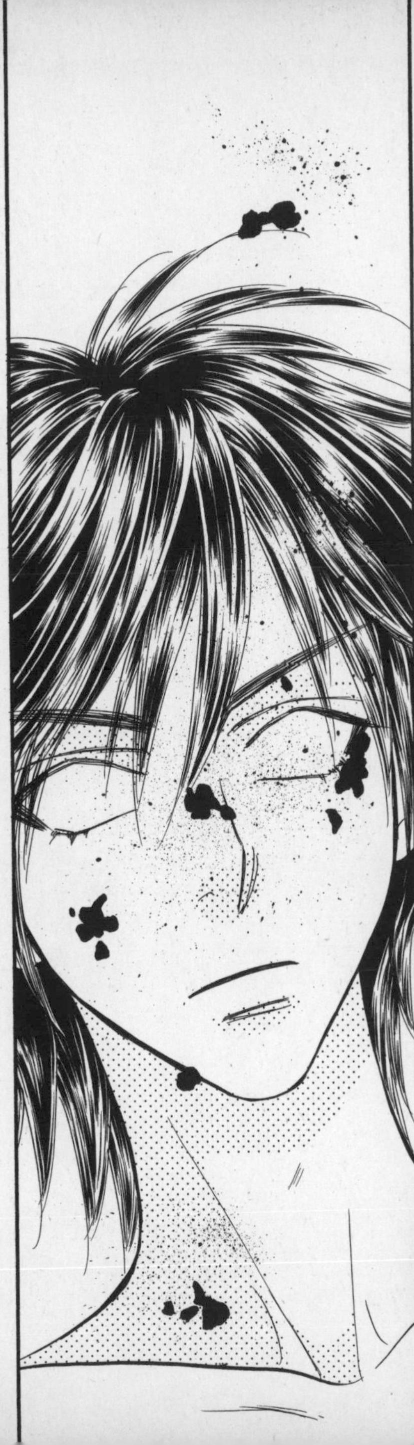

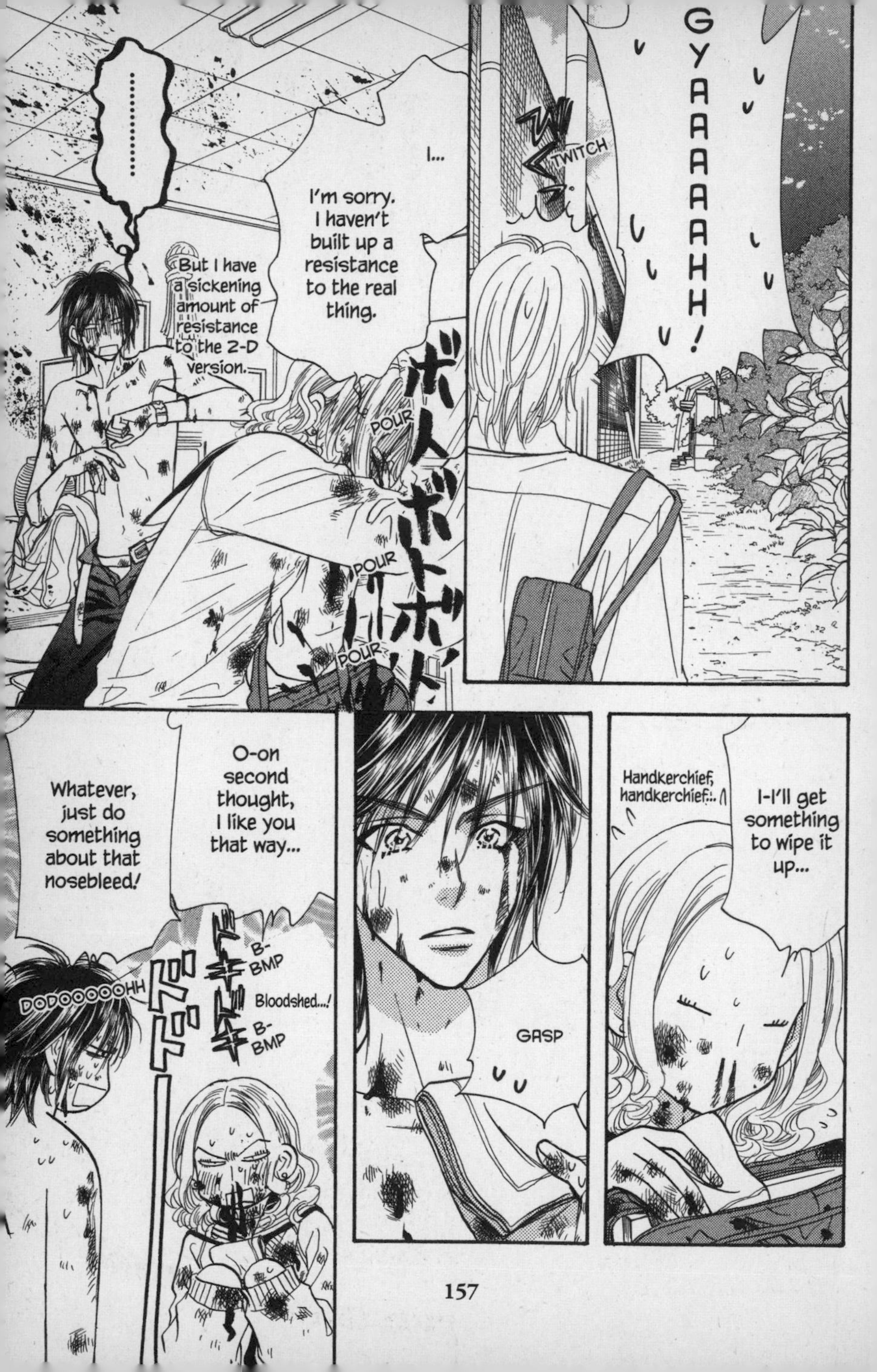
GYAAAAAAHH!
TWITCH
I...
I'm sorry. I haven't built up a resistance to the real thing.
....
But I have a sickening amount of resistance to the 2-D version.
ボ人ボトボトボト
POUR
POUR
POUR
I-I'll get something to wipe it up...
Handkerchief, handkerchief...
GASP
O-on second thought, I like you that way...
Whatever, just do something about that nosebleed!
ドキドキ
B-BMP
Bloodshed...!
B-BMP
ドドドド
DODOOOOOOHH

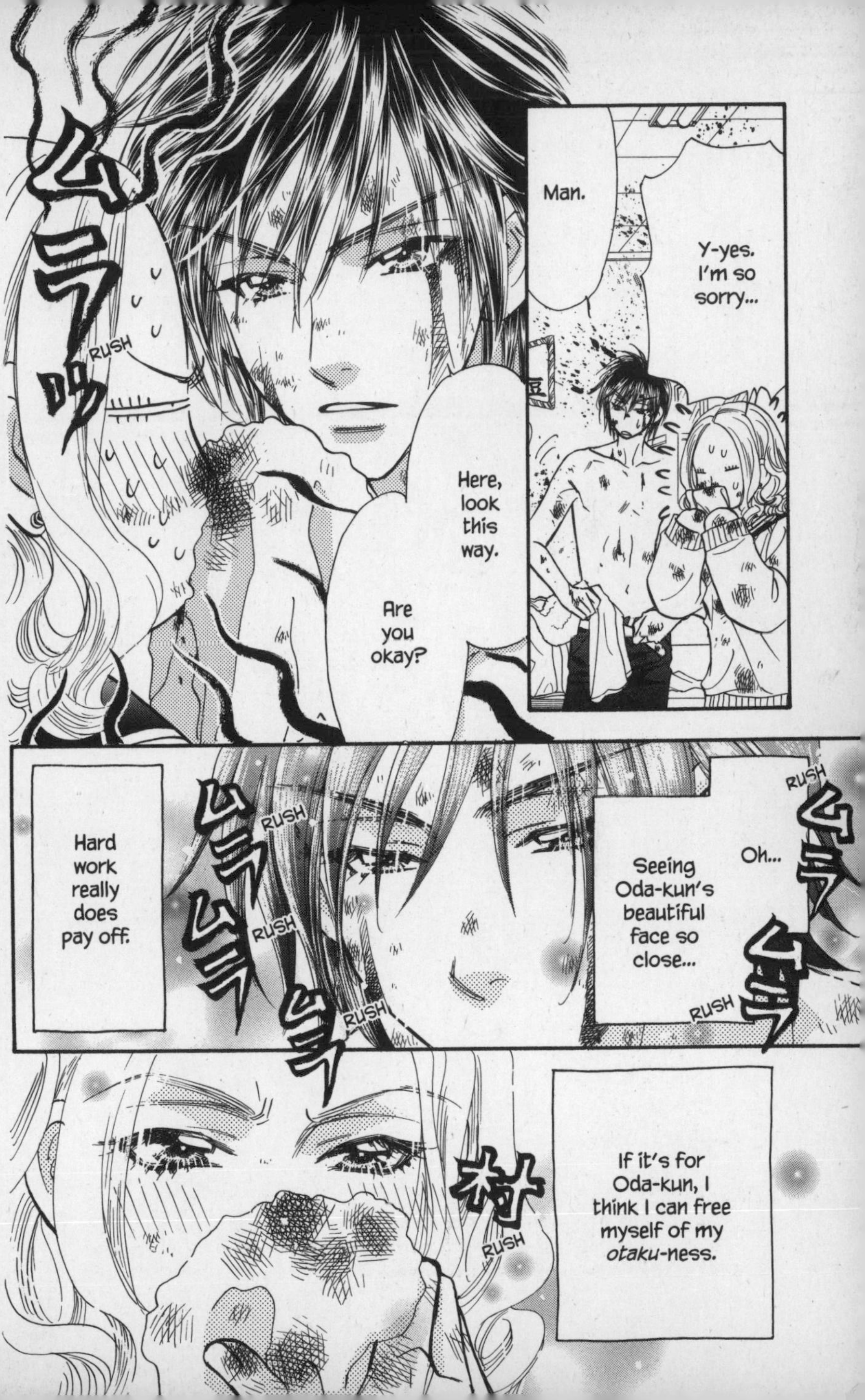

Man.
Y-yes. I'm so sorry...
Here, look this way.
Are you okay?
RUSH
RUSH
Oh...
Seeing Oda-kun's beautiful face so close...
RUSH
RUSH
RUSH
Hard work really does pay off.
If it's for Oda-kun, I think I can free myself of my *otaku*-ness.
RUSH

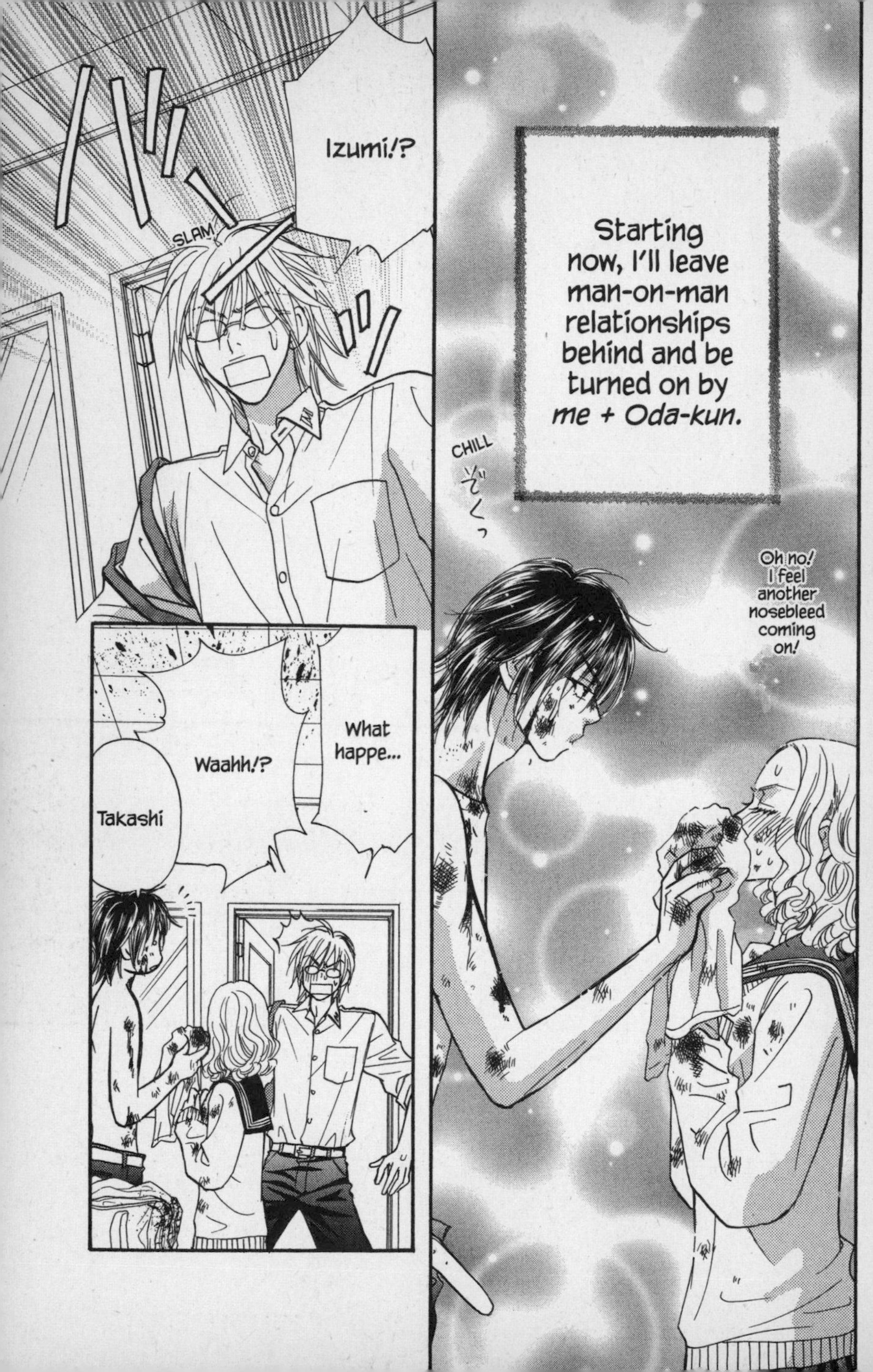
Starting now, I'll leave man-on-man relationships behind and be turned on by *me + Oda-kun.*
CHILL
ぞくっ
Oh no! I feel another nosebleed coming on!
SLAM
Izumi!?
What happe...
Waahh!?
Takashi

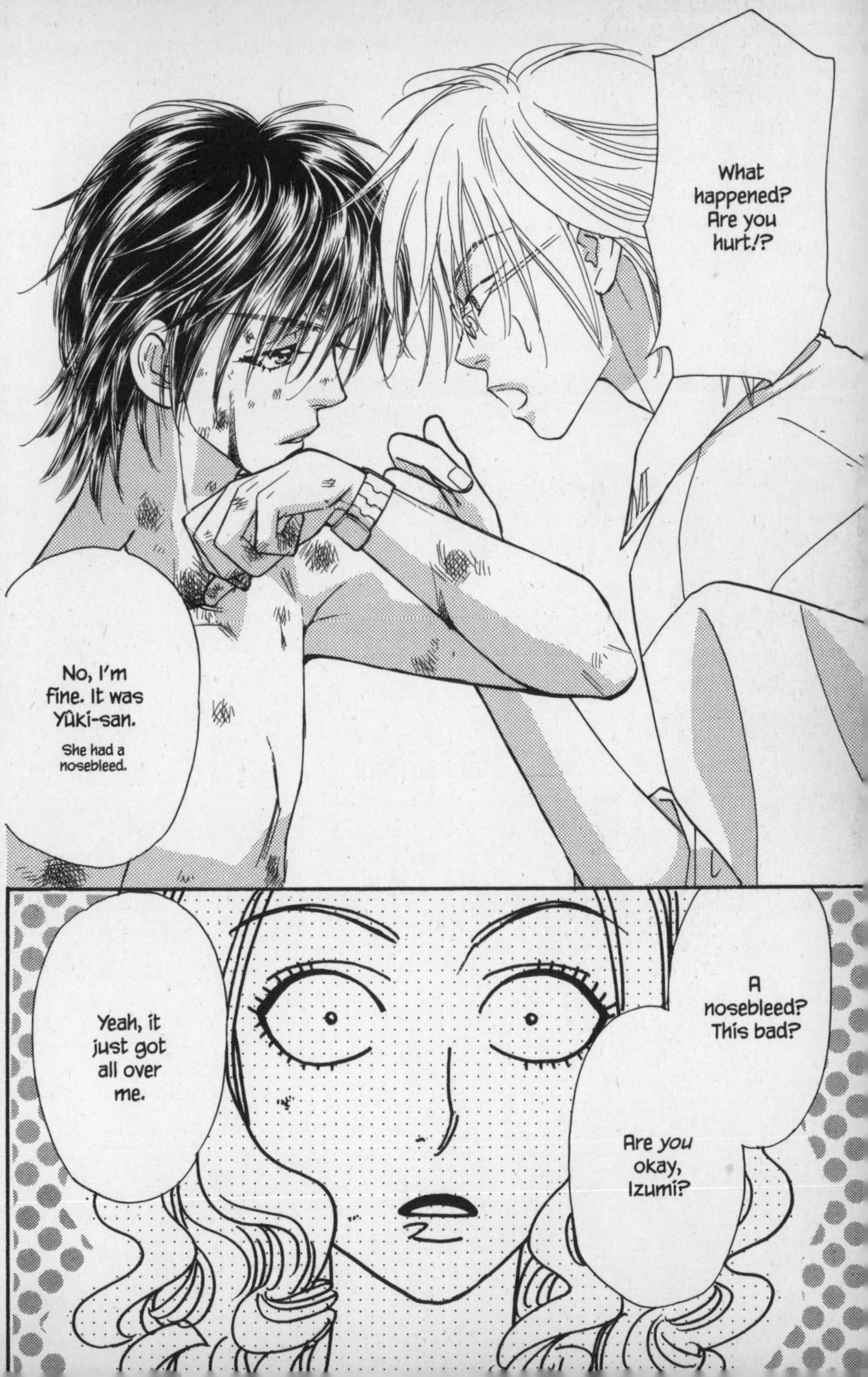
What happened? Are you hurt!?
No, I'm fine. It was Yûki-san.
She had a nosebleed.
A nosebleed? This bad?
Are *you* okay, Izumi?
Yeah, it just got all over me.

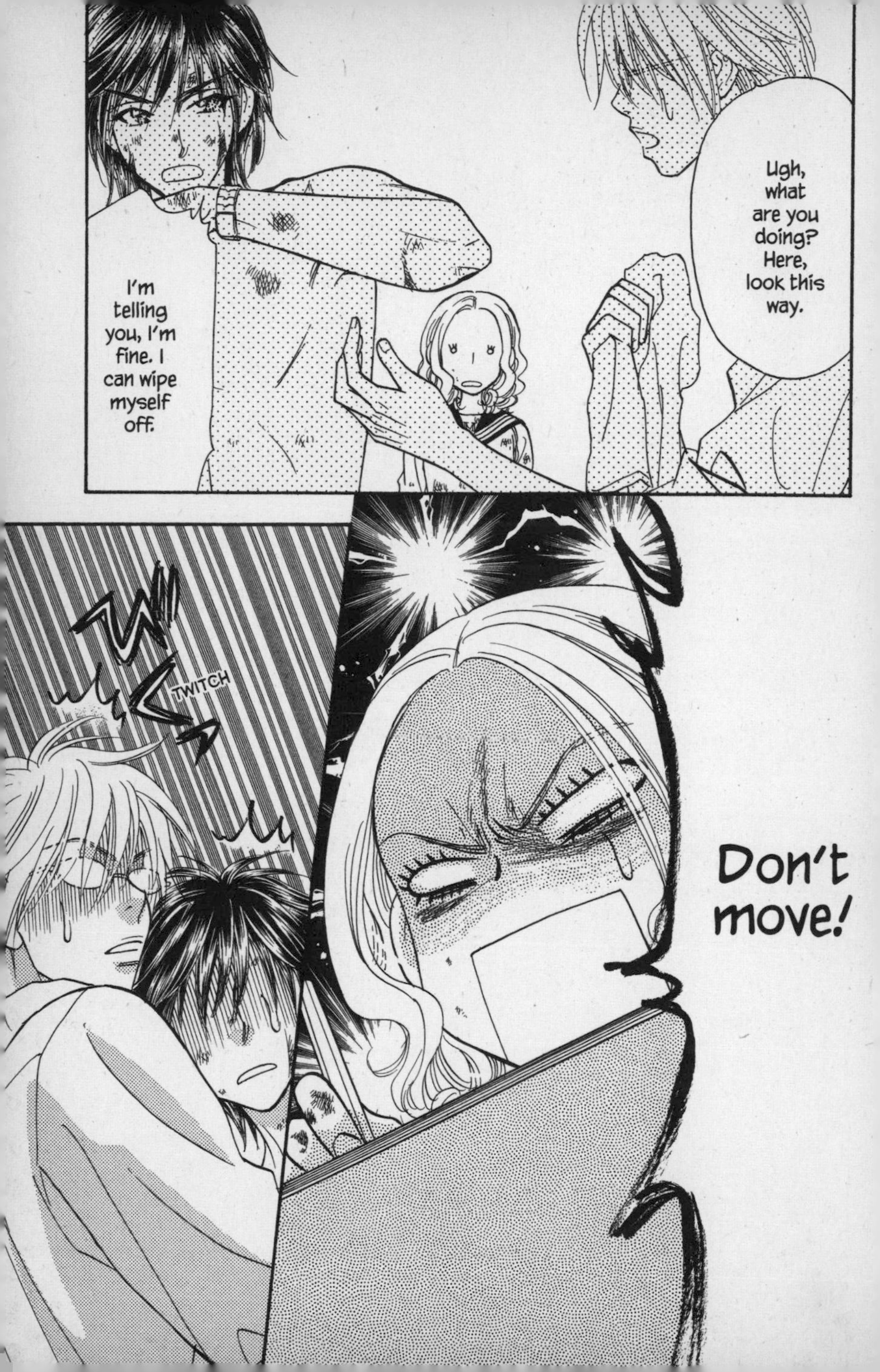
Ugh, what are you doing? Here, look this way.
I'm telling you, I'm fine. I can wipe myself off.
Don't move!
TWITCH

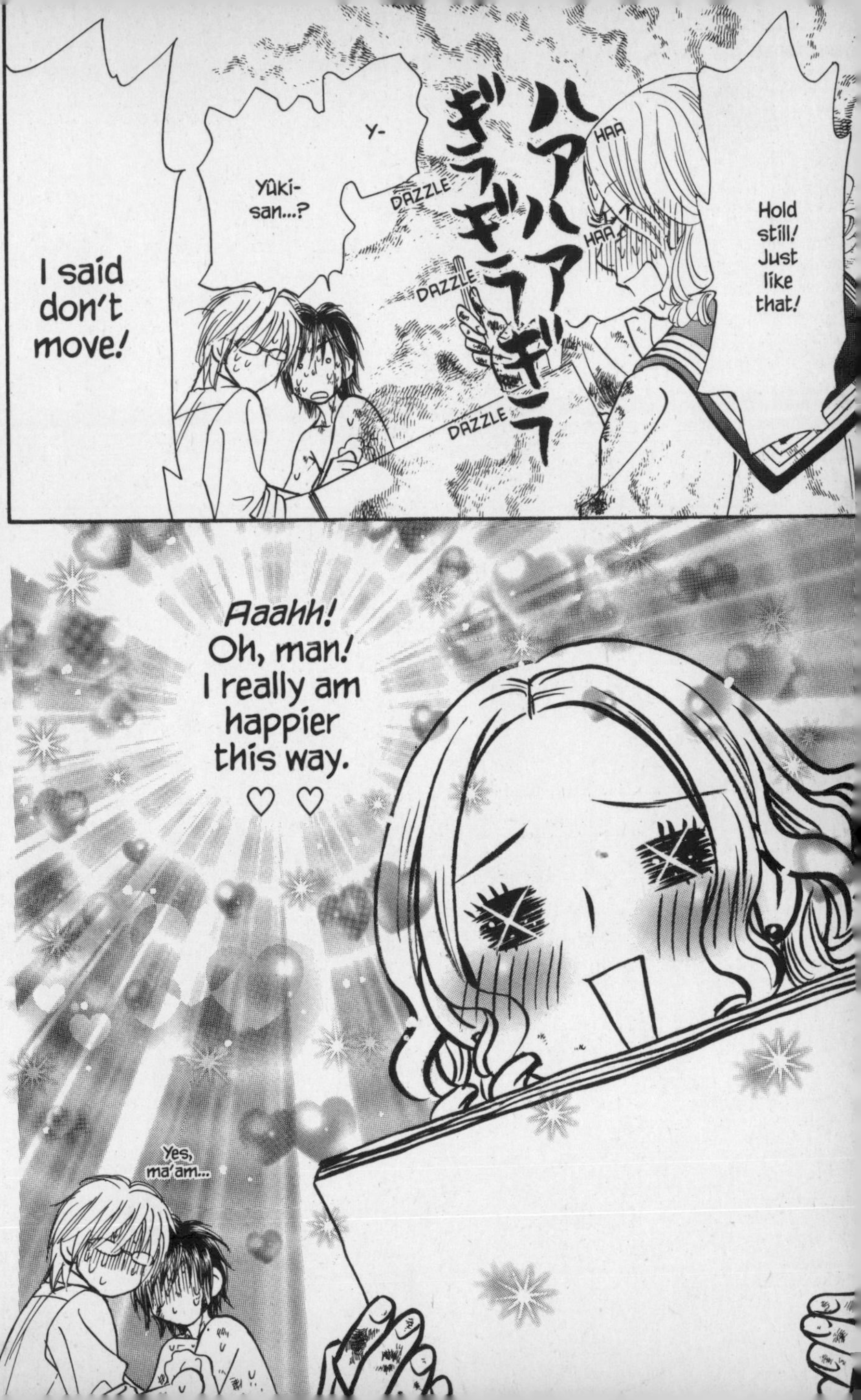
Hold still! Just like that!
ハアハア
HAA
HAA
ギラギラギラ
DAZZLE
DAZZLE
DAZZLE
Y-
Yûki-san...?
I said don't move!
Aaahh! Oh, man! I really am happier this way. ♡ ♡
Yes, ma'am...

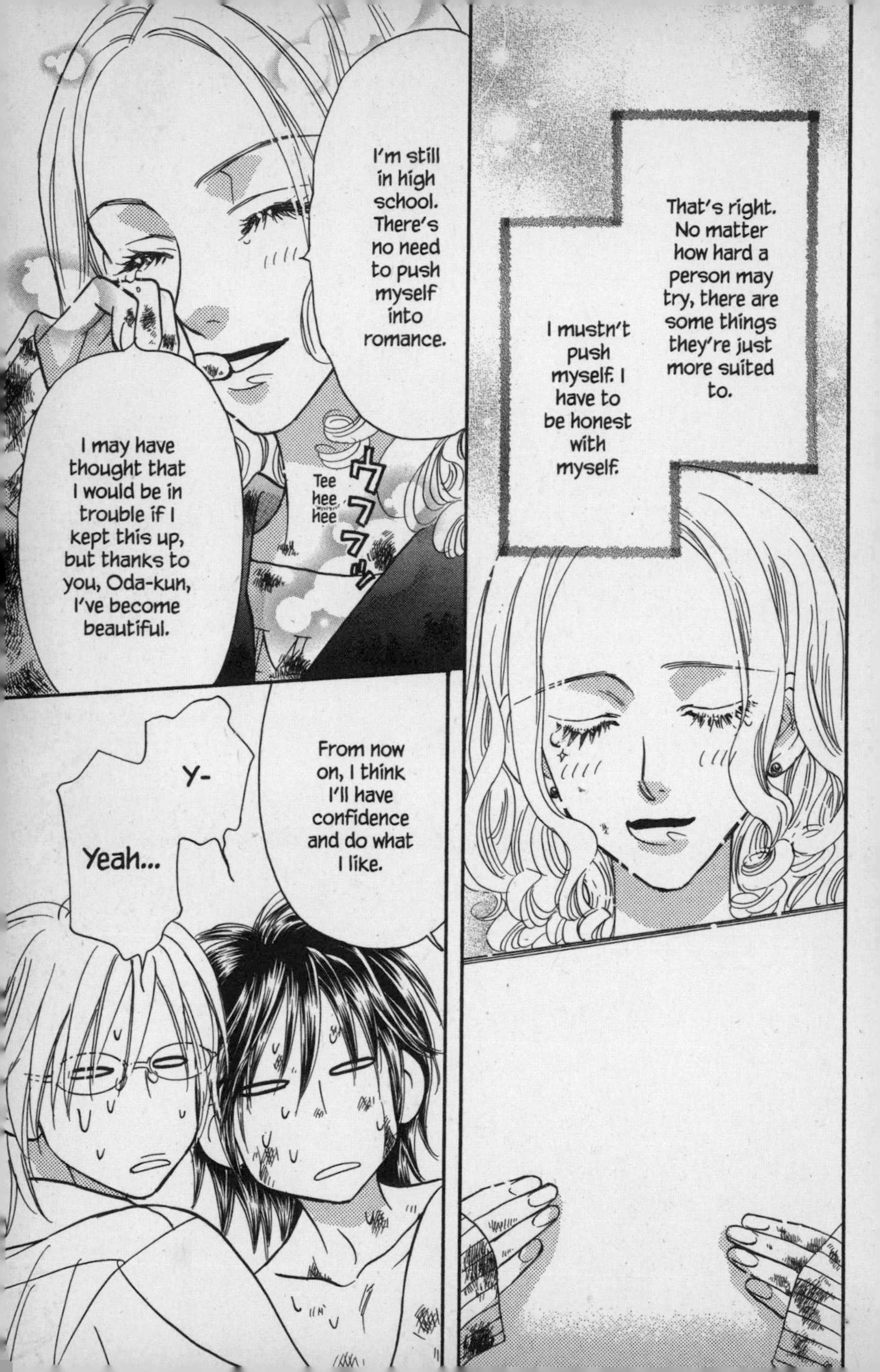
That's right. No matter how hard a person may try, there are some things they're just more suited to.
I mustn't push myself. I have to be honest with myself.
I'm still in high school. There's no need to push myself into romance.
Tee hee hee
I may have thought that I would be in trouble if I kept this up, but thanks to you, Oda-kun, I've become beautiful.
From now on, I think I'll have confidence and do what I like.
Y-
Yeah...

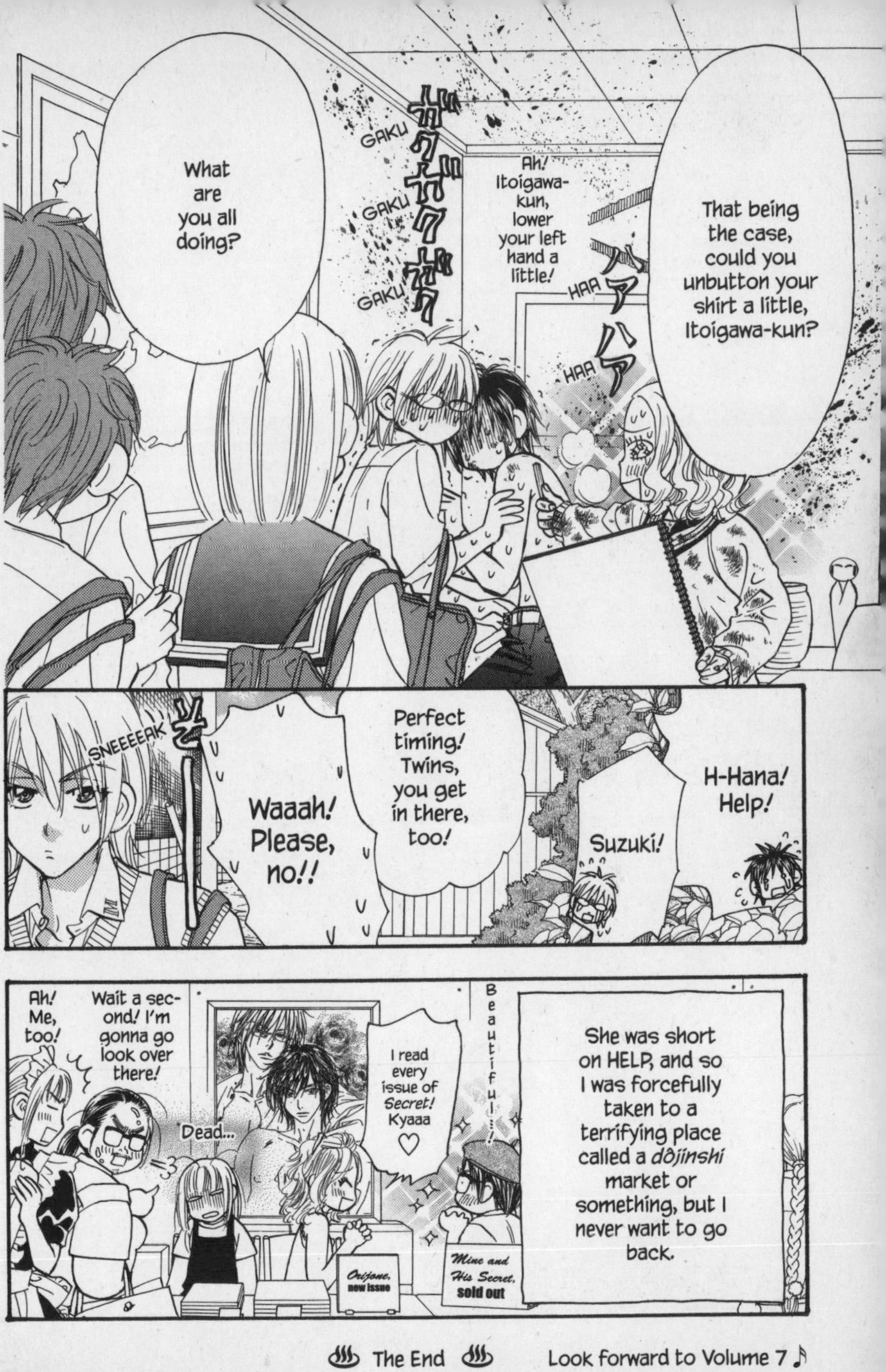
That being the case, could you unbutton your shirt a little, Itoigawa-kun?
HAA
HAA
Ah! Itoigawa-kun, lower your left hand a little!
GAKU
GAKU
GAKU
What are you all doing?
H-Hana! Help!
Suzuki!
Perfect timing! Twins, you get in there, too!
Waaah! Please, no!!
SNEEEEAK
She was short on HELP, and so I was forcefully taken to a terrifying place called a *dōjinshi* market or something, but I never want to go back.
Beautiful...!
Mine and His Secret. sold out
I read every issue of *Secret!* Kyaaa ♡
Orijone. new issue
Dead...
Wait a second! I'm gonna go look over there!
Ah! Me, too!

♨ The End ♨ Look forward to Volume 7 ♪

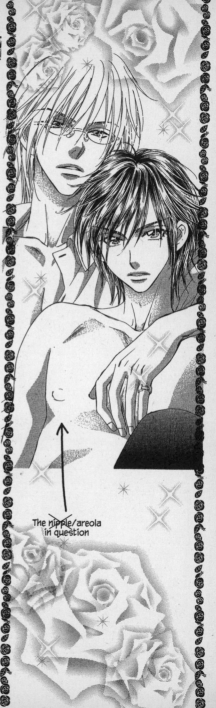

Afterword

Hello! We're already at volume 6, Madame. I get one page for an afterword, so this time, I would like to discuss something that happened at work. A discussion between my assistants, M-san and T-san, after seeing the cover page for chapter 24.

This

T: "Izumi-sempai's nipple is too big."

M: "Let me see. It really is huge. But isn't that the areola? Not the nipple."

T: "Oh, okay! Ah ha ha."

Me: "You're all so mean...!"

Poor me

~I ran off crying~

~Fin~

As expected, nipples are not that big. It's scary. This has been a very frightening story. After writing this far, I wonder about this afterword, but since I'm out of time, we'll say it's good enough.

The nipple/areola in question

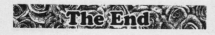

The End

Hockey Club ♨ Character Profile No.7

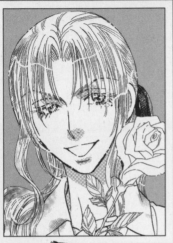

Full Name Yukio François de Saint-Martin

Nickname Mar-tan

Birthday	February 29
Blood type	AB
Height	181 cm (about 5'11")
Hobbies	Himself
Special skill	Beauty, being loved by all
Favorite food	Anything with eggs
Least favorite food	Sea cucumber
Favorite subjects	Anything involving Japanese language
Least favorite subjects	Anything involving any other language
Favorite type of girl	A girl who loves *me*
Other (notes)	Anyway, he loves himself

Everyone, look at me!!

♨ Famous Scene Selections ♨

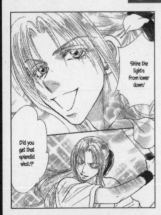

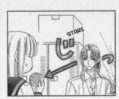

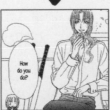

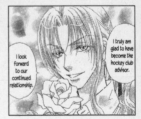

I truly am glad to have become the hockey club advisor.
I look forward to our continued relationship.

▲ This is the joyous occasion when he became the hockey club's advisor.♥

STARE
How do you do?

◀ "I am so beautiful that things with beautiful flavor are drawn to me."♥

Shine the lights from lower down!
Did you get that splendid shot!?

▲ "(Me playing) Hockey truly is magnificent......!!"

Hockey Club ♨ Character Profile No.8

Bakawk!!

Wacky

Birthday	Secret ♥ Born in autumn
Overall length	Just under 40 cm (about 16")
Weight	How rude–asking a woman a question like that!
Hobby	Takashi Itoigawa
Special skill	She's a chicken, but she can coil her poo.
Favorite food	Anything Takashi Itoigawa feeds her
Least favorite food	*Nattô*
Favorite type of guy	Tall, cool, wimpy types with glasses
Charm point	Eyelashes
Things that had been bothering her lately	Izumi Oda and dogs are eyesores
Other (notes)	Takashi Itoigawa is her life

♨ Famous Scene Selections ♨

▼ The origin of Wacky's name. But Izumi was the one who raised her as an egg...

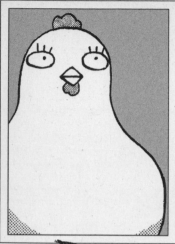

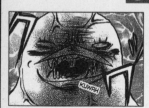

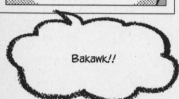

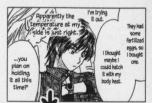

They had some fertilized eggs, so I bought one.
I thought maybe I could hatch it with my body heat.
I'm trying it out.
Apparently the temperature at my side is just right.
...you plan on holding it all this time?

Cheep
Ah.

▲ The first person Wacky saw was Takashi!! It was a fateful encounter!!

KUWAH

◀ "I won't forgive anyone who takes Takashi from me!!"

BURI BURI BOOÓOO
Oh!

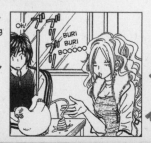

▶ "Finishing move!! Winding poo attack!!"

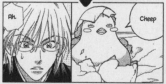

Translation Notes

Japanese is a tricky language for most Westerners, and translation is often more art than science. For your edification and reading pleasure, here are notes on some of the places where we could have gone in a different direction with our translation of the work, or where a Japanese cultural reference is used.

Kintoki, page 5
Kintoki is a kind of red bean. In this case, it's been made into a jam and put into a roll with cream.

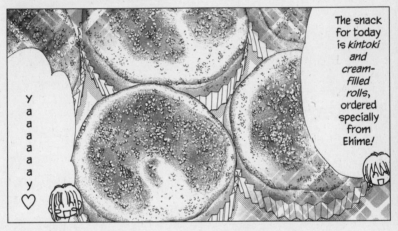

Y
a
a
a
a
a
a
a
y
♡

The snack for today is *kintoki* and cream-filled rolls, ordered specially from Ehime!

Anko, page 5
Anko is the general term for red bean paste or jam.

Maru-chan, Mar-tan, page 13
Because Martin is originally French, his name is pronounced more like "Martan." In Japanese, "-tan" is kind of a cutesy way of saying "-chan," so it's no wonder Hana would hear it and think of the instant ramen brand Maru-chan. Fanboys in reference to their favorite female characters also use "-tan," hence Martin's later comment.

Classical Japanese, page 13

Classical Japanese literature is all written in Japanese so old that it's almost like a completely different language. Martin's familiarity with this language is a rare attainment—one that shows just how committed a Japanophile this Frenchman is.

Yukio Mishima, page 16

Yukio Mishima is a famous Japanese author from the '50s and '60s, known for such works as *Haru no Yuki* (*Spring Snow*). He committed ritual suicide in 1970.

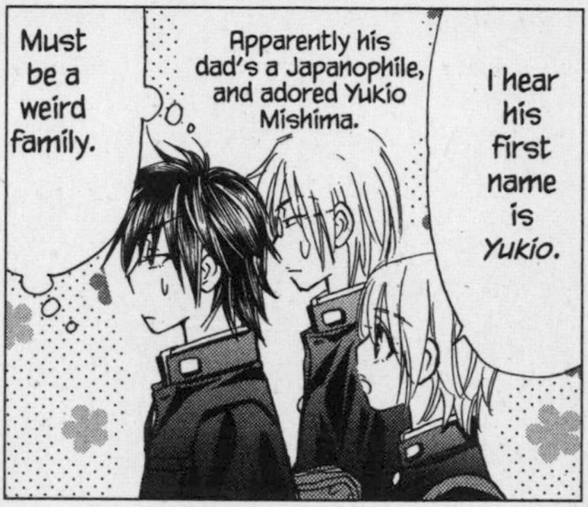
I hear his first name is *Yukio*.
Apparently his dad's a Japanophile, and adored Yukio Mishima.
Must be a weird family.

Kinpachi-sensei, page 41

Kinpachi-sensei is the main character of the Japanese soap opera of the same name. Despite having many of his own serious problems, he is constantly helping his students with their social and psychological problems, which are often quite extreme.

Spiritualism, page 43

Spiritualism refers to a religious movement that asserts that spirits can be contacted through a medium.

Oni underpants, page 49

Much like we have "On Top of Spaghetti" and "Found a Peanut," the Japanese have altered the lyrics to the familiar song "Funiculì Funiculà" to make it a song about wearing *oni* underpants. An *oni* is a Japanese demon known for its horns and tiger stripes, so *oni* underpants have a tiger-stripe pattern.

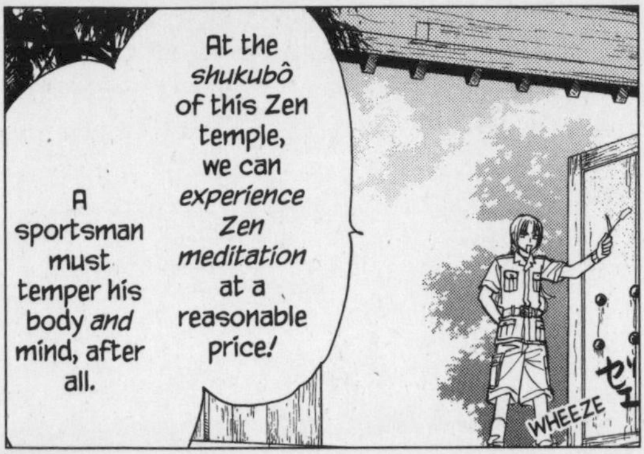
At the *shukubô* of this Zen temple, we can *experience* Zen *meditation* at a reasonable price!
A sportsman must temper his body *and* mind, after all.
WHEEZE

Zen meditation experience, page 50

It isn't uncommon in Japan for organizations to take their members to a Zen temple to meditate, thus improving their concentration and performance.

Shôjin ryôri, page 54

Japanese for "purification cooking," this is a style of vegetarian cuisine eaten by priests and other devout Buddhists.

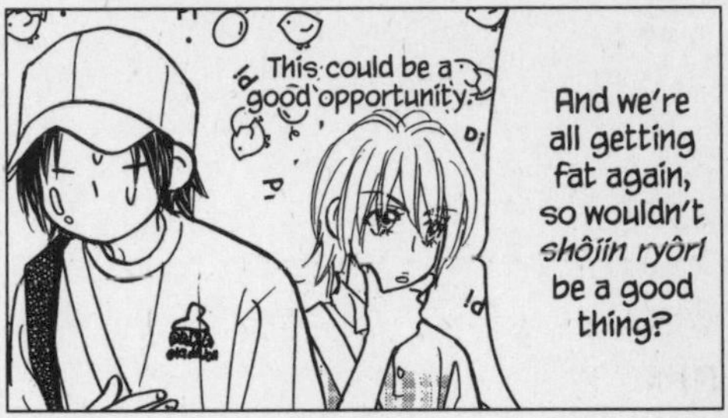
And we're all getting fat again, so wouldn't *shôjin ryôri* be a good thing?
This could be a good opportunity.

Ume, page 57

The Japanese sometimes use a three-tier ranking system of *shouchikubai* (pine bamboo plum), where the ranks are *matsu* (pine), *take* (bamboo), and *ume* (plum). *Ume* indicates the lowest rank, or in this case, a small-sized meal. *Take* and *matsu* would be medium and large, respectively.

WHAP, page 57

When doing Zen meditation at a retreat, there is usually a priest overseeing your meditation who will hit you when you are not meditating properly so that you will learn to improve your focus.

Jîya, page 58

A *jîya* is an elderly servant, kind of like a nanny, but male.

Shuriken, page 62

Also known as ninja throwing stars.

Isn't made for being a ninja, page 62

Ninja, in Japanese, literally means "person with stealth," and a good ninja would be able to stay invisible at all times. Martin calls attention to himself in everything he does, and so would not make a very good ninja.

Call 119, page 64

119 is the Japanese equivalent of 911.

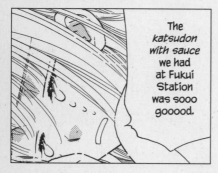

The *katsudon* with sauce we had at Fukui Station was sooo gooood.

Katsudon, page 66

Breaded pork on rice.

Wakasa beef, page 66

Wakasa is a town in Fukui Prefecture, where the club is staying, and one of several places in the Kansai area where the beef is especially good because of the fresh water there for the cattle to drink.

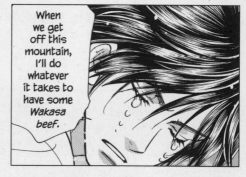

When we get off this mountain, I'll do whatever it takes to have some *Wakasa beef.*

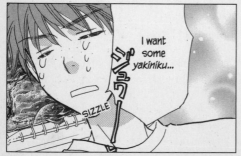

I want some yakiniku...

SIZZLE

Yakiniku, page 66

A Japanese dish of fried meat.

Butamin, page 68

Butamin is a combination of "*buta* (pig)" and "vitamin." Martin is referring to the vitamins one gets from pork.

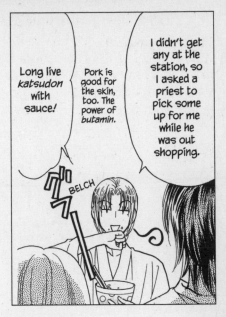

I didn't get any at the station, so I asked a priest to pick some up for me while he was out shopping.
Pork is good for the skin, too. The power of *butamin*.
Long live *katsudon* with sauce!
BELCH

Bara Shuriken Attack, page 76

Rose Throwing Star Attack.

Shinkansen, page 82

The *shinkansen* is the bullet train.

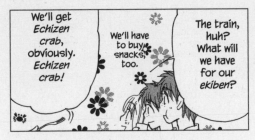

The train, huh? What will we have for our *ekiben*?
We'll have to buy snacks, too.
We'll get *Echizen* crab, obviously. *Echizen* crab!

Ekiben, page 82

Ekiben comes from *eki* (train station) and *bentô* (or *obentô*—boxed lunch). In other words, it's a lunch that you buy at the station.

Echizen crab, page 82

Echizen is another place in Fukui, known for its seafood, especially crab.

Tarezô, page 84

Tareru means "to hang" or "dangle," and *zô* is a suffix to make it a name. This may be a reference to the egg that Wacky started to lay, so it was sort of dangling.

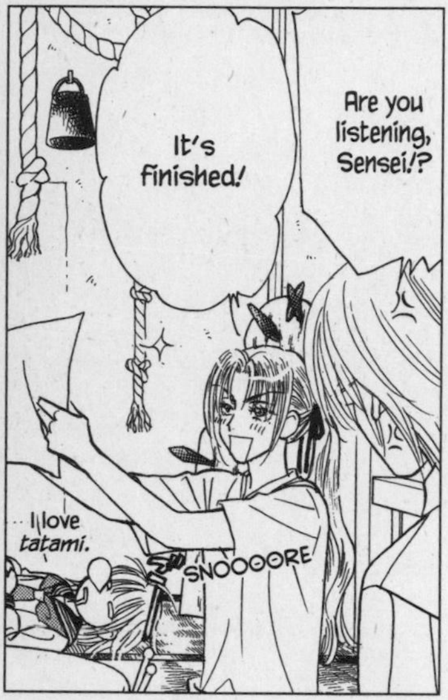
Are you listening, Sensei!?
It's finished!
...I love tatami.
SNOOOORE

Tatami, page 87

A straw floor covering used for Japanese-style rooms. Because ninja are from Japan, it's only natural that they would have a Japanese-style room.

Kokkuri-san, page 87

Kokkuri-san is the Japanese name for Ouija board. Because in Japanese tradition foxes, or *kitsune*, are thought to have supernatural powers, it is believed that the marker, often a coin, is moved not by a spirit of the dead, but by a spirit of a fox, called Kokkuri-san. In most legends, foxes are female. The board the hockey club is using uses Japanese characters instead of the alphabet.

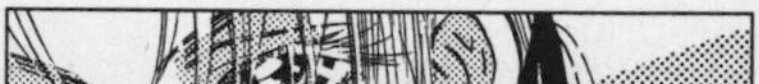
Gentlemen, the club activity for today is *Kokkuri-san!*
Yes
4 5 6 7 8
Ma Ha Na Ta Sa
Mi Hi Ni Chi Shi
Nu Tsu Su

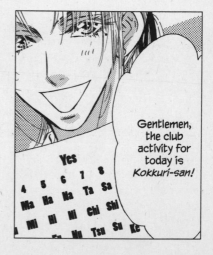

Johnny Depp, page 90
The way Japanese writing works, "Johnny Depp" would be written "Shi Yo Ni Te Tsu Fu." The Shi and Te would have marks looking like quotation marks to alter the sounds, making them Ji and De, and the Fu would have a mark like a degree symbol to make it Pu. The Yo is made smaller to make the Ji a Jyo, and the Tsu would be smaller to emphasize the first sound of Pu, so it ends up like Jyoni Deppu. The Kokkuri-san board doesn't have smaller characters, quotation marks, or degree symbols.

***Aho*, page 92**
Aho is one of many ways to call someone an idiot in Japanese.

***Maccha dorayaki*, page 95**
Dorayaki is a Japanese pastry made of two sponge cakes with a filling between them, kind of like a jelly donut. *Maccha* is green tea and refers to the flavor of the filling.

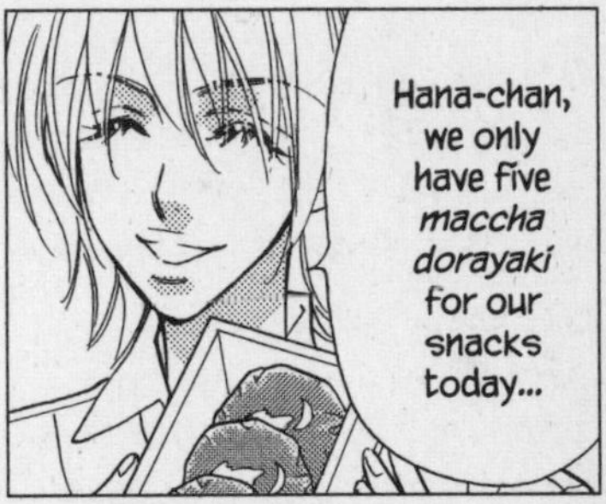
Hana-chan, we only have five *maccha dorayaki* for our snacks today...

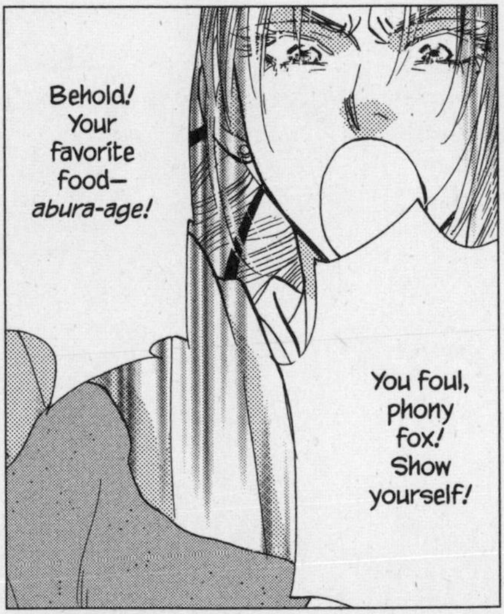
You foul, phony fox! Show yourself!
Behold! Your favorite food—*abura-age!*

***Abura-age*, page 97**
Abura-age is fried tofu. According to legend, as Martin says, it is a favorite food of foxes.

Inarizushi, page 106

Sushi rice in a pouch of fried tofu. It is named after the deity Inari, who is represented as a fox.

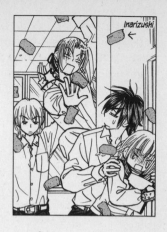

Inarizushi

Shown your tail, page 117

Because foxes and the like were thought to disguise themselves as humans, the phrase "to show one's tail" has come to refer to when someone shows their true colors.

Seimei, page 118

Abe no Seimei is a famous Onmyôji, or Yin-Yang Master. Onmyôji were in charge of protecting the capital from evil spirits. It's no wonder Martin would want to name his dog after him.

Kinds of *inari*, page 123

Gomoku inari is *inarizushi* with *gomoku* rice, or rice mixed with vegetables. *Takowasa inari* is *inarizushi* with *tako* (octopus) and wasabi. *Rebanira* means "liver-leek," so *rebanira inari* would be *inarizushi* with liver and leeks.

Bishônen, page 130

Pretty boy.

Dôjinshi, page 132

A magazine published by fans, often fan-fiction manga.

***Otaku*, page 134**
Japanese for "geek" or "nerd", especially one who is obsessed with something.

***Shishô*, page 140**
A master or teacher.

My name is not helping, page 141
Moé is a phrase used by fanboys and fangirls to describe the type of character from an anime or video game that they have a particular attraction to, and the strong feelings that those characters inspire.

***Omamori*, page 145**
Omamori comes from *mamoru* (to protect) and refers to a protective charm.

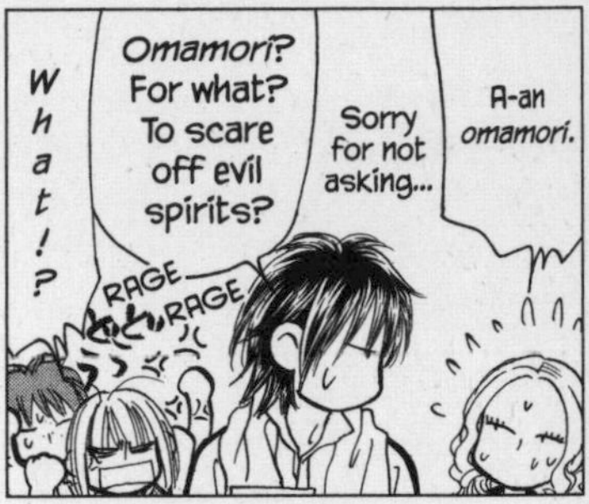
A-an *omamori.*
Sorry for not asking...
Omamori? For what? To scare off evil spirits?
What!?
RAGE RAGE

***Nattô*, page 167**
Fermented soybeans.

Wacky's name, page 167
In this scene, Izumi tells Takashi that he will keep the egg containing Wacky by his side, or in Japanese, by his *waki*, and that's where Hana got the idea to call the egg Wacky.

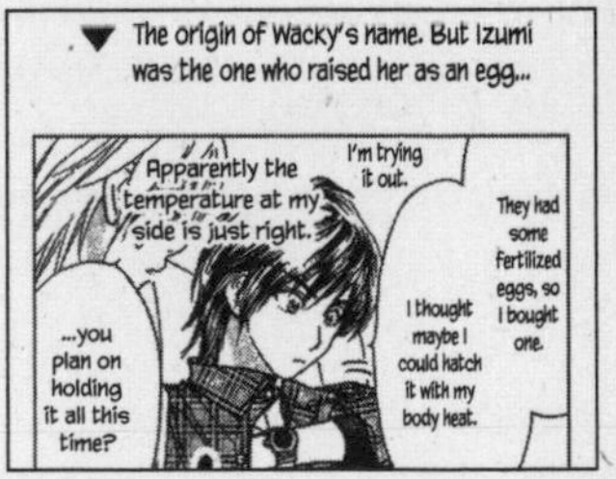
▼ The origin of Wacky's name. But Izumi was the one who raised her as an egg...
They had some fertilized eggs, so I bought one.
I'm trying it out.
I thought maybe I could hatch it with my body heat.
Apparently the temperature at my side is just right.
...you plan on holding it all this time?

Preview of Volume 7

We're pleased to present you a preview from volume 7. Please check our website (www.delreymanga.com) to see when this volume will be available in English. For now you'll have to make do with Japanese!

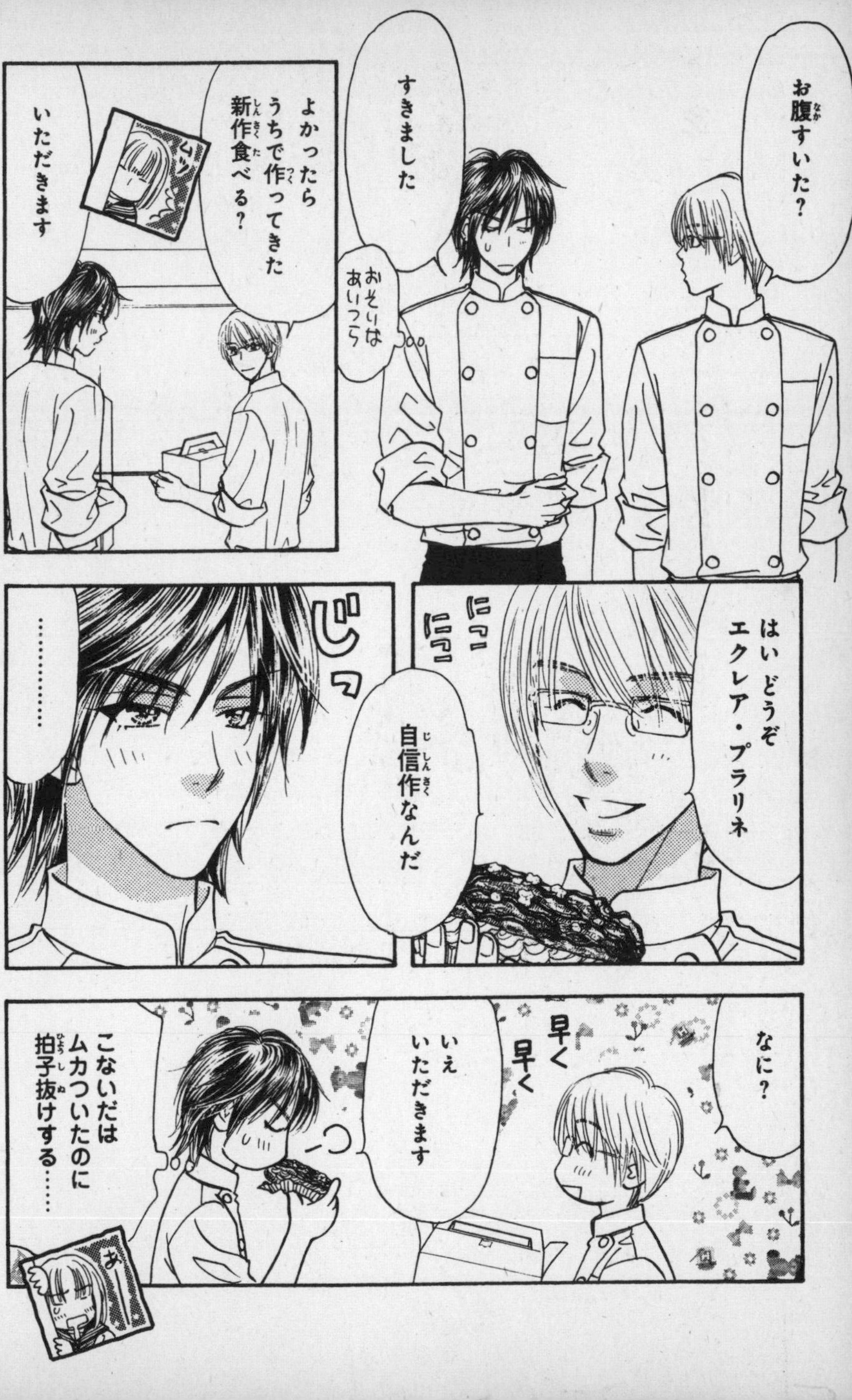
お腹すいた？
すきました
おそりは ありつら
よかったら うちで作ってきた 新作食べる？
ムッ
いただきます
はい どうぞ エクレア・プラリネ
にっこ にっこ
自信作なんだ
じっ
………
なに？
早く 早く
いえ いただきます
こないだは ムカついたのに 拍子抜けする……
あー

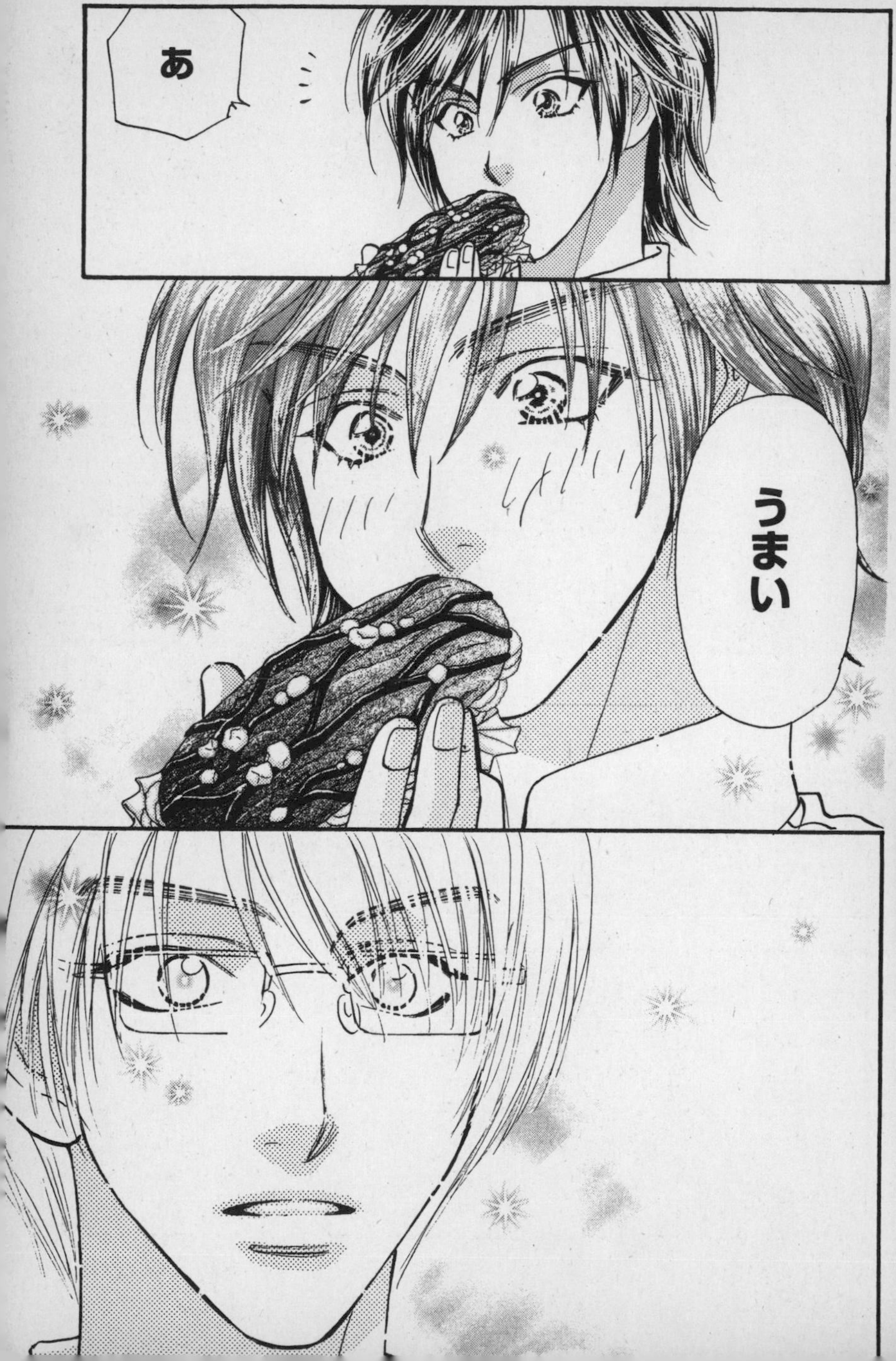
あ
うまい

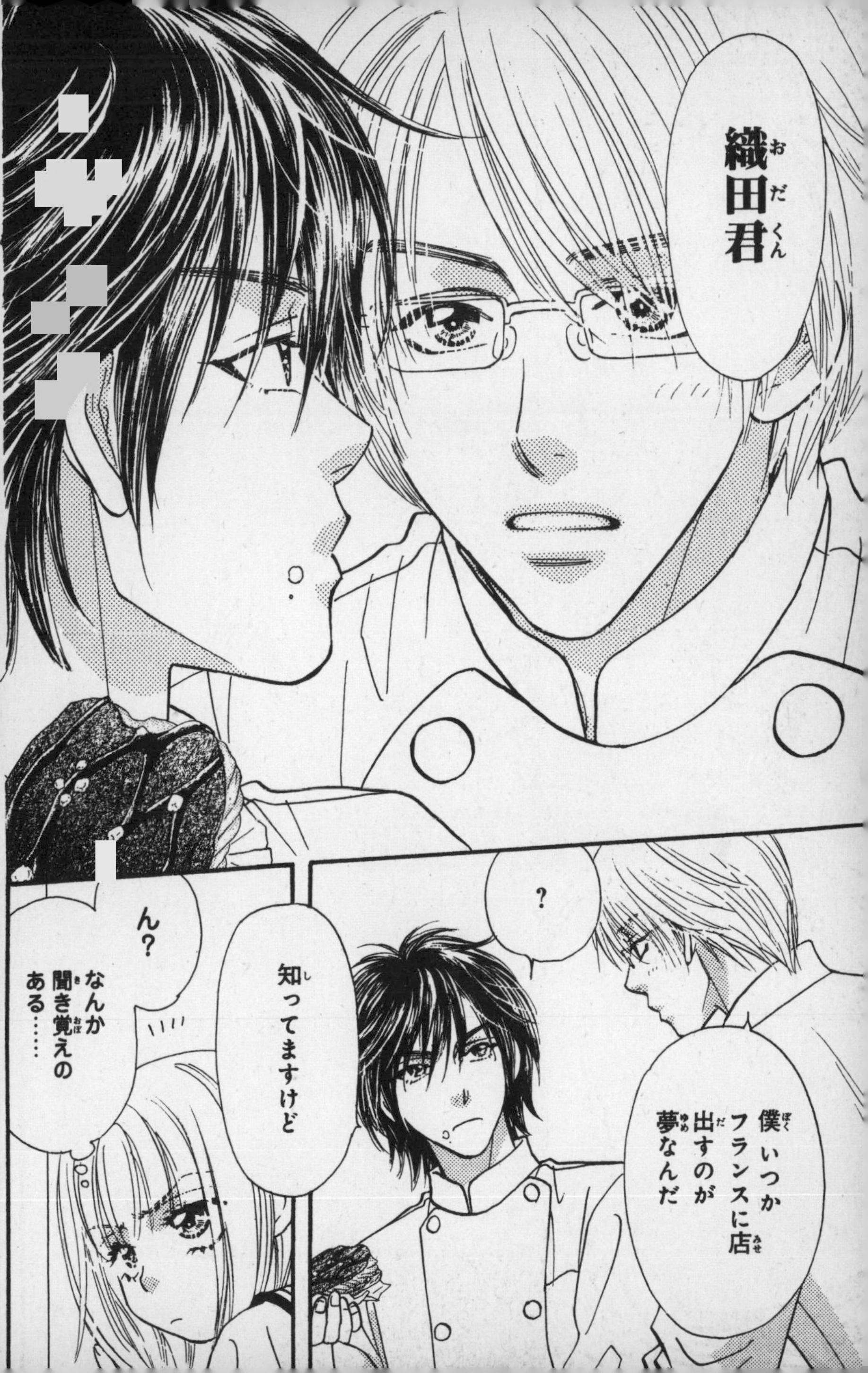
織田君
僕いつかフランスに店出すのが夢なんだ
?
知ってますけど
ん?
なんか聞き覚えのある……

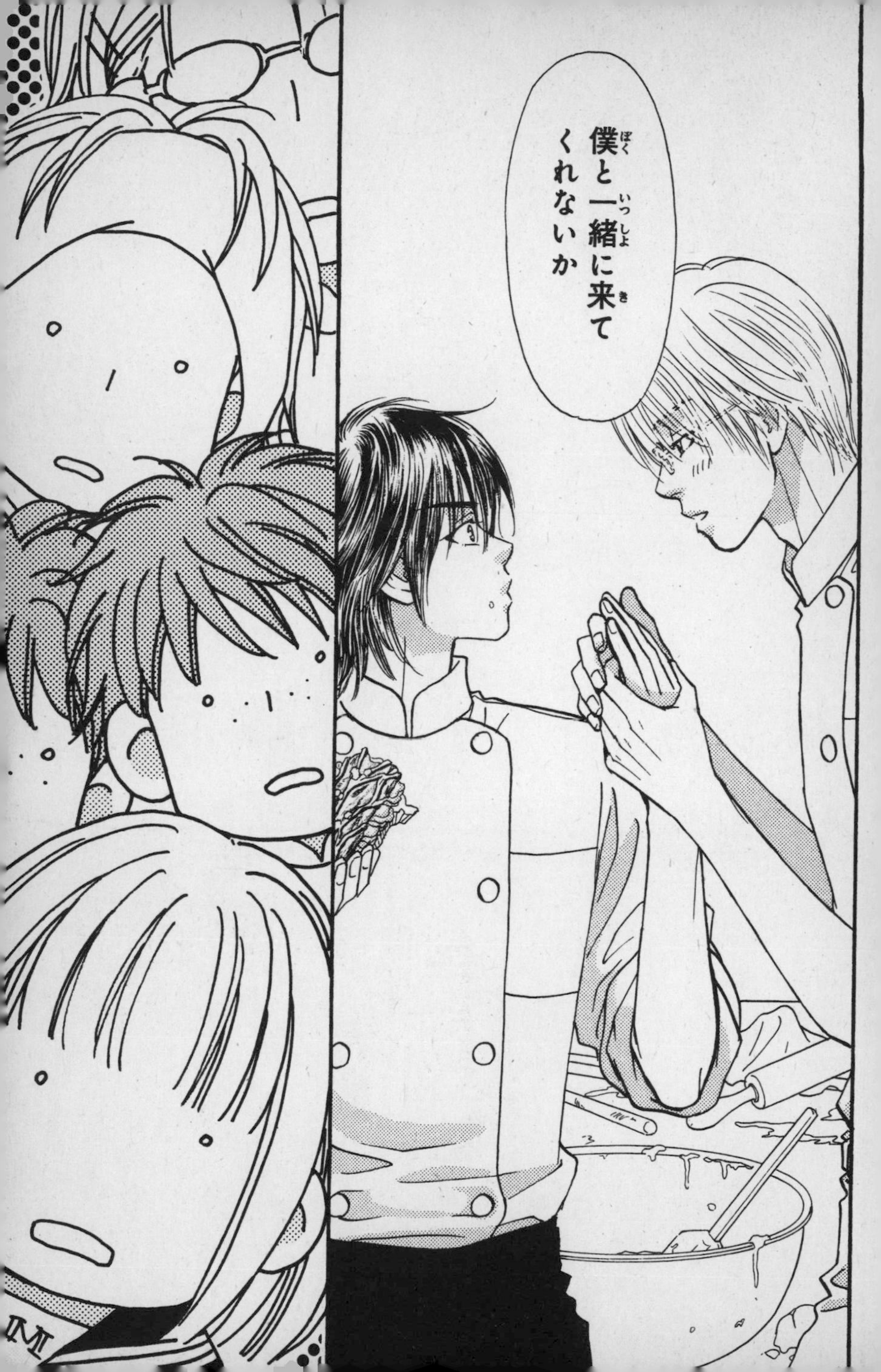
僕と一緒に来てくれないか

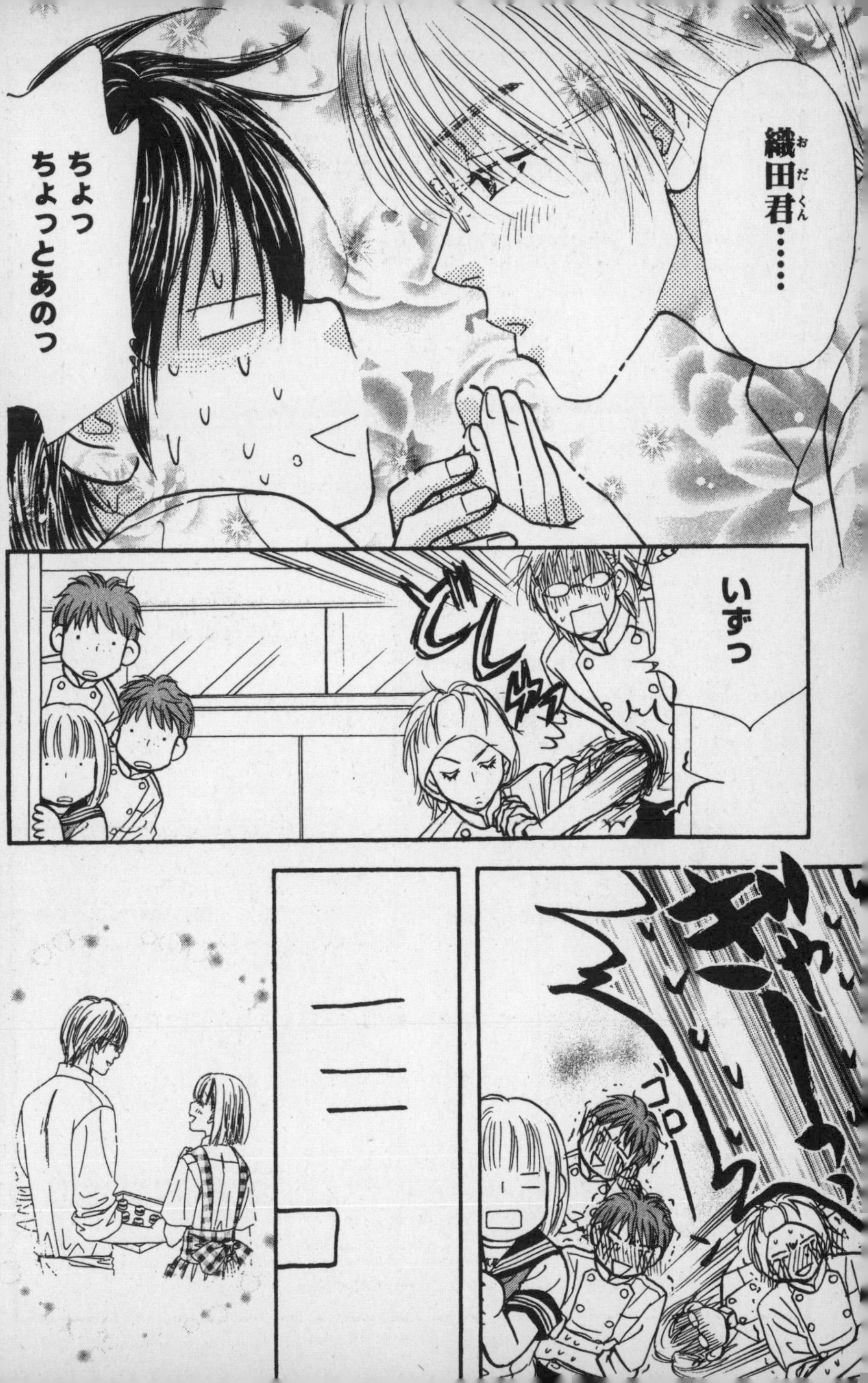
織田君……
ちょっ
ちょっとあのっ
いずっ
ぎゃーっ
ゴロー

Kamichama Karin Chu

BY KOGE-DONBO

A GODDESS IN LOVE!

Karin is your lovable girl next
door—if the girl next door
also happens to be a goddess!
Karin has a magic ring that gives
her the power to do anything
she'd like. Though what she'd
like most is to live happily ever
after with Kazune, the boy of her
dreams. Magic brought Kazune to
her, but it also has a way of
complicating things. It's not easy
to be a goddess and a girl in
love!

• Sequel series to the
fan-favorite *Kamichama Karin*

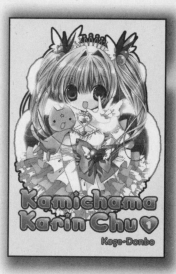

Special extras in each volume! Read them all!

VISIT WWW.DELREYMANGA.COM TO:
• Read sample pages
• View release date calendars for upcoming volumes
• Sign up for Del Rey's free manga e-newsletter
• Find out the latest about new Del Rey Manga series

RATING T AGES 13+

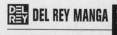

DEL REY MANGA デルレイ

The Otaku's Choice™

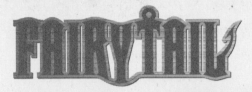
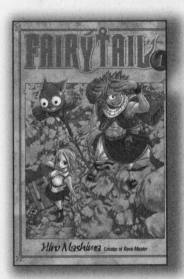 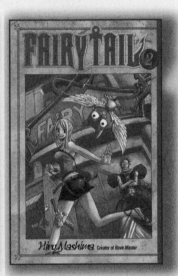

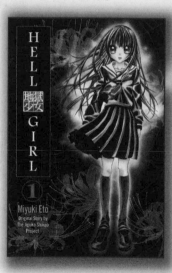

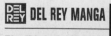
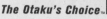

TOMARE!

✓ P9-DDM-412

止まれ

[STOP!]

You're going the wrong way!

Manga is a completely different
type of reading experience.

To start at the *beginning*,
go to the *end*!

That's right! Authentic manga is read the traditional Japanese way—
from right to left. Exactly the opposite of how American books are
read. It's easy to follow: Just go to the other end of the book, and read
each page—and each panel—from right side to left side, starting at
the top right. Now you're experiencing manga as it was meant to be!